language, discourse and social psychology

edited by
ann weatherall
victoria university of wellington

bernadette m. watson
university of queensland

cindy gallois
university of queensland

Editorial matter and selection © Ann Weatherall,
Bernadette M. Watson and Cindy Gallois 2007
Chapters © their authors 2007

All rights reserved. No reproduction, copy or transmission of
this publication may be made without written permission.

No paragraph of this publication may be reproduced, copied or transmitted
save with written permission or in accordance with the provisions of the Copyright,
Designs and Patents Act 1988,
or under the terms of any licence permitting limited copying issued by
the Copyright Licensing Agency,
90 Tottenham Court Road, London W1T 4LP.

Any person who does any unauthorised act in relation to this publication may be
liable to criminal prosecution and civil claims for damages.

The authors have asserted their rights to be identified as the authors
of this work in accordance with the Copyright, Designs and
Patents Act 1988.

First published 2007 by
PALGRAVE MACMILLAN
Houndmills, Basingstoke, Hampshire RG21 6XS and
175 Fifth Avenue, New York, N.Y. 10010
Companies and representatives throughout the world

PALGRAVE MACMILLAN is the global academic imprint of the
Palgrave Macmillan division of St. Martin's Press, LLC and of
Palgrave Macmillan Ltd.
Macmillan® is a registered trademark in the United States,
United Kingdom and other countries. Palgrave is a registered
trademark in the European Union and other countries.

ISBN-13   978–1–4039–9594–0 hardback
ISBN-10   1–4039–9594–X hardback
ISBN-13   978–1–4039–9595–7 paperback
ISBN-10   1–4039–9595–8 paperback

This book is printed on paper suitable for recycling and made from
fully managed and sustained forest sources. Logging, pulping
and manufacturing processes are expected to conform to the
environmental regulations of the country of origin.

A catalogue record for this book is available
from the British Library.

Library of Congress Cataloging-in-Publication Data
Language discourse and social psychology / edited by Ann Weatherall,
Bernadette M. Watson, Cindy Gallois.
p. cm.
Includes bibliographical references and index.
ISBN-13: 978–1–4039–9594–0 (cloth)
ISBN-10: 1–4039–9594–X (cloth)
ISBN-13: 978–1–4039–9595–7 (pbk.)
ISBN-10: 1–4039–9595–8 (pbk.)
1. Discourse analysis—Social aspects. 2. Social psychology. I. Weatherall, Ann,
1964– II. Watson, Bernadette M. III. Gallois, Cynthia.
P302.84.L363 2007
401'.41—dc22

2006053003

10 9   8   7   6   5   4   3   2   1
16 15 14 13 12 11 10 09 08 07

Printed and bound in Great Britain by
Antony Rowe Ltd, Chippenham and Eastbourne

Swansea University
WITHDRAWN FROM STOCK
Information Services
UNIVERSITY OF WALES
LIBRARY
SWANSEA

UNIVERSITY OF WALES SWANSEA
PRIFYSGOL CYMRU ABERTAWE
LIBRARY / LLYFRGELL

Classmark   P 302.84.L363 2007

Location

LIC Main

Swansea University
WITHDRAWN FROM STOCK
Information Services & Systems

Palgrave Advances in Linguistics

Consulting Editor:
Christopher N. Candlin,
Macquarie University, Australia

Titles include:

Monica Heller (*editor*)
BILINGUALISM: A SOCIAL APPROACH

Martha E. Pennington (*editor*)
PHONOLOGY IN CONTEXT

Ann Weatherall, Bernadette M. Watson and Cindy Gallois (*editors*)
LANGUAGE, DISCOURSE AND SOCIAL PSYCHOLOGY

Forthcoming:

Noel Burton-Roberts (*editor*)
PRAGMATICS

Susan Foster-Cohen (*editor*)
LANGUAGE ACQUISITION

Palgrave Advances
Series Standing Order ISBN 1–4039–3512–2 (Hardback) 1–4039–3513–0 (Paperback)
(*outside North America only*)

You can receive future titles in this series as they are published by placing a standing order.
Please contact your bookseller or, in the case of difficulty, write to us at the address below
with your name and address, the title of the series and the ISBN quoted above.

Customer Services Department, Macmillan Distribution Ltd, Houndmills, Basingstoke,
Hampshire RG21 6XS, England

contents

series preface

christopher n. candlin

This new *Advances in Linguistics Series* is part of an overall publishing programme by Palgrave Macmillan aimed at producing collections of original, commissioned articles under the invited editorship of distinguished scholars.

The books in the Series are not intended as an overall guide to the topic or to provide an exhaustive coverage of its various sub-fields. Rather, they are carefully planned to offer the informed readership a conspectus of perspectives on key themes, authored by major scholars whose work is at the boundaries of current research. What we plan the Series will do, then, is to focus on salience and influence, move fields forward, and help to chart future research development.

The Series is designed for postgraduate and research students, including advanced level undergraduates seeking to pursue research work in Linguistics, or careers engaged with language and communication study more generally, as well as for more experienced researchers and tutors seeking an awareness of what is current and in prospect in adjacent research fields to their own. We hope that the some of the intellectual excitement posed by the challenges of Linguistics as a pluralistic discipline will shine through the books!

Editors of books in the Series have been particularly asked to put their own distinctive stamp on their collection, to give it a personal dimension, and to map the territory, as it were, seen through the eyes of their own research experience.

With its focus on the key domains of gender, ethnicity, inter-generational communication, and public and political discourses,

Language, Discourse and Social Psychology edited by Ann Weatherall, Bernadette M. Watson and Cindy Gallois provides a cutting-edge map of an interdisciplinary territory now essential to the study of discourse in social life. Through the voices of its distinguished international contributors and the broad experience of its editors, it charts the discursive turn in studies of human communication and brings to such studies an essential combination of experimental rigour and social and ethnographic understanding. In doing so, it defines for a wide audience the underpinning theoretical principle and the empirical practice of grounded and evidence-based analysis of the conditions of production and reception of human communicative interaction.

Christopher N Candlin
Senior Research Professor
Department of Linguistics
Macquarie University, Sydney

list of tables and figures

tables

figures

notes on contributors

Martha Augoustinos is Professor and Co-Director of the Discourse and Social Psychology unit (DASP) in the School of Psychology, University of Adelaide, where she teaches social psychology. She has written extensively on racist discourse in Australia and is coeditor with Kate Reynolds (Australian National University) of *Understanding Prejudice, Racism and Social Conflict* (Sage Publications, 2001).

Valerie Barker (PhD, University of California, Santa Barbara) is a lecturer in the School of Communication, San Diego State University. Her research interests focus on intergenerational communication from an intergroup perspective, as well as the role of mass media in shaping and reflecting social identity. Publications have appeared in *Language and Communication*, the *Journal of Multilingual and Multicultural Development*, *Health Communication*, and *Journal of Communication*.

Richard Y. Bourhis was educated in the French and English school system in Montreal, obtaining a BSc in Psychology at McGill University in 1971. He pursued his graduate studies in Social Psychology at the University of Bristol with Howard Giles where he obtained a PhD in 1977. In Bristol, Richard Bourhis was also a member of the 'Social Identity Theory' research group headed by Henri Tajfel during the 1970s. As Associate Professor, Bourhis taught Social Psychology at McMaster University in Ontario and then joined the Psychology Department at the Université du Québec à Montréal (UQÀM) where he is now full professor. Richard Bourhis has published extensively in English and French on topics such as cross-cultural communication, discrimination and intergroup relations, acculturation and language planning. He has served as consultant on language policy issues for various governments including: Canada, Québec, the Basque

Autonomous Community and Catalonia in Spain. Richard Bourhis was elected Fellow of the Canadian Psychological Association in 1988 and member of the Society for Experimental Social Psychology (SESP) in 1991. In 1996 he was elected Director of the Concordia-UQÀM Chair in Ethnic Studies and is also a member of the Immigration and Metropolis research group at the Université de Montréal, Canada.

Peter Bull (PhD University of Exeter, United Kingdom) is a Senior Lecturer in the Department of Psychology at the University of York, United Kingdom. He has over 70 academic publications, principally in the form of articles in internationally recognized academic journals; he has also written five books, as well as numerous book chapters. His published output has been primarily concerned with the analysis of interpersonal communication. His most recent books are *The Microanalysis of Political Communication: Claptrap and Ambiguity* (2003) and *Communication under The Microscope: The Theory and Practice of Microanalysis* (2002).

Michelle Chernikoff Anderson, a member of the California State Bar Association, is the Director of Research and Education for the Center on Police Practices and Community (COPPAC) at the University of California, Santa Barbara. Her research focuses on the intersections of law, social science, and policy. Her work has been published in journals of criminal justice, law and social science and law reviews, and she has taught courses in Criminal Justice and Law and Social Science.

Richard Clément (PhD University of Western Ontario) is Professor of Psychology at the University of Ottawa. His current research interests include issues related to bilingualism, second language acquisition and identity change and adjustment in the acculturative process. In 2001 he was awarded the Otto Klineberg Intercultural and International Relations Prize by the Society for the Psychological Study of Social Issues; and in 2002 he received the Robert C. Gardner Award from the International Association of Language and Social Psychology. He is a fellow of both the Canadian and the American Psychological Association.

Shaha El-Geledi received her early education in Arabic in Libya and Saudi Arabia. Following her immigration to Quebec, she finished her secondary schooling in French and pursued her education in English at McGill University where she obtained a BA in psychology in 2002. She is presently doing her PhD in social psychology with Richard Y. Bourhis at the Université du Québec à Montréal (UQÀM). She is pursuing her doctoral studies on intergroup relations focusing on cross-cultural communication and immigration and acculturation issues in multiethnic societies. In 2004, she published a paper entitled: 'The Impact of Cultural Internalization and Integration on Well-Being Among Tricultural Individuals' which appeared in *Personality and Social Psychology Bulletin*.

Danielle Every is a PhD candidate in the School of Psychology, University of Adelaide. Her thesis explores counter-arguments in talk about asylum seekers, particularly those challenging discourses of race and nationalism, from a critical discourse analysis perspective.

Cindy Gallois is Professor of Psychology at the University of Queensland, and Director of Research in the Faculty of Social and Behavioural Science. In 2002, she became the founding Director of the Centre for Social Research in Communication, which was established to promote research and postgraduate training in health, organizational, intergroup, and mass/online communication. Her research focuses on intergroup communication, particularly on the process of communication accommodation. In the health area, she has studied decision-making, identity and blaming in HIV transmission and prevention, as well as communication between health professionals and patients. Her recent research has examined identity and communication accommodation and their influence on hospital staff members' adjustment to major organizational change. She has published ten books and monographs, and well over a hundred chapters and journal articles. She is a Fellow of the Academy of the Social Sciences in Australia, past President of the International Communication Association, current President of the International Association of Language and Social Psychology, Charter Fellow of the Intercultural Studies Academy, and a member of a number of professional associations in communication and social psychology. She is a past Editor of *Human Communication Research*, and is on the editorial boards of many journals in communication and psychology.

Howard Giles (PhD, DSc, University of Bristol) is Professor of Communication at the University of California, Santa Barbara. He is also founding Executive Director of that institution's Center on Police Practices and Community (COPPAC). His work has encompassed many different spheres of intergroup communication and, most recently, has focused on civilian–police interactions.

Christopher Hajek (PhD University of California, Santa Barbara) is an assistant professor at the University of Texas, San Antonio. His research regards the effect of group identity on interpersonal communication outcomes and social attitudes. His research agenda encompasses diverse intergroup phenomena in areas that range from ageing, sexuality, and health, to law enforcement.

Alexa Hepburn is a Senior Lecturer in Social Psychology in the Social Sciences Department at Loughborough University. She has had a long-standing interest in children's rights, and has published on constructions of authority, control and bullying in school situations. Her focus on school bullying has looked at how problems arise through the hierarchical relationship between adults and children in general, and teachers and pupils in particular. This focus on the construction of young people and their rights and competences has continued in her current research into the NSPCC Helpline. She was recently awarded a Leverhulme fellowship for this work. Her research has developed a critical perspective on more traditional forms of psychology, reflected in her recently published book *An Introduction to Critical Social Psychology*, where she highlights taken-for-granted assumptions about the person and society in psychology, and argues for a greater focus on everyday social contexts and applied work. She has published scholarly articles in *British Journal of Social Psychology*, *Discourse and Society*, *Research on Language and Social Interaction* and a range of other journals, as well as contributing book chapters to a range of edited collections. She is currently coediting a special issue of *Discourse and Society* on discursive psychology, and is coeditor of a similar collection for Cambridge University Press – *Discursive Research in Practice: New Approaches to Psychology and Interaction*. Her publications reflect the dual focus on methodological innovation in psychology, and a call for greater theoretical sophistication.

Mary Lee Hummert (PhD, University of Kansas) is a Professor of Communication Studies and Vice Provost for Faculty Development at the University of Kansas. Her research focuses on the social cognitive processes linking age stereotypes and communication, with funding from the National Institute on Ageing/National Institutes of Health.

Anna Janssen is a lecturer in the Faculty Education Unit at the Faculty of Medical and Health Sciences, University of Auckland. She has a PhD in psychology from the University of Otago. This investigated the roles that gender and context play in styles of expression and perceptions of other people and their messages. Anna completed post-doctoral research on the topic of postgraduate research supervision. Her research interests include communication in the clinical setting, end-of-life care, and the effectiveness of clinical teaching and supervision.

Celia Kitzinger is Professor of Conversation Analysis, Gender and Sexuality in the Department of Sociology at the University of York, UK. She has published nine books and around 80 articles and chapters on issues related to language, sexuality and gender. Her books include *The Social Construction of Lesbianism* (Sage, 1987), *Changing Our Minds* (co-authored with Rachel Perkins, New York University Press, 1993) and *Lesbian and Gay Psychology* (co-edited with Adrian Coyle), the last of which was awarded a Distinguished Publication Award from the American Psychological Association Division 44. She is currently completing a book on feminism and conversation analysis and analysing 350 calls to a crisis line for women in trauma after childbirth.

Mei-Chen Lin (PhD, University of Kansas) is an assistant professor in the School of Communication Studies at Kent State University. Her research interests are in ageing, identity, culture and communication, and grandparent–grandchild relationships. Her recent work is published in *Journal of Aging Studies*, *Journal of Cross-Cultural Gerontology*, and *Journal of Social and Personal Relationship*.

Peter D. MacIntyre (PhD, University of Western Ontario) is Professor of Psychology at Cape Breton University. His current research interests focus on the study of emotional and cognitive processes underlying second language acquisition and communication, in particular the role that willingness to communicate, language learning motivation, language anxiety, and personality processes play in second language. He has received the awards from the Modern Language Association, the International Association for Language and Social Psychology, and the Canadian Psychological Association.

Tamar Murachver is Senior Lecturer in Psychology at the University of Otago in New Zealand. Her research interests include the development of social competence, and the use of language in establishing and maintaining social groups. She also conducts research on the influence of linguistic support on children's event memories, and on the development of social stereotypes.

Kimberly A. Noels (PhD, University of Ottawa) is an associate professor in the Social and Cultural Psychology area of the Department of Psychology at the University of Alberta, Canada. Her research concerns the social psychology of language and communication processes, with a focus on intercultural communication. Her publications include articles on motivation for language learning, the role of communication in the process of cross-cultural adaptation, and intergenerational communication from a cross-cultural perspective. Her research has been recognized through awards from the Modern Language Association, the International Association of Language and Social Psychology, and the Society for the Psychological Study of Social Issues.

Jonathan Potter is Professor of Discourse Analysis in the Social Sciences Department at Loughborough University. He has studied topics such as scientific argumentation, current affairs television, racism, relationship counselling and child protection helplines. His main focus recently has been on the study of professional client interaction in a variety of settings. He is an international authority on qualitative methods and has written on discourse analysis and discursive psychology, focus groups, the study of psychological issues and he has taught short courses on analysis in ten different countries. His books include: *Mapping the Language of Racism* (Columbia University Press, 1992, with Margaret Wetherell) which studied the way racial inequalities are discursively legitimated; and *Discursive Psychology* (Sage, 1992, with Derek Edwards) that developed foundational principles for discursive psychology illustrated through a set of analyses of political controversies. In *Representing Reality* (Sage, 1996) he attempted to provide a systematic overview, integration and critique of constructionist research in social psychology, postmodernism, rhetoric and ethnomethodology. He has a book in press on the nature of interaction in focus groups (*Focus Group Practice*, Sage, with Claudia Puchta); and he has coedited a forthcoming book on the relationship between cognition and interaction (*Talk and Cognition*, CUP, with Hedwig te Molder). He has published ten books, more than 40 book chapters and 60 journal articles, and is on the editorial board of 15 journals. His work has been cited nearly 3,000 times in journals surveyed by the ISI. He is advisory editor to the journal *Theory and Psychology*.

W. Peter Robinson is currently Professor of Social Psychology Emeritus and Senior Research Fellow at the University of Bristol. He has been contributing to the study of language and communication from a social psychological perspective for most of his academic career. His latest general consideration of the field is published in *Language in Social Worlds* (Blackwell, 2002) and his latest special concern with the use of mistaken beliefs and inadequate arguments in *Arguing to Better Conclusions* (Erlbaum, 2006).

Ellen Bouchard Ryan is Professor in the Department of Psychiatry and Behavioural Neurosciences and in the Centre for Gerontological Studies at McMaster University in Hamilton, Canada. She focuses her psychological research on social cognitive aspects of communication and ageing. Working within adaptations of the Communication Predicament of Ageing Model, she and colleagues continue to examine communication predicaments experienced by vulnerable older adults with sensory, cognitive and physical impairments and the roles of empowering communication in fostering personhood and successful ageing with a disability.

Itesh Sachdev did his undergraduate work in Psychology at the University of Bristol (UK) and his doctoral work at McMaster University (Canada). He is a Reader in the Social Psychology of Language and Groups at Birkbeck College, University of London. He is the current President of the British Association of Canadian Studies and the editor of the *London Journal of Canadian Studies*. He has published on the social psychology of intergroup relations as well as on issues of multilingualism and multiculturalism with diverse sets of participants originating from many parts of the world including Bolivia, Canada, France, Hong Kong, India, Taiwan, Thailand, Tunisia and the UK.

Marie Savundranayagam is an Assistant Professor in the Helen Bader School of Social Welfare at the University of Wisconsin-Milwaukee. Her research interests maintain an ageing and health outcomes perspective. Specifically, her research focuses on dementia-related stressors, including communication problems, and their effect on burden for family caregivers. Her research is also on professional caregivers and the impact of communication enhancing strategies, including personhood, on perceptions of long-term care staff and residents.

Bernadette Watson (PhD, 2000) is an Australian Research Council Postdoctoral fellow in the Centre for Social Research in Communication (CSRComm) at the University of Queensland. She is a social psychologist who studies communication. Her research focuses on effective communication between health professionals and patients and good patient health outcomes. This includes research on the influence of identity and intergroup processes both on patient-health professional communication and on communication in multidisciplinary health teams. She is currently a chief investigator on a project examining communication issues for nurses and the impact on job satisfaction, stress and retention. Her other research focus is on organizational change, where she is looking at how information technology affects the working environment. She is a member of the executive of the International Association of Language and Social Psychology. She has published in the journals *Health Communication*, *Journal of Language and Social Psychology*, and *International Journal of Psycholinguistics*, as well as a number of book chapters.

Ann Weatherall is a Reader in the School of Psychology at Victoria University of Wellington, New Zealand. Her research interests lie in the general areas of language, discourse and social psychology; gender, and feminist psychology. Ann Weatherall has published numerous articles and book chapters including some that review and evaluate developments in the social psychology of language and discourse. Her books include: *Sex and the Body* (Dunmore Press, 2004, co-edited with Nicola Gavey and Annie Potts) which explores the discursive constructions of sex, gender and the body; *Gender, Language and Discourse* (Routledge, 2002) which uniquely examines the contribution that psychological research has made to questions about the relationships between gender and language; and *Ages Ahead* (Victoria University Press, 1998, co-edited with Sik Hung Ng, James Liu and Cynthia Loong), a volume that explores the roles of communication in different cultural approaches to intergenerational relationships. Her current discursive research takes a more distinctively conversation analytic approach to the study of psychological phenomena in talk.

Sue Wilkinson is Professor of Feminist and Health Studies in the Department of Social Sciences at Loughborough University. She is the founding editor of *Feminism & Psychology: An International Journal*, and has published widely in the areas of gender, sexuality and health. Her books include: *Feminist Social Psychologies* (Open University Press), *Feminism and Discourse*, *Heterosexuality* and *Representing the Other* (all Sage Publications). Her current research interests include women's experience of breast cancer, the social construction of same-sex marriage and civil partnerships, and the use of reaction tokens in conversation.

Yan Bing Zhang (PhD, University of Kansas) is an assistant professor in the Department of Communication Studies at the University of Kansas. Her research focuses on intercultural/intergenerational communication with particular regards to cultural values, age group stereotypes, conflict management, and media effects. Frequently, she examines these issues from a cross-cultural perspective. Her work has been published in journals such as *Communication Monographs*, *Journal of Communication*, *Journal of Broadcasting & Electronic Media*, *Journal of Asian Pacific Communication*, *Journal of Cross-Cultural Gerontology*, *New Media & Society*, and *Hallym International Journal of Aging*.

introduction
theoretical and methodological
approaches to language and
discourse in social psychology

ann weatherall, cindy gallois and bernadette watson

This book contains a range of chapters in the area of language and discourse, all from scholars who identify with the broad concerns of the field of social psychology. The study of language in social psychology has a long history, going back to close observational work of language done from the 1930s on (see Ball, Gallois & Callan, 1989; Markel, 1998). Nevertheless, language and discourse have for a long time been located away from the mainstream of social psychology. Not too many years ago, it was common for senior social psychologists to ask what contribution the study of language, the most social of all human behaviours, could make to social psychology or to psychology more generally. This may be because, as Ball et al. note, the rise of social cognition meant a loss of focus within social psychology on actual behaviour, and a privileging, or arguably even reifying, of thoughts, beliefs and cognitive processes. Thus, it is fair to say that the approach of language and social psychology came *from* social psychology, in that researchers in one way or another emphasize social-psychological themes like motivation, attitudes, and beliefs. At the same time, however, it can also be said that language and social psychology came *out of* social psychology, as a reaction to the increasingly intra-personal and cognitivist bias of that field in the 1970s and 1980s. So, the study of language and discourse in social psychology also owes great theoretical and methodological debts to sociology, sociolinguistics, anthropology, and communication studies (see Gallois, McKay & Pittam, 2004).

In its early incarnation, a language and social psychology approach involved an effort to do two things. The first was to bring a psychological perspective to the close analysis of the more social factors in language and communication, which in the 1950s and 1960s was mainly the province of sociology and sociolinguistics. Therefore, psychological aspects of interactions such as identification and status, and processes such as cognition and affect, were introduced as being consequential for language use and communication. The second was to bring an intergroup perspective to the, at that time, resolutely interpersonal psychological research on communication across roles and social identities (e.g., doctor–patient interaction, interethnic encounters). For this reason, theories of effective communication and communication skills in applied contexts were challenged as not taking adequate account of the socio-historical dimensions of interaction. Over time, social psychological research on language and communication has developed a greater focus and theoretical consideration of the emergent aspects of communication, a more qualitative approach, and greater emphasis on the reciprocal relations among contexts (intergroup and interpersonal, motives, and the interaction process itself).

The area of language and social psychology research grew its own identity over time, aided by the International Conference on Language and Social Psychology that began in Bristol in 1979 that continues to the present day, and the establishment of an International Association for Language and Social Psychology in 1997. There have been two Handbooks (Giles & Robinson, 1990; Robinson & Giles, 2001) that have comprehensively reviewed the area, and the *Journal of Language and Social Psychology* is an important publishing outlet for ongoing original cutting-edge research. There has been a further expansion of research over the past decade. Thus, in this book we have brought together the latest developments in this field, in order to demonstrate the range of topics and methodologies that are currently being undertaken. Our goal in this introduction is to provide an overview of the general field of language, discourse and social psychology and to situate each of the topic areas covered in this book within that field. Furthermore we wish to point to issues that straddle and divide the approaches in each of the chapters in this book.

In general, research in language and social psychology is comprised of related approaches based on the contextualized negotiation of social relations and action, as well as the manipulation and/or production of identity and language to those ends. Research has focused on a variety of groups and intergroup processes, including gender, age, ethnicity, and institutional role, placing increasing importance on negotiated identities or identities mobilized in the service of social actions in interaction (see particularly the chapters by Augoustinos & Every, Potter & Hepburn, Wilkinson & Kitzinger, this volume). More recently, in recognition that individuals belong to multiple groups simultaneously and thus need to manage multiple identities, researchers have begun to examine the impact of multiple identities on intergroup communication (see Giles et al., this volume, for an approach using communication accommodation theory, and Gallois et al., 2004, for a review in several contexts).

Shared concerns aside, it would be misleading to ignore the distinctiveness of different research traditions falling within the broad scope of language and social psychology. These can be crudely glossed as falling into two camps: social cognition and discursive psychology. The former can be credited as demonstrating the relevance of language to social psychology (e.g., Giles & Powesland, 1975; Giles & St Clair, 1979) and, as previously mentioned, bringing a psychological perspective into studies of language attitudes and linguistic variation. However, the psychological perspective imported into early research in language and social psychology was a cognitive one. Put crudely, the dominant view was that internal mental constructs such as attitudes, expectations and identities were the underlying causes of patterns of language use and speech perception. A quantitative approach using experiments and/or surveys, also imported from 'mainstream' psychology, was another characteristic of early work on language and social psychology.

The publication of *Discourse and Social Psychology: Beyond Attitudes and Behaviour* (Potter & Wetherall, 1987) introduced a new research approach that established itself, partly, in contra-distinction to *Language and Social Psychology* (Giles & St Clair, 1979). An anti- or post-cognitivist position is a hallmark of this perspective. For example, attitude as a cognitive notion has been respecified as the study of discourse practices that simultaneously construct and evaluate social objects, for personal or political ends (see Augoustinos & Every; Potter & Hepburn, this volume). A discursive approach uses qualitative analytic tools and techniques, which marks a radical methodological departure from mainstream social psychology.

The crude contrast just presented provides a starting point for understanding historical research trajectories of language and discourse in social psychology. The stamp of the more traditional social cognitive perspective, for example, is illustrated by the widespread use, development and application of Communication Accommodation Theory (see

Savundranayagam, Ryan & Hummert; Watson & Gallois; Giles et al., this volume). However, the contrast belies points of convergence between the two approaches, as well as distinctive threads within each approach. For example, communication accomodation theory (CAT) developed in part out of social identity theory (SIT), which itself is distinctive from more mentalistic approaches to social cognition. SIT and discursive approaches to identity are similar insofar as they both emphasize the emergent and interactionally contingent nature of social identities. Within discursive psychology there are at least two research threads; one that examines how psychological themes are handled and managed in talk and texts (e.g. Augoustinos & Every, this volume) and another that focuses more on how social life is accomplished through the recurrent structural features of mundane and/or institutionalized interactions that exist independently of the characteristics of individual speakers (see Wilkinson & Kitzinger, this volume).

The existence of distinctive approaches within a subject area of a discipline has benefits and risks. A benefit is that it provides fertile grounds for lively debate that can act as a catalyst for further development in research practices. For example, a discursive approach staunchly advocates the study of natural language use (Potter & Wetherell, 1995). Consequently, the use of qualitative data is becoming increasingly widespread. The methodological rigour characteristic of quantitative research has spurred the development of more explicit standards for judging discursive work. However, a risk of trying to embrace approaches that are in some respects fundamentally incompatible is that they diverge and follow separate paths with little, if any, cross-fertilization. In our view, volumes such as this one are important for maximizing the benefits and minimizing the risks associated with having two compelling approaches within the same general disciplinary area.

The chapters in this book show a range of international perspectives looking at American (including the major Canadian influences), British, European and Australasian literatures. We have included topics that reflect traditional and contemporary research topics and diverse methodological approaches to language, discourse and social psychology. The inclusion of original and innovative research using diverse methodologies is consistent with our desire to support diversity and discussion across differing approaches. There are four parts to the book, which we canvass briefly below. In doing this, we aim to give a flavour of the theoretical and methodological approaches taken by the authors in that part, their intersections and their discontinuities.

language, accommodation and intercultural encounters

Part One concerns a topic that has been at the heart of language and social psychology since its beginnings in the 1950s: the intersection of language, cultural and ethnic identity, and intergroup prejudice and discrimination. This section of the book provides both an overview of relevant theory and research and an up-to-date account of the cutting edge ideas in this field of enquiry. The two chapters in this section are written by scholars with long-standing expertise in the interpersonal, intergroup and structural factors influencing language use and attitudes in a multilingual world.

In the first chapter, Bourhis, El-Geledi and Sachdev consider the social psychological processes affecting which language is used and in what contexts in multilingual and multiethnic societies. Bourhis and his colleagues describe the theoretical state of the art in explaining code-switching behaviours. They do this by bringing together the elements that are currently known to predict and explain relationships between language and society. They review some of the core theories in the more experimental approach in language and social psychology, including communication accommodation theory and the variants of ethnolinguistic vitality theory. These theories posit that the processes involved in language choice and use in intercultural encounters include structural influences (e.g., levels of institutional and legislative support for languages), intergroup dynamics (e.g., the relative social status of the language or variety in the larger society), and interpersonal factors (e.g., liking). Bourhis et al. then add intercultural adaptation theory (e.g., Berry, 1997), which aims to predict cultural attitude and interaction with majority and minority cultures in a multicultural society at the individual level. Bourhis and his colleagues review extensions of this work to include the position of majority members as well as minority members of a society, so that the interactive acculturation model becomes intergroup as well as interpersonal. The combination of these four theories gives a comprehensive account of language choice and use, from the sociohistorical context through to individual orientation.

The second chapter takes up a separate but related issue of language use in intercultural encounters: that of second language (L2) learning. Clément, Noels and MacIntyre discuss recent developments in social-psychological research on bilingualism and second-language learning. The authors first give a brief history of theory and methodology in this area, which (like the research described by Bourhis et al. in Chapter 1) has been largely questionnaire-based and quantitative. Clément and his colleagues document a shift in the social psychology of bilingualism from a focus on the role of intergroup attitudes to a greater concern with the motivational processes involved in second language use. This shift includes the introduction to this area of an older concept in communication studies, willingness to communicate (WTC). Clément and colleagues have over the past few years extended WTC to intergroup contexts as WTC in L2 (and more recently health WTC; see Watson & Gallois, this volume). In this chapter, Clément et al. note that researchers in this area have also broadened the context of their work from second language learning and language survival/revival to foreign language learning and the learning of English as a global language. These authors contend that motivational aspects of language learning and use are key elements in cultural definition and identity, as well as personal and social identification. They present a general heuristic, the pyramid model, which organizes the wide variety of influences on a willingness to communicate in a second language. This model is new, but provides a research agenda for testing, based both on survey studies of language attitudes and use among second- and foreign-language learners (e.g., EFL/ESL students) and arguably for experimental tests of learning outcomes based on manipulation of variables in the model.

language and discourse in institutional talk

The chapters presented in Part two represent a sample of papers showcasing studies that examine language use in institutional settings. The strong influence of communication accommodation theory on research in language and social psychology is evidenced in this section, with three of the four chapters taking the conceptual framework of CAT as a stepping-stone for their work. Like the previous section, this one includes work by scholars who have significantly influenced theory and research in this area. For instance, Giles (see Chapter 5) was the originator of speech accommodation theory (Giles & Powesland, 1975; Giles, Mulac, Bradac & Johnson, 1987), the forerunner of CAT, and he has remained the guiding force in the development of this theory (which now includes a plethora of colleagues, among them many of the authors in this volume). Ryan and Giles were key figures in developing the communication predicament model of ageing (CPA; Ryan, Giles, Bartolucci & Henwood, 1986; see Savundranayagam, Ryan & Hummert, this volume), which is itself an extension of SAT/CAT. Hummert has been a leading collaborator in this research and has advanced understandings of 'elder-speak' or patronizing communication (see Hummert & Ryan, 2001, as well as Chapter 3 here, for reviews of this work).

In contrast to the research tradition described above, Chapter 6 takes the approach of discursive psychology. Potter (see Potter & Hepburn, this volume; Augoustinos & Every, this volume) was one of the founders of this distinctive approach to social psychology (e.g., Potter & Wetherell, 1987; Edwards and Potter, 1992). This meta-theory and meta-methodology revolutionized thinking in much of social psychology, especially in the UK. Standard social psychological topics such as attitudes, attribution and identity are respecified as discourse practices, rather than as cognitive processes underlying communicative events. Furthermore, this is a perspective that examines the ways psychological matters such as self-interest and knowledge are implicated in talk and interaction. Discursive psychology also stands in contrast to more experimental theories related to social identity theory (e.g., Tajfel & Turner, 1979), including CAT. In recent years, this divide has been (arguably) crossed to some extent by changes in CAT to accommodate a more discursive perspective (see Gallois, Ogay & Giles, 2005; Weatherall & Gallois, 2003). As a group, the chapters in this section exemplify the diverse settings now attracting research in language, discourse and social psychology.

In Chapter 3, Savundranayagam and her colleagues consider how positive interaction can empower older adults and reverse the negative impacts described in the communication predicament model. The authors tease out how empowerment can be operationalized in terms of assertive communication strategies for older people, particularly those who experience multiple losses in health and relationships. This chapter touches on health interactions, which are often three-way affairs among (older) care receivers, health professionals and third parties involved with the care receiver (e.g., younger relatives). The authors stress the potentially harmful effect for older adults if they accept the role of passive receiver of care. The chapter revisits the traditional work of the communication enhancement model, linking it with recent work on health care partnerships. This chapter also highlights applied research that provides practical ways for older people to practise assertive communication. This chapter includes an exciting evaluation of the ways in which older adults can achieve empowerment and communicative competence through the use of varying interactional strategies.

Continuing the theme of health, in Chapter 4 Watson and Gallois briefly review the range of topics in health communication research. In particular, they acknowledge a move away from atheoretical research towards studies that adopt theoretical frameworks to understand and predict communication behaviours and outcomes. They examine the implications for patients and health professionals of shifts in the level of patient empowerment and patient participation. They also describe new developments in understanding the ways in which supportive affect can be communicated to patients. Furthermore this chapter takes up the issue of communication in multi-disciplinary health teams and the intergroup dynamics involved. Chapter 4 uses an explicitly intergroup lens (as do Savundranayagam et al. in Chapter 3) in an area that has tended to be constructed largely in interpersonal terms.

Chapter 5, by Giles, Hajek, Barker, Lin, Zhang, Hummert and Cherinikoff, moves into a new and socially significant research context of law enforcement and communication. Giles and his colleagues discuss the psychologically salient aspects of encounters between individual speakers and larger social institutions. They then describe the more specific context of encounters between individuals and law enforcement officers. Detailed in this chapter is the importance of communication accommodation by police officers on attitudes to the police among members of the general public, and they begin a discussion of how these results might be applied in the training of police officers and the life-saving impact this could have. Their methodology is based on surveys (at least in this chapter, where they present some new data), but a likely direction of future research efforts will be explorations of discourse and language behaviour in context.

In Chapter 6, the final chapter of this section, Potter and Hepburn examine communication between individuals and social institutions, this time in the context of children's help lines. Like Giles et al., they present some new data and review older work in this important area, taking the perspective of discursive psychology. Here we see the increasing influence of conversation analysis in contemporary discursive psychology. Their micro-analysis of help line communication indicates the way concerned adults position themselves in calls of concern about neglect and abuse of children, and has potential applications for informing communication training for those working on the help lines.

gender and sexuality

In Part Three, the two chapters examine gender and language from two very different perspectives. Chapter 7, by Murachver and Janssen, takes up the issue of sex differences in language and the ways in which they interact with gendered language style and context. Although the concept of sex differences in language came from sociolinguistics (see Lakoff, 1990, for a review), this area has in more recent years attracted considerable interest from experimental social psychologists (even after it went out of fashion among sociolinguists: see Holmes & Meyerhoff, 2003, and more discursively oriented social psychologists: see Weatherall, 2002). The research, reviewed by Murachver and Janssen, is used to make a case for reliable sex differences in language, some of which are relatively stable and others highly dependent upon context. Murachver and Janssen aim to elucidate the complex interactions among gender, style, and context. This is an area that is well-suited to an experimental approach, because of the control over extraneous variables that experiments provide and because each key variable (actual gender, gendered style, context) can be independently manipulated. Murachver and her colleagues have cleverly used email communication to do this convincingly, without introducing the artificiality that often detracts from experimental work. In this chapter, Murachver and Janssen take a social-cognitive approach to consider the impact of gender stereotypes on evaluations of language. In addition, they canvass a number of experimental studies (including their own work using email exchanges) that manipulate biological sex, gendered language study, and context, noting the strength of style as a source of impressions and attributions.

In stark contrast, in Chapter 8 Wilkinson and Kitzinger argue for the value that conversation analysis can add to our understanding of the everyday and mundane practices that produce oppressive forms of gender and sexuality. Through a series of close analyses of conversational texts, they consider the ways in which sexual refusals are organized and structured in interaction; as well as the ways a social identity as a lesbian can be made relevant and consequential to interaction and how the organization of turn-taking can be mobilized to 'come out' as lesbians. For the latter, Wilkinson and Kitzinger show that far from being a grand announcement, coming out as an everyday event is something 'slipped' into conversation. Wilkinson and Kitzinger show the value of the very detailed methodological approach that conversation analysis prescribes.

discourse, rhetoric and politics

In the fourth and final part of this book, we present three chapters that are both current and controversial. Chapter 9, by Augoustinos and Every, takes up the issue of racist language. In contrast to Potter and Hepburn's, Augoustinos and Every's approach uses a thread of discursive psychology that examines both broad patterns and themes within talk as well as the more detailed linguistic strategies used to accomplish local actions. An important aspect of this chapter is that it outlines the value of discursive psychology for the study of prejudice and racism. These authors review work on implicit or 'new' racism, which shows its face while simultaneously denying its existence. Augoustinos and Every show how close interpretive analysis of texts on issues such as indigenous rights claims and immigration reveals the ways majority group members position themselves as non-prejudiced while at the same time justifying and rationalizing negative evaluations of minority ethnic groups. An original aspect of this chapter is the authors' consideration of the ways accusations of racism are framed in indirect and subtle ways.

In Chapter 10, Bull draws on his own as well as established empirical research to test propositions on three facets of the language of politics: equivocation, invited applause, and metaphor. First, on the topic of equivocation, he investigates the style of questioning that politicians face from interviewers and concludes that politicians use equivocation as a response to conflictual questions to lessen their personal and public threat to face. Second, he presents his extension of Atkinson's (1983, 1984) groundbreaking work on applause, where he reassigns the importance of a politician's use of speech content, spontaneous applause and delivery. This critical reassessment of Atkinson's work may concern some researchers, but at the same time it provides a forum for further debate. On the topic of metaphor, Bull argues that social psychologists of language have not seriously investigated how political metaphor can unify and engage people with a particular movement and view. Bull argues that a coming together of the study of political language and persuasion will serve to invigorate and extend current work in these two fields.

Finally, in Chapter 11, Robinson takes us on a journey that examines the presentation of arguments from the Thatcher era of the late 1970s to the current 'new Labour' government of Tony Blair. Robinson extends his earlier work on big lies, or the deliberate fabrications of politicians and the mass media that are so comprehensive that they are believed without question (Robinson, 1996). He situates his text in everyday life, questioning the concept of truth as it can be understood through rational and irrational argument. This chapter gives a trenchant appraisal of the influence of power and politics in society. Through revisiting economic and social history, Robinson demonstrates how the arguments put forward to the general public are often misrepresentative and flawed. He draws on modern historical examples of discourse to alert readers to likely ulterior motives.

This chapter sends a clear signal to researchers in language and discourse that we have a responsibility to make politicians, policy makers, media providers, and others in powerful positions accountable, through the rigorous examination of everyday discourse and media texts. His call to action shows the immediate application of the research approaches in the two previous chapters. Augoustinos and Every show that racism can be hidden in apparently neutral discussions of indigenous people, refugees and in similar contexts: Robinson gives salient and powerful examples of the consequences. Bull reviews and extends work on the strategies of politicians to attract positive appraisals from the public, and Robinson points to the consequences of these rhetorical devices. The next step is for researchers to engage with this important area. In addition to the discursive approach and the close analysis of verbal and non-verbal behaviour reviewed in Chapters 10 and 11, Robinson's earlier work (Robinson, 1996) points to a research agenda. There he notes that individual research projects must be particularistic, but researchers must not lose sight of the larger picture in policy and politics.

concluding comment

Taken as a whole the chapters show the diversity and importance of research in language, discourse and social psychology. There are now some established research topics and traditions that are being further developed, and some new areas for study of alternative methodological approaches are promoted. Editing this volume has shown us that an ongoing challenge for research in this area is to continue both cross-disciplinary and intra-disciplinary dialogues to ensure cross-fertilization of ideas. To our minds it is crucial to support a diversity of approaches, because that diversity is needed for developing better understandings of the complex ways language produces and reproduces the realities (warts and all) of social life.

references

Atkinson, J.M. (1983). Two devices for generating audience approval: A comparative study of public discourse and text. In K. Ehlich & H. van Riemsdijk (Eds.), *Connectedness in sentence, text and discourse* (pp.199–236). Tilburg, Netherlands: Tilburg Papers in Linguistics.

Atkinson, J.M. (1984). Public speaking and audience responses: Some techniques for inviting applause. In J.M. Atkinson & J.C. Heritage (Eds.), *Structures of social action: Studies in conversation analysis* (pp.370–409). Cambridge and New York: Cambridge University Press.

Ball, P., Gallois, C. & Callan, V.J. (1989). Language attitudes: Perspectives from social psychology. In P. Collins & D. Blair (Eds.), *Australian English: The language of a new society* (pp.89–102). Brisbane: University of Queensland Press.

Berry, J.W. (1997). Immigration, acculturation, and adaptation. *Applied Psychology: An International Journal, 46*, 5–68.

Edwards, D. & Potter, J. (1992). *Discursive psychology.* London: Sage.

Gallois, C., McKay, S. & Pittam, J. (2004). Intergroup communication and identity: Intercultural, health, and organisational communication. In K. Fitch & R. Sanders (Eds.), *Handbook of language and social interaction* (pp.231–250). Mahwah, NJ: Erlbaum.

Gallois, C., Ogay, T. & Giles, H. (2005). Communication accommodation theory: A look back and a look ahead. In W. Gudykunst (Ed.), *Theorizing about intercultural communication* (pp.121–148). Thousand Oaks, CA: Sage.

Giles, H., Mulac, A., Bradac, J.J. & Johnson, P. (1987). Speech accommodation theory: The first decade and beyond. In M. McLaughlin (Ed.), *Communication Yearbook, 10* (pp.13–48). Newbury Park, CA: Sage.

Giles, H. & Powesland, P.F. (1975). *Speech style and speech evaluation.* London: Academic Press.

Giles, H. & Robinson, W.P. (Eds.) (1990). *Handbook of language and social psychology.* Chichester: Wiley.

Giles, H. & St Clair, R. (Eds.) (1979). *Language and social psychology.* Oxford: Blackwell.

Holmes, J. & Meyerhoff, M. (Eds.) (2003). *The handbook of language and gender.* Malden, MA: Blackwell.

Hummert, M.L. & Ryan, E.B. (2001). Patronizing. In W.P. Robinson & H. Giles (Eds.), *The new handbook of language and social psychology* (pp.253–269). London: Wiley.

Lakoff, R.T. (1990). *Talking power: The politics of language.* New York: Basic Books.

Markel, N.N. (1998). *Semiotic psychology.* New York: Peter Lang Press.

Potter, J. & Wetherell, M. (1987). *Discourse and social psychology: Beyond attitudes and behaviour.* London: Sage.

Potter, J. & Wetherell, M. (1995). Rethinking Methods in Psychology. In J. Smith, Rom Harré & Luk Van Langenhow (Eds.), *Rethinking psychology* (pp.80–92). London: Sage.

Robinson, W.P. (1996). *Deceit, delusion, and detection.* Thousand Oaks, CA: Sage.

Robinson, W.P. & Giles, H. (Eds.) (2001). *The new handbook of language and social psychology* (pp.561–584). London: Wiley.

Ryan, E.B., Giles, H., Bartolucci, G. & Henwood, K. (1986). Psycholinguistic and social psychological components of communication by and with the elderly. *Language and Communication, 6*, 1–24.

Tajfel, H. & Turner, J.C. (1979). An integrative theory of intergroup conflict. In W. G. Austin & S. Worchel (Eds.), *The social psychology of intergroup relations* (pp.33–53). Belmont, CA: Wadsworth.

Weatherall, A. (2002). *Gender, language and discourse.* London: Routledge.

Weatherall, A. & Gallois, C. (2003). Gender and identity: Representation and social action. In J. Holmes & M. Meyerhoff (Eds.), *Handbook of language and gender* (pp.487–508). Oxford: Blackwell.

part one
language, accommodation and intercultural encounters

1
language, ethnicity and intergroup relations

richard y. bourhis, shaha el-geledi and itesh sachdev

The main goal of this chapter is to provide a framework for understanding the sociolinguistic and social psychological processes affecting language attitudes and language behaviours in multiethnic societies. The empirical research reviewed in the chapter focuses mainly on language behaviours related to code switching in encounters between members of contrasting ethnolinguistic groups. The first part of the chapter reviews intergroup processes affecting the development of language communities by focusing on the ethnolinguistic vitality of linguistic minorities and majorities in contact situations. Using the interactive acculturation model (IAM; Bourhis 2001a), the second part of the chapter provides an analysis of the language policies regulating the status of language communities in multilingual societies. The IAM proposes that the acculturation orientations of minority and majority group speakers can have an impact on the intergroup communication strategies they adopt during their intercultural encounters, resulting in harmonious, problematic or conflictual relational outcomes. The third part of the chapter provides an overview of communication accommodation theory (CAT; Giles & Coupland, 1991) which complements the IAM model in detailing the subtleties of the intergroup communication strategies used by minority and majority group speakers in their cross-cultural encounters.

ethnolinguistic vitality and language behaviour

Sociolinguists and social psychologists concerned with issues of language attitudes, code switching behaviour, language shift and language loss must inevitably deal with the relative strength and weaknesses of the language communities they are investigating (Johnson, Giles & Bourhis, 1983). Sociostructural factors such as group vitality can fundamentally affect the nature and quality of intergroup communications between speakers of contrasting language groups. This is likely to be the case especially in settings where accent, dialect and language not only provide important cues for the categorization of speakers on the social map (Giles & Powesland, 1975; Scherer & Giles, 1979) but also serve as the most salient dimension of ethnolinguistic identity (Bourhis, Giles & Tajfel, 1973; Fishman, 1977; Sachdev & Bourhis, 1990).

objective group vitality

The notion of *ethnolinguistic vitality* provides a conceptual tool to analyse the sociostructural variables affecting the strength of language communities within multilingual settings. The vitality of an ethnolinguistic group is defined as 'that which makes a group likely to behave as a distinctive and collective entity within the intergroup setting' (Giles, Bourhis & Taylor, 1977, p.308). The more vitality an ethnolinguistic group has, the more likely it is that it will survive and thrive as a collective entity in the multilingual setting. Conversely, ethnolinguistic groups that have little or no vitality are more likely to eventually cease to exist as distinctive language groups within the intergroup setting.

Three broad dimensions of sociostructural variables influence the vitality of ethnolinguistic groups: demographic, institutional support, and status. *Demographic* variables are those related to the absolute number of speakers composing the language group and their distribution throughout the urban, regional, or national territory. Number factors refer to the language community's absolute group numbers, their birth rate, mortality rate, age pyramid, endogamy/exogamy, and their patterns of immigration and emigration in and out of the ancestral territory. Distribution factors refer to the numeric concentration of speakers in various parts of the territory, their proportion relative to outgroup speakers, and whether or not the language community still occupies its ancestral territory. These demographic factors can be based on one or a combination of the following linguistic indicators often found in census data: first language as mother tongue, knowledge of a first (L1) or second (L2) language, L1 and/or L2 language use at home. Taken together, these indicators can be used to monitor demolinguistic trends such as language maintenance, language shift, language loss and intergenerational transmission of the L1 mother tongue. Within democracies, demographic factors constitute a fundamental asset for ethnolinguistic groups as *'strength in numbers'* can be used as a legitimizing tool to grant language communities with the institutional support they need to ensure their intergenerational continuity within multilingual societies.

Institutional control is defined as the degree of control one group has over its own fate and that of outgroups, and can be seen as the degree of social power enjoyed by one language group relative to salient outgroups (Sachdev & Bourhis, 2001). Institutional control is the dimension of vitality 'par excellence' needed by language groups to maintain and assert their ascendancy relative to competing language groups. Language groups need to achieve and maintain a favourable position on the institutional control front if they wish to survive as distinctive collective entities within multilingual states (Fishman, 1991, 2001). The extent to which a language group has gained formal and informal representation in the institutions of a community, region, state, or nation constitutes its institutional support. Informal support refers to the degree to which a language community has organized itself as a pressure group to represent and safeguard its own language interests in various state and private domains. Formal support refers to the degree to which members of a language group have gained positions of control at decision-making levels of the government apparatus, in education, in health care, in business, the mass media and within cultural, sport and religious institutions. Language planning adopted by regional or national governments can also contribute to the institutional support of language communities by legislating the use of competing languages in the government administration, in education, the mass-media, as the language of work and across the linguistic landscape (Bourhis, 1984a, 1994a, 2001b; Bourhis & Landry, 2002; Cooper, 1989; Landry & Bourhis, 1997).

The presence and quality of leaders who can head the formal and informal institutions representing language groups also contributes to the institutional support of language communities. Gains in institutional support often depend on the emergence of activists and charismatic leaders who succeed in mobilizing language groups to struggle for greater institutional control within multilingual states. The absence of quality leadership can undermine gains achieved by previous generations of group members on the institutional control front and can mortgage future gains needed for the language survival of the next generation of group members. Taken together, language groups who have gained strong institutional control within state and private institutions are in a better position to safeguard and enhance their collective language and cultural capital than language communities who lack institutional control in these domains.

Language groups that have gained ascendancy on institutional support factors are also likely to benefit from considerable social status relative to less dominant groups within multilingual states. The *status variables* are those related to a language community's social prestige, its socio-historical status within the state, and the prestige of its language and culture locally, nationally and internationally. The more status a language community is ascribed to have, the more vitality it is likely to possess as a collectivity. Social psychological evidence shows that speakers of high-status groups enjoy a more positive social identity and can more readily mobilize to maintain or improve their vitality position within the state (Giles & Johnson, 1987). Conversely, being a member of a disparaged low-status linguistic group can sap the collective will of minorities to maintain themselves as distinctive language communities leading to linguistic assimilation. The experience of belonging to a high- vs. low-status language community is more vivid to the degree that status differentials between ethnolinguistic groups are perpetuated through language stereotypes (Bourhis & Maass, 2005; Ryan, Giles & Sebastian, 1982) and/or enshrined through the adoption of language laws that legislate the relative status of language communities within multilingual states (Bourhis, 1984b, 1994a, 2001a; Kaplan & Baldauf, 1997; Ricento & Burnaby, 1998).

These three dimensions combine to affect in one direction or the other the overall strength or vitality of ethnolinguistic groups (Giles et al., 1977). A language community may be strong on demographic variables but weak on institutional support and status factors resulting in a medium vitality position relative to a language majority strong on all three vitality dimensions. Strength on only one dimension of vitality may be undermined by weakness on other dimensions as was illustrated in a study examining the objective vitality of Euro-Americans and Hispanic minorities in the USA (Barker, Giles, Noels, Duck, Hecht & Clément, 2001). Current US Census data show that Euro-Americans are now a demographic minority in key immigration states such as California, Texas, and Florida. The US Census Bureau predicts that, while the Euro-American population is expected to grow by 5 per cent in the coming decade, the Hispanic population is expected to triple during this period. Therefore, demographic vitality of Hispanic minorities is becoming stronger than that of Euro-Americans in key border states whose economy is also the most dynamic. However, Hispanic minorities remain weaker on both institutional and status vitality dimensions than Euro-Americans (Barker et al., 2001). The Hispanic minorities have a lower socioeconomic status, higher unemployment rate, and weaker educational achievement than Euro-Americans (Johnson, 2000). On the status dimension the 'English Only Movement' succeeded in declaring English as the only official language in the very states where Hispanics have the most demographic vitality. Therefore, while the demographic vitality of Hispanic minorities is increasing, their vitality on the institutional and status dimensions remains weak.

The objective vitality framework was used to describe the relative position of language groups in numerous bilingual and multilingual settings such as: the French and the English of Quebec and Canada (Bourhis, 2001b; Bourhis & Lepicq, 2004; Johnson & Doucet, 2006); the Acadians in New Brunswick (Landry & Allard, 1994b); the Cajuns in Louisiana (Landry, Allard & Henry, 1996); the Basques, Catalans and Gallicians in Spain (Atkinson, 2000; Ros, Huici & Cano, 1994; Ytsma, Viladot & Giles, 1994); Arabophones, Francophones and Anglophones in Lebanon (Shaaban & Ghaith, 2002); ethnolinguistic groups in Nigeria (Mann, 2000), and Black/White communities in South Africa (Bornman & Appelgryn, 1997).

subjective perceptions of group vitality

How speakers perceive the vitality of their own language community relative to salient linguistic outgroups may be as important as 'objective' assessments of group vitality based on demolinguistic and census data. The subjective vitality questionnaire (SVQ) was designed to measure group members' assessments of in/outgroup vitality on each of the items constituting the demographic, institutional support, and status dimensions of the objective vitality framework (Bourhis, Giles & Rosenthal, 1981). A review of the vitality research using the SVQ showed that overall group members are realistic in perceiving their vitality position along the lines suggested by 'objective' assessments of ethnolinguistic vitality (Harwood, Giles & Bourhis, 1994). However, studies have also shown that ethnolinguistic group members can be biased in their assessments of ingroup and outgroup vitalities. Such biases do not emerge on obvious differentials between ingroup/outgroup vitality, but are documented on objectively minor vitality differences between contrasting language communities. Three basic types of subjective vitality biases were identified based on the review of the literature (Harwood et al., 1994). Perceptual distortions in favour of ingroup vitality occur when language groups exaggerate the strength of their own group's vitality while underestimating the vitality of the outgroup. This pattern was found among Greek- and Anglo-Australians (Giles, Rosenthal & Young, 1985), Italian- and English-Canadians (Bourhis & Sachdev, 1984), and Arab and Jewish Israelis (Kraemer & Olshtain, 1989). Perceptual distortions in favour of outgroup vitality involve language groups who underestimate the vitality of their own group while exaggerating the vitality of the outgroup. Such perceptions were found among first generation Chinese immigrants in London and Toronto (Sachdev & Bourhis, 1987, 1990) and German students in francophone Switzerland (Young, Bell & Giles, 1988). Non-consensual vitality perceptions occur when language groups disagree not only on the degree of difference between groups, but also on the direction of such difference. Both motivational (ingroup bias) and cognitive factors (availability and vividness heuristics) help account for these perceptual distortions of group vitality (Sachdev & Bourhis, 1993).

Empirical studies have also shown that the vitality items listed within each dimension of the objective vitality framework are not necessarily seen by perceivers as falling within the demographic, institutional and status dimensions of the model. Vitality items are perceived as belonging to configurations of dimensions that reflect current harmonious or problematic relations between language communities within specific cultural settings. Noting such trends, Giles (2001) pointed out that 'vitality is not a static given but, rather, a malleable social construction depending on social group membership and fluctuating sociopolitical circumstances' (p.473). Overall, studies show that perceivers are quite sensitive to the relative position of their own language group relative to outgroups on each vitality element making up the three dimensions of objective and subjective vitality.

subjective vitality as a predictor of language attitudes and behaviours

A combination of both objective and subjective vitality information constitutes a more sensitive method of predicting the language behaviour of group members than simply relying on objective assessments of group vitality (Giles & Johnson, 1987). Studies combining features of objective and subjective vitality have shown that ethnolinguistic vitality is related to a broad range of language attitudes and language behaviours. For instance, studies have shown that ethnolinguistic vitality was related to self-reports of French language use in everyday activities by Acadians in New Brunswick (Landry & Allard, 1994b), self-report of Italian language use amongst first and second generation Italian-Canadians in Ontario (Bourhis & Sachdev, 1984), self-reported Turkish usage amongst immigrants from Turkey in France (Yagmur & Akinci, 2003), self-reported use of Bengali and attitudes to English use by Sylheti-Bangladeshi pupils in London (Lawson & Sachdev, 2004), evaluative reactions to language switching in Montreal and Quebec city (Genesee & Bourhis, 1988), positive/negative attitudes towards outgroups amongst Blacks and Afrikaans-speaking Whites in South Africa (Bornman & Appelgryn, 1997), Anglo-American support for the English-only movement in the USA (Barker & Giles, 2004), ingroup favouritism attitudes and bilingual language use by Castillians and speakers of regional languages in the bilingual communities of Spain (Azurmendi, Bourhis, Ros & Garcia, 1998; Ros et al., 1994; Ros, Azurmendi, Bourhis & Garcia, 1999), second language competence of Francophones and Anglophones in Ontario and willingness to communicate in L2 (Clément, Baker & MacIntyre, 2003; Noels & Clément, 1996), and presence of French linguistic landscape perceived by Francophones across Anglo-Canada (Landry & Bourhis, 1997).

While the SVQ monitors 'general exocentric beliefs' about the perceived vitality of ingroup/outgroup language communities (Bourhis et al., 1981), the BEVQ (beliefs about ethnolinguistic vitality questionnaire) monitors 'egocentric beliefs' made up of self-beliefs and goal beliefs concerning ingroup/outgroup vitality (Allard & Landry, 1986). Group members may perceive that their language community is weak on most vitality factors as per SVQ ratings. However, BEVQ ratings may show that most group members may do little personally to assert their own group vitality (self-beliefs) and may have no intention to act personally in favour of improving their own group vitality (goal beliefs). In contrast, other group members may also perceive that their own group vitality is weak but may endorse self- and goal beliefs in favour of mobilizing personally and collectively to improve their ingroup vitality on strategic institutional control, demographic and status factors. Thus, a combination of general beliefs (SVQ) and egocentric beliefs (BEVQ) may better predict language attitudes and behaviours in multilingual settings. Allard and Landry (1994) compared the predictive value of their BEVQ with the SVQ, which they had administered to a large sample of Francophone minorities across Canada. Though their results showed that the BEVQ was the more powerful predictor of French language behaviour, strong support in favour of the SVQ as a predictive measure was also obtained.

To the degree that ethnolinguistic group members accurately perceive the vitality of their own group and that of salient outgroups, the SVQ can be used as a descriptive measure that can help validate the choice of ethnolinguistic groups used by researchers to conduct their sociolinguistic and social psychological studies. Combining objective and subjective vitality can be used as a tool of social analysis for addressing a broad range of empirical and theoretical issues related to language behaviours within both sociolinguistics and social psychology.

public policies and the survival of language minorities

In multilingual settings, 'free market forces' usually favour the ascendancy of the dominant language majority, often to the disadvantage of linguistic minorities and national minorities. National minorities are language communities established within the national territory before the creation of the state. Examples of national minorities are Aborigines in Australia; first nations people in Canada, the USA and South America; the Basque, Catalan and Gallicians of Spain, or the Palestinian Arab minority in Israel. As a counterpoint to 'free market forces', linguistic minorities and national minorities often need the support of state language planning to provide the institutional support they need to maintain the institutional vitality of their minority communities, foster minority language use in prestige public functions, and minimize the erosion of their demolinguistic base (Fishman, 1991, 2001; Kaplan & Baldauf, 1997).

The interactive acculturation model (IAM) proposes that it is high vitality majority groups that have the institutional control and demographic base to impose the state language policies which best serve the interests of their own linguistic community (Bourhis, 2001a; Bourhis, Moïse, Perreault & Senécal, 1997). Though low vitality language minorities can be given a say in the development of such language policies in democratic states, their weaker vitality position undermines their capacity to influence the adoption of the language policies they need to sustain the use of minority languages in key institutional domains such as education, health and public services, mass media and the work world. As can be seen in Figure 1.1, linguistic minorities depend on dominant language majorities to approve language laws that in the long run help limit the intergenerational language loss of minorities. The cumulative effects of favourable language laws providing institutional support for minority languages improve the prospects of language maintenance for linguistic minorities, who gain a better chance of transmitting their minority language from one generation to the other, thus contributing to demographic vitality (Fishman, 1991). The IAM is an intergroup acculturation model which proposes that high vitality language majorities and low vitality language minorities often compete to promote the vitality, development and public use of their respective languages (Bourhis, 2001a, b). The outcome of this competition is reflected in the language policies that are eventually adopted in multilingual states (Bouchard & Bourhis, 2002; Bourhis, 1984a, 1994a, Kaplan & Baldauf, 1997).

As seen in Figure 1.1, the IAM proposes four clusters of state ideologies which shape the language policies ensuring the predominance of the language majority and the survival of linguistic minorities (Bourhis, 2001a). These ideologies can be situated on a continuum including the pluralism, the civic, the assimilationist and the ethnist ideology. Each of the ideological clusters produces specific language and cultural policies

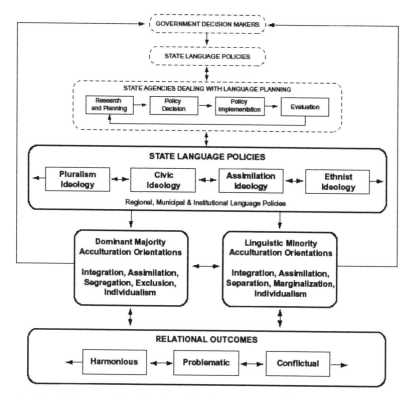

Figure 1.1 State language policies as they relate to the Acculturation Orientations of linguistic minority members and dominant majority members (based on Bourhis, Moïse, Perreault & Sénécal, 1997 and Bourhis, 2001a).

concerning the maintenance of language minorities within a given region or state. This ideological continuum provides the public policy backdrop needed to contextualize the ethnolinguistic vitality and multilingual communication strategies of minority and majority group speakers in the intergroup setting. The cumulative and sustained implementation of these pro-diversity (pluralism) to intolerant (ethnist) language policies can have a decisive impact on the linguistic identity of high/low vitality community speakers, their identity management strategies, their bilingual/multilingual communication strategies and their intergenerational language transmission thus affecting the language maintenance vs. language loss prospects of linguistic minorities.

The *pluralism ideology* implies that in modern states, language majorities and minorities should adopt *public values* including acceptance of the democratic process, obedience to Civil and Criminal codes, endorsement of the Constitution, and/or Charters of Rights and Freedoms. Such values may also include the responsibility of all citizens to learn one or more languages adopted as official or co-official languages of the state. The pluralism ideology upholds that the state has no right to regulate the private values of citizens whose individual liberties in personal domains must be respected. *Private values* include freedom of association in the linguistic, cultural, political spheres, as well as freedom for linguistic minorities to learn and transmit languages of their choice for use at home, private schools, in interpersonal communication, in community and economic activities, and for cultural productions.

The pluralism ideology implies that the state is also willing to support financially and socially the maintenance of the linguistic distinctiveness of its minorities. Such minorities are seen to enhance the linguistic diversity and economic dynamism of mainstream society. The pluralism ideology proposes that because high and low vitality language communities pay taxes, some state funds should be allocated to support the cultural and linguistic activities of minorities, including heritage language schooling and some government services offered in minority languages at the local, regional and national level (Fleras & Elliot, 1992). The ideology assumes that the endogenous culture and institutions of the dominant majority may need to be transformed through 'reasonable accommodation' to serve the linguistic needs of its linguistic minorities (Kymlicka, 1995). However, it is recognized that by virtue of their weaker vitality position, linguistic minorities are more likely to be transformed through assimilation, than the high vitality majority. An example of a language policy inspired by the pluralism policy is Canada's Official Languages Act, which recognizes the equality of French and English as co-official languages in Canada (Bourhis, 1984a, 1994a; Bourhis & Marshall, 1999; Schmidt, 1998). This policy was recognized as paving the way for the adoption of the 1988 Multiculturalism Act, the first official pluralism policy adopted for immigrant cultural communities in the world (Driedger, 1996; Fleras & Elliot, 1992).

As in the case of the pluralism ideology, the *civic ideology* assumes that both majority and minority linguistic communities should share common public values. Unlike the pluralism ideology, the civic ideology enshrines as a principle that the state does not fund or endorse the private values of groups, including linguistic minorities. Thus, this ideology is characterized by official state policies of non-intervention and non-support of minority languages and cultures. However this ideology does respect the right of individuals to organize as community groups, using their own private financial means, in order to maintain or promote their respective languages through after-hours schooling, cultural and religious activities, and own group entrepreneurship. In multilingual states, the civic ideology amounts to state funding of the linguistic and cultural interests of the dominant language group, often portrayed as the 'neutral' unifying embodiment of the nation and its common destiny. It is in the name of a 'neutral state' that the civic ideology legitimizes the absence of official recognition and financial support of its linguistic minorities (Bourhis, 2001a). The survival of linguistic minorities is thus left up to 'free market forces', which, as the language planning literature has demonstrated, usually favour the dominant language of the majority (Fishman, 1991, 2001). Under the pretext of 'neutral non-intervention' on linguistic issues, dominant majorities can in effect accelerate the language shift and language loss of linguistic minorities in multilingual states. Great Britain has traditionally espoused a civic ideology towards its immigrant minorities (Schnapper, 1992). In this case, no state support is granted for the recognition or maintenance of distinctive immigrant languages and cultures. However, state support has been provided to promote more harmonious relations between members of the dominant host society and immigrant communities. For example, funding was provided to develop and apply anti-discrimination laws and to help immigrants integrate more easily within the host society. After centuries of non-recognition of its national minorities (Welsh, Scots, Irish), Britain recently shifted towards a more pluralist orientation by recognizing the distinctiveness of its national minorities through constitutional changes establishing regional Parliaments in Scotland and Wales. It is expected that these regional Parliaments will be in a position to recognize and support financially the revival and maintenance of their ancestral cultures and languages.

The *assimilation ideology* expects language minorities to abandon their own linguistic and cultural distinctiveness for the sake of adopting the language and values of the dominant language group. Some countries expect this linguistic and cultural assimilation to occur voluntarily and gradually over time, but other states impose assimilation through regulations that repress the linguistic and cultural distinctiveness of its minorities in public domains such as the school system and the mass media. Usually, it is the economically and politically dominant language group that is more successful in imposing its language and culture as the unifying 'founding myth' of the nation state (Citron, 1987; Lodge, 1993). For the 'greater cause' of 'national unity', assimilationist policies are designed to accelerate the language loss of national minorities (Fishman, 1991, 2001). Dominant language majorities who endorse assimilationist policies often portray language minorities as a threat to the authenticity, homogeneity and indivisibility of the national state (Crawford, 2000; Safran, 1999; Schmidt, 1998). For instance, Barker and Giles (2004) found that, among Euro-Americans, perceptions of 'threat' caused by a decreasing gap between Anglo-American majority vitality and Hispanic minority vitality was related to support for the English-only movement. Euro-Americans who more strongly identified as Anglo-Americans were the ones most likely to support the English-only movement in their region.

Linguistic minorities sometimes face a dilemma when at the local level, a civic or a pluralist language policy is adopted, but at the state level an assimilationist policy is imposed by the language majority (Wiley & Wright, 2004). For instance, Trujillo (2005) studied the case of Crystal City Independent School District in Texas, USA, where Chicanos gained local control of the school district in the early 1970s. At the local level Hispanics succeeded in adopting a language policy that promoted the teaching of both English and Spanish in the school district (Carter & Segura, 1979). However, the local bilingual language policy was eroded by interventions at the Texas State level which had adopted the unilingualism policies promoted by the English-only movement (Trujillo, 2005).

State policies encouraging or enforcing linguistic assimilation have resulted in the assimilation of not only second and third generation immigrants established in Australia and the United States (Clyne, 2001; Ricento, 1998) but also of aboriginal national minorities of Australia, Canada, the USA and Latin America (Crawford, 1998; Fettes, 1998; Garcia, 1999; Hornberger & King, 2001; Lee & McLaughlin, 2001; Lo Bianco & Rhydwen, 2001; Sachdev, 1998; Taylor, Wright, Ruggiero & Aitchison, 1993), and of national minorities such as the Basque, the Breton and the Occitant in France and Spain (Azurmendi, Bachoc & Zabaleta, 2001; Lodge, 1993; Strubell, 2001; Tabouret-Keller, 1999).

As in the case of the assimilationist ideology, the *ethnist ideology* encourages or forces linguistic minorities to give up their own language and culture for the sake of adopting the language of the dominant majority. Unlike the assimilationist ideology, the ethnist ideology makes it difficult for linguistic minorities to be accepted legally or socially as authentic members of the majority, no matter how much such minorities assimilate linguistically and culturally to the dominant group. Unlike the other ideologies discussed so far, the ethnist ideology usually defines 'who can be' and 'who should be' citizens of the state in ethnically or religiously exclusive terms. This ideology is sometimes enshrined in the notion of 'blood belonging' whereby only members of selected racial groups can gain full legal access to citizenship (Kaplan, 1993). In such states the nation is defined as being composed of a 'kernel' ancestral ethnolinguistic group as determined by birth and kinship. Linguistic minorities and immigrants who do not share this kinship may never be accepted as legitimate citizens of the state.

Important features of German immigration policies illustrate the ethnist ideology. Until recently, German citizenship laws reflected a founding myth based on common blood ties (*volkisch, volschen kern*) binding all Germans by virtue of their kinship (Peralva, 1994). For instance 'German returning immigrants' from Eastern Europe (*Volksdeusche*) are granted full citizenship within months of entry in the country by virtue of 'blood ties' (Wilpert, 1993). In contrast, non-German blood immigrants recruited as 'guest workers' (*Gastarbeiter*), such as Turks and their descendants, have tenuous claim to full citizenship and are denied the right to vote in regional and national elections (Esser & Korte, 1985). However, as a result of growing criticism, aspects of German citizenship law are becoming less restrictive (Hoerder, 1996). Germany adopted a new citizenship and nationality law in 2001. It is now possible to obtain German citizenship as a result of being born in the country (*jus soli*). However, children who are born in Germany to foreign nationals do not automatically receive citizenship. One of the child's parents must reside lawfully in Germany for at least eight years and must hold entitlement to residence or hold an unlimited residence permit for at least three years. Furthermore, the new law offers a shorter mandatory waiting period for naturalization (8 years instead of 15 years).

In democracies, language policies usually reflect the most prevalent ideological orientations endorsed by the dominant language majority (Figure 1.1). In a given state, the majority of the population may endorse the assimilationist ideology, while the civic ideology receives moderate support, and the ethnist and pluralist ideologies are endorsed by only a minority. Depending on economic, political, demographic and military events occurring at the national and international level, politicians elected by the majority of citizens can shift language policies from one ideological orientation to the other. Political tensions may emerge between factions of the dominant population holding rival ideological views on language policies. The polarization of ideological positions regarding such issues may lead to the formation of political parties whose main platform relates to state policies on language as was the case in Quebec, Wales and Belgium in the 1970s (Bourhis, 1984a, 2001b; Bourhis & Giles, 1977; Bourhis, Giles, Leyens & Tajfel, 1979). Backlash movements or xenophobic political parties within the dominant majority may succeed in shifting language policies from the pluralism position to the assimilationist or ethnist ideology (e.g., English-only movement in the USA, Crawford, 2000; Barker & Giles, 2004; Bourhis & Marshall, 1999). However, mobilized linguistic minorities with efficient leadership may succeed in convincing regional or national governments to change existing assimilationist language policies to more tolerant approaches such as the pluralist or the civic language policies. In his influential language planning model known as Reversing Language Shift (RLS), Fishman (1991, 2001) identified the sequence of language policies needed to stem the tide of assimilation suffered by language minorities. Once the language policies are adopted by the state at the local or national level, the government apparatus applying the language laws can help legitimize the use of minority languages not only in private everyday discourse but also in public domains of language use such as the educational system, the public administration, and the mass media. Thus, both top-down and bottom-up pressures can shift language policies from one pole of the ideological continuum to the other over time and across regions. Taken together, language policies applied at the local and national levels can have a substantial impact on multilingual communication, language maintenance, language shift and on the acculturation orientations of both linguistic minorities and members of the dominant language group (Bourhis, 2001a).

acculturation orientations and relations between linguistic minorities and majorities

The struggle of linguistic minorities to maintain their own language and culture may not depend only on state language policies and the objective/subjective vitality positions of such minorities, but may also depend on the acculturation orientations endorsed by individuals from each side of the language divide. A fundamental premise of the IAM model is that not all members of a language community share the same attitudes and orientations about how minorities and majorities should relate with each other (Bourhis, 2001a). The IAM seeks to integrate within a common theoretical framework the following components of linguistic minority and majority intergroup relations: 1) linguistic and acculturation orientations adopted by language minorities; 2) linguistic and acculturation orientations adopted by the dominant majority towards specific linguistic minority groups; 3) interpersonal and intergroup relational outcomes which may be harmonious, problematic or conflictual. Relational outcomes between linguistic minorities and language majority speakers include language choice strategies during cross-cultural communication as well as longer-term outcomes such as language maintenance, language shift and language loss.

defining acculturation orientations

Linguistic minorities can adopt one of five acculturation orientations depending on their desire to maintain their heritage language and culture and their wish to adopt the language and culture of the dominant majority. Using a variant of the immigrant acculturation scale (IAS), linguistic minority acculturation can be measured as an individual difference orientation or can be assessed at the group level as an orientation preferred by subgroups of the language community (Berry, 1997; Berry, Kim, Power, Young & Bujaki, 1989).

The *integrationism* orientation reflects a desire to maintain key features of the linguistic and cultural identity while adopting aspects of the majority culture including its dominant language. Linguistic minorities who adopt the *assimilationism* orientation essentially relinquish their own linguistic and cultural identity for the sake of adopting the language and culture of the dominant majority. Those who adopt the *separatism* orientation have a desire to maintain their heritage language and culture while rejecting key aspects of the dominant culture and sometimes its language. The *marginalization* orientation characterizes minority individuals who feel estranged from both their own heritage language community and that of the dominant language majority. In contrast, linguistic minority members who dissociate themselves from both their ethnolinguistic origin and the dominant majority may do so not because they feel marginalized but simply because they prefer to identify themselves as individuals rather than as members of either a linguistic minority or majority. Such *individualists* reject group ascriptions *per se* and prefer to treat others as individual persons rather than as members of group categories. These five acculturation orientations can be adopted by individuals or by most members of a particular linguistic minority. A majority of individuals from a linguistic minority may endorse an integrationist orientation while the assimilationist and separatist orientations may be preferred by only a few individual immigrants. Furthermore, individuals from a particular ethnolinguistic origin may overwhelmingly adopt the assimilationist orientation, while the majority of individuals from another national minority may prefer the separatist orientation.

The IAM model proposes that by virtue of their strong vitality position in the control of the state, dominant language majorities play a major role in shaping the acculturation orientations of linguistic minorities. Two key questions can be used to situate the acculturation orientations of dominant language majority members. These two prototypic questions are: 1) 'Do you find it acceptable that minorities maintain their linguistic and cultural identity?' 2) 'Do you accept that minorities adopt the linguistic and cultural identity of your majority group?' The acculturation orientations of majority language groups can be monitored using a variant of the host community acculturation scale (HCAS; Bourhis & Bougie, 1998; Montreuil & Bourhis, 2001, 2004). This scale is made up of items that address these two questions in key domains such as language use at home, cultural maintenance, endogamy/exogamy, etc. Responses to the HCAS questionnaire allow the following classification of language majority members as regards their acculturation orientations towards linguistic minorities: integrationists, assimilationist, segregationist, exclusionist and individualists.

Dominant language group members who endorse the *integrationism* orientation accept and value the maintenance of the language and culture of linguistic minorities and also accept that such minorities adopt important features of the majority culture including knowledge and use of the dominant language. This orientation implies that dominant majority members value a stable bilingualism amongst linguistic minorities that may in the long term contribute to cultural and linguistic pluralism as an enduring feature of the mainstream society. The integrationist orientation implies that the dominant majority is willing to transform some of its state and private institutions to accommodate the linguistic and cultural needs of its linguistic and national minorities (e.g., languages of schooling, government services such as health care and social services offered in minority languages).

The *assimilationist* orientation corresponds to the traditional concepts of absorption, whereby dominant group members expect linguistic minorities to relinquish their heritage language and culture for the sake of adopting the language of the majority society. The assimilationist orientation implies that dominant group members will eventually consider linguistic minorities who have assimilated as full-fledged members of the majority society and treat them as equal citizens of the state. Members of the dominant majority who prefer a *segregationist* orientation distance themselves from linguistic minorities by not wishing them to adopt or transform the dominant culture though they accept that national minorities and immigrants maintain their heritage language and culture. Majority group individuals who adopt the segregationist orientation disfavour cross-cultural contacts with linguistic minorities, feel threatened by the presence of linguistic outgroups, prefer such minorities to remain together in separate urban or regional enclaves and are ambivalent regarding the status of linguistic minorities as rightful members of mainstream society. Members of the dominant majority who endorse the *exclusionist* orientation are not only intolerant of the maintenance of minority languages and cultures but also refuse to allow linguistic minorities to adopt features of the dominant culture. Basically, exclusionists believe that linguistic minorities can never be incorporated culturally or linguistically as rightful members of the majority society. Exclusionists are most likely to deny linguistic minorities the right to maintain or use their language in both public and private domains.

Individualists define themselves and others as individuals rather than as members of group categories such as linguistic minorities or dominant majority group members. For individualists it is the personal character-istics of each individual that count most rather than belonging to one group or another. Such individualists, therefore, tend to downgrade the importance of maintaining the language of national minorities or the need to adopt the dominant culture and language as criteria of successful integration. Given that it is personal characteristics that count most, individualists tend to interact with linguistic minorities in the same way they would with other individuals who happen to be members of the dominant majority.

So far the HCAS has been tested empirically with language majority undergraduate students in the following cities: Montreal (Bourhis & Bougie, 1998; Montreuil & Bourhis, 2001, 2004), Los Angeles (Barrette, Bourhis, El-Geledi & Schmidt, 2005), Paris (Barrette, Bourhis, Personnaz & Personnaz, 2004), Geneva (Ogay, Bourhis, Barrette & Montreuil, 2001), Leuven, Belgium (Montreuil, Bourhis & Vanbeslaere, 2004) and Tel Aviv (Bourhis & Dayan, 2004). Results show that the integrationism and the individualism orientations were the most strongly endorsed orientations. The assimilationism orientation was only somewhat endorsed, while the segregationism and exclusionism orientations were least endorsed. However across these studies, results show that individualism and inte-grationism is more strongly endorsed for linguistic minorities that are 'valued' socially than for minorities that are seen as 'devalued'. Conversely, the assimilationism, segregationism and exclusionism orientations tend to be even less strongly endorsed for valued minorities than for devalued minorities.

In the above studies conducted with majority group undergradu-ates across different cities of North America, Europe and Israel, it was possible to draw the social psychological profile of people endorsing each acculturation orientations towards linguistic and national minorities. Results showed that individualism and integrationism are two 'live

and let live' acculturation orientations. Individualists and integrationists enjoyed a secure social identity as majority group members, felt
more comfortable with minorities, wanted close relations with both
valued and devalued minorities and felt that minorities wanted good
relations with the majority language community. Integrationists and
individualists did not endorse the authoritarianism, social dominance
and ethnocentric ideologies, were more likely to identify with 'left of
centre' political parties and were more likely to endorse 'civic belonging'
rather than 'ethnic belonging' beliefs about who can be considered a 'true
member' of the majority society. In contrast, majority group members
who endorsed the assimilationism, segregationism and exclusionism
orientations shared in common the rejection of linguistic minorities and
their culture while wishing to avoid minorities as colleagues at work,
as neighbours or as best friends. Assimilationists, segregationists and
exclusionists were more likely to feel that their ingroup identity was
threatened by the presence of linguistic minorities, especially devalued
ones. They were more likely to feel insecure culturally, linguistically and
economically as members of their own majority group. They also tended
to endorse social dominance orientations, authoritarian and ethnocentric
ideologies, were more likely to identify with right-wing political parties
and were more likely to endorse 'ethnic belonging' beliefs. In each
cultural setting specific social psychological variables differentiated the
endorsement of each acculturation orientation. Taken together, these
social psychological correlates of acculturation orientations attest to the
construct validity of the HCAS and confirm that language majorities can
be quite differentiated in their orientations towards valued and devalued
linguistic minorities.

How are dominant language community acculturation orientations
related to our proposed continuum of ideologies regarding language
policies? As proposed in Figure 1.1, state language policies are expected
to influence the acculturation orientation of both minority and majority
language communities. Tentatively, the simplest hypothesis is that a match
should exist between the type of acculturation orientation preferred by
language majority members and their support for the corresponding state
ideologies depicted on the continuum. Thus, language majority members
whose acculturation orientation is *integrationist* are likely to favour the
pluralism ideology of providing publicly funded institutional support
for the maintenance of minority languages and cultures. Individualists are more likely to support language policies which range from the
pluralism to civic part of the continuum than from the assimilationist to
ethnist pole of the continuum. Individualists would support institutional

support for linguistic minorities especially if such services were mainly funded by the linguistic communities themselves. Language majority members who endorse the *assimilationist* orientation are likely to endorse language policies along the civic to assimilationist range of the ideological continuum. Consequently, assimilationists are unlikely to support any state funding for minority language services such as schooling, health care or the judiciary. Assimilationists may be tempted to support government measures designed to erode the intergenerational transmission and use of minority languages thus accelerating the assimilation process. However, assimilationists may tolerate efforts by linguistic minorities to promote the maintenance of their minority language in private settings (e.g., Sunday language schooling), as long as such efforts are funded only by members of the minority groups themselves. *Segregationists* are likely to support language policies that range from the assimilationist to the ethnist pole of the continuum. As such they are likely to oppose state funding for the maintenance of minority languages (e.g. schooling). However, segregationists could tolerate efforts by linguistic minorities to fund their own private schools or language services, as long as such activities were conducted within the separate enclaves traditionally occupied by such minorities. *Exclusionist* majority members are likely to prefer language policies that repress the use and transmission of minority languages and would encourage measures designed to accelerate language shift resulting in complete language loss for linguistic minorities.

The IAM model proposes that language majority acculturation orientations are not uniform, but rather will vary depending on the linguistic background of each of the national minorities and immigrant groups being assessed. For instance, results obtained using the adapted HCAS may yield contrasting patterns for the valued national minority A vs. the devalued recently established immigrant group B. Finer analysis of majority acculturation orientation could be conducted with targeted subgroups of the dominant majority, such as members of pluralist political parties contrasted with members of nationalist xenophobic associations and parties. The proportion of language majority members adopting each of the acculturation orientations may vary across time for the same target linguistic minority, depending on changing demographic, economic and political circumstances. For instance, dominant majority orientations towards a particular national minority may be mostly integrationist at first, then shift towards the segregationist pole as the national minority becomes more militant in claiming institutional support for its language in the school system and in government services.

Different subgroups of linguistic minorities are expected to adopt different configurations of acculturation orientations, depending on their ethnolinguistic origin, social class background, and degree of ingroup identification and linguistic militancy, degree of contact with the dominant majority, and state language policies supporting or repressing their minority language. The proportion of linguistic minorities from the same origin favouring each acculturation orientation may also change from one generation to the other, depending on the pattern of upward or downward mobility experienced by linguistic minorities during the lifespan and across the generations. The acculturation orientations of linguistic minorities may also change in line with improvements or declines in minority group vitality across time. For instance, as the vitality of a national minority improves, thanks to sustained intergenerational transmission of the mother tongue (Fishman, 1991, 2001) coupled with stronger institutional support in favour of minority language schooling, the profile of acculturation orientations within this national minority may shift from a mainly integrationist orientation to a predominantly separatist orientation.

acculturation orientations and relational outcomes

It is by combining the five acculturation orientations of linguistic minorities with the five language majority ones that the interactive nature of the IAM framework becomes most evident (Figure 1.1). *Relational outcomes* include patterns of intercultural communication between linguistic minority and dominant majority group speakers, interethnic attitudes and stereotypes, acculturative stress, and discrimination between dominant majority group members and linguistic minority individuals in domains such as housing, employment, schooling and the police. It is the interaction of linguistic minority and language majority group acculturation orientations that determines whether relational outcomes are harmonious, problematic or conflictual in different settings.

The most *harmonious relational outcomes* are predicted when both high vitality majority group speakers and linguistic minority speakers share either the integrationist, assimilationist or individualist acculturation orientations. It is under such circumstances that the IAM model predicts positive relational outcomes including positive and effective verbal and non-verbal cross-cultural communications; mutually positive interethnic attitudes and stereotypes, low intergroup tension, low acculturative stress and virtually no discrimination between dominant majority and linguistic minority group members.

Problematic relational outcomes emerge when members of the dominant majority and the linguistic minority experience both partial agreement and partial disagreement as regards their preferred profile of acculturation orientations. Problematic outcomes emerge when linguistic minority speakers favour assimilationism while language majority speakers prefer linguistic minorities to adopt the integrationism orientation, and conversely when speakers of the linguistic minority prefer integrationism but dominant group speakers insist that minorities assimilate linguistically to mainstream society. Such relational outcomes may trigger communication breakdown between minority/majority speakers, foster negative intergroup stereotypes, lead to discriminatory behaviours, and cause both language shift pressures and acculturative stress amongst speakers of the linguistic minority. Problematic relational outcomes are also likely to emerge for linguistic minority speakers whose acculturation orientation is marginalization or individualism in a majority society which favours integrationism or assimilationism. Likewise, majority group speakers who endorse the individualism orientation are likely to have problematic relational outcomes with minority speakers who highlight their linguistic identity as group members during their encounters.

Linguistic minority speakers who endorse the separatism orientation are likely to experience *conflictual relational outcomes* with most dominant majority speakers, especially those who have a segregationist and exclusionist acculturation orientation. Majority speakers who endorse the segregationism or exclusionism orientation are likely to foster the most conflictual relational outcomes with targeted national minorities regardless of the acculturation orientations they endorse. In addition to miscommunicating with linguistic minorities, exclusionists and segregationists are likely to hold negative stereotypes towards linguistic minorities, to discriminate against them in many domains including employment and housing while opposing institutional support in favour of linguistic minorities. Finally, exclusionists are the speakers of the dominant majority most likely to launch racist attacks against linguistic minorities and to organize politically to disparage the language and culture of linguistic minorities.

Under such circumstances, linguistic minorities who have very low vitality are likely to be more vulnerable and suffer more acculturative stress and language shift than medium vitality linguistic minorities whose strength in numbers and institutional support can better shield them against abuses from segregationist and exclusionist language majorities. Of the linguistic minorities that are targeted by exclusionists it is those with a separatist orientation and medium vitality that are most likely to resist and even retaliate against linguistic majority persecutions. Thus, the IAM model predicts the most intergroup conflict in encounters between segregationist/exclusionist majority speakers and linguistic minorities who have a separatist orientation. As implied in Figure 1.1, it is proposed that conflictual relational outcomes may be attenuated by state language policies that are situated toward the pluralistic and civic end of the continuum. Conversely, conflictual relational outcomes may be accentuated by language policies that are situated toward the assimilation and especially ethnist pole.

language switching strategies as relational outcomes

Language switching strategies adopted in encounters between linguistic minority and majority speakers can reflect or contribute to harmonious vs. problematic vs. conflictual relational outcomes. When cross-cultural conversations involve code-switching (CS), different languages may be used within the same sentence, or between sentences, or between speaker turns (Bourhis, 1979; Gardner-Chloros, 1991; Milroy & Muysken, 1995; Myers-Scotton, 1997; Ng & He, 2004; Sachdev & Bourhis, 2001, 2005; Sachdev & Giles, 2004). Linguistic competence, desires to increase communication accuracy, sociolinguistic norms, and social identity needs have been identified as important factors governing code-switching in conversations between linguistic minorities and majorities (Beebe & Giles, 1984; Giles & Coupland, 1991; Sachdev & Bourhis, 2001, 2005). A key contribution in our understanding of the complexity and dynamic nature of multilingual communication has been the development of communication accommodation theory (CAT; Bourhis, 1979; Coupland & Giles, 1988; Gallois, Giles, Jones, Cargile & Ota, 1995; Giles, Taylor & Bourhis, 1973; Niedzielski & Giles, 1996; Reid & Giles, 2005; Sachdev & Giles, 2004).

CAT was developed partly as a counterpoint to the sociolinguistic tradition of explaining code-switching strictly in terms of language norms determining who speaks what to whom and when (Myers-Scotton, 1997; Sachdev & Bourhis, 2001). Without ignoring normative factors, CAT sought to account for language use in terms of interlocutors' motives, attitudes, perceptions and group loyalties in a broad range of experimental and applied settings (Crabtree & Sapp, 2004; Giles, Coupland & Coupland, 1991; Giles, Mulac, Bradac & Johnson, 1987; De Montes, Semin & Valencia, 2003; Ng & He, 2004; Shepard, Giles & Le Poire, 2001).

CAT proposes that most communicative behaviours involve either an approach or an avoidance orientation between speakers, a process known as interpersonal accommodation (Giles et al., 1973). The three basic communicative strategies proposed within CAT are convergence, divergence and maintenance, although other strategies have also been investigated (Shepard et al., 2001; Ng & He, 2004; Lin & Harwood, 2003). Briefly, *convergence* was defined as a strategy whereby individuals adapt their communicative behaviours in terms of a wide range of linguistic (e.g., languages, accents, speech rates), paralinguistic (e.g., pauses, utterance length), and nonverbal features (e.g., smiling, gazing) in such a way as to become more similar to their interlocutor's behaviour (Giles et al., 1973; Giles & Coupland, 1991). Within the IAM, language convergence strategies can be associated mostly with harmonious relational outcomes. Conversely, *divergence* is defined as a dissociative strategy where individuals change their communicative behaviours to become less similar to their interlocutor's behaviour (Bourhis & Giles, 1977). Language *maintenance* is a speech act involving non-convergence with the other but, instead, sustaining one's own personal or own group language usage (Bourhis, 1979, 1984b). Within the IAM, language maintenance can be associated with a problematic relational outcome, while language divergence is more closely associated with conflictual relational outcomes. It is noteworthy that these three communicative strategies have been found to occur simultaneously on a variety of linguistic and paralinguistic levels and that minority and majority speakers are not always aware that they are modifying their communicative behaviours (Giles et al., 1977, 1987; Hecht, Jackson & Pitts, 2005). Compared to convergence, levels of awareness about divergence and maintenance tends to be higher given their willful dissociative intent as a way of expressing interpersonal dislike and/or group affirmation and differentiation (Bourhis, 1985; Bourhis, Giles & Lambert, 1975; Street, 1982).

CAT attempts to explain and predict convergence, maintenance and divergence in terms of social psychological processes operating at both the interindividual level (e.g., similarity-attraction; Byrne, 1969) and at the intergroup level where social identity processes are of primary importance (Giles, 1978; Giles et al., 1977; Giles & Johnson, 1987; Tajfel & Turner, 1986).

At the interindividual level, motivations for social approval are thought to underlie communication convergence (Giles et al., 1987). Using research on similarity-attraction (Byrne, 1969) as a starting point, it was argued that as interlocutors become more similar in their speech styles they grow to like each other more. Furthermore, if interlocutors wish to highlight their similarities, they are more likely to converge linguistically and non-verbally (Coupland, Coupland, Giles & Henwood, 1988;

Janssen & Murachver, 2004). In support of this, studies have suggested that language convergence facilitates interpersonal and intergroup interaction where linguistic dissimilarities may otherwise be a barrier to effective communication (Bourhis, 1979). Linguistic convergence has the effect of increasing interlocutors' intelligibility (Triandis, 1960), predictability (Berger & Bradac, 1982) and interpersonal involvement (LaFrance, 1979). Additionally, convergence is perceived more favourably if it can be attributed internally to the converger's personal intentions rather than to external pressures such as sociolinguistic norms (Simard, Taylor & Giles, 1976). In a classic study, Montreal Anglophone bilinguals who made an effort to converge to the French mother tongue of their interlocutor were more likely to find their Francophone interlocutor reciprocate the effort through language convergence in English (Giles et al., 1973).

Convergence may also reflect motivations to maximize rewards and minimize costs (Homans, 1961). For instance, in conversations between bilingual Francophone and Anglophone civil servants of the Canadian Federal Administration working in provinces where Anglophones are in the majority (New Brunbswick and Ontario), Francophones were more likely to converge to English than Anglophones were to converge to French (Bourhis, 1994b, 2004; Clément & Bourhis, 1996). The enduring prestige of English as the language of work and upward mobility in Anglo-Canadian society contributed to the reward power of English use for both Anglophone and Francophone civil servants, even in an organizational setting promoting official bilingualism. However, in the Province of Quebec, where Francophones are the dominant majority, it was Anglophone civil servants who were more likely to converge to French than Francophones were to converge to English (Bourhis, 2005). Language planning favouring French rather than English as the dominant language of Quebec society over the last thirty years (Bourhis, 1984a, 2001b) contributed to the reward power of French as the language of work even in the Canadian Federal Administration whose language policy promotes the equal use of French and English as the language of work. The reward power of competing languages also affects language choice strategies in public situations not regulated by official bilingualism regulations. In his field study, Van den Berg (1986) observed that bilingual customers converged 'downward' by using the local vernacular (Southern Min, Hakka) with street market attendants, yet converged 'upward' by using Mandarin in their dealings with bank clerks, again maximizing their reward potential in each communication situation.

At the intergroup level, social identity theory (SIT) proposes that individuals prefer to belong to groups that provide them with a positive social identity (Tajfel & Turner, 1986). In the language attitude literature, studies have consistently shown that speakers who identify with their own group tend to evaluate speakers of their ingroup more favourably than outgroup speakers (Ryan & Giles, 1982). This 'ingroup favouritism effect' was obtained on ratings of both status and solidarity traits and enhanced the positive social identity of speakers whether they were differentiated by ethnicity, social class, or regional or national origin (Giles & Ryan, 1982). Experimental studies show that positive social identification with the ingroup is related to the positive evaluation of language maintenance and language divergence voiced by ingroup members in conversations with rival outgroup speakers (Bourhis, Giles & Lambert, 1975; Genesee & Bourhis, 1988). A field study conducted in Hong Kong one year before its handover to the PRC showed that Chinese respondents who identified with Hong Kong evaluated ingroup members who diverged (by using Cantonese) from Mandarin speakers more favourably than did Chinese participants who identified with mainland China (Tong, Hong, Lee & Chiu, 1999).

SIT proposes that minority and majority group speakers engage in personal and collective strategies for achieving and maintaining a 'positive distinctiveness' vis-à-vis salient or rival linguistic outgroups. Language maintenance and divergence are ideal strategies of psycholinguistic distinctiveness, as they contribute to the establishment of favourable social comparisons with outgroup speakers on language dimensions (Abrams, O'Conner & Giles, 2002; Crabtree & Sapp, 2004; Giles et al., 1977, 1987; Reid & Giles, 2005). When a speaker's linguistic identity is made salient by a threatening outgroup speaker, members are likely to perceive the encounter in intergroup terms and strategically use language divergence and language maintenance in order to maintain or assert their positive social identity. For instance, a language laboratory study conducted in Wales had Welsh learners respond verbally to an outgroup English speaker who had voiced a culturally threatening message using the 'Queen's English' accent (Bourhis & Giles, 1977). Results showed that the Welsh learners not only disagreed verbally with the English outgroup speaker but also expressed their dissociative reaction by diverging linguistically through emphasizing their Welsh accent in English. Similarly, a language laboratory study conducted in Belgium examined how trilingual Flemish undergraduates responded to a French-background confederate who voiced a series of questions in English and then in French (Bourhis et al., 1979). When the French confederate used English to voice content neutral questions, the Flemish students converged to English. However, when the confederate switched to French to voice a culturally threatening message, all the Flemish undergraduates demonstrated linguistic and content divergence by switching to Flemish, vehemently disagreeing with the disparaging statements about the Flemish language, and using insulting epithets to describe the French confederate.

Language strategies proposed by CAT may be investigated by using not only synchronic methodologies but also by using broader diachronic approaches. For instance, a series of field studies were conducted in bilingual Montreal from 1977 to 1997 to monitor bilingual communication between Francophone and Anglophone pedestrians following the adoption of the Bill 101 language law designed to increase the status of French relative to English in Quebec (Bourhis, 1984b, 2001a). Local Francophone and Anglophone pedestrians were randomly accosted in downtown Montreal by a female confederate who voiced a plea for directions in either fluent French or fluent English. While controlling for the bilingual skills of respondents, results showed that Francophone pedestrians systematically converged to English (95–100 per cent) when responding to the plea voiced in English by the confederate in the four studies conducted from 1977 to 1997. In contrast, as many as 30 per cent to 40 per cent of Anglophone pedestrians maintained English when responding to pleas for directions voiced in French in the studies conducted from 1977 to 1991 (Bourhis, 1984b; Moïse & Bourhis, 1994). Results obtained in favour of English usage during this period reflected the lingering power advantage of the elite Anglophone minority relative to the low status Francophone majority in Montreal. It was only in a 1997 study that 95 per cent of Anglophone pedestrians converged to French when providing directions to the Francophone confederate (Amiot & Bourhis, 1999). That both Anglophones and Francophones overwhelmingly converged to each other's linguistic needs by 1997 suggested that such multilingual exchanges were being emptied of their former tense intergroup symbolism, while being redefined as encounters that were more neutral, functional and interpersonal in nature. Thus, when linguistic identities are less salient in an intergroup encounter, both linguistic minorities and majorities may converge to one or the other language in order to maximize effective communication rather than accentuate the salience of their respective linguistic distinctiveness.

concluding note

Multilingualism rather than unilingualism is the rule in most modern states. As implied in the ethnolinguistic vitality framework, it is the stratification of language communities rather than their statutory equality which is the rule in most multilingual societies. We have seen with the interactive acculturation model (IAM) that linguistic majorities and minorities more often compete than collaborate to gain the institutional support they need to ensure their control of the public and private institutions of the state. Gaining ground on the institutional support front has the immediate effect of improving the social and economic fate of ingroup speakers while in the long run contributing to the intergenerational transmission of the ingroup language, thus contributing to the future vitality of the language community. Given the limited organizational and financial resources of most regions and states it is not surprising that contrasting language communities must compete to improve their respective institutional support. Language laws can accentuate or attenuate rivalries between competing language communities. To the degree that language laws giving some protection to language minorities become consensual, they can at least stabilize the vitality position of linguistic minorities who in a free market environment would otherwise be faced with language loss or even language death. By differentiating subgroups of language community members according to their acculturation orientations, we may be in a better position to identify the subgroup of community leaders most likely to promote more fruitful compromises between competing language communities, thus reducing tensions between linguistic minorities and majorities. As seen in communication accommodation theory (CAT), language strategies such as convergence, maintenance and divergence provide a vivid reflection of relational outcomes emerging between speakers of contrasting language communities. Current research should help uncover the acculturation orientations most likely to yield harmonious, problematic and conflictual relational outcomes as expressed through the code-switching strategies proposed within CAT.

author note

Comments are welcome and can be addressed to Richard Y. Bourhis and Shaha El-Geledi, Département de psychologie, Université du Québec à Montréal, Canada, CP 8888, Succ.Centre-Ville, Montreal, Canada, H3C 3P8. bourhis.richard@uqam. ca; el-geledi.shaha@courrier.uqam.ca, or to Itesh Sachdev, School of Oriental and African Studies, University of London, Thornhaugh Street, Russell Square, London, England, WC1H 0XG. I.sachdev@soas.ac.uk

references

Abrams, J., O'Conner, J. & Giles, H. (2002). Identity and intergroup communication. In W. B. Gudykunst & B. Mody (Eds.), *Handbook of international and intercultural communication* (2nd ed., pp.225–240). Thousand Oaks, CA: Sage.

Allard, R. & Landry, R. (1986). Subjective ethnolinguistic vitality viewed as a belief system. *Journal of Multilingual and Multicultural Development, 7,* 1–12.

Allard, R. & Landry, R. (1994). Subjective ethnolinguistic vitality: A comparison of two measures. *International Journal of the Sociology of Language, 108,* 117–144.

Amiot, C. & Bourhis, R.Y. (1999). Ethnicity and French-English Communication in Montréal. *Poster presented at the 60th convention of the Canadian Psychological Association,* Halifax, NS, Canada.

Atkinson, D. (2000). Minorisation, identity and ethnolinguistic vitality in Catalonia. *Journal of Multilingual and Multicultural Development, 21,* 185–197.

Azurmendi, M.J., Bachoc, E. & Zabaleta, F. (2001). Reversing language shift: The case of Basque. In J.A. Fishman (Ed.), *Can threatened languages be saved? Reversing Language shift, revisited: A 21st century perspective* (pp.234–259). Clevedon, Avon, UK: Multilingual Matters.

Azurmendi, M.J., Bourhis, R.Y., Ros, M. & Garcia, I. (1998). Identidad etnolinguistica y construccion de ciudadania en las Comunidades Autonomas Bilingues (CAB) de Espana. *Revista de Psycologia Social, 13 (3),* 559–589.

Barker, V., Giles, H., Noels, K., Duck, J., Hecht, M. & Clément, R. (2001). The English-only movement: A communication analysis of changing perceptions of language vitality, *Journal of Communication, 51,* 3–37.

Barker, V. & Giles, H. (2004). English-only policies: Perceived support and social limitation. *Language and Communication, 24,* 77–95.

Barrette, G., Bourhis, R.Y., Personnaz, M. & Personnaz, B. (2004). Acculturation orientations of French and North African undergraduates in Paris. *International Journal of Intercultural Relations, 28,* 415–438.

Barrette, G., Bourhis, R.Y., El-Geledi, S. & Schmidt, R. Sr. (2005). Acculturation and relations between immigrants and host communities. Manuscript under revision: *Journal of Cross-Cultural Psychology.*

Beebe, L. & Giles, H. (1984). Speech accommodation theories: A discussion in terms of second language acquisition. *International Journal of the Sociology of Language, 46,* 5–32.

Berger, C.R. & Bradac, J.J. (1982). *Language and social knowledge.* London: Edward Arnold.

Berry, J.W. (1997). Immigration, acculturation and adaptation. *Applied Psychology: An International Review, 46,* 5–34.

Berry, J.W., Kim, U., Power, S., Young, M. & Bujaki, M. (1989). Acculturation attitudes in plural societies. *Applied Psychology: An International Review, 38,* 185–206.

Bornman, E. & Appelgryn, A.E. (1997). Ethnolinguistic vitality under a new political dispensation in South Africa. *The Journal of Social Psychology, 137,* 690–707.

Bouchard, P. & Bourhis, R.Y. (2002). L'aménagement linguistique au Québec: 25 ans d'application de la Charte de la langue française. (Language planning in Quebec: 25 years of implementing the Charter of the French language). *Revue d'Aménagement Linguistique.* Québec: Publications du Québec.

Bourhis, R.Y. (1979). Language and ethnic interaction: A social psychological approach. In H. Giles & B. Saint-Jacques (Eds.), *Language and Ethnic Relations.* Oxford: Pergamon Press.

Bourhis, R.Y. (1984a). Language policies in multilingual settings. In R.Y. Bourhis (Ed.). *Conflict and language planning in Quebec.* Clevedon: Multilingual Matters.

Bourhis, R.Y. (1984b). Cross-cultural communication in Montreal: Two field studies since Bill 101. *International Journal of the Sociology of Language, 46,* 33–47.

Bourhis, R.Y. (1985). The sequential nature of language choice in cross-cultural communication. In R.L. Street, Jr. & J.N. Cappella (Eds.), *Sequence and pattern in communicative behavior* (pp.120–141). London: Edward Arnold.

Bourhis, R.Y. (1994a). Introduction and overview of language events in Canada. *International Journal of the Sociology of Language, 105–106,* 5–36.

Bourhis, R.Y. (1994b). Bilingualism and the language of work: The linguistic work environment survey. *International Journal of the Sociology of Language, 105–106,* 217–266.

Bourhis, R.Y. (2001a). Reversing language shift in Quebec. In J.A. Fishman (Ed.), *Can threatened languages be saved?* (pp.101–141). Clevedon, England: Multilingual Matters.

Bourhis, R.Y. (2001b). Acculturation, language maintenance and language shift. In J. Klatter-Falmer and P. Van Avermaet (Eds.), *Theories on language maintenance and loss of minority languages: Towards a more integrated explanatory framework* (pp.5–37). New York: Waxmann Verlag.

Bourhis, R.Y. (2004). *Organizational and sociolinguistic determinants of official language use in the Canadian Public Service: A survey of six departments in the NCR.* Ottawa, Canada: Office of the Commissioner of Official Languages.

Bourhis, R.Y. (2005). *Sociolinguistic and organizational correlates of French-English use in the Federal Public Service of Québec.* Ottawa, Canada: Office of the Commissioner of Official Languages.

Bourhis, R.Y., Giles, H. & Tajfel, H. (1973). Language as a determinant of Welsh Identity. *European Journal of Social Psychology, 3,* 447–460.

Bourhis, R.Y., Giles, H. & Lambert, W.E. (1975). Social consequences of accommodating one's style of speech: a cross-national investigation. *International Journal of the Sociology of Language, 6,* 55–72. Reprinted in: *Linguistics, 166,* 55–71.

Bourhis, R.Y. & Giles, H. (1977). The language of intergroup distinctiveness. In H. Giles (Ed.), *Language, ethnicity and intergroup relations* (pp.119–135). London: Academic Press.

Bourhis, R.Y., Giles, H., Leyens, J-P. & Tajfel, H. (1979). Psycholinguistic distinctiveness: Language divergence in Belgium. In H. Giles & R.N. St. Clair (Eds.), *Language and Social Psychology* (pp.158–185). Oxford: Basil Blackwell.

Bourhis, R. Y., Giles, H. & Rosenthal, D. (1981). Notes on the construction of a 'Subjective Vitality Questionnaire' for ethnolinguistic groups. *Journal of Multilingual and Multicultural Development, 2,* 144–155.

Bourhis, R.Y. & Sachdev, I. (1984). Vitality perceptions and language attitudes: Some Canadian data. *Journal of Language and Social Psychology, 3,* 97–126.

Bourhis, R.Y., Moïse, L. C., Perreault, S. & Senécal, S. (1997). Towards an interactive acculturation model: A social psychological approach. *International Journal of Psychology, 32,* 369–386.

Bourhis, R.Y. & Bougie, E. (1998). Le modèle d'acculturation interactif: Une étude exploratoire. *Revue québécoise de psychologie, 19,* 75–114.

Bourhis, R.Y. & Marshall, D. (1999). The United States and Canada. In J. Fishman (Ed.), *Handbook of Language and Ethnic Identity* (pp.244–264). Oxford: Oxford University Press.

Bourhis, R.Y. & Landry, R. (2002). La loi 101 et l'aménagement du paysage linguistique au Québec. *Revue d'aménagement linguistique, 105–106*, 107–132.

Bourhis, R.Y. & Dayan, J. (2004). Acculturation orientations towards Israeli Arabs and Jewish immigrants in Israel. *International Journal of Psychology, 39*, 118–131.

Bourhis, R.Y. & Lepicq, D. (2004). *La vitalité des communautés francophone et Anglophone du Québec: Bilan et perspectives depuis la loi 101*. Cahier de recherche No.11 Montréal, Québec: Chaire Concordia-UQÀM en études ethniques.

Bourhis, R.Y. & Maass, A. (2005). Linguistic prejudice and stereotypes. In U. Ammon, N. Dittmar, K.J. Mattheir & P. Trudgill (Eds.), *Sociolinguistics: An international handbook of the science of language and society*, 2nd edition. Berlin and New York: Walter De Gruyter.

Byrne, D. (1969). Attitudes and attraction. *Advances in Experimental Social Psychology, 4*, 35–89.

Carter, T.P. & Segura, R.D. (1979). *Mexican Americans in school: A decade of change*. New York: College Entrance Examination Board.

Citron, S. (1987). *Le Mythe National: l'histoire de France en question*. (The National Myth: A reappraisal of the History of France). Paris: Les Éditions Ouvrières.

Clément, R., Baker, S.C. & MacIntyre, P.D. (2003). Willingness to communicate in a second language: The effect of context, norms and vitality. *Journal of Language and Social Psychology, 22*, 190–209.

Clément, R. & Bourhis, R.Y. (1996). Bilingualism and intergroup communication. *International Journal of Psycholinguistics, 12*, 171–191.

Clyne, M. (2001). Can the shift from immigrant languages be reversed in Australia? In J.A. Fishman (Ed.), *Can threatened languages be saved?* (pp.364–390). Clevedon, England: Multilingual Matters.

Cooper, R.L. (1989). *Language planning and social change*. Cambridge: Cambridge University Press.

Coupland, N., Coupland, J., Giles, H. & Henwood, K. (1988). Accommodating the elderly: Invoking and extending a theory. *Language in Society, 17*, 1–41.

Coupland, N. & Giles, H. (Eds.) (1988). Communicative accommodation: Recent developments. *Language and Communication, 8*, 175–327.

Crabtree, R.D. & Sapp, D.A. (2004). Your culture, my classroom, whose pedagogy? Negotiating effective teaching and learning in Brazil. *Journal of Studies in International Education, 8*, 105–132.

Crawford, J. (1998). Endangered Native American languages: What is to be done, and why? In T. Ricento & B. Burnaby (Eds.), *Language and Politics in the United States and Canada: Myths and Realities* (pp.151–165). Mahwah, New Jersey: Lawrence Erlbaum.

Crawford, J. (2000). *At war with diversity: US language policy in an age of anxiety*. Clevedon, England: Multilingual Matters.

De Montes, L.G., Semin, G.R. & Valencia, J.F. (2003). Communication patterns in interdependent relationships. *Journal of Language and Social Psychology, 22*, 259–281.

Driedger, L. (1996). *Multi-ethnic Canada: Identities and inequalities*. Toronto: Oxford University Press.

Esser, H. & Korte, H. (1985). Federal Republic of Germany. In T. Hammar (Ed.), *European immigration policy: A comparative study* (pp.165–205). Cambridge: Cambridge University Press.

Fettes, M. (1998). Life on the edge: Canada's Aboriginal languages under official bilingualism. In T. Ricento & B. Burnaby (Eds.), *Language and politics in the United States and Canada: Myths and realities* (pp.117–149). Mahwah, New Jersey: Lawrence Erlbaum.

Fishman, J.A. (1977). Language and ethnicity. In H. Giles (Ed.), *Language, ethnicity and intergroup relations*, (pp.15–57). London: Academic Press.

Fishman, J.A. (1991). *Reversing language shift.* Clevedon, Avon, England: Multilingual Matters.

Fishman, J.A. (Ed.) (2001). Why is it so hard to save a threatened language? In J.A. Fishman (Ed.), *Can threatened languages be saved?* (pp.1–22). Clevedon, England: Multilingual Matters.

Fleras, A. & Elliot, J.L. (1992). *The challenge of diversity: Multiculturalism in Canada.* Scarbourough: Nelson Canada.

Gallois, C., Giles, H., Jones, E., Cargile, A.C. & Ota, H. (1995). Accommodating intercultural encounters: Elaborations and extensions. In R. Wiseman (Ed.), *Theories of intercultural communication*, 19th International and Intercultural Communication Annual (pp.115–147). Thousand Oaks, CA: Sage.

Garcia, O. (1999). Latin america. In J. Fishman (Ed). *Handbook of language and ethnic identity* (pp.226–243). Oxford: Oxford University Press.

Gardner-Chloros, P. (1991). *Language selection and switching in Strasbourg.* Oxford: Clarendon Press.

Genesee, F. & Bourhis, R. Y. (1988). Evaluative reactions to language choice strategies: The role of sociostructural factors. *Language and Communication, 8*, 229–250.

Giles, H. (1978). Linguistic differentiation between ethnic groups. In H. Tajfel (Ed.), *Differentiation between social groups* (pp.361–393). London: Academic Press.

Giles, H. (2001). Ethnolinguistic vitality. In Mesthrie R. (Ed.), *Concise encyclopedia of Sociolinguistics*. Elsevier, Oxford.

Giles, H., Taylor, D.M. & Bourhis, R.Y. (1973). Toward a theory of interpersonal accommodation through speech: Some Canadian data. *Language in Society, 2*, 177–192.

Giles, H. & Powesland, P. (1975). *Speech style and social evaluation*. London: Academic Press.

Giles, H., Bourhis, R.Y. & Taylor, D. (1977). Towards a theory of language in ethnic group relations. In H. Giles (Ed.), *Language, ethnicity and intergroup relations* (pp.307–348). London: Academic Press.

Giles, H. & Ryan, E.B. (1982). Prolegomena for developing a social psychological theory of language attitudes. In E.B. Ryan & H. Giles (Eds.), *Attitudes toward language variation*. London: Academic Press.

Giles, H., Rosenthal, D. & Young, L. (1985). Perceived ethnolinguistic vitality: The Anglo- and Greek-Australian setting. *Journal of Multilingual and Multicultural Development, 6*, 253–269.

Giles, H. & Johnson, P. (1987). Ethnolinguistic identity theory: A social psychological approach to language maintenance. *International Journal of the Sociology of Language, 68*, 69–99.

Giles, H., Mulac, A., Bradac, J.J. & Johnson, P. (1987). Speech accommodation theory: The first decade and beyond. In M.L. Mclaughlin (Ed.), *Communication yearbook 10* (pp.13–48). Beverly Hills: Sage.

Giles, H. & Coupland, N. (1991). *Language: Contexts and consequences*. Milton Keynes: Open University Press.

Giles, H. Coupland, J. & Coupland, N. (Eds.) (1991). *Contexts of accommodation: Developments in applied sociolinguistics*. Cambridge: Cambridge University Press.

Harwood, J., Giles, H. & Bourhis, R.Y. (1994). The genesis of vitality theory: Historical patterns and discoursal dimensions. *International Journal of the Sociology of Language, 108*, 167–206.

Hecht, M., Jackson, R. & Pitts, M. (2005). Culture: Intersection of intergroup identity theories. In J. Harwood & H. Giles (Eds.), *Intergroup communication: Multiple perspectives* (pp.21–42). New York: Peter Lang Publishers.

Hoerder, D. (1996). *Nation and multiculturalism in German past and present: Comparative perspectives*. Paper presented at the Nation-State, Multi-Ethnicity and Citizenship Conference. Montreal, Quebec, Canada.

Homans, G. (1961). *Social behavior: Its elementary forms*. New York: Harcourt, Brace and World.

Hornberger, N.H. & King, K.A. (2001) Reversing quechua language shift in South America. In J.A. Fishman (Ed.), *Can threatened languages be saved? Reversing language shift, revisited: A 21st century perspective*. (pp.166–194). Clevedon, Avon, UK: Multilingual Matters.

Janssen, A. & Murachver, T. (2004). The role of gender in New Zealand literature: Comparisons across periods and styles of writing. *Journal of Language and Social Psychology, 23*, 180–203.

Johnson, F.L. (2000). *Speaking culturally: Language diversity in the United States*. Thousand Oaks, CA: Sage.

Johnson, M.L. & Doucet, P. (2006). *A sharper view: Evaluating the vitality of official language minority communities*. Office of the Commissioner of Official Languages, Montreal, Quebec, Canada.

Johnson, P., Giles, H. & Bourhis, R.Y. (1983). The viability of ethnolinguistic vitality: A reply, *Journal of Multilingual and Multicultural Development, 4*, 255–269.

Kaplan, W. (1993). Who belongs? Changing concepts of citizenship and nationality. In W. Kaplan (Ed.), *Belonging: The meaning and future of Canadian citizenship*. Montreal: McGill-Queen's University Press.

Kaplan, R.B. & Baldauf, R.B. (1997). *Language planning: From practice to theory*. Clevedon, England: Multilingual Matters.

Kraemer, R. & Olshtain, E. (1989). Perceived ethnolinguistic vitality and language attitudes: The Israeli setting. *Journal of Multilingual and Multicultural Development, 10*, 197–212.

Kymlicka, W. (1995). *Multicultural citizenship: A liberal theory of minority rights*. Oxford: Oxford University Press.

LaFrance, M. (1979). Nonverbal synchrony and rapport: Analysis by the cross-lag panel technique. *Social Psychology Quarterly, 42*, 66–70.

Landry, R. & Allard, R. (1994a). Diglossia, ethnolinguistic vitality and language behavior. In R.Y. Bourhis (Ed.), *International Journal of the Sociology of Language, 108*, 15–42.

Landry, R. & Allard, R. (1994b). The Acadians of New Brunswick: demolinguistic realities and the vitality of the French language. *International Journal of the Sociology of Language, 105–106*, 181–215.

Landry, R., Allard, R. & Henry, J. (1996). French in South Louisiana: Towards language loss. *Journal of Multilingual and Multicultural Development, 17*, 442–468.

Landry, R. & Bourhis, R.Y. (1997). Linguistic landscape and ethnolinguistic vitality: An empirical study. *Journal of Language and Social Psychology, 16*, 23–49.

Lawson, S. & Sachdev, I. (2004). Identity, language use, and attitudes: Some Sylheti-Bangladeshi data from London, UK. *Journal of Language and Social Psychology, 23*, 49–69.

Lee, T. & McLaughlin, D. (2001). Reversing Navajo language shift, revisited. In J.A. Fishman (Ed.), *Can threatened languages be saved? Reversing language shift, revisited: A 21st century perspective* (pp.23–43). Clevedon, Avon, UK: Multilingual Matters.

Lin, M. & Harwood, J. (2003). Accommodation predictors of grandparent–grandchild relational solidarity in Taiwan. *Journal of Social and Personal Relationships, 20*, 537–563.

Lo Bianco J. & Rhydwen, M. (2001) Is the extinction of Australia's indigenous languages inevitable? In J.A. Fishman (Ed.), *Can threatened languages be saved? Reversing language shift, revisited: A 21st century perspective* (pp.391–422). Clevedon, Avon, UK: Multilingual Matters.

Lodge, R.A. (1993). *French: From dialect to standard.* London: Routledge.

Mann, C. (2000). Reviewing ethnolinguistic vitality: The case of Anglo-Nigerian Pidgin. *Journal of Sociolinguistics, 4/3*, 458–474.

Milroy, L. & Muysken, P. (1995). Introduction: Code-switching and bilingualism research. In L. Milroy & P. Muysken (Eds.), *One speaker, two languages: Cross-disciplinary perspectives on code-switching* (pp.1–14). Cambridge: Cambridge University Press.

Moïse, L.C. & Bourhis, R.Y. (1994). Langage et ethnicité: Communication inter-culturelle à Montréal, 1977–1991. (Language and ethnicity: Intercultural communication in Montreal: 1977–1991). *Canadian Ethnic Studies/Études Ethniques au Canada, 26*, 86–107.

Montreuil, A. & Bourhis, R.Y. (2001). Majority acculturation orientations toward 'valued' and 'devalued' immigrants. *Journal of Cross-Cultural Psychology, 32*, 698–719.

Montreuil, A. & Bourhis, R.Y. (2004). Acculturation orientations of competing host communities toward valued and devalued immigrants. *International Journal of Intercultural Relations, 28*, 507–532.

Montreuil, A., Bourhis, R.Y. & Vanbeslaere, N. (2004). Perceived threat and host community acculturation orientations towards immigrants: Comparing Flemings in Belgium and Francophones in Quebec. *Canadian Ethnic Studies Journal, 36*, 113–136.

Myers-Scotton, C. (1997). Code-switching. In F. Coulmas (Ed.), *The handbook of sociolinguistics* (pp.217–237). Oxford: Blackwell.

Ng, S.H. & He, A. (2004). Code-switching in tri-generational family conversations among Chinese immigrants in New Zealand. *Journal of Language and Social Psychology, 23*, 28–48.

Niedzielski, N. & Giles, H. (1996). Linguistic accommodation. In H. Goebl, P. Nelde, H. Zdenek, S. Zdenek & W. Wölck (Eds.), *Contact linguistics. An international handbook of contemporary research* (pp.332–342). Berlin, New York: Walter de Gruyter.

Noels, K.A. & Clément, R. (1996). Communicating across cultures: Social determinants and acculturative consequences. *Canadian Journal of Behavioural Science, 28,* 214–228.

Ogay, T., Bourhis, R.Y., Barrette, G. & Montreuil, A. (2001). Orientations d'acculturation de Suisse romands envers des immigrés 'valorisés' et 'dévalorisés'. *Actes du VIIIe Congrès de l'Association pour la Recherche Interculturelle (ARIC), Université de Genève, Genève, Suisse,* 24–28 septembre 2001.

Peralva, A. (1994). Racisme et xénophobie dans l'Allemagne contemporaine. In M. Wieviorka (Ed.), *Racisme et xénophobie en Europe: Une comparaison internationale,* (pp.157–212). Paris: Edition la Découverte.

Reid, S.A. & Giles, H. (2005). Intergroup relations: Its linguistic and communicative parameters. *Group Processes and Intergroup Relations, 8,* 211–214.

Ricento, T. (1998). National language policy in the United States. In T. Ricento & B. Burnaby (Eds.), *Language and politics in the United States and Canada: Myths and realities* (pp.85–112). Mahwah, New Jersey: Lawrence Erlbaum.

Ricento, T. & Burnaby, B. (1998). *Language and politics in the United States and Canada: Myths and realities.* Mahwah, NJ: Lawrence Erlbaum Associates.

Ros, M., Huici, C. & Cano, J.I. (1994). Ethnolinguistic vitality and social identity: Their impact on ingroup bias and social attribution. *International Journal of the Sociology of Language, 108,* 145–166.

Ros, M., Azurmendi, M-J., Bourhis, R.Y. & García, I. (1999). Cultural and linguistic identities in the Bilingual Autonomous Communities (BAC) of Spain: Antecedents and consequences/Identidades culturales y lingüísticas en las Communidades Autónomas Bilingües (CAB) de España: antecedents y consecuencias. *Revista de Psicología Social, 14,* 69–86.

Ryan, E.B. & Giles, H. (Eds.) (1982). *Attitudes toward language variation.* London: Academic.

Ryan, E.B., Giles, H. & Sebastian, R. (1982). An integrative approach for the study of attitudes toward language variation. In E.B. Ryan & H. Giles (Eds.) *Attitudes toward language variation: Social and applied contexts,* London: Arnold.

Sachdev, I. (1998). Language use and attitudes amongst the Fisher River Cree in Manitoba. *Canadian Journal of Native Education, 22,* 108–119.

Sachdev, I. & Bourhis, R.Y. (1987). Status differentials and intergroup behaviour. *European Journal of Social Psychology, 17,* 277–293.

Sachdev, I. & Bourhis R.Y. (1990). Language and social identification. In D. Abrams & M. Hogg (Eds.), *Social identity theory: Constructive and critical advances* (pp. 33–51). Hemel Hempstead, UK: Harvester Wheatsheaf.

Sachdev, I. & Bourhis, R.Y. (1993). Ethnolinguistic vitality: Some motivational and cognitive considerations. In M. Hogg & D. Abrams (Eds.), *Group motivation: Social psychological perspectives.* New York and London: Harvester/Wheatsheaf.

Sachdev, I. & Bourhis, R.Y. (2001). Multilingual communication. In W.P. Robinson & H. Giles (Eds.), *The new handbook of language and social psychology* (pp.407–428). Chichester: Wiley.

Sachdev, I. & Giles, H. (2004). Bilingual accommodation. In T.K. Bhatia & W. Ritchie (Eds.), *Handbook of bilingualism* (pp.353–378). Oxford: Blackwell.

Sachdev, I. & Bourhis, R.Y. (2005). Multilingual communication and social identification. In J. Harwood & H. Giles (Eds.), *Intergroup communication: Multiple perspectives* (pp.65–91). New York: Peter Lang Publishers.

Safran, W. (1999). Nationalism. In J.A. Fishman (Ed.), *Handbook of language and ethnic identity* (pp.77–93). New York: Oxford University Press.

Scherer, K.R. & Giles, H. (1979) (Eds.), *Social markers in speech*. Cambridge: Cambridge University Press.

Schmidt, R. (1998). The politics of language in Canada and the United States: Explaining the differences. In T. Ricento and B. Burnaby (Eds.), *Language and politics in the United States and Canada: Myths and Realities*. Mahwah, NJ: Lawrence Erlbaum Associates.

Schnapper, D. (1992). *L'Europe des immigrés*. Essai sur les politiques d'immigration. Paris: François Bourin.

Shaaban, K. & Ghaith, G. (2002). Univeristy students' perceptions of the ethnolinguistic vitality of Arabic, French and English in Lebanon. *Journal of Sociolinguistics, 6*, 557–574.

Shepard, C.A., Giles, H. & Le Poire, B.A. (2001). Communication accommodation theory. In W.P. Robinson & H. Giles (Eds.), *The new handbook of language and social psychology* (pp.33–56). Chichester, UK: Wiley.

Simard, L., Taylor, D.M. & Giles, H. (1976). Attribution processes and interpersonal accommodation in a bilingual setting. *Language and Speech, 19*, 374–387.

Street, R.L., Jr. (1982). Evaluation of noncontent speech accommodation. *Language and Communication, 2*, 13–31.

Strubell, M. (2001). Catalan a decade later. In J. Fishman (Ed.), *Can threatened languages be saved?* (pp.260–283). Clevedon, England: Multilingual Matters.

Tabouret-Keller, A. (1999). Western Europe. In J.A. Fishman (Ed.), *Handbook of language and ethnic identity* (pp.334–349). New York: Oxford University Press.

Tajfel, H. & Turner, J.C. (1986). The social identity theory of intergroup behavior. In S. Worchel & W. Austin (Eds.), Psychology of intergroup relations (pp.7–24). Chicago: Nelson-Hall.

Taylor, D.M., Wright, S.C., Ruggiero, K.M. & Aitchison, M.C. (1993). Language perceptions among the Inuit of Arctic Quebec: The future role of the heritage language. *Journal of Language and Social Psychology, 12*, 195–206.

Tong, Y-Y., Hong, Y-Y., Lee, S-L. & Chiu, C-Y. (1999). Language use as a carrier of social identity. *International Journal of Intercultural Relations, 23*, 281–296.

Triandis, H.C. (1960). Cognitive similarity and communication in a dyad. *Human Relations, 13*, 175–183.

Trujillo, A. (2005). Politics, school philosophy, and language policy: The case of Crystal City schools. *Educational Policy, 19*, 621–654.

Van den Berg, M.E. (1986). Language planning and language use in Taiwan: Social identity, language accommodation, and language choice behavior. *Special Issue: Chinese Language Planning: Perspectives from China and Abroad, 59*, 97–115.

Wiley, T.G. & Wright, W.E. (2004). Against the undertow: Language-minority education policy and politics in the 'age of accountability'. *Educational Policy, 18*, 142–168.

Wilpert, C. (1993). Les fondements institutionnels et idéologiques du racisme dans la République Fédérale d'Allemagne. In M. Wieviorka (Ed.), *Racisme et modernité*. Paris: Édition la Découverte.

Yagmur, K. & Akinci, M. (2003). Language use, choice, maintenance, and ethno-linguistic vitality of Turkish speakers in France: Intergenerational differences. *International Journal of the Sociology of Language, 164*, 107–128.

Young, L., Bell, N. & Giles, H. (1988). Perceived vitality and context: A national majority in a minority setting. *Journal of Multilingual and Multicultural Development, 9,* 285–289.

Ytsma, J., Viladot, M.A. & Giles, H. (1994). Ethnolinguistic vitality and ethnic identity: Some Catalan and Friesian data. *International Journal of the Sociology of Language, 108,* 63–78.

2
three variations on the social psychology of bilinguality: context effects in motivation, usage and identity

richard clément, kimberly a. noels and peter d. macintyre

For many humans, bilinguality is a fact of life. It has been estimated that there are over 6,000 languages spoken in the 193 countries of the world (Anderson, 2005). Given that there are 30 times the number of languages than there are nation states to house them (Sadlak, 2000; Valdes, 2005), it follows that persons in many nations must negotiate their daily interactions with others in multiple languages. Indeed, it has been estimated that approximately two-thirds of the world's population is bi- or multilingual (Sadlak, 2000).

Bilingualism is, therefore, the normative state of affairs for many people on the planet. There is, however, much variation in terms of its distribution across nations. This heterogeneity introduces, in our view, a new class of variables moderating the relationship between individual characteristics and bilingualism. Specifically, how do social and cultural characteristics of communities affect how bilingualism is played? The specific purpose of this chapter is to highlight some recent developments in social psychological research on bilinguality in different social contexts, with a focus on the social psychology of developing bilingual competence (particularly the role of motivation), the willingness to use one's bilingual capacity, and some potential implications of bilingualism for ethnic identity and adjustment.

motivational aspects of developing bilingual competence

While many factors determine the eventual level of bilingualism that a learner will attain, including aptitude, opportunity to use the language, educational experience, and so on, a construct that has captured the attention of many social psychologists is motivation (see Dörnyei & Schmidt, 2001, for overview). Motivation has been shown to be at least as important as language aptitude in predicting linguistic competence in a second language (Gardner, 1985), but unlike aptitude, motivation is hypothesized to be influenced by the social environment. Hence, by better understanding the social dynamics of language learning motivation, it may be possible to strengthen learners' bilinguality.

intergroup attitudes and motivation

Historically, models of language learning motivation have defined the social context in terms of relations between ethnolinguistic groups, and scholars have pointed out that this influence from outside the immediate classroom context makes learning another language unique from learning other academic subjects (e.g., Giles & Byrne, 1982; Leets & Giles, 1995). The most prominent of these models is Gardner's (1985) socio-educational model of language learning. The model posits that *integrativeness*, corresponding to positive attitudes towards the language community and towards learning the language, along with a desire to learn the second language in order to have contact and possibly identify with members of the second language group, are important predictors of the amount of effort (motivational intensity) that a learner will exert. This notion of integrativeness (and its opponent process, fear of assimilation) is also evident in Clément's (1980; Clément & Gardner, 2001) socio-contextual model of motivation and in Schumann's (1978a; 1978b; 1986) acculturation model of language learning.

Despite the similarities in terminology, subtle differences between scholars' definitions of integrativeness must be noted (cf., Noels, 2005a). While Gardner (1985) emphasizes positive contact and increased cultural understanding of the second language community, Clément (1988) stresses understanding and behaving like (even acculturating towards) members of that community. Although each of these terms reflects an underlying concern with intergroup relations, their nuances render their use more or less appropriate depending upon the intergroup context in which they are applied.

Considerable empirical research supports the idea that intergroup attitudes and motives play an important part in sustaining motivated effort. By way of example, the integrative motivation has been shown to predict language classroom behaviour (Gliksman, Gardner & Smythe, 1982), motivational intensity (MacIntyre & Charos, 1996), language class dropout (Gardner, 1983), and the rate of learning (Gardner, Lalonde &

Moorcroft, 1985; Gardner & MacIntyre, 1991; see Masgoret & Gardner, 2003, for a meta-analytic overview of this research programme). Yashima (2002) demonstrated that international posture predicts not only Japanese students' motivation to learn English but also their willingness to communicate in the English language.

While continuing to recognize the significant role of intergroup attitudes in second language learning and use, since the 1990s there has been a shift to considering how other motivational models might inform understanding of language learning and bilingualism (see Dörnyei, 2003, for overview): specifically a call for models that could at once reflect both the classroom and the wider societal context of L2 acquisition.

self-determination and language learning

In one such model, Noels and her colleagues (e.g., Noels, 2001a, 2001b, 2005a, 2005b; Noels, Clément & Pelletier, 2001) have argued that an understanding of language learning motivation is enhanced by incorporating tenets of Deci and Ryan's self-determination theory (Deci & Ryan, 1985, 2002; Deci, Vallerand, Pelletier & Ryan, 1991) into a model alongside intergroup processes. This approach maintains that motivation can be broadly categorized in terms of three types of orientations: amotivation, intrinsic motivation and extrinsic motivation, following a self-determination continuum. Amotivation refers to the lack of any intention to act (Deci & Ryan, 2002), either because individuals feel that their behaviour has no systematic way of influencing the outcome, because of feelings of low competence, or because the activity and/or its outcomes are not valued. Intrinsic motivation refers to the desire to perform an activity because of the inherent interest and enjoyment of performing the behaviour for its own sake. These feelings of pleasure are proposed to derive from the fulfilment of three basic needs – autonomy, competence and relatedness. Thus, intrinsic motivation is sustained when individuals perceive that they have voluntarily chosen to perform an activity in which they can exercise and express their capacities, and that they and their decision to engage in the activity is securely supported by others.

In contrast to intrinsic motivation, extrinsic motivation refers to the state in which a goal external to the activity itself serves as the rationale for performing the activity. Deci and Ryan (1985) suggest that there are several types of extrinsic motivation that vary in the extent to which the goal is controlled by the self or by external contingencies. The least self-determined form of extrinsic motivation is external regulation, in which the person performs the activity to achieve some instrumental end, such as to gain a reward or to avoid punishment. Externally regulated students have not chosen the activity of their own free will, and hence are unlikely to incorporate second language learning into their identities. A second type of extrinsic motivation, somewhat more internally regulated, is introjected regulation. A student whose motivational orientation is described as introjected performs an activity because of a self-induced pressure, such as a desire to avoid guilt or for ego-enhancement reasons. Somewhat more self-governed is identified regulation, which refers to carrying out an activity because it is important to attaining a goal valued by the individual. The activity is not, in itself, particularly important, but it will help to achieve some goal that is highly desired. Finally, the most internally regulated form of extrinsic motivation is integrated regulation. At this point, the behaviour fits in with the rest of the person's values and aspirations, and the performance of the activity is an expression of who that individual is. Although integrated regulation is posited to be similar to intrinsic motivation in that it is associated with positive emotions, increased engagement, and creative productivity, it is distinct from intrinsic motivation because the reason for performing the activity remains external to the activity per se.

An important claim of this theory is that, over time, an externally regulated activity may become more internally regulated to the extent that students feel that they have freely chosen to participate in the learning process, that their skills and competence are improving, and that they are supported in these activities by significant others. Although highly self-determined students remain extrinsically motivated, they are similar to intrinsically motivated students in that they are likely to engage in the activity longer and more productively, because their needs for autonomy, competence and relatedness are fulfilled.

A growing body of research supports the claim that self-determined and intrinsic motivations are associated with a variety of language learning outcomes. More self-determined and/or intrinsically oriented language learners are more persistent and exhibit greater motivational intensity (Noels, Clément & Pelletier, 1999; Noels, 2001b; Ramage, 1990), use the language more often, and have greater speaking and reading proficiency (Ehrman, 1996; Noels et al., 1999, 2001; Tachibana, Matsukawa & Zhong, 1996). In addition, these learners have greater grammatical sensitivity and better language learning strategy preferences (Ramage, 1990), feel less anxiety, and have more positive attitudes towards language learning and increased feelings of self-efficacy (Ehrman, 1996; Schmidt, Boraie & Kassabgy, 1996). Finally, they are more likely to pursue post-secondary education in the second language and to identify with the second language community (Goldberg & Noels, 2005).

It would seem that these motivational orientations are relatively independent of those associated with intergroup processes. Noels and her colleagues (Noels, 2001a, 2005b; Noels et al., 2001) demonstrated that although the integrative orientation (e.g., learning L2 to befriend members of the L2 group) is correlated with intrinsic and self-determined orientations, these two categories of variables predict different language learning-related variables. The integrative orientation predicts intergroup variables, such as contact with the second language group and ethnic identity, whereas intrinsic/self-determined orientations more strongly predict immediate outcomes, including motivational intensity, persistence in language learning and attitudes towards learning the language. Noels (2005a) further showed that while intrinsic and extrinsic motivational orientations reflected a motivational substrate common to both heritage[1] and non-heritage language learners, an intergroup substrate which included identified regulation and the integrative orientation was unique to heritage language learners. There is, therefore, evidence that the influence of motivational predispositions of the type discussed above may be modulated by context.

the context of self-determination

Self-determination theory claims that intrinsic and self-determined motivation are sustained to the extent that significant others foster a sense of autonomy, competence and relatedness, by providing choice, informative feedback, and a warm and caring environment. We will consider this hypothesis at three levels of social context which have been shown to influence the language learning experience.

The first level of social context involves interpersonal interactions with many significant others in the learners' social network. The most obvious person is the instructor, who is employed to structure and provide feedback on the learning process. Some research has pointed out that perceptions of the language teacher are related to language learners' motivation (see Gardner, 1985, for review), and particularly that the teacher can foster feelings of intrinsic and self-determined motivation by supporting a sense of autonomy and competence in the learner (Noels et al., 1999; Noels, Pelletier, Clément & Vallerand, 2000; see also Schmidt et al., 1996).

Perceptions of parents' and other family members' attitudes and behaviours regarding language learning have also been linked, generally positively, with learners' motivation (e.g. Gardner, Tremblay & Masgoret,

1997; Gardner, 1985). Some results, however, have been more complex. For instance, Colletta, Clément, and Edwards (1983) found weak negative correlations between parents' active encouragement of their children's involvement in language learning and the children's attitudes towards language learning. They suggest that active involvement may be perceived as pressure, which may cause the child to feel less favourable about the learning experience and the L2 group, consistent with the notion that a perceived lack of control can dampen intrinsic motivation.

Finally, members of the second language community may affect learners' motivation and eventual L2 achievement. Genesee, Rogers and Holobow (1983) suggest that the learner's perception of the L2 community's support of language learning, in addition to the learner's motivation, accounts for a significant amount of the variance in linguistic competence, use, and social affiliation with the target language group (see also Leets & Giles, 1992). In their investigation of English learners of Spanish, Noels and Rollin (1998) found that perceptions of criticism and uninvolvement from the Spanish community were associated with decreased feelings of self-determined motivation, and perceptions of pressure to learn the language increased external and introjected regulation.

The second level of social context, the intergroup level, pertains to the nature of the relationship between the learner's ethnolinguistic group and the target language group. Clément and Kruidenier (1983) identified two aspects of context that affect the emergence and predictive power of motivational orientations. The first is the opportunity for immediate contact with members of the target language community. The second is the relative dominance or nondominance of the language learner's group in comparison to that of the target language group (cf. 'ethnolinguistic vitality': Harwood, Giles & Bourhis, 1994). A third aspect of context is the ethnolinguistic background of the learner (cf. Noels, 2005a; Noels & Clément, 1989). In some cases, learners desire to learn an ancestral language which is not the language of the dominant society, including indigenous, colonial, and immigrant languages (Cummins, 1998; Cummins & Danesi, 1990). These heritage language learners may or may not use the language regularly in the home and the community (Fishman, 2001), but the language has some personal relevance to them.

It might further be suggested that the first and second levels of social context interact, such that certain individuals play a stronger role in certain intergroup contexts than in others. For instance, while the teacher may play a strong role in motivational support for learners of foreign languages, second language community members may be more influential for students who have more immediate access to that language community (e.g., Asian ESL students in Australia, French Canadians outside Quebec). Consistent with this hypothesis, Noels (2005a) found that the autonomy, competence and relatedness needs of non-heritage learners of German were supported most by their language instructor, but these needs in heritage learners of German were supported most by members of the German community. Moreover, the fundamental needs were differentially linked to intrinsic/self-determined motivation depending upon the background of the student. Whereas autonomy needs most strongly predicted intrinsic/self-determined motivation for non-heritage learners, relatedness needs most strongly predicted this type of motivational orientation for heritage learners.

The third, less well examined, level of social context posited to have a bearing on motivational experience is the cultural origin of the learner. Much of the scholarship on motivation to date has focused on Western nations (e.g., Canada, USA, Western Europe) and failed to consider learners in other cultural contexts. According to cross-cultural psychologists (e.g., Hofstede, 1984), people in Western cultures tend to hold relatively individualistic values which emphasize the importance of personal aspirations over interpersonal and group relationships. In other cultures, people are suggested to hold more collectivistic values, which prioritize the harmony and structure of interpersonal and group relationships over individualistic goals. While the distinction between individualistic and collectivistic tendencies has been linked to many social and educational variables (see Kagitçibasi, 1997, for an overview), only recently has the relation between cultural values and language learning motivation been addressed.

Although they do not necessarily address self-determination theory per se, some accounts of teaching styles in many East Asian nations suggest that the support of autonomy is not a central concern in the classroom. In many nations (e.g., People's Republic of China, Japan, Hong Kong, and until very recently Taiwan), English is a requirement for university entrance examinations and courses are often oriented to ensuring good success on these exams, often using decontextualized grammar-translation approaches that are relatively teacher-centred and authoritarian, rather than communication-oriented approaches that can be more learner-centred (Campbell & Yong, 1993; Ho, 1998; Kobayashi, 2001; Warden & Lin, 2000). Some scholars working with students in East Asia argue that authoritarian education systems and stringent assessment criteria are detrimental to students' sense of competence, and maintain that emphasizing learner autonomy would improve learning (e.g., Wen

& Clément, 2003; Yang, 1998). Others claim that autonomy may be incompatible with certain cultural values (cf. Farmer, 1994; Ho & Crookall, 1995; Jones, 1995; Riley, 1998a). Still others argue that autonomy in non-Western cultures need not entail an individualistic orientation, but rather can be developed from pedagogical approaches that stress collaboration and interdependent learning (Aoki, 1999; Aoki & Smith, 1999).

In sum, research on the social psychology of developing bilingualism has evolved from a focus on how intergroup attitudes influence linguistic and nonlinguistic outcomes to a broader incorporation of motivational processes. As researchers move beyond the second language context to consider foreign language learning and the learning of English as a global language, cultural differences in the construction and dynamics of motivation become a central issue. Attention to the social context, on several levels, does not imply that individual differences between learners are not important determinants of language behaviour. Rather the interactions among such intergroup and individual differences factors create a set of dynamics in the immediate situation that affects intergroup processes at the ethnolinguistic level, interpersonal processes between second language communicators, and activities within language classrooms.

using the second language

Modern language pedagogy places strong emphasis on communicative approaches to instruction on the basis that language acquisition is determined by language usage. The above considerations regarding the role of motivation can, therefore, be placed within the wider context of defining the condition leading to language usage. Indeed, many of the factors evoked in the context of our discussion of motivation are also relevant to the willingness to engage in communication using the second language. The concept of willingness to communicate (WTC) has been a recent addition to the literature on second language learning. WTC has been defined as the intention to initiate communication, specifically talk, when given the opportunity (McCroskey & Baer, 1985), and was originally developed with reference to native language use. The WTC concept captures the predisposition to approach or avoid oral communication across situations (McCroskey & Richmond, 1991). Whereas WTC has been viewed as a stable characteristic of a person, other researchers view it as a situationally-determined volitional choice to speak at a particular time with a specific person or group (MacIntyre, Clément, Dörnyei & Noels, 1998). The trait level conceptualization has been advanced in studies of both native and second language use, with the situational conceptualization discussed most often with respect to second language use, where the range of factors affecting communication is more diverse. Conceptualizing WTC as a state of readiness to speak allows for both an examination of its effects on the language learning process and an examination of WTC as a non-linguistic language learning outcome.

In this section, we will first consider how WTC was adapted to second language contexts. We will next review the fairly consistent pattern of correlations with WTC obtained for its two key antecedents, perceived competence and anxiety. Finally, the section concludes with a broad look at WTC in social contexts.

the 'pyramid' model of L2 WTC

The origins of the concept of WTC lie in the interpersonal communication literature, most directly the work by Burgoon (1976) on unwillingness to communicate, and McCroskey and Richmond (1987; McCroskey & Richmond 1991) who hypothesized that a regular pattern whereby a person avoids or devalues communication is related to both social and individual factors. In adapting the concept to second language communication, MacIntyre et al. (1998) provided a more comprehensive, heuristic model that organizes the diversity of influences on second language WTC. That model, nicknamed the pyramid model (Figure 2.1), captures a wide range of intergroup, interpersonal, intrapersonal, linguistic, communication, and situational factors that culminate in the decision to initiate or not L2 communication.

At the base of the pyramid are intergroup climate and the personality of the speaker, contextual variables that are handed down to the individual over which they have little influence. Moving to a more proximal level, the next layer of the pyramid captures the individual's usual affective and cognitive context. Setting the tone for motivation to learn the second language is the tension between a desire to approach the target language group and a sense of hesitation or fear of the implications of doing so. The final layer of enduring influences are specifically related to language learning, including specific motives for acquiring the language and cognition about oneself as a language learner. These foundational layers capture intergroup motives that stem from membership in a particular social group and interpersonal motives stem from the social roles one plays within the group. Issues of affiliation and control are the most basic of motives. Roles and motives combine with L2 self-confidence; perceptions of communicative competence coupled with a lack of anxiety.

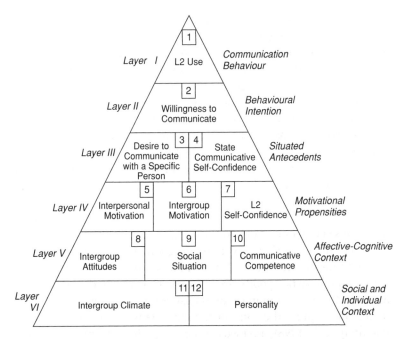

Figure 2.1 Schematic representation of the 'pyramid' model. (From MacIntyre, Clément, Dörnyei & Noels, 1998).

When moving to the next layer of the pyramid, a transition is made from enduring influences to situational ones. The sense of time is coming to focus on the here-and-now. At this level of the pyramid model is the desire to communicate with a specific person, as well as a state of self-confidence. The culmination of the processes described thus far is the willingness to communicate, to initiate second language discourse on a specific occasion with a specific person. This represents the level of behavioural intention (Ajzen & Fishbein, 1980) to speak if one has the opportunity. Dörnyei and Ottó (1998) have likened this to 'crossing the Rubicon', a point of no return where one commits to act in the L2. There are times when one crosses such a threshold in the flow of conversation mindlessly without hesitation or concern; at other times L2 communication is initiated with reluctance, hesitation, even trepidation.

the empirical evidence

The empirical evidence pertaining to the pyramid model has been consistent in supporting its key tenets. Theoretically, the most immediate influences on WTC are perceived competence and anxiety, and both have shown consistent relationships with WTC across several studies.

MacIntyre and Charos (1996), who studied a group of Anglophone adults taking an evening course in conversational French, were the first to report a significant correlation between WTC and perceived competence in the second language (r = .56). A subsequent study (MacIntyre, MacMaster & Baker, 2001) of high school students taking French-as-a-second-language courses found a similar relationship between WTC and perceived competence in the second language (r = .56). In a cross-sectional study of late French immersion students, correlations between WTC and perceived competence of .34, .56 and .40 were obtained in grades 7, 8 and 9 respectively (MacIntyre, Baker, Clément & Donovan, 2002). Baker and MacIntyre (2000) reported a non-significant correlation between WTC and perceived competence among high school immersion students (r = .17), but a strong correlation among non-immersion students (r = .72) in the same school. Yashima, Zenui-Nishide & Shimizu (2004) reported a correlation of .53 in a sample of Japanese students learning English. Overall, the results consistently point to perceived competence as a significant source of impetus for WTC.

Given that WTC is an internal psychological state, the speaker's self-perception of competence is considered more relevant than objective measures of linguistic skill, for two major reasons. First, the specific linguistic skills we might test (vocabulary, grammar, comprehension, sentence construction, etc.) are subordinated to the interpersonal goal of making oneself understood *in situ*. Whereas assessment of second language proficiency usually requires specific tests of pre-selected ability, the pyramid model recognizes that nonverbal cues, conversational management strategies, etc., exert a substantial influence on communication behaviour. Therefore, the specific 'objective' ability to be tested is so closely tied to the situation that traditional tests of competence do not seem particularly useful. A second concern is for systematic biases in the perception of competence that lead to either overestimating or underestimating one's ability, as demonstrated by MacIntyre, Noels and Clément (1997). Being 'able' and 'willing' to communicate are two different issues. Even in the native language, McCroskey and Richmond (1991, p.27) acknowledge the importance of communication skills, but emphasize the importance of the individual's perception of her or his skill level. 'Since the choice of whether to communicate is a cognitive one, it is likely to be more influenced by one's perceptions of competence (of which one usually is aware) than one's actual competence (of which one may be totally unaware).'

A second consistent finding in studies of WTC is that anxiety has a negative effect. Baker and MacIntyre (2000) found negative correlations for non-immersion students (r = –.29) and among immersion students (r = –.44). MacIntyre at al. (2001), who tested junior high school immersion students found correlations ranging between –.22 and –.45. MacIntyre and Charos (1996) found a correlation of –.46 between WTC and anxiety. Yashima et al. (2004) found that anxiety about communicating correlated negatively with WTC in the second language (r = –.25).

Anxiety works primarily as a restraining force on L2 communication. Previous research on language anxiety has demonstrated its pervasive and subtle effects on both language use (Horwitz, Horwitz & Cope, 1986) and language learning (MacIntyre & Gardner, 1994a, 1994b). The emotional arousal that accompanies high levels of anxiety can distract attention from the cognitive demands of the task at hand. Anxiety is especially disruptive when the speaker has little experience in the L2 and can lead to an unwillingness to take on communicative tasks or to abandon them after they begin (MacIntyre & Gardner, 1994a, 1994b; MacIntyre, Noels & Clément, 1997).

The decision to take on or abandon ongoing communication plays out naturally during conversations. If we consider that each turn taken in conversation is another point at which one initiates action, then WTC may operate on both the choices made within the situation as well as the choice to enter situations in the first place. Dörnyei and Kormos (2000) predicted that task engagement would be necessary for speech to be produced in the L2 in a structured conversation task. They studied 46 Hungarian students in intermediate English courses at Budapest secondary schools. Participants were paired off and given a school-related communication task to complete, first in the L2 and then in the L1. Performance was assessed by the number of words produced and the number of turns taken. WTC significantly correlated with the number of turns that were taken, but not with the number of words that were produced. Similar results were obtained by MacIntyre, Babin and Clément (1999) using only L1 tasks. WTC has been shown to affect conversations by increasing the likelihood that one speaks more frequently (MacIntyre & Charos, 1996; Yashima, 2002), and it is therefore relevant to setting the interpersonal social context in which L2 interactions take place.

WTC in context

Both variations and consistencies are observed in the effects of social context and culture on WTC. Given the intricate relationship between language learning and language usage, the pyramid model allows for WTC to be seen as both a facilitator and an outcome of learning. This duality is clear in the context of educational programmes that emphasize linguistic and cultural immersion as a pedagogical tool.

In Canada, where the intergroup climate has been a prominent social and educational issue for decades, second language immersion programmes have been introduced with the broad purpose of increasing intercultural contact and intergroup harmony (Clément, 1994). MacIntyre et al. (1998) questioned whether engendering WTC might be the ultimate but often unstated goal of language learning. If that notion has validity, it would appear that second language *communication* should be given centre stage in the evaluation of the effectiveness of immersion, especially given the broad view of the bilingual person we have advocated above.

A handful of studies emphasize the communicative outcomes of second language learning in French immersion programmes among Anglophone Canadian students. Within this context, the students are coming from a majority group learning the language of a minority group. One such study (MacIntyre, Baker, Clément & Donovan, 2002) found that WTC was substantially higher among students in their second and third year (grades 8 and 9) of a late immersion programme, as compared to students in their first year (grade 7). Differences in perceived competence that mirrored the pattern of WTC differences also were observed. Language anxiety showed a more complex pattern of results (girls' anxiety levels decreased but boys' anxiety levels remained constant) that the authors attribute to gender differences in the timing of psychological and physical maturation during adolescence. In addition to the group comparisons, correlations within the three grade-levels showed that students higher in WTC communicated more frequently in the L2 (see also MacIntyre, Baker, Clément & Conrod, 2001). There is also some evidence that the positive communicative effects of immersion education are maintained after the programme is completed (MacIntyre, Baker, Clément & Donovan, 2003). This collection of studies, therefore, shows the influence of the context on the development of WTC, namely that more intensive programmes, more advanced courses and maturation are influential factors.

Reliable variations in WTC observed across cultures (Sallinen-Kuparinen, McCroskey & Richmond, 1991), further attest to their strong impact. Wen and Clément (2003) propose that among many Chinese persons, a willingness to communicate is not necessarily sufficient to initiate action at the first available opportunity. Based on Confucian philosophy, issues of face and connectedness intervene between willingness to communicate and the initiation of speech. For Chinese speakers in this tradition, the responsibility to the group and fear of losing face converge to create an atmosphere that promotes silence over talk, a preference for mindful quiet over mindless conversation. In contrast, Daly and McCroskey (1975) have noted that unwillingness to communicate leads to negative attributions about the reluctant speaker in American culture (see also Miczo, 2004). Such differences between cultures highlight the operation of various motives underlying communication, the forceful impact of social and psychological processes, and the omnipresent effect of social contexts that must be negotiated by bilingual speakers.

Normative constraints are one aspect through which contextual effects operate. Clément, Baker and MacIntyre (2003) examined the effects of context, norms and ethnolinguistic vitality on WTC in Ottawa, Canada, in a bilingual (French–English) institution where both groups have equal status and where bilingual contact is frequent. In this context, Anglophones show higher ethnolinguistic vitality than Francophones. Surprisingly, in both groups, the expected effect of normative pressure for L2 communication did not emerge as a predictor of L2 WTC, but L2 WTC did significantly predict the frequency of L2 communication. Further, in both groups, L2 confidence, which is defined by a lack of anxiety and high perceived competence, predicted L2 communication independently of WTC. The impact of L2 confidence on WTC was, however, much stronger for majority than for minority group members. In the latter case, a minority status implies more frequent and pleasant contact with the other group and generally a much better command of the other language. In these circumstances, willingness to communicate may no longer hinge on linguistic factors. Furthermore, an institutional context imposing equal status norms may limit the extent to which WTC will directly impact L2 usage. Both societal and institutional status of the language groups can, therefore, influence the ways in which WTC influences communicative action. Furthermore, the normative constraints imposed by an institution contribute to a climate that promotes extrinsic as opposed to intrinsic orientations to the learning of the second language.

In sum, studies of WTC have demonstrated its applicability to both native and second language communication situations, making it a useful construct in the study of bilingualism. Beyond that, in the process of developing second language, WTC draws upon a number of social, psychological and linguistic features that operate whenever a person chooses to act in the second language. The pyramid model organizes these influences in a time-sensitive, layered approach that emphasizes the background and foreground processes that affect the decision to speak up or be silent. This development has improved our understanding of the decision-making process undertaken when a person has the opportunity to use a second language. Consistent with the model, enduring factors located at the lower levels of the pyramid – which include intergroup climate and motives for contact, individual difference factors, and the development of linguistic competence with the accompanying changes in self-confidence – combine to influence the communication context. By understanding the dynamics underlying these moment-by-moment actions, we can get a better handle on the larger processes that help to define the ways in which culture itself is enacted when groups come into contact.

L2 learning and use as cultural appropriation

Research and theorizing bearing on issues of self-determined motivation and willingness to communicate underline the eminently social nature of these phenomena. As shown above, motivation to learn a second language and its usage are rooted in the factors affecting socialization, interpersonal, and intergroup relations, as well as personal predispositions. What then might be some social consequences of motivation and usage? We contend that they are important vectors of cultural definition and development affecting self identification.

ethnic identity

There is little consensus about what constitutes ethnic belonging (Leets, Giles & Clément, 1996) or ethnic identity (Phinney, 1990; Ross, 1979). Since Barth's (1969) analysis, a definition corresponding to subjective feelings of belonging has been used by researchers. Furthermore, after Isajiw (1985, see also Berry, 1990) ethnic identity has been defined according to multiple dimensions: with reference to one's own group and with reference to at least one other significant group (Clément, Singh & Gaudet, in press). As an added feature of this definition of ethnic identity, it is assumed to be situationally variable. Hraba and Hoiberg (1983) suggest that ethnic identity is an attitude which may cue identification behaviour. The manifest display of ethnic identity will only occur in certain situations, during intergroup contact, for example. The motivation to show or conceal an ethnic identity is rooted in the desire to maintain a positive self-image either through intergroup comparisons (Tajfel, 1978) or through the adherence to contextually defined norms (Alexander & Beggs, 1986). Ethnic identity is, therefore, highly variable and responds to contingencies of the situation in which it is played.

Our first attempt at assessing situational effects was in a Canadian university context defined by the presence of two linguistic groups (French and English), each originating from settings in which they constituted either a majority or a minority (Clément & Noels, 1992). Among other things, the results show that profiles of identification are linked to the status of the groups, with majority Anglophones showing the greatest difference between their French and English identity and the minority Francophones showing the least difference. Furthermore, the majority Francophones' results resemble those of the minority Francophones more than those of the majority Anglophones, attesting to the North American prevalence of English. These results hark back to those evoked in our earlier discussion of motivation and WTC. They foster the expectation that the relation between language and language-related outcomes may be subject to variations attributable to the relative status of language groups.

the consequences of bilingualism

These outcomes were not unforeseen by social psychologists dealing with bilingualism. As early as 1974, Lambert proposed a distinction between additive and subtractive bilingualism. Originally defined from a cognitive point of view, additive bilingualism corresponds to the capacity to use two languages as cognitive tools, whereas subtractive bilingualism corresponds to the loss of the first language as a result of the acquisition of the second language. Subtractive bilingualism would occur in the cases where minority group members would learn the language of a dominant group, whereas additive bilingualism would result when majority group members would learn the language of a minority.

Our development of the social corollary of this hypothesis (e.g., Clément, 1980, 1984; Clément & Noels, 1991) applies the same construct to the maintenance or loss of ethnic identity. Following the original model (Clément, 1980; Clément & Kruidenier, 1985), second language confidence developed through frequent and positive contacts with outgroup members is hypothesized to mediate the effects of contact on identity and wellbeing. The results obtained by Noels and Clément (1996) support both this hypothesis and the preceding considerations regarding status. As can be seen in Figure 2.2, majority Anglophones (i.e., Anglophones originating from settings where they are a majority) show an additive pattern: better identification with the Francophones and better psychological adjustment as a result of greater language confidence in French and no erosion of English identity.

These results contrast with those obtained by Noels, Pon & Clément (1996). In this research, rather than involving participant members of the two Canadian chartered language groups, Chinese university students were invited to participate. As in many areas of the world, the Chinese

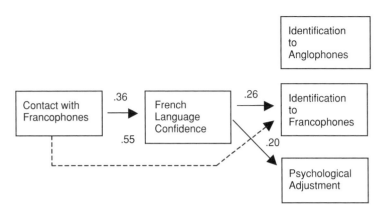

Figure 2.2 Path analytic solution: majority Anglophones. (From Noels & Clément, 1996)

community is old and well established, with its own institutions and living area. It is also a visible minority, with all the attendant difficulties related to individual integration into the mainstream. For these reasons, they would be expected to be relatively resistant to the erosive forces affecting their identity. As Figure 2.3 shows, however, this is not the case. English language confidence not only leads to a subtractive identity profile but also to better psychological adjustment, thus aggravating the influence of erosive forces on identification to the Chinese community. This research supports the original contention pertaining to the potentially subtractive effects of second language competence, and further demonstrates its implications for psychological adjustment. Finally, the results obtained with majority Francophone and Chinese students support the powerful impact of second language confidence as a determinant of identity.

Yet it is obvious that minority communities survive and even thrive for long periods without the appearance of a final obliteration. Understanding the dynamics of such resilience requires a broadening of the definitions of contact and communication beyond those above. Direct contact with members of the outgroup may be only one of the multiple aspects in which intergroup communication is manifested. Another aspect of contact corresponds to contact with the ingroup. Although the work depicted above hinges on definitions of contact with members of the outgroup, maintaining harmonious and involved relations with the ingroup should be a factor in ingroup identity maintenance.

Furthermore, indirect contact via the media may be as important as direct contact, particularly with respect to ensuring first language usage among linguistic minorities. Clément, Baker, Josephson and Noels (2005) recently reported results supporting cultivation (Gerbner, 1969) and

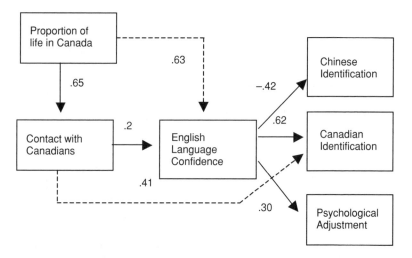

Figure 2.3 Path analytic solution: Chinese students. (From Noels, Pon & Clément, 1996)

erosion (Varan, 1998) theories to the effect that media have an immediate impact on culture. Specifically, their longitudinal design showed that L2 audio-visual and written media had an impact on degree of identification with the outgroup, mediated by second language confidence.

Although these results further support the key role filled by language confidence, they also suggest that the mediation process linking aspects of contact on the one hand, and on the other hand identity and adjustment, may require some degree of added complexity. Figures 2.2 and 2.3 show an unexpected path from contact to identity, by-passing language confidence. It is, therefore, possible that another mechanism may act as a mediator. Besides developing language confidence, intergroup contact contributes to the development of networks, themselves a source of social support. The influence of social support on wellbeing has received much support in previous research (Stroebe & Stroebe, 1996). Its effect on ethnic identification has, however, received little attention.

A study by Gaudet and Clément (2005), therefore, aimed to test this conjecture among the Francophone community of the Province of Saskatchewan (Canada). These people, known as the *Fransaskois*, are descendants of the early French settlers originating from French areas of Eastern Canada as well as the United States. They are made up of remote pockets of small French communities, largely self-sustaining. Contacts with the majority Anglophone group as well as inter-marriage has, however, brought their population from 4.4 per cent in 1951 to 2 per cent in 1996.

The results of the study are presented in Figure 2.4. As can be seen, two concurrent processes seem to be operating here. The paths from Anglophone contact and media through English language confidence to identity and adjustment replicate the subtractive situation discussed earlier. Francophone involvement and social support result, however, in an additive situation, sustaining Francophone identity and self-esteem. Furthermore, Francophone social support fosters Anglophone social support and, eventually, self-esteem as well. An examination of involvement with one's community and social support provides a hint at the complex processes governing minority identity and adjustment. Expanding the definition of contact as well as that of the mediational process has proved useful in improving our understanding of resistance to assimilation pressures shown by extreme minority groups. Nevertheless, that social support as a psychological phenomenon is dependent on communication patterns which remain to be delineated.

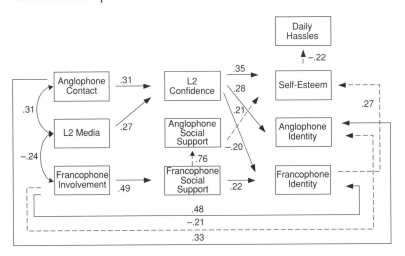

Figure 2.4   Path analytic solution: the *Fransaskois* (From Gaudet & Clément, 2005)

conclusion

Whether it is the *Fransaskois* or any other group discussed here, the issue of communication is a keystone to understanding contextual effects. The results reported above, while supporting the role of individual characteristics such as self-determination, willingness to communicate and language confidence, highlight at the same time the interpersonal, intergroup and societal aspects of context as they impinge on the motivation, usage and consequences of bilinguality. In all cases, however, and in spite of the rather wide scope of this review, the understanding of contextual effects lies with an adequate comprehension of the transactions between individuals embedded in specific cultural contexts.

Although not specific to bilingualism or second languages, Bourdieu (1977) made the point that languages only convey meaning in a specific context which acts to lift the ambiguity inherent to utterances or lexical items taken out of context. This semiotic function is, furthermore, intimately tied to the power relation between interlocutors. 'The value of a language is equivalent to the value of its speakers', (p.22, author translation). In interactions, the meaning of an utterance is what is understood and intended by the most powerful individual, who may legitimately use an array of discursive strategies to orient and dominate the conversation (e.g., Ng & Bradac, 1993). Conversely, if a conversation is to persist, the non-dominant participant must also subscribe to the dominance rules. Finally, given changing contexts dominance relations and strategies are likely to change to maximize individual gains.

Applied to bilingualism, this approach to communication thrives on context effects of the type described above. Learning and using a second language, as well as their consequences, are optimized in situations where these activities act to support the relative dominance of the speaker. A learning environment supporting autonomy fosters more self-determined motivation to acquire a language; a high degree of language confidence in a given context promotes willingness to communicate; additive forms of bilingualism are found among dominant group members. The common thread here is not so much social dominance but rather the individual's appraisal that, given a specific context, the conversation will evolve according to his or her goals and expectations.

But what about minority groups? Obviously, their acquisition of a majority language plays out along with their goals and expectations to direct interactions with members of the majority group. To the extent that they achieve close to perfect mastery of the language they may legitimately claim ascendancy in the conversation, such as was the case in the Clément et al. (2003) study with highly bilingual Francophones. But for them, societal erosion of their first language poses another challenge, that of maintaining positive relationships with their own non-dominant group. As shown by Gaudet and Clément (2005), however, that too is resolved through the establishment of community communication networks.

The recourse to and maintenance of speech characteristics that are considered non-dominant, or the refusal to interact in the second language evidenced by the Asian students, is the product of cultural norms that define what is a desirable outcome. The Western hierarchically organized society described by Bourdieu (1977) may foster relatively well-defined power relations based on social class. A collective ideology favouring plurality, as is the case for the Canadian examples, or the need to conserve face and respect for the teachers in the Chinese case, dictate approaches to language transactions which are quite different. In the end, it is the broader cultural tapestry of values which determines the contextual conditions for mastery.

acknowledgements

Production of this paper was facilitated by a grant from the Social Sciences and Humanities Research Council of Canada to the three authors. We would like to thank Susan Baker, Sophie Gaudet and Sara Rubenfeld for their assistance in completing this project. Correspondence concerning this chapter should be addressed to R. Clément, School of Psychology, University of Ottawa, Ottawa, Ontario, Canada K1N 6N5 (rclement@uottawa.ca).

note

1. Heritage language students are those learning a language once spoken by their ancestors whereas this is not the case for non-heritage language students.

references

Ajzen, Icek & Fishbein, Martin (1980). *Understanding attitudes and predicting social behavior.* Englewood-Cliffs, NJ: Prentice Hall.

Alexander, Norman C. & Beggs, John J. (1986). Disguising personal inventories: A situated identity strategy. *Social Psychology Quarterly, 49,* 192–200.

Anderson, Stephen R. (2005). How many languages are there in the world? Retrieved June 27, 2005, from the website of the Linguistic Society of America: http://www.lsadc.org/pdf_files/howmany.pdf.

Aoki, Naoko (1999). Affect and the role of teachers in the development of learner autonomy. In J. Arnold (Ed.), *Affect in language learning* (pp.142–154). New York: Cambridge University Press.

Aoki, Naoko & Smith, Richard C. (1999). Learner autonomy in cultural context: The case of Japan. In S. Cotterall & D. Crabbe (Eds.), *Learner autonomy in language learning: Defining the field and effecting change* (pp.19–28). Frankfurt am Main: Lang.

Baker, Susan & MacIntyre, Peter D. (2000). The role of gender and immersion in communication and second language orientations. *Language Learning, 50,* 311–341.

Barth, Frederic (1969). *Ethnic groups and boundaries.* London, UK: Allen & Unwin.

Berry, John W. (1990). Psychology of acculturation. In J.J. Berman (Ed.), *Cross-cultural perspectives: Nebraska symposium on motivation Vol. 37* (pp.201–234). Lincoln: University of Nebraska Press.

Bourdieu, Pierre (1977). L'Économie des échanges linguistiques. [The economie of linguistic exchanges]. *Langue Française, 34,* 17–34.

Burgoon, Judith K. (1976). The Unwillingness-to-Communicate Scale: Development and validation. *Speech Monographs, 43,* 60–69.

Campbell, Keith P. & Zhao, Yong (1993). The dilemma of English language instruction in the People's Republic of China. *TESOL Journal, 2,* 4–6.

Clément, Richard (1980). Ethnicity, contact and communicative competence in a L2. In H. Giles, W.P. Robinson & P.M. Smith (Eds.), *Language: Social psychological perspectives.* Oxford: Pergamon Press.

Clément, Richard (1984). Aspects socio-psychologiques de la communication inter-ethnique et de l'identité culturelle, *Recherches sociologiques, 15,* 293–312.

Clément, Richard (1988). *Échelles d'attitude et de motivation reliées aux raports inter-éthniques.* [Scales of attitude and motivation related to inter-ethnic relations]. (Tech. Rep.). Ottawa: University of Ottawa.

Clément, Richard (1994). The acquisition of French as a second language in Canada: Towards a research agenda. In J.W. Berry & J.A. Laponce (Eds.), *Ethnicity and culture in Canada: The research landscape* (pp.410–434). Toronto: University of Toronto Press.

Clément, Richard, Baker, Susan C., Josephson, Gordon & Noels, Kimberly A. (2005). Media effects on ethnic identity among linguistic majorities and minorities: A longitudinal study of a bilingual setting. *Human Communication Research, 31,* 399–422.

Clément, Richard, Baker, Susan C. & MacIntyre, Peter D. (2003). Willingness to communicate in a second language: The effects of context, norms and vitality. *Journal of Language and Social Psychology, 22,* 190–209.

Clément, Richard & Gardner, Robert C. (2001). Second language mastery. In H. Giles & W.P. Robinson (Eds.), *Handbook of language and social psychology* (pp.489–504). London, UK: Wiley.

Clément, Richard & Kruidenier, Bastian G. (1983). Orientations in second language acquisition: The effects of ethnicity, milieu and target language on their emergence. *Language Learning, 33,* 272–291.

Clément, Richard & Kruidenier, Bastian G. (1985). Aptitude, attitude and motivation in second language proficiency: A test of Clément's model. *Journal of Language and Social Psychology, 4,* 21–37.

Clément, Richard & Noels, Kimberly. A. (1991). Langue, statut et acculturation: Une étude d'individus et de groupes en contact. In M. Lavallée & F. Larose (Eds.), *Identité, culture et changement social: Actes du 3ième colloque de l'Association pour la recherche interculturelle* (pp.315–326). Paris: L'Harmattan.

Clément, Richard & Noels, Kimberly A. (1992). Towards a situated approach to ethnolinguistic identity: The effects of status on individuals and groups. *Journal of Language and Social Psychology, 11,* 202–232.

Clément, Richard, Singh, Sonya & Gaudet, Sophie (in press). 'Identity and adaptation among minority Indo-Guyanese: Influence of generational status, gender, reference group and situation'. *Group Processes and Intergroup Relations.*

Colletta, Salvator P., Clément, Richard & Edwards, Henry P. (1983). *Community and parental influence: Effects on student motivation and French second language proficiency*. Quebec: International Centre for Research on Bilingualism.

Cummins, James (1998). The teaching of international languages. In J. Edwards (Ed.), *Language in Canada* (pp.293–304). Cambridge, UK: Cambridge University Press.

Cummins, James & Danesi, Marcel. (1990). *Heritage languages: The development and denial of Canada's linguistic resources*. Toronto: Our Schools/Our Selves Education Foundation: Garamond Press.

Daly, John A. & McCroskey, James C. (1975). Occupational desirability and choice as a function of communication apprehension. *Journal of Counseling Psychology, 22*, 309–313.

Deci, Edward L. & Ryan, Richard M. (1985). *Intrinsic motivation and self-determination in human behaviour*. New York: Plenum.

Deci, Edward L. & Ryan, Richard M. (2002). *Handbook of self-determination research*. New York: The University of Rochester Press.

Deci, Edward L., Vallerand, Robert J., Pelletier, Luc G. & Ryan, Richard M. (1991). Motivation in education: The self-determination perspective. *The Educational Psychologist, 26*, 325–346.

Dörnyei, Zoltan (2003). *Attitudes, orientations, and motivations in language learning*. Malden, USA: Blackwell Publishing.

Dörnyei, Zoltan & Kormos, Judit (2000). The role of individual and social variables in oral task performance. *Language teaching research, 4(3)*, 275–300.

Dörnyei, Zoltan & Ottó, Istvan. (1998). Motivation in action: A process model of L2 motivation. *Working Papers in Applied Linguistics (Thames Valley University, London, England), 4*, 43–69.

Dörnyei, Zoltan & Schmidt, Richard (2001). *Motivation and second language acquisition*. Honolulu, HI: University of Hawai'i Press.

Ehrman, Madelaine E. (1996). An exploration of adult language learner motivation, self-efficacy, and anxiety. In R.L. Oxford (Ed.), *Language learning motivation: Pathways to the new century* (pp.81–104). Honolulu, HI: University of Hawai'i Press.

Farmer, Richard (1994). The limits of learner independence in Hong Kong. In D. Gardner & L. Miller (Eds.), *Directions in self-access language learning* (pp.13–27). Hong Kong: Hong Kong University Press.

Fishman, Joshua (2001). 300-plus years of heritage language education in the United States. In J.K. Peyton, D.A. Ranard & S. McGinnis (Eds.), *Heritage languages in America: Preserving a national resource* (pp.29–36). McHenry, IL: The Center for Applied Linguistics and Delta Systems.

Gardner, Robert C. (1983). Learning another language: A true social psychological experiment. *Journal of Language and Social Psychology, 2*, 219–239.

Gardner, Robert C. (1985). *Social psychology and second language learning*. London: Edward Arnold.

Gardner, Robert C., Lalonde, Richard N. & Moorcroft, Regina (1985). The role of attitudes and motivation in second language learning: Correlational and experimental considerations. *Language Learning, 35*, 207–227.

Gardner, Robert C. & MacIntyre, Peter D. (1991). An instrumental motivation in language study: Who says it isn't effective? *Studies in Second Language Acquisition, 13*, 57–72.

Gardner, Robert C., Tremblay, Paul F. & Masgoret, Anne-Marie (1997). Towards a full model of second language learning: An empirical investigation. *Modern Language Journal, 81*, 344–362.

Gaudet, Sophie & Clément, Richard (2005). Ethnic identity and psychological adjustment among the *Fransaskois*. *Canadian Journal of Behavioural Science, 37*, 110–122.

Genesee, Fred, Rogers, Pierre & Holobow, Naomi (1983). The social psychology of second language learning: Another point of view. *Language Learning, 33*, 209–224.

Gerbner, George (1969). Toward cultural indicators: Analysis of mass mediated public message systems. *AV Communication Review, 17*, 137–148.

Giles, Howard & Byrne, Jane L. (1982). An intergroup approach to second language acquisition. *Journal of Multilingual and Multicultural Development, 3*, 17–40.

Gliksman, Louis, Gardner, Robert C. & Smythe, Padric C. (1982). The role of the integrative motive on students' participation in the French classroom. *Canadian Modern Language Review, 38*, 625–647.

Goldberg, Erin & Noels, Kimberly A. (2005). Motivation, ethnic identity and post-secondary education choices of graduates of intensive French language high school programs. *Canadian Modern Language Review*. Manuscript submitted for review.

Harwood, Jake, Giles, Howard & Bourhis, Richard (1994). The genesis of vitality theory: Historical patterns and discoursal dimensions. *International Journal of the Sociology of Language, 108*, 167–206.

Ho, Judy & Crookall, David (1995). Breaking with Chinese cultural traditions: Learner autonomy in English language teaching. *System, 23*, 235–243.

Ho, Meng-Ching (1998). Culture studies and motivation in foreign and second language learning in Taiwan. *Language, Culture, and Curriculum, 11*, 165–182.

Hofstede, Geert (1984). *Culture's consequences*. Beverly Hills, CA: Sage.

Horwitz, Elaine K., Horwitz, Michael B. & Cope, Jo A. (1986). Foreign language classroom anxiety. *Modern Language Journal, 70*, 125–132.

Hraba, Joseph & Hoiberg, Eric (1983). Ideational origins of modern theories of ethnicity: Individual freedom vs. organizational growth. *Sociological Quarterly, 24*, 381–391.

Isajiw, Wsevolod (1985). Definitions of ethnicity. In R. Bienvenue & J. Goldstein (Eds.), *Ethnicity and ethnic relations in Canada* (pp. 5–17). Toronto: Butterworth.

Jones, Jeremy F. (1995). Self-access and culture: Retreating from autonomy. *ETL Journal, 49*, 228–234.

Kagitçibasi, Cigdem (1997). Individualism and collectivism. In J.W. Berry, M.H. Segall & C. Kagitçibasi (Eds.) *Handbook of cross-cultural psychology: Vol. 3: Social behavior and applications* (pp.1–49). Needham Heights, MA: Allyn and Bacon.

Kobayashi, Yoko (2001). The learning of English at academic high schools in Japan: Students caught between exams and internalization. *Language Learning Journal, 23*, 67–72.

Lambert, Wallace (1974). Effects of bilingualism on the individual: Cognitive and socio-cultural consequences. In P.A. Hornby (Ed.), *Bilingualism: Psychological, social and educational implications* (pp.15–28). New York: Academic Press.

Leets, Laura & Giles, Howard (1995). Dimensions of minority language survival/non-survival: Intergroup cognitions and communication climates. In W. Fase,

K. Jaspaert & S. Kroon (Eds.), *The state of minority languages* (pp. 37–71). Lisse, Netherlands: Swets & Zeitlinger.

Leets, Laura, Giles, Howard & Clément, Richard (1996). Explicating ethnicity in theory and communication research. *Multilingua, 15,* 115–147.

MacIntyre, Peter D., Babin, Patricia A. & Clément, Richard (1999). Willingness to communicate: Antecedents and consequences. *Communication Quarterly, 47,* 215–229.

MacIntyre, Peter D., Baker, Susan C., Clément, Richard & Conrod, Sarah (2001). Willingness to communicate, social support and language learning orientations of immersion students. *Studies in Second Language Acquisition, 23,* 369–388.

MacIntyre, Peter D., Baker, Susan C., Clément, Richard & Donovan, Leslie A. (2002). Sex and age effects on willingness to communicate, anxiety, perceived competence, and motivation among junior high school French immersion students. *Language Learning, 52,* 537–564.

MacIntyre, Peter D., Baker, Susan C., Clément, Richard & Donovan, Leslie A. (2003). Talking in order to learn: Willingness to communicate and intensive language programs. *The Canadian Modern Language Review, 59,* 587–605.

MacIntyre, Peter D. & Charos, Catherine (1996). Personality, attitudes, and affect as predictors of second language communication. *Journal of Language and Social Psychology, 15,* 3–26.

MacIntyre, Peter D. Clément, R., Dörnyei, Zoltan & Noels, Kimberly A. (1998). Conceptualizing willingness to communicate in a L2: A situational model of L2 confidence and affiliation. *Modern Language Journal, 82,* 545–562.

MacIntyre, Peter D. & Gardner, Robert C. (1994a). The subtle effects of language anxiety on cognitive processing in the second language. *Language Learning, 44,* 283–305.

MacIntyre, Peter D. & Gardner, Robert C. (1994b). The effects of induced anxiety on cognitive processing in computerised vocabulary learning. *Studies in Second Language Acquisition, 16,* 1–17.

MacIntyre, Peter D. MacMaster, Keith & Baker, Susan C. (2001). The convergence of multiple models of motivation for second language learning: Gardner, Pintrich, Kuhl and McCroskey. In Z. Dörnyei & R. Schmidt (Eds.), *Motivation and second language acquisition* (pp.461–492). Honolulu, HI: The University of Hawai'i, Second Language Teaching & Curriculum Center.

MacIntyre, Peter D., Noels, Kimberly A. & Clément, Richard (1997). Biases in self-ratings of second language proficiency: The role of language anxiety. *Language Learning, 47,* 265–287.

Masgoret, Anne-Marie & Gardner, Richard C. (2003). Attitudes, motivation and second language learning: A meta-analysis of studies conducted by Gardner and associates. In Z. Dörnyei (Ed.), *Attitudes, orientations, and motivations in language learning* (pp.167–210). Oxford, UK: Blackwell.

McCroskey, James C. & Baer, J. Elaine (1985, November). *Willingness to communicate: The construct and its measurement.* Paper presented at the annual convention of the Speech Communication Association, Denver, CO.

McCroskey, James C. & Richmond, Virginia P. (1987). Willingness to communicate. In J.C. McCroskey & J.A. Daly (Eds.), *Personality and interpersonal communication* (pp.129–156). Newbury Park, CA: Sage Publications.

McCroskey, James C. & Richmond, Virginia P. (1991). *Willingness to communicate: A cognitive perspective.* In M. Booth-Butterfield (Ed.), *Communication, cognition and anxiety* (pp.19–37). Newbury Park, CA: Sage.

Miczo, Nathan (2004). Humor ability, unwillingness to communicate, loneliness, and perceived stress: Testing a security theory. *Communication Studies, 55,* 209–226.

Ng, Sik Hung & Bradac, James J. (1993). Power in language: Verbal communication and social influence. Thousand Oaks, CA: Sage Publications, Inc.

Noels, Kimberly A. (2001a). Learning Spanish as a second language: Learners' orientations and perceptions of teachers' communicative style. *Language Learning, 51,* 107–144.

Noels, Kimberly A. (2001b). New orientations in language learning motivation: Towards a model of intrinsic, extrinsic and integrative orientations. In Z. Dörnyei & R. Schmidt (Eds.), *Motivation and second language acquisition* (pp.43–68). Honolulu, HI: University of Hawai'i, Second language Teaching and Curriculum Center.

Noels, Kimberly A. (2005a). Orientations to learning German: Heritage language background and motivational processes. *Canadian Modern Language Review.* Manuscript submitted for publication.

Noels, Kimberly A. (2005b). *Fostering self-determination and intrinsic motivation in heritage-and non-heritage learners of German.* Manuscript in preparation.

Noels, Kimberly A. & Clément, Richard (1989). Orientations to learning German: The effect of language heritage on second language acquisition. *The Canadian Modern Language Review, 45,* 245–257.

Noels, Kimberly A. & Clément, Richard (1996). Communicating across cultures: Social determinants and acculturative consequences. *Canadian Journal of Behavioural Science, 28,* 214–228.

Noels, Kimberly A., Clément, Richard & Pelletier, Luc G. (1999). Perceptions of teacher communicative style and students' intrinsic and extrinsic motivation. *Modern Language Journal, 83,* 23–34.

Noels, Kimberly A. Clément, Richard & Pelletier, Luc G. (2001). Intrinsic, extrinsic and integrative orientations of French Canadian learners of English. *Canadian Modern Language Review, 57,* 424–442.

Noels, Kimberly A., Pelletier, Luc G., Clément, Richard & Vallerand, Robert J. (2000). Intrinsic and extrinsic motivation and second language learning: Extending self-determination theory. *Language Learning, 50,* 57–85.

Noels, Kimberly A., Pon, Gordon & Clément, Richard (1996). Language, identity and adjustment: The role of linguistic self-confidence in the adjustment process. *Journal of Language and Social Psychology, 15,* 246–264.

Noels, Kimberly A. & Rollin, Emma (1998). *Communicating in a second language: The importance of support from the Latino community for Anglo-Americans' motivation to learn Spanish.* Paper presented at the 1998 Congress of the International Association for Cross-Cultural Psychology, Bellingham, WA.

Phinney, Jean S. (1990). Ethnic identity in adolescents and adults: Review of research. *Psychological Bulletin, 108,* 499–514.

Ramage, Katherine (1990). Motivational factors and persistence in foreign language study. *Language Learning, 40,* 189–219.

Riley, Philip (1988). The ethnography of autonomy. In A. Brookes & P. Grundy (Eds.), *Individualisation and autonomy in language learning* (pp.12–34). London: Modern English Publications in association with the British Council (Macmillan).

Ross, Jeffrey A. (1979). Language and mobilization of ethnic identity. In H. Giles and B. Saint-Jacques (Eds.), *Language and ethnic relations.* Oxford: Pergamon Press.

Sadlak, Jan (2000). *The Bilingual University: Its origins, mission and functioning: Opening remarks.* Retrieved May 31, 2005, from www.cepes.ro/hed/policy/biling_univ/Sadlak.htm

Sallinen-Kuparinen, Aino, McCroskey, James C. & Richmond, Virginia P. (1991). Willingness to communicate, communication apprehension, introversion, and self-reported communication competence: Finnish and American comparisons. *Communication Research Reports, 8,* 55–64.

Schmidt, Richard, Boraie, Deena & Kassabgy, Omneya (1996). Foreign language motivation: Internal structure and external connections. In R.L. Oxford (Ed.), *Language learning motivation: Pathways to the new century* (pp.14–87). Honolulu, HI: University of Hawai'i Press.

Schumann, John H. (1978a). The acculturation model for second language acquisition. In R.C. Gingras (Eds.), *Second language acquisition and foreign language teaching.* Arlington, VA: Center for Applied Linguistics.

Schumann, John H. (1978b). *The Pidgination process: a model for second language acquisition.* Rowley, MA: Newbury House.

Schumann, John H. (1986). Research on the acculturation model for second language acquisition. *Journal of Multilingual and Multicultural Development, 7,* 379–392.

Stroebe, Wolfgang & Stroebe, Margaret (1996). The social psychology of social support. In E. Tory Higgins & A.W. Kruglanski (Eds.), *Social psychology: Handbook of basic principles* (pp.597–621). New York: The Guilford Press.

Tachibana, Yoshiharu, Matsukawa, Reiko & Zhong, Qu X. (1996). Attitudes and motivation for learning English: A cross-national comparison of Japanese and Chinese high school students. *Psychological Reports, 79,* 691–700.

Tajfel, Henry (1978). *The Social Psychology of Minorities.* London: Minority Rights Press.

Valdes, Guadalupe (2005). *Multilingualism.* Retrieved June 27, 2005 from the website of the Linguistic Society of America at www.lsadc.org/fields/index.php?aaa+multiling.htm

Varan, Duana (1998). The cultural erosion metaphor and the transcultural impact of media systems. *Journal of Communication, 48,* 58–85.

Warden, Clyde A. & Lin, Hsiu J. (2000). Existence of integrative motivation in an Asian EFL setting. *Foreign Language Annals, 33,* 535–545.

Wen, Wei-Ping & Clément, Richard (2003). A Chinese conceptualization of willingness to communicate in ESL. *Language, Culture and Curriculum, 16,* 18–38.

Yang, Nae-Dong (1998). Exploring a new role for teachers: Promoting learner autonomy. *System, 26,* 127–135.

Yashima, Tomoko (2002). Willingness to communicate in a second language: The Japanese EFL context. *Modern Language Journal, 86,* 55–66.

Yashima, Tomoko, Zenui-Nishide, Lori & Shimizu, Kazuaki (2004). The influence of attitudes and affect on willingness to communicate and second language communication. *Language Learning, 54,* 119–152.

part two
language and discourse in institutional talk

3
communication, health and ageing: promoting empowerment

marie y. savundranayagam,
ellen bouchard ryan and mary lee hummert

> Don't call me a young woman;
> it's not a compliment or courtesy
> but rather a grating discourtesy.
> Being old is a hard won achievement
> not something to be brushed aside
> treated as infirmity or ugliness
> or apologized away by 'young woman'.

(Ruth Harriet Jacobs, 1997, p.8)

Negative stereotypes of old age remain salient in North American and other societies despite worldwide improvements in health and longevity and educational efforts regarding positive ageing (Harwood et al., 1996, 2001; Kite & Wagner, 2002; Levy & Banaji, 2002). Accordingly, the adverse impact of ageism on older adults continues to be productively studied (Nelson, 2002, 2005; Palmore, 1999). The communication predicament of ageing model (CPA) conceptualized by Ryan, Giles, Bartolucci, and Henwood in 1986 examined age stereotypes and ageism through the lens of language and social psychology, specifically communication accommodation theory (CAT; Giles, Coupland & Coupland, 1991). The CPA has had profound heuristic value in guiding research on how age stereotypes constrain intergenerational interactions, thereby reducing the degree to which older adults can demonstrate competent behaviours and experience a positive sense of personhood (Coupland, Coupland &

Giles, 1991; Hummert, Garstka, Ryan & Bonnesen, 2004; Williams & Nussbaum, 2001).

Age-biased communication tends to reduce opportunities to demonstrate competence and to contribute to satisfying conversations. Moreover, the predicament is deepened by the reinforcing of age-stereotyped behaviours such as painful self-disclosures, talk about the past, and age excuses (Coupland, Coupland & Giles, 1991; Ryan, Bieman-Copland, Kwong See, Ellis & Anas, 2002). Within this negative feedback model, repeated experiences of thwarted communication lead increasingly to feelings of reduced capability, withdrawal from activities, and loss of personal control (Baltes & Wahl, 1996; Rodin & Langer, 1980; Ryan, Anas & Gruneir, in press; Ryan, et al., 2002).

Such experiences can be especially harmful in health care interactions and for frail older persons. Within health care interactions, poor communication can lead to inadequate diagnosis, inappropriate treatment, and reduced compliance with life style, exercise, and medication prescriptions (Adelman, Greene & Ory, 2000; Street, 2001). The presence of age-related disabilities (e.g., sensory impairments, motor impairments, dementia) can have the effect of lowering the threshold at which age-stereotyped expectations are triggered. Hence, older persons with disabilities are more likely to experience stronger variants of the communication predicament due to the reactions of others to the cues associated with their disability than do older persons without disabilities (see Hummert et al., 2004; Pichora-Fuller & Carson, 2001; Ryan, Bajorek, Beaman & Anas, 2005).

purpose

As this discussion suggests, age biases and inappropriate communication can make it difficult for older persons to communicate effectively, to show their competence, and to maintain self-esteem and a sense of control. Yet communication also offers older persons a powerful means of countering age biases and inappropriate communication so that they can avoid, or at least reduce, these negative consequences (Hummert & Nussbaum, 2001). Our purpose in this chapter is to examine the role of communication in empowering older adults, especially those with physical, sensory or cognitive impairments. Specifically, we consider how assertiveness strategies can serve as a resource in coping with communication predicaments. From the perspective of communication accommodation theory (Giles et al., 1991), assertiveness strategies may be viewed as appropriate accommodations designed to interrupt (even reverse) the negative feedback cycle conceptualized in the CPA model (Hummert et al., 2004). We focus especially on strategies that older adults can use to influence health care situations where power differences are inevitable, and where the consequences of poor communication can be so critical to their wellbeing and that of their caregivers.

empowerment and communication in later life

> I am an old woman, a long liver.
> I'm proud of it. I revel in it.
> I wear my grey hair and wrinkles
> as badges of triumphant survival
> and I intend to grow even older.
>
> (Ruth Harriet Jacobs, 1997, p.8)

empowerment of older adults

Empowerment has been defined as a process that helps people gain control over their lives (Solomon, 1976). Moreover, researchers have suggested that this process is not only limited to the personal/individual level (Zimmerman, 1995), but is strengthened by interaction with others and by supportive environments (Petterman, 2002; Zimmerman & Warschausky, 1998). From a health promotion perspective that goes beyond self-care, empowerment can involve the individual in mutual aid and in advocacy for healthy environments (Epp, 1986; Ryan, Meredith, MacLean & Orange, 1995). While group-level strategies involving advocacy by older adults themselves are an important part of empowerment, this chapter focuses primarily on individual and interpersonal strategies.

The process of becoming empowered has three components: participation, context awareness, and personal control (Cox & Parsons, 1994; Perkins & Zimmerman, 1995). One who is empowered is able to participate in decisions and activities that are important to both self and others. Therefore, participation is considered to be the ultimate indicator of empowerment, moving a person or group from awareness to action. Moreover, the three components of successful ageing outlined by Rowe and Kahn (1998) in their influential model all involve participation: minimizing disease and disability, maintaining physical and mental function, and continued engagement with life.

In order to take action, individuals must be aware of the context. Context awareness involves understanding the factors that enable or hinder goal achievement. This process involves seeking knowledge, developing skills and networking with others in order to evaluate the factors that contribute to goal achievement. Context awareness informs the setting of realistic goals, including the reshaping of goals after age-related losses of social roles, physical and mental health, and family and friends (Baltes & Carstensen, 1999; Carstensen, Isaacowitz & Charles, 1999). In order to make choices and participate in important everyday activities, one needs timely access to high quality, relevant information that will enable oneself to decide which goal to pursue and make accurate judgements about how to achieve them (Miller, 2000).

Participation in decisions that affect one's life and in the desired activities associated with successful ageing also requires a sense of personal control. Empowerment for older adults often involves regaining personal control over situations, outcomes and self-care after age-related losses in status, roles, health and opportunities (Miller, 2000). Individuals feeling powerless need to find new motivations by determining what can and cannot be controlled. In most cases, this can be done by controlling interpretations of events instead of the events themselves and by choosing action goals that optimize existing abilities while compensating for age-related losses (Heckhausen & Schulz, 1995). As described in the quotations above, ageing brings with it the achievement of survival. Older adults have a wealth of resources, including the wisdom of life history and personal connections, which can help in regaining personal control over life events. Communication offers a primary means of using those resources to regain the personal control that will enable them to negotiate successfully the challenges of ageing (Hummert & Nussbaum, 2001).

assertive communication

As part of empowerment, assertive communication involves responding proactively in difficult situations rather than reacting passively or aggressively (Rakos, 1991). Assertiveness entails calm, direct, honest expression of feelings and needs. As seen in Table 3.1, assertive communication flows from responsible choices and is characterized by a poised, confident style conveyed verbally, vocally, and nonverbally (Doty, 1987; Paterson, 2000; Rakos, 1991; Ryan et al., 2005a; Wilson & Gallois, 1993). Assertive communication is particularly relevant to the following key aspects of older adults' control over their own lives: obtaining needed information, making decisions, making and declining requests, managing help, managing privacy, dealing with inappropriate talk to or about oneself, and caregiving (Gambrill, 1994; Northrop & Edelstein, 1998; Ryan et al., 2005b).

Table 3.1   Assertive communication*

	Passive	Assertive	Aggressive
Choices	follow others	choose responsibly for self	force choices upon others
Benefits	avoid risks, stay safe	engage in desired activities, self-respect, growth	control others
Outcome	fail to meet goals, frustration, helplessness	meet goals, finish tasks, self-confidence, respect	fail to meet goals, alienate others
Emotion	resignation, frustration, guilt	confidence, calm, in control, positive self-esteem	anger, frustration, feeling out of control, resentment, guilt
Style	timid, closed, inhibited, dishonest, self-denying, apologetic	poised, open, direct, honest, self-expressive, empowered	pushy, closed, explosive, self-righteous, over-expressive
Language	hidden meaning, filled with excuses, indirect, overly polite	clear message, express what is wanted, use 'I' language, direct, acknowledge positive behaviours	blunt message, demand what is wanted, use 'You' language, attacking, rude
Humour	self-deprecating, giggle	contextually sensitive	target others
Voice	weak, monotone, flat	firm, naturally expressive	loud, harsh, over-expressive
Posture	stooped, sagging, fidgety	upright, relaxed, fluid	stiff, towering, threatening
Hands	fluttering, clammy	open, smooth motions, gentle gestures	clenched, abrupt, pointing, arms crossed, over-gesture
Eyes	avoid eye contact, look down	Make frequent eye contact	stare, glare
Face	lack of expression, frowning, tense	open expression, smiling, relaxed	over-expressive, frowning, tense, high colour

* Adapted from Doty, 1987; Paterson, 2000; and others

Assertive behaviour can lead to greater likelihood of meeting personal needs and to more positive self concept. Originally designed for patients in clinical psychology, assertiveness training has been successfully extended to groups in the community traditionally accorded less status such as women, people with disabilities, and older adults (Doty, 1987; Engels, 1991; Franzke, 1987; Northrop & Edelstein, 1998; Rakos, 1991).

Since assertive behaviour can be interpreted as aggressive or selfish, it is associated with risks. Wilson and Gallois (1993) indicate that assertiveness is often associated with lower ratings of friendliness and appropriateness. They interpret this typical finding in terms of confusion between aggression and assertiveness and restrictive role expectations for members of particular social groups (e.g., women, medical patients). Assertiveness is less common among women and among older cohorts (Gallois, 2004; Rakos, 1991; Wilson & Gallois, 1993; Twenge, 2001). Older people are less assertive than younger peers because they never were as assertive and also because they may have lost the confidence to use assertiveness skills (Furnham & Pendleton, 1983). The 'me first' association with mislabelled assertiveness (actually aggressiveness) is a deterrent to groups socialized to be other-oriented. In addition, assertive behaviour may be especially avoided in health care encounters, given that non-assertive behaviour is encouraged in such hierarchical contexts (Adler, McGraw & McKinlay, 1998).

We have used the term *selective assertiveness* to characterize the main strategy for recipients to interrupt the negative feedback cycle of the communication predicament model (Ryan et al., 2005a; see also Doty, 1987; Paterson, 2000; Taylor & Epstein, 1999). Assertive speakers communicate clearly while taking responsible control over meeting their goals. They neither defer passively to others nor impose on them aggressively. They are neither a pushover nor pushy. In line with socio-emotional selectivity theory, speakers make choices about important, realistic goals to fit the circumstances (Carstensen et al., 1999). Within a health promotion framework, assertiveness becomes part of managing one's health within a social environment. It is a matter of taking care of oneself, not a matter of being selfish.

Whether assertiveness is effective depends on its appropriateness in the specific situation. Lack of attention to contextual specificity is one reason for limited transfer to real life situations after assertiveness training (Rakos, 1991; Wilson & Gallois, 1993). The assertive speaker is tactful: aware of the social context and the other person's perspective; knows when to be direct or indirect; and acknowledges the communication partner's positive behaviours when appropriate (Ryan et al., 2005a; Wilson & Gallois, 1993). Older adults with age-related impairments can use these skills selectively for self advocacy and group advocacy (Gallois, 2004; Hickson & Worrall, 2003; Orr & Rogers, 2003).

The concept of selective assertiveness would encourage older adults to choose carefully when to voice their desires or concerns after assessing benefits and risks and to focus on fitting words and manner to the goals, speaker and situation (Ryan et al., 2005b). Teaching selective assertiveness would involve contingent communication strategies in terms of situational features, goals and behaviours (e.g., 'In a situation of . . . if you wish to . . . then try . . . .': Ohlsson, 1996, cited by Lizzio, Wilson, Gilchrist & Gallois, 2003).

Research by Birditt and Fingerman (2005) on choosing one's battles shows that older adults favour passive, accepting responses as compared to young adults, who are more likely to react aggressively in situations of interpersonal conflict. Training, including support groups, could assist older adults with disabilities to work out assertive strategies for use when the battle is especially important to reduce the frustrations associated with persistently avoiding such battles.

empowerment in health contexts: the challenge of disability

The wounds, I suppose, teach – force to resolve, to surmount, to transcend. I will not be put down permanently like a dying animal. I can recover and go on creating. (Sarton, 1988, pp.230–231)

My years with failing vision have prompted me to learn about the nature of the eye and the incredible gift of sight, which I had always taken for granted until it began to slip away. But I also learned about living within limits and overcoming disability. This, then, is not merely a story about seeing but also about living. It is a story not merely about losing sight but about gaining insight as well. (Grunwald, 2003, p.102)

I would love to see some people with Alzheimer's not trying to stay in the shadows all the time but to say, damn it, we're people too. And we want to be talked to and respected as if we were honest to God real people. (Henderson & Andrews, 1998, p.7)

I can be a care-partner with you, communicating my true feelings, my true needs, so that you can walk alongside me adjusting and compensating for these expressed needs as we face this struggle together. (Bryden, 2005, p.150)

Empowerment has been facilitated by the societal move toward interpreting disability as an interaction between a person and the demands of the environment rather than a deficiency solely within the person. Worrall and Hickson (2003) have elaborated on the World Health Organization International Classification of Functioning specifically in the context of age-related communication disabilities. We offer a slight adaptation here in terms of communication by people with varying disabilities. The WHO model emphasizes how the physical impairment and/or chronic health condition can limit activities and restrict participation in valued social domains. Key activities, for this chapter, are communication and interpersonal relationships. Limitations in these activities can restrict participation in domains such as personal maintenance, mobility, exchange of information, social relationships, occupation, economic life, and community life. Personal strengths and resources, as well as environmental threats and supports, can have a great influence on participation given any range of specific disabilities. Thus, stages of dementia or degrees of aphasia or levels of visual impairment might not always predict participation restrictions. Communication predicaments, for example, might well reduce success of communication and interpersonal relationships, thereby exacerbating the disability in terms of participation restrictions. On the other hand, empowering environments might well compensate for much of the potential activity limitations usually associated with particular impairments. Relating back to our emphasis on goal setting, participation restrictions can be defined in terms of the individual's own goals.

empowered care receiving

The research programme of Greene and Adelman has identified a number of risks for older patients in health care situations that show the need for empowerment of older patients: being ignored in three-way conversations, little time to express concerns, and low responsiveness of physicians to their psychosocial concerns. Because they are often passive seekers of health information, older patients are less likely to use non-traditional sources of medical information (e.g., internet), instead relying heavily on their health care professionals for medical advice and decision-making (Bilodeau & Degner, 1996; Cassileth, Zupkis, Sutton-Smith & March, 1980). Older adults also ask fewer questions about their diagnoses and participate less actively in their health decisions than younger adults (Cameron & Horsburgh, 1998; Thompson, Robinson & Beisecker, 2004).

Older adults seeking health care, especially those who are frail or experiencing impairments, are in the position of asking for help. Research on communication and disability has identified helping situations as prime contexts for communication predicaments (Braithwaite & Eckstein, 2003; Braithwaite & Thompson, 2000). For instance, older persons are likely to find themselves in three-way conversations in which their health provider may speak mainly to an accompanying family member (Adelman et al., 2000). Older adults are even more likely to be excluded when their English (or main language of the culture) is not native, when they suffer from communication or cognitive impairments, or when they are seated in a wheelchair while others are standing (Frank, 1995; Hallberg, Norberg & Erikson, 1990; Ryan, Anas & Gruneir, 2006). Once providers and family members become comfortable speaking on behalf of older persons, it becomes all the more difficult for older individuals to regain their voice in future encounters (Braithwaite & Thompson, 2000). Another major source of communication difficulties is the pressure to disclose personal information – to fend off unwanted help, to account for help requests, or simply to satisfy the curiosity of non-disabled communication partners (Braithwaite & Thompson, 2000; Ryan et al., 2005b). Helping behaviours incongruent with one's needs create excess disability, threaten personhood, and limit the potential for successful ageing through premature relinquishment of goals (Baltes & Carstensen, 1999).

Much of the literature on health provider–older adult relationships has focused on how the provider's communication should change to reduce these risks and to meet the individual needs of older adults (Clark, 1996; Ryan et al., 1995). This focus on the provider implicitly reflects a power differential in this relationship. However, consumers of health care, including older adults, are not powerless during the health encounter. In fact, the information provided by older adults about their health situation enables providers to make the best assessment (Brorsson & Rastam, 1993). Accessing relevant information for their health situation can improve the value of their questions to the providers, adherence to treatment, and health outcomes. Therefore, older adults have a responsibility to share their health concerns (Lambert, Street, Cegala, Smith, Kurtz & Schofield, 1997) and use that as an opportunity to empower themselves and their health provider. Below is a discussion of how older adults can actively participate when receiving care.

Previous research has shown that the more actively involved patients are in their health care, the better their health outcomes (Kaplan, Greenfield, Gandek, Rogers & Ware, 1996; Kreps & O'Hair, 1995). Street and Voigt (1997) found that participants who were more active in their health care believed they had more control over their situation and decision-making. Therefore, the natural next question is what communication strategies can empower older adults to take a more active role in their health care? Empowering communication strategies for older adults include asking questions to get clarification, expressing concerns, and being assertive (McGee & Cegala, 1998; Street, 2003). By expressing expectations for care and making suggestions for treatment, one can inform the health provider's choices of the best-fitting approach.

person-perception studies of communication strategies

The effectiveness of assertiveness as a strategy to communicate expectations of care while maintaining the face of health providers has been examined by person-perception studies. These studies have shown that assertive speakers are characterized as more competent compared to non-assertive speakers (Hummert & Mazloff, 2001) and less satisfied with patronizing communication (Ryan, Kennaley, Pratt & Shumovich, 2000). To further examine perceptions of assertiveness, Ryan, Anas and

Friedman (in press) compared assertive, aggressive and passive responses in problematic health care encounters (i.e., being ignored by a physician in favour of a companion, difficulty following a medication message delivered too quickly by a pharmacist, or misunderstanding a physiotherapist's exercise message because of noise). Older adults selecting assertive responses were rated as most competent and likely to be satisfied with future health encounters by both young and older participants. This finding suggests that assertiveness is a potentially useful response that is not bounded by contrasting ingroup or outgroup perceptions. The selective aspect, however, is critical. The assertive response was viewed as less polite than a passive response while being more polite than an aggressive one. The risk of crossing the line to aggressive and the social cost of standing up for oneself need to be weighed along with the benefits. Also, the health professional in the scenarios was rated more negatively when the older adult responded assertively or aggressively. This can be valuable in the sense that one avoids reinforcing the continuing negative feedback cycle.

Ryan, Anas, and Mays (2005a) took two steps in exploring the contextual variations on evaluations of older adult assertiveness within problematic health care encounters. This study examined the appropriateness of assertive responses by visually impaired older adults under different circumstances (serious or moderate) and in different contexts (community or institution). Both young and old participants rated conversational scenarios in which a visually impaired older adult responded either passively or assertively after requesting assistance with reading health-related information and not receiving it. Both older and young participants viewed the assertive older adult as more competent and responding more positively than the passive older adult. However, the appreciation for assertive responding was higher in the non-hierarchical community setting than in the hierarchical hospital setting (see Harwood et al., 1993; Harwood, Ryan, et al., 1997; Hummert et al., 1998 for similar findings). When the situation was of a serious nature, the assertive older adult was rated as even more competent and as having handled the situation better. Having the knowledge of when and where older adults will benefit most from an assertive style will work to alleviate the negative consequences of constantly being stereotyped and reinforcing those stereotypes with a passive style.

Directly assertive responses tend to threaten the face of health care professionals, who could retaliate intentionally or unconsciously. Some indirectly assertive approaches (e.g., humorous and appreciative) have elicited favourable reactions and can be especially useful for older adults dependent upon others for care (Hummert & Mazloff, 2001; Hummert & Ryan, 2001; Hummert et al., 2004; Ryan et al., 2000). Hence, future research is needed to determine the suitability of different forms of older adult assertiveness in specific contexts.

communication interventions and training programmes

Being able to communicate competently does not always come naturally, especially when it can be an uphill battle due to communication predicaments in hierarchical health care settings. Some researchers also suggest that older adults find it more difficult to seek useful health information during a health encounter (Greene, Adelman, Charon & Hoffman, 1986; Rost & Frankel, 1993). Therefore, it is important to prepare and practise appropriate communication (Street, 2003). Preparation and practice enables one to develop a repertoire of communication behaviours/ skills that can be easily accessed depending on the situation (Parks, 1994). In an empowerment intervention for cancer patients, participants in the experimental group thought about the information needed from their doctor, generated questions, and searched for information in a packet they received (Davison & Degner, 1997). The control group only received the information packet. Compared to the control group, participants in the experimental group were more active in treatment decisions and less anxious about their health in a six-week follow-up. Community workshops on communicating with health providers have been helpful in teaching older adults about the need to prepare and present information effectively, and to express concerns and ask questions (Towle, Godolphin, Manklow & Wiesinger, 2003).

Cegala and colleagues' PACE programme (2001) trained older adults how to ask questions, provide information and verify information in medical interviews using a 30-minute one-on-one session prior to a medical visit. The older adults learned to organize and present medical information and questions using the PACE acronym as a guide: Present, Ask, Check, Express. Specifically, older persons were taught to Present their feelings in detail, Ask questions when the information they required was not provided, Check their understanding of information that was communicated to them, and Express concerns regarding suggested treatments. Results showed that in comparison to a control group, those who experienced the PACE training were more active participants in a subsequent medical interview, asking more questions about medically related topics and providing more detailed responses to the doctor's questions. In short, the PACE group, after only the briefest of training experiences, exhibited the participation that is the hallmark of empowerment and which positioned them as shared decision makers in their health care planning.

Tennstedt's (2000) intensive two-hour group community-based intervention also stressed active participation by older adults. The programme involved modelling desirable and ineffective patient behaviours, and taught older adults to record medical information and prioritize their health concerns. The negative consequences of passive interactions during a health visit were discussed and participants received cue cards with a list of active behaviours to try before, during and after the visit. Examples include preparing a list of prioritized concerns, discussing medications, expressing preferences for treatment, and following up with the physician regarding side-effects of treatments. Programme outcomes included active participation and patient satisfaction with the medical visit. Compared with an untrained control group, older adults in the programme reported a greater number of active behaviours and were more likely to be satisfied with their health encounter.

Training for older individuals with disability can be empowering in facilitating growth and use of skills of self-advocacy as well as mutual support. Such training is often conducted in small groups for the advantages of sharing ideas and emotions, role play, and feedback on possible strategies. Worrall and Hickson (2003) review several studies with the Keep on Talking approach of assisting older individuals in small groups to identify their own communication skills learning priorities and to learn and practise relevant strategies. This community approach has been successful in reaching older adults with hearing impairments who would not otherwise access help. Many seniors are interested in this proactive approach to prepare for possible future communication difficulties for themselves or for family members.

Orr and Rogers (2003) have produced a programme tested across the USA for facilitating learning groups of older individuals with visual impairment to gain self-advocacy skills. These individuals can learn to ensure their needs are met as they continue to age with visual difficulties through knowledge, practice, and feedback concerning various strategies to find targeted information in a timely manner, manage health care, interact with family caregivers, retain and share decision making, and handle the crises of life. The training package is sufficiently detailed and available in alternative formats so that the groups can be led by peer trainers, an especially empowering approach.

computer-mediated communication

Supporting existing strengths is vital to engendering personal control. Seeing oneself as separate from the disease process (i.e., a person is more than the disease itself) and viewing disability as a difference instead of as dependence or disadvantage is key to maintaining personal control (Orr & Rogers, 2003; Ryan et al., 2005b; Schulz, 2000). Acquiring skills that enable better communication (e.g., lip reading, using adaptive technologies such as computers) can help older adults regain confidence and control over their changing environments. For instance, if older adults with sensory difficulties associated with vision or hearing are equipped with assistive devices and communication skills that help them to navigate their social environments, they are more likely to resume former roles or gain new ones (Orr & Rogers, 2003).

Computers are useful assistive devices that help older adults with mobility restrictions. Such restrictions can physically and socially isolate individuals, leaving them homebound and experiencing a loss of control in their day-to-day activities. Wright (2000) found that computer-mediated communication can be an important source of social support in coping with such challenges. McMellon and Schiffman (2002) assert that the internet can empower older adults on personal and social levels. Specifically, the internet can personally empower older adults by allowing them to engage with others, reconnect with past pleasures, be a source of information gathering, and increase personal control. The internet also empowers older adults on a community level because it allows them to interact with other individuals, institutions or interest groups. This type of interaction allows older adults to discuss current events, share experiences, be more informed, and find support. McMellon and Schiffman (2002) also contend that internet empowerment contributes to successful ageing because learning computer skills keeps older adults mentally active. Moreover, older adults are more actively engaged with life when they connect with family/friends, develop social networks and explore interests on the internet (Rowe & Kahn, 1998). The potential is great for personal computer usage by older adults, especially with improvements in ease of software usage, teaching approaches, and valuable accessibility options for those with physical and visual impairments (see Charness, Park & Sabel, 2001).

writing for oneself and for publication

Most of the empowerment strategies we have discussed come from within and build on existing abilities of older adults. One of the most empowering communication strategies has been the publication of life stories by older authors, some with disabilities. These provide engaging narratives of age-related losses and specific journeys of coping as well as heartfelt acknowledgement of age-related gains that surprise even the authors themselves. Writing a journal or a memoir or an illness narrative has great power in helping an individual to transform their sense of their life story – to take a broader perspective, to grow from 'why me' to 'why not me', to accept their life as their own, to recreate the beauty that they have experienced and to reap the lessons from their lives (Kenyon, Clark & de Vries, 2001; Smyth & Pennebaker, 1999). Berman (1994) has analysed five personal journals (including the well-known journals of May Sarton and Florida Scott-Maxwell), giving a year-to-year sense of how ageing voices talk about their changing/continuing sense of self across age. Autobiographies or memoirs can teach us about life span development, family history, local and world history, and spiritual growth. In publishing their stories, older adults can reach a wider audience, reporting back from the frontier about what their life is like after many decades. These reports can open hearts and transform the readers' views of ageing and of loss and of illness.

For older adults with an acquired disability or progressive chronic illness, writing in a journal can be an important part of finding a new sense of identity. Such individuals can find the inner voice that underlies key elements of assertiveness (i.e., calm, confidence, what to say). When they choose to convey their messages in writing (in a letter or email message or for publication), writing can facilitate selective assertiveness through greater control, away from the shaping power of the communication predicaments experienced in conversation (Ryan, 2006, in press).

empowered caregiving by older adults

Caregiving involves advocating on behalf of the care receiver, especially when he/she cannot self-advocate due to communication difficulties. Kahana and Kahana (2003) suggest that family members can help care receivers be proactive by gathering information on health conditions. Family members can influence health beliefs of care receivers by being for or against certain treatments or practices. They influence care receivers' participation in their own self-care by helping them adhere to treatment plans, providing emotional support, allowing time to learn and practise new techniques (support without pressure), and taking part in instruction of rehabilitation techniques. This description represents the empowered caregiver. However, caregiving is effortful. The enormity of juggling multiple care-tasks while dealing with possible changes in relationships and lifestyles can easily engender a sense of powerlessness.

Older adults, especially spouses, assume new roles as caregivers to other older adults with complex and often multiple chronic conditions that affect communication. These conditions include losses in hearing and vision, and dementia. Over the past few decades, there has been considerable research on the deleterious psychosocial and physical impact of caregiving (Schulz, O'Brien, Bookwala & Fleissner, 1995; Schulz, 2000).

Caregiving often becomes an all-consuming role, especially with complex conditions such as Alzheimer's disease that affect cognitive-communicative, physical and behavioural health. As a result, caregivers who do not receive necessary and timely support are at risk of dis-empowerment. Specifically, unsupported caregivers are likely to feel overwhelmed by the numerous day-to-day tasks associated with cognitive-communicative and physical declines. Moreover, the unpredictability of disruptive behaviours, such as agitation and aggression, only adds to the diminished sense of personal control caregivers experience (McCarty et al., 2000). This lack of caregiving mastery has been identified as an important factor in a caregiver's physical and psychological decline, and in strained relationships with their family member with dementia (Narayan, Lewis, Tornatore, Hepburn & Corcoran-Perry, 2001; Pearlin & Schooler, 1978).

Consequently, interventions have focused on empowering caregivers with instrumental issues such as increasing knowledge and problem-solving skills about disease processes affecting their loved ones, knowing how to advocate for them, effective communication, and accessing health care and community services (Burns, Nichols, Martindale-Adams, Graney & Lummus, 2003; Brodaty, Green & Koschera, 2003; Kahana & Kahana, 2003; Ostwald, Hepburn, Caron, Burns & Mantell, 1999; Ripich, Ziol, Fritsch & Durand, 1999; Schulz et al., 2002). Additionally, many interventions also targeted relational issues such as caregiver burden, depression, and improved caregiver–care receiver relationships (McCallion, Toseland & Freeman, 1999; Mittleman, Ferris, Shulman, Steinberg & Levin, 1996). Burns and colleagues (2003) found that interventions including both educational and relational components are more effective than those that only consider one aspect.

The outcomes of such interventions are not only limited to empowering the older caregiver but extend to simultaneously increasing participation of the older care receiver. Bourgeois and colleagues' communication interventions trained family caregivers to use external memory aids (e.g., memory wallets) to increase the use of on-topic statements about personal information and decrease repetitive verbalizations by individuals with dementia (Bourgeois, 1992; Bourgeois, Burgio, Schulz, Beach & Palmer, 1997; Bourgeois, Schulz, Burgio & Beach, 2002). Similarly, another communication intervention by Ripich and others (1999) showed that changing the way caregivers asked questions when communicating with their family members with dementia led to improved conversation exchange. These interventions show that by teaching caregivers to communicate effectively with their family members with dementia, they not only empower themselves but also enable their family members to participate on a level that suits their abilities.

Empowered caregiving is also not limited to the individual family caregiver or care receiver. Some interventions target feelings of powerlessness by connecting individuals with others who are in similar life situations. Caregiver support groups are excellent examples of mutual aid, where individuals experiencing similar challenges share their concerns and problem solve together. Czaja and Mark (2002) developed a telecommunications system that enhanced caregivers' access to formal and informal support services. The system also facilitated linkages among caregivers and between caregivers and other family members. Online discussion groups and resource guides helped caregivers connect with others sharing similar experiences and also helped them remain up-to-date on opportunities and technologies that might assist them. Again, it is likely that caregivers benefited from the *combination* of instrumental coping skills with shared personal experiences. Although information is powerful, the vast amount of health information available can overload caregivers. Therefore, being able to discuss the practicality and relevance of the available information with other caregivers is an invaluable resource.

enabling environments: role of health/social provider

Empowering older clients to cope with age biases and inappropriate communication is one avenue for avoiding the negative feedback cycle of the communication predicament of ageing model. Another equally important avenue, however, is developing the communication competencies of physicians and other health professionals because they play influential roles in creating health care interactions that facilitate empowerment. Prior research shows that through their communication practices, physicians and other health professionals may contribute to the negative feedback cycle of the communication predicament model. These practices may reflect stereotyped-based stylistic modifications such as exaggerated intonation, high pitch, increased loudness, simpler vocabulary, increased redundancy, and reduced grammatical complexity (Caporael, 1981; Coupland et al., 1991; Kemper, 2001; Sachweh, 1998), as well as content modifications such as restricted topic selection (e.g., avoidance of explicit reference to long-term prognosis), reduced time allotment, and frequent interruptions (Adelman, Greene, Charon & Friedmann, 1992; Greene, Adelman & Rizzo, 1996; Meyer, Russo & Talbot, 1995). For example, physicians and oncologists often do not communicate in as much detail with older patients as they do with younger patients (Greene et al., 1996). Such speech modifications can be driven by a dismissive or impatient task orientation, but they often arise from a nurturing, overprotective concern (Hummert & Ryan, 1996, 2001; Kemper, 2001). Regardless of the motivation, a patronizing manner of communication implicitly primes negative self-stereotypes held by the older recipients. Levy's innovative research on implicit priming of either negative or positive old age stereotypes has documented corresponding behavioural changes in memory, gait, cardiovascular indicators, and handwriting (Levy, 2003).

The communication enhancement model (Ryan et al., 1995) outlines how social partners, especially health care professionals, can modify their communication to meet the actual needs of older adults. The model suggests that interventions focus on appropriate speech accommoda-tions, supportive physical environments, and creating positive social environments. This process, involving individualized assessment and repeated cycles of adjusting manner and content of communication, empowers both the care provider and older adult. Empowerment in this model is linked to health provider facilitation of the three intervention domains of health promotion: self-care, mutual aid, and healthy environments (Epp, 1986).

Kahana and Kahana's (2003) health care partnership (HCP) model also acknowledges the important role of providers in affecting patient outcomes. Content and relational aspects of physicians' communication are expected to affect especially patients' satisfaction with their health care encounter and participation in health promotion and prevention. Content of communication includes information about prevention, diagnosis, health maintenance, and corrective action. Relational aspects of the physician's communication include support, reassurance, hope, respectfulness and shared decision making. Older patients gain more control when the content of physician's communication is presented using jargon-free information that accounts for their health beliefs and concerns. In turn, older adults are more likely to participate in decision making (Mills & Sullivan, 1999). Research also suggests that the quality of physician communication is associated with patient adherence to physician's treatment plans, instructions and advice (Kahana & Kahana, 2003). Although the content of physician communication is often highlighted in discussions of the quality of interactions with patients, relational aspects of the communication are equally important but often overlooked (Cegala, McGee & McNellis, 1996; Greene, Adelman, Rizzo & Friedmann, 1994).

Research by Watson and Gallois (2004) illustrates that managing relational needs of patients deserves as much attention as providing accurate information. Using written retrospective accounts of satisfactory and unsatisfactory medical encounters, the authors examined health professionals' use of communication strategies, including emotional expression. In satisfactory health care encounters, patients described health professionals as treating them as individuals, listening to their concerns, allowing them to negotiate topic selection and expressing emotions. Conversely, in unsatisfactory encounters, health professionals did not express any positive emotions, were not responsive, did not show concern and even showed displeasure towards patients. As a result, patients in unsatisfactory encounters were perceived as having less control.

Thus far, we have discussed the need for facilitative environments to counter stereotypes of incompetence and dependence associated with normal ageing. The communication predicament becomes more pronounced for individuals with cognitive-communicative impairments (e.g., dementia), especially those in social contexts that invoke negative age stereotypes (e.g., long-term care facilities). Health providers, especially long-term care staff, tend to maintain misperceptions of poor interactions by using patronizing speech, by neglecting remaining abilities, and by promoting dependent behaviours (Baltes & Wahl, 1996; Richter, Bottenberg & Roberto, 1993; Orange, Ryan, Meredith & MacLean, 1995).

Researchers continue to develop the groundwork for interventions that can prevent or reduce patronizing communication. Baltes and Wahl (1996) demonstrated that training nursing home staff to change the usual independence-ignore script by rewarding independent behaviours led to more independent self-care behaviours by the residents. Other researchers have proposed incorporating personhood (Kitwood, 1997) and simplifying language (Kemper & Harden, 1999) to communicate clearly with people with dementia while minimizing the patronizing tone. Using a vignette evaluation method, Savundranayagam, Ryan, Anas and Orange (2005) investigated whether long-term care staff depicted using personhood strategies would be perceived more positively than those using directive language. They also investigated whether perceptions of the resident depicted identically in the scenarios would differ in personhood versus directive conversations. Finally, they examined whether simplifying complex language and adding repetitions would influence the positive effect of personhood on perceptions of LTC staff and residents. Results showed that personhood-based language had positive effects on both perceptions of staff and residents. Simplified language strengthened those effects by showing staff as less patronizing, and residents as more competent. Therefore, in support of the CEM, changing staff communication alone empowers both staff and residents.

conclusions

In this chapter we have focused on older adults as care receivers and caregivers, noting that empowerment has a function in both roles. Moreover, we have highlighted the importance of facilitative social environments that provide opportunities for older adults to be active participants in important decisions, especially within health care encounters. Acknowledging that power differentials exist in everyday encounters for older adults, we have argued that communication can be a useful resource in narrowing gaps in power. Older adults can use the strategies we have outlined, notably assertiveness, to participate in activities that matter to them. Learning such strategies engenders confidence, which can help older adults resume former roles or gain new ones, as well as select appropriate goals. Although we have focused on empowering older individuals, many of the strategies considered in this chapter can also be extended to other vulnerable groups, including women in male-dominated settings, ethnic minorities, and individuals with chronic diseases and disabilities (Hummert & Ryan, 2001).

Future research should consider the impact of different communication strategies on personal control, and also investigate the extent to which increasing personal control affects older adults' participation in activities that are important to them. Additionally, future research should consider the longer-term impact of communication skills training. Currently, it appears that communication skills training is effective before a health encounter; more research is needed on whether such training programmes affect older adults' decisions to follow-up with a health provider and use the learned skills. Certainly, systematic, longitudinal studies are needed to evaluate the role of communication on context awareness, personal control and participation, and to consider the interplay between those aspects of empowerment.

Our goal in this chapter was to promote opportunities for vulnerable older adults to age successfully through their own enhanced communication skills and through the improved communication skills of those interacting with them. We hope that readers agree that older adults and health providers alike need to examine whether expectations go beyond age and/or disability stereotypes to consider older adults in individualized interactions. The quotations throughout this chapter illustrate that the accomplishment of ageing must be embraced and that empowerment comes from within the individual and from healthy interactions with others.

We who are old know that age is more than a disability. It is an intense and varied experience, almost beyond our capacity at times, but something to be carried high. If it is a long defeat it is also a victory, meaningful for the initiates of time, if not for those who have come less far. (Scott-Maxwell, 1979, p.5)

acknowledgements

We would like to thank Ann Anas, Jake Harwood and the editors for comments on this chapter. We also acknowledge financial support from a grant to E. Ryan from the Social Sciences and Humanities Research Council of Canada.

references

Adelman, R.D., Greene, M.G., Charon, R. & Friedmann, E. (1992). The content of physician and elderly patient interaction in the medical primary care encounter. *Communication Research, 19*, 370–380.

Adelman, R.D., Greene, M.G. & Ory, M.G. (2000). Communication between older patients and their physicians. *Clinics in Geriatric Medicine, 16*, 1–24.

Adler, S.R., McGraw, S.A. & McKinlay, J.B. (1998). Patient assertiveness in ethnically diverse older women with breast cancer: Challenging stereotypes of the elderly. *Journal of Aging Studies, 12(4)*, 331–350.

Baltes, M.M. & Carstensen, L. (1999). Social-psychological theories and their applications to aging: From individual to collective. In V.L. Bengtson & K.W. Schaie (Eds.), *Handbook of theories of aging* (pp.209–226). New York, NY: Springer.

Baltes, M. & Wahl, H-W. (1996). Patterns of communication in old age: The dependency-support and independence-ignore script. *Health Communication, 8*, 217–232.

Berman, H.J. (1994). *Interpreting the aging self*. New York: Springer.

Bilodeau, B.A. & Degner, L.F. (1996). Information needs, sources of information, and decisional roles in women with breast cancer. *Oncology Nursing Forum, 23(4)*, 691–696.

Birditt, K.S. & Fingerman, K.L. (2005). Do we get better at picking our battles? Age group differences in descriptions of behavioral reactions to interpersonal tensions. *Journal of Gerontology, 60,* P121–P128.

Bourgeois, M. (1992). Evaluating memory wallets in conversations with patients with dementia. *Journal of Speech and Hearing Research, 35,* 1344–1357.

Bourgeois, M.S., Burgio, L.D., Schulz, R., Beach, S. & Palmer, B. (1997). Modifying repetitive verbalizations of community-dwelling patients with AD. *The Gerontologist, 37,* 30–39.

Bourgeois, M.S., Schulz, R., Burgio, L.D. & Beach, S. (2002). Skills training for spouses of patients with Alzheimer's disease: Outcomes of an intervention study. *Journal of Clinical Geropsychology, 8,* 53–73.

Braithwaite, D.O. & Eckstein, N. (2003). Reconceptualizing supportive interactions: How persons with disabilities communicatively manage assistance. *Journal of Applied Communication Research, 31(1),* 1–26.

Braithwaite, D. & Thompson, T. (Eds.) (2000). *The handbook of communication and physical disability.* Mahwah, NJ: Erlbaum.

Brodaty, H., Green, A. & Koschera, A. (2003). Meta-analysis of psychosocial interventions for caregivers of people with dementia. *Journal of the American Geriatrics Society, 51,* 657–664.

Brorsson, A. & Rastam, L. (1993). The patient's family history: A key to the physician's understanding of patient's fears. *Family Practice, 10,* 197–200.

Bryden, C. (2005). *Dancing with dementia: My story of living positively with dementia.* Vancouver: University of British Columbia Press.

Burns, R., Nichols, L.O., Martindale-Adams, J., Graney, M.J. & Lummus, A. (2003). Primary care interventions for dementia caregivers: 2-year outcomes from the REACH study. *The Gerontologist, 43,* 547–555.

Cameron, S. & Horsburgh, M.E. (1998). Comparing issues faced by younger and older women with breast cancer. *Canadian Oncology Nursing Journal, 8(1),* 40–44.

Caporael, L.R. (1981). The paralanguage of caregiving: Baby talk to the institutionalized aged. *Journal of Personality and Social Psychology, 40,* 876–884.

Carstensen, L.L., Isaacowitz, D.M. & Charles, S.T. (1999). Taking time seriously: A theory of socioemotional selectivity. *American-Psychologist, 54,* 165–181.

Cassileth, B.R., Zupkis, R.V., Sutton-Smith, K. & March, V. (1980). Information and participation preferences among cancer patients. *Annals of Internal Medicine, 92,* 832–836.

Cegala, D.J., McGee, D.S. & McNellis, K.S. (1996). Components of patients' and doctors' perceptions of communication competence during a primary care interview. *Health Communication, 8,* 1–27.

Cegala, D.J., Post, D.M. & McClure, L. (2001). The effects of patient communication skills training on the discourse of older patients during a primary care interview. *Journal of the American Geriatrics Society, 49(11),* 1505–11.

Charness, N., Park, D.C. & Sabel, B.A. (Eds.) (2001). *Communication, technology and aging: Opportunities and challenges for the future.* New York: Springer.

Clark, P.G. (1996). Communication between provider and patient: Values, biography, and empowerment in clinical practice. *Ageing and Society, 16,* 747–774.

Cox, E.O. & Parsons, R.J. (1994). *Empowerment oriented social work practice with the elderly.* Pacific Grove, CA: Brooks/Cole.

Coupland, N., Coupland, J. & Giles, H. (1991). *Language, society and the elderly.* Cambridge: Basil Blackwell.

Czaja, S.J.R. & Mark, P. (2002). Telecommunications technology as an aid to family caregivers of persons with dementia. *Psychosomatic Medicine, 64,* 469–476.

Davison, B.J. & Degner, L.F. (1997). Empowerment of men newly diagnosed with prostate cancer in treatment decision making. *Cancer Nursing, 20,* 187–196.

Doty, L. (1987). *Communication and assertion skills for older adults.* Washington: Hemisphere Publishing Corporation.

Engels, M.L. (1991). The promotion of positive social interaction through social skills training. In P.A. Wisocki (Ed.), *Handbook of clinical behavior therapy with the elderly client.* (pp.185–202), New York: Plenum Press.

Epp, J. (1986). Achieving health for all: A framework for health promotion. Ottawa: Minister of Supplies and Services Canada.

Frank, A.W. (1995). *The wounded storyteller: Body, illness, and ethics.* Chicago: University of Chicago Press.

Franzke, A.W. (1987). The effects of assertiveness training on older adults. *The Gerontologist, 27,* 13–16.

Furnham, A. & Pendleton, D. (1983). The assessment of social skills deficits in the elderly. *International Journal of Aging and Human Development, 17,* 29–38.

Gallois, C. (2004). Communicating disability: Stereotypes, identity, and motivation. In S.H. Ng, C.N. Candlin & C.Y. Chiu (Eds.), *Language matters: Communication, identity, and culture.* (pp.355–374). Hong Kong: City University of Hong Kong Press.

Gambrill, E. (1994). Assertion skills training. In W. O'Donohue & L. Krasner (Eds.) et al., *Handbook of psychological skills training: Clinical techniques and applications* (pp.81–118). Boston, MA: Allyn & Bacon.

Giles, H., Coupland, J. & Coupland, N. (1991). Accommodation theory: Communication, context, and consequence. In H. Giles, J. Coupland & N. Coupland (Eds.) *Contexts of accommodation. Developments in applied sociolinguistics.* Cambridge: Cambridge University Press.

Greene, M.G., Adelman, R., Charon, R. & Hoffman, S. (1986). Ageism in the medical encounter: An exploratory study of the doctor–elderly patient relationship. *Language and Communication, 6(1–2),* 113–124.

Greene, M.G., Adelman, R.D. & Rizzo, C. (1996). Problems in communication between physicians and older patients. *Journal of Geriatric Psychiatry, 29,* 13–32.

Greene, M.G., Adelman, R.D., Rizzo, C. & Friedmann, E. (1994). The patient's presentation of self in an initial medical encounter. In M.L. Hummert, J.M. Wiemann & J.F. Nussbaum (Eds.), *Interpersonal communication in older adulthood: Interdisciplinary theory and research* (pp.226–250). Thousand Oaks, CA: Sage Publications, Inc.

Grunwald, H. (2003). Twilight: Losing sight, gaining insight. *Generations, 27* (spring), 102–104.

Hallberg, I.R., Norberg, A. & Eriksson, S. (1990). A comparison between the care of vocally disruptive patients and that of other residents at psychogeriatric wards. *Journal of advanced nursing, 15,* 410–416.

Harwood, J., Giles, H., McCann, R.M., Cai, D., Somera, L.P., Ng, S.H., Gallois, C. & Noels, K. (2001). Older adults' trait ratings of three age-groups around the Pacific rim. *Journal of Cross-Cultural Gerontology, 16,* 157–171.

Harwood, J., Giles, H., Ota, H., Pierson, H.D., Gallois, C., Ng, S.H., Lim, T.S. & Somera, L. (1996). College students' trait ratings of three age groups around the Pacific rim. *Journal of Cross-Cultural Gerontology, 11*, 307–317.

Harwood, J., Giles, H., Fox, S., Ryan, E.B. & Williams, A. (1993). Patronizing young and elderly adults: Response strategies in a community setting. *Journal of Applied Communication Research, 21*, 211–226.

Harwood, J., Ryan, E.B., Giles, H. & Tysoski, S. (1997). Evaluations of patronizing speech and three response styles in a non-service-providing setting. *Journal of Applied Communication Research, 25*, 170–184.

Heckhausen, J. & Schulz, R. (1995). A life-span theory of control. *Psychological Review, 102*, 284–304.

Henderson, C.S. & Andrews, N. (1998). *Partial view: An Alzheimer's journal.* Dallas: Southern Methodist University.

Hickson, L. & Worrall, L. (2003). Beyond hearing aid fitting: Improving communication for older adults. *International Journal of Audiology, 42*(Suppl2), 2S84–2S91.

Hummert, M.L., Garstka, T.A., Ryan, E.B. & Bonnesen, J.L. (2004). The role of age stereotypes in interpersonal communication. In J.F. Nussbaum & J. Harwood (Eds.), *The handbook of communication and aging* (2nd ed., pp.91–114). Mahwah, NJ: Erlbaum.

Hummert, M.L. & Mazloff, D.C. (2001). Older adults' responses to patronizing advice: Balancing politeness and identity in context. *Journal of Language and Social Psychology, 20*, 168–196.

Hummert, M.L. & Nussbaum, J.F. (2001). Introduction: Successful aging, communication, and health. In M.L. Hummert & J.F. Nussbaum (Eds.), *Aging, communication, and health: Linking research and practice for successful aging* (pp. xi–xix). Mahwah, NJ: Lawrence Erlbaum.

Hummert, M.L. & Ryan, E.B. (1996). Toward understanding variations in patronizing talk addressed to older adults: Psycholinguistic features of care and control. *International Journal of Psycholinguistics, 12*, 149–169.

Hummert, M.L. & Ryan, E.B. (2001). Patronizing. In W.P. Robinson & H. Giles (Eds.), *The new handbook of language and social psychology* (pp.253–269). London: Wiley.

Hummert, M.L., Shaner, J.L., Garstka, T.A. & Henry, C. (1998). Communication with older adults: The influence of age stereotypes, context, and communicator age. *Human Communication Research, 25*, 124–151.

Jacobs, R.H. (1997). *How to be an outrageous woman.* New York: Harper Perennial.

Kahana, E. & Kahana, B. (2003). Patient proactivity enhancing doctor–patient–family communication in cancer prevention and care among the aged. *Patient Education and Counseling, 50*, 67–73.

Kaplan, S.H., Greenfield, S., Gandek, B., Rogers, W.H. & Ware, J.E., Jr. (1996). Characteristics of physicians with participatory decision-making styles. *Annals of Internal Medicine, 124*, 497–504.

Kemper, S. (2001). Over-accommodations and under-accommodation to aging. In N. Charness, D.C. Parks & B. Sabel (Eds.), *Communication, technology, and aging: Opportunities and challenges for the future* (pp.30–46). New York: Springer.

Kemper, S. & Harden, T. (1999). Experimentally disentangling what's beneficial about elderspeak from what's not. *Psychology and Aging, 14*, 656–670.

Kenyon, G., Clark, P. & de Vries, B. (2001). *Narrative gerontology: Theory, research, and practice*. New York: Springer.

Kite, M.E. & Wagner, L.S. (2002). Attitudes toward older adults. In T.D. Nelson (Ed.), *Ageism: Stereotyping and prejudice against older persons* (pp.129–162). Cambridge, MA: MIT Press.

Kitwood, T. (1997). *Dementia reconsidered: The person comes first*. Philadelphia: Open University Press.

Kreps, G.L. & O'Hair, D. (1995). *Communication and health outcomes*. Cresskill, NJ: Hampton Press.

Lambert, B.L., Street, R.L., Jr., Cegala, D.J., Smith, D.H, Kurtz, S. & Schofield, T. (1997). Provider patient communication, patient-centered care, and the mangle of practice. *Health Communication, 9*, 27–43.

Levy, B.R. (2003). Mind matters: Cognitive and physical effects of aging self-stereotypes. *Journal of Gerontology: Psychological Sciences, 58B*, P203–P211.

Levy, B.R. & Banaji, M.R. (2002). Implicit ageism. In T.D. Nelson (Ed.), *Ageism: Stereotyping and prejudice against older persons* (pp.49–76). Cambridge, MA: MIT Press.

Lizzio, A., Wilson, K.L., Gilchrist, J. & Gallois, C. (2003). The role of gender in the construction and evaluation of feedback effectiveness. *Management Communication Quarterly, 16*, 341–379.

McCallion, P., Toseland, R.W. & Freeman, K. (1999). An evaluation of a family visit education program. *Journal of the American Geriatrics Society, 47*, 203–214.

McCarty, H.J., Roth, D.L., Goode, K.T., Owen, J.E., Harrell, L., Donovan, K. et al. (2000). Longitudinal course of behavioral problems during Alzheimer's disease: Linear versus curvilinear patterns of decline. *Journal of Gerontology, 55A*, M200–M206.

McGee, D. & Cegala, D. (1998). Patient communication skills training for improved communication competence in the primary care medical consultation. *Journal of Applied Communication Research, 26*, 412–430.

McMellon, C.A. & Schiffman, L.G. (2002). Cybersenior empowerment: How some older individuals are taking control of their lives. *Journal of Applied Gerontology, 21(2)*, 157–175.

Meyer, B.J., Russo, C. & Talbot, A. (1995). Discourse comprehension and problem solving: decisions about the treatment of breast cancer by women across the life span. *Psychology and Aging, 10*, 84–103.

Miller, J.F. (2000). *Coping with chronic illness: Overcoming powerlessness*. Philadelphia: F.A. Davis Company.

Mills, M.E. & Sullivan, K. (1999). The importance of information giving for patients newly diagnosed with cancer: A review of the literature. *Journal of Clinical Nursing, 8*, 631–642.

Mittleman, M.S., Ferris, S.H., Shulman, E., Steinberg, M.S. & Levin, B. (1996). A family intervention to delay nursing home placement of patients with Alzheimer's disease. *Journal of the American Medical Association, 276*, 1725–1731.

Narayan, S., Lewis, M., Tornatore, J., Hepburn, K. & Corcoran-Perry, S. (2001). Subjective responses to caregiving for a spouse with dementia. *Journal of Gerontological Nursing, 27*, 19–28.

Nelson, T.D. (Ed.) (2002). *Ageism: Stereotyping and prejudice against older persons*. Cambridge, MA: MIT Press.

Nelson, T.D. (Ed.) (2005). Ageism. *Journal of Social Issues, 61(2)*.

Northrop, L.M.E. & Edelstein, B.A. (1998). An assertive-behavior competence inventory for older adults. *Journal of Clinical Geropsychology, 4*, 315–331.

Orange, J.B., Ryan, E.B., Meredith, S.D. & MacLean, M.J. (1995). Application of the Communication Enhancement Model for long term care residents with Alzheimer's disease. *Topics in Language Disorders, 15(2)*, 20–35.

Orr, A.L. & Rogers, P. (2003). *Self-advocacy skills training for older individuals: Training manual, participant manual, family guide to self-advocacy.* AFB Press.

Ostwald, S.K., Hepburn, K.W., Caron, W., Burns, T. & Mantell, R. (1999). Reducing caregiver burden: A randomized psychoeducational intervention for caregivers of persons with dementia. *The Gerontologist, 39*, 299–309.

Palmore, E.B. (1999). *Ageism: Negative and positive* (2nd ed.). New York: Springer.

Paterson, R.J. (2000). *The assertiveness workbook: How to express your ideas and stand up for yourself at work and in relationships.* Oakland, CA: New Harbinger.

Pearlin, L.I. & Schooler, C. (1978). The structure of coping. *Journal of Health and Social Behavior, 19(1)*, 2–21.

Perkins, D.D. & Zimmerman, M.A. (1995). Empowerment theory: Research and applications. *American Journal of Community Psychology, 23*, 569–579.

Petterman, D.M. (2002). Empowerment evaluation: Building communities of practice and culture building. *American Journal of Community Psychology, 30(1)*, 89–102.

Pichora-Fuller, K. & Carson, A. (2001). Hearing health and the listening experiences of older communicators. In M.L. Hummert & J.F. Nussbaum (Eds.), *Aging, communication and health: Linking research and practice for successful aging* (pp.43–74). Mahwah NJ: Erlbaum.

Rakos, R.F. (1991). *Assertive behavior: Theory, research, and training.* London, England: Routledge.

Richter, J., Bottenberg, D. & Roberto, K. (1993). Communication between formal caregivers and Alzheimer's impaired residents. *The American Journal of Alzheimer's and Related Disorders Care & Research, 8*, 20–26.

Ripich, D.N., Ziol, E., Fritsch, T. & Durand, E.J. (1999). Training Alzheimer's disease caregivers for successful communication. *Clinical Gerontologist, 21(1)*, 37–56.

Rost, K. & Frankel, R. (1993). The introduction of the older patient's problems in the medical visit. *Journal of Aging and Health, 5*, 387–401.

Rodin, J. & Langer, E. (1980). Aging labels: The decline of control and the fall of self-esteem. *Journal of Social Issues, 36(2)*, 12–29.

Rost, K. & Frankel, R. (1993). The introduction of the older patient's problems in the medical visit. *Journal of Aging and Health, 5*, 387–401.

Rowe, J.W. & Kahn, R.L. (1998). *Successful aging.* New York: Pantheon/Random House.

Ryan, E.B. (2006, in press). Finding a new voice: Writing through health adversity. *Journal of Language and Social Psychology.*

Ryan, E.B., Anas, A.P. & Friedman, D.B. (in press). Evaluations of older adult assertiveness in problematic clinical encounters. *Journal of Language and Social Psychology.*

Ryan, E.B., Anas, A.P. & Gruneir, A.J.S. (2006). Evaluations of overhelping and underhelping communication: Do old age and physical disability matter? *Journal of Language and Social Psychology.*

Ryan, E.B., Anas, A.P. & Mays, H. (2005a). When to be assertive: Evaluations of response alternatives for older adults with visual impairment. McMaster University, unpublished ms.

Ryan, E.B., Bajorek, S., Beaman, A. & Anas, A.P. (2005b). I just want you to know that 'them' is me: Intergroup perspectives on communication and disability. In J. Harwood & H. Giles (Eds.), *Intergroup communication: Multiple perspectives.* New York: Peter Lang Publishing Group.

Ryan, E.B., Bieman-Copland, S., Kwong See, S.T., Ellis, C.H. & Anas, A.P. (2002). Age excuses: Conversational management of memory failures in older adults. *Journal of Gerontology, 57B,* P256–P267.

Ryan, E.B., Giles, H., Bartolucci, G. & Henwood, K. (1986). Psycholinguistic and social psychological components of communication by and with the elderly. *Language and Communication, 6,* 1–24.

Ryan, E.B., Kennaley, D.E., Pratt, M.W. & Shumovich, M.A. (2000). Evaluations by staff, residents, and community seniors of patronizing speech: Impact of passive, assertive, or humorous responses. *Psychology and Aging, 15,* 272–285.

Ryan, E.B., Meredith, S.D., MacLean, M.J. & Orange, J.B. (1995). Changing the way we talk with elders: Promoting health using the communication enhancement model. *International Journal of Aging and Human Development, 41(2),* 89–107.

Sachweh, S. (1998). Granny darling's nappies: Secondary babytalk in German nursing homes for the aged. *Journal of Applied Communication Research, 26,* 52–65.

Sarton, M. (1988). *After the stroke: A journal.* New York: Norton.

Savundranayagam, M.Y., Ryan, E.B., Anas, A. & Orange, J.B. (2005). Communication and dementia: Staff perceptions of conversational strategies. Paper presented at the 58th annual meeting of the Gerontological Society of America.

Schulz, R.E. (2000). *Handbook on dementia caregiving: Evidence-based interventions for family caregivers.* New York: Springer.

Schulz, R., O'Brien, A.T., Bookwala, J. & Fleissner, K. (1995). Psychiatric and physical morbidity effects of dementia caregiving: Prevalence, correlates, and causes. *The Gerontologist, 35,* 771–791.

Schulz, R., O'Brien, A., Czaja, S., Ory, M., Norris, R., Martire, L.M., Belle, S.H., Burgio, L., Gitlin, L., Coon, D., Burns, R., Gallagher-Thompson, D. & Stevens, A. (2002). Dementia caregiver intervention research: In search of clinical significance. *Gerontologist, 42(5),* 589–602.

Scott-Maxwell, F. (1979). *The measure of my days.* New York: Penguin Books.

Smyth, J.M. & Pennebaker, J.W. (1999). Sharing one's story: Translating emotional experiences into words as a coping tool. In C.R. Snyder (Ed.), *Coping: The psychology of what works.* New York: Oxford University.

Solomon, B.B. (1976). *Black empowerment.* New York: Columbia University Press.

Street Jr., R.L. (2001). Active patients as powerful communicators. In W.P. Robinson & H. Giles (Eds.), *The new handbook of language and social psychology* (pp.541–560). London: Wiley.

Street, Jr., R.L. (2003). Interpersonal communication skills in health care contexts. In J. Greene and B. Burleson (Eds.), *Handbook of communication and social interaction skills* (pp.909–933). Thousand Oaks, CA: Sage Publications.

Street, Jr., R.L. & Voigt, B. (1997). Patient participation in deciding breast cancer treatment and subsequent quality of life. *Medical Decision-Making, 17,* 298–306.

Taylor, S. & Epstein, R. (1999). *Living well with a hidden disability: Transcending doubt and shame and reclaiming your life*. Oakland, CA: New Harbinger Publications.

Tennstedt, S.L. (2000). Empowering older patients to communicate more effectively in the medical encounter. In A.D. Adelman & M.G. Greene (Eds.), *Clinics in Geriatric Medicine (Communication between older patients and their physicians)*, *16(1)* (pp.61–70). London: W.B. Saunders Co.

Thompson, T.L., Robinson, J.D., Beisecker, A.E. (2004). The older patient–physician interaction. In J.F. Nussbaum and J. Coupland (Eds.), *Handbook of communication and aging research* (2nd ed.) (pp.451–478). Hillsdale, NJ: Lawrence Erlbaum.

Towle, A., Godolphin, W., Manklow, J. & Wiesinger, L. (2003). Patient perceptions that limit a community-based intervention to promote participation. *Patient Education and Counseling, 50*, 231–233.

Twenge, J.M. (2001). Changes in women's assertiveness in response to status and roles: A cross-temporal meta-analysis, 1931–1993. *Journal of Personality and Social Psychology, 81*, 133–145.

Watson, B. & Gallois, C. (2004). *Emotional expression as a sociolinguistic strategy: Its importance in medical interactions*. In S.H. Ng, C.N. Candlin & C.Y. Chiu (Eds.), Language matters: Communication identity and culture (pp 63–84). Hong Kong: City University of Hong Kong Press.

Williams, A. & Nussbaum, J.F. (2001). *Intergenerational communication across the life span*. Mahwah, NJ: Erlbaum.

Wilson, K. & Gallois, C. (1993). *Assertion and its social context*. New York: Pergamon Press.

Worrall, L. & Hickson, L. (2003). *Communication disability in ageing: Prevention to intervention*. San Diego: Singular Press.

Wright, K.B. (2000). Computer-mediated social support, older adults, and coping. *Journal of Communication, 50*, 100–118.

Zimmerman, M. (1995). Psychological empowerment: Issues and illustrations. *American Journal of Community Psychology, 23*, 581–599.

Zimmerman, M.A. & Warschausky, S. (1998). Empowerment theory for rehabilitation research: Conceptual and methodological issues. *Rehabilitation Psychology, 43*, 3–16.

4

language, discourse, and communication about health and illness: intergroup relations, role, and emotional support

bernadette watson and cindy gallois

It is no understatement to say that research into communication in health contexts is vast. Finnegan and Viswanath (1990) identified five areas of health communication: professional–patient relations, lifestyle campaigns, interprofessional relations, health professional training, and health information systems. More recently, Beck et al. (2004) reviewed research between 1990 and 2000. They identified three main areas of published research: individuals seeking health information, public health campaigns, and health care delivery. This huge scope reflects the salience and importance to most of society inherent in all aspects of health and illness. Furthermore, in recent times, demographic and technological changes such as the ageing of the population and lower mortality from traumatic injury have produced consequent changes in the relative balance between acute illness on one hand and chronic illness and disability on the other. These changes have led to an increased emphasis on the social and psychological features of the contexts. For example, the Australian National Health and Medical Research Council now asks for a statement of the social impact of each piece of research that is proposed for funding. Similarly, there are now targeted calls for research in most Western countries on specific social or psychological aspects of health, illness and disability.

As the health context changes, the complexity of health communication becomes more obvious. The topics above indicate that this is already a complex arena. The complexity doubles and redoubles as people begin to deal with long-term health issues (prevention, treatment and management) and become more informed (and more demanding) of health professionals. The recent emphasis on liability for error and patient safety is only one outcome of this change. Another is the perceived loss of status by health professionals, with the attached lower morale, sense of threat, and high turnover. All these things highlight the increased salience of the intergroup context.

It is clearer now than previously that doctors, nurses, allied health professionals, ancillary health workers, and patients alike are communicating as group members and also as individuals. In spite of this, relatively few studies have taken an explicitly intergroup perspective in considering health communication. We believe that the approach of language and social psychology, with its core assumption of an intergroup context, has much to offer in this area. In this chapter, we aim to highlight some of the contribution this approach can make. We concentrate on two areas where we ourselves have done research: patient–health professional interactions and interprofessional communication in the health sector. First, however, we briefly review key research over the past decade, to give a sense of the scope and consistent considerations in this area.

research in health communication: language and discourse

In the spirit of language and social psychology, Larkey et al. (1999) investigated the ways in which health education programmes were applied in the field. They classified communication strategies as either group- or individual-based, and found that different strategies were employed at these different levels. This research established an empirical basis for investigating the relationship between peer influence and health education programmes in achieving positive behaviour change. More recently, Walther, Pingree, Hawkins and Buller (2005) explored the value of interactive online health information systems, drawing on a range of theoretical frameworks to question whether these systems are helpful and effective for the target users.

Parrott (2004) addressed health communication at the macro level, and investigated how health and illness emerge in discourse. She identified three key groups in discourse: societal, expert and lay. While the medical interaction was not a focal part of Parrott's paper, she highlighted a lack of connection between the discourse used by policy makers to promote specific health risk programmes and day-to-day consultations between doctors and patients. Parrott described the socio-historical context within which individuals form their views about society and culture. In turn, this information provides people with a common understanding of the norms and societal mores about how they should act in the role of patient or doctor. In later sections where we discuss interprofessional communication, the socio-historical context within which medical interactions occur can be seen as a critical component of the communication dynamic.

In the arenas of ageing and disability, Ryan and her colleagues (Hummert & Ryan, 2001; Ryan, Bajorek, Beaman & Anas, 2005; see also Savundranayagam, Ryan & Hummert, this volume) present the communication predicament model originally developed for inter-generational communication (Hummert, Garstka, Ryan & Bonnesen, 2004; Ryan, Giles, Bartolucci & Henwood, 1986). This model, like communication accommodation theory (CAT; see Gallois, Ogay & Giles, 2005, for a review), is aimed at explaining dynamics and processes in communication encounters. This work has tended to focus on the impact of the non-aged or non-disabled person in the encounter (often a health professional) and thus to theorize the communication process in terms of the reaction of the aged or disabled person. Barker and Giles (2003) argued that the communication predicament model assumes that the older (or disabled) person is a passive player in the encounter. They proposed an 'enhanced predicament' model that takes account of the agency of the older (or disabled) person and the two-way dynamics of an intergroup interaction. Savundranayagam and colleagues (this volume) have taken this up in terms of the potential for assertive communication by older or disabled adults and thence to patient participation and empowerment.

In a similar way, Gallois (2004) argued that people with disabilities adapt differently to the larger society, depending in part on the type and severity of the disability and the age at which the disability was acquired (and thus whether new or altered identities need to be managed). Gallois adapted Berry's model of intercultural adaptation (e.g., Berry, 1997) to characterize several major types of adaptation. These include *assimilation*, where the person desires to return as nearly as possible to a non-disabled identity; *integration*, where the person strives to switch from an identity as a person with a disability to another identity, or to blend the identities; *separation*, where the person mainly interacts from the identity of disability and chooses to avoid people without disabilities; and *individuation*, where the person strives to be treated as an individual person or emphasizes a completely different identity. The different adaptation styles entail different levels and types of communication accommodation. For example, a person oriented to assimilation may try to converge to a non-disabled interlocutor, whereas a person oriented to separation may diverge or even counter-accommodate through hostility. Gallois argued that these adaptation styles are likely to be important in motivation and desire (or not) for rehabilitation; they all imply active participation by the person with a disability as well as the non-disabled person. This greater emphasis on the symmetry of interlocutors is characteristic of the intergroup approach.

In a more general exploration of communication relationships in the health context, Fitzpatrick and Vangelisti (2001) emphasized the importance of social interaction in health encounters, and investigated common threads in communication across a wide range of illness types. They proposed a model of health communication that takes account of the role that communication plays in the lives of patients. Fitzpatrick and Vangelisti argued that studying interpersonal communication has an important role in prolonging and improving quality of life, examining the different ways in which patients with different levels of chronicity and in differing socio-historical contexts respond to their illness and health professionals, and thus experience different outcomes.

Considering patients in terms of their social groupings, whether they are explicit (e.g., gender, ethnicity) or more implicit (e.g., level of chronicity) is part of our ongoing research. We are examining these dimensions of (potentially) group identity across a broad range of health professionals and contexts. In doing this, we aim to take account of both the health provider and patient, and to emphasize the agency of speech partners. We work from the perspective of social identity theory (see Haslam, 2001; Tajfel & Turner, 1979) and more specifically communication accommodation theory (see Gallois, Ogay & Giles, 2005) because these theories explicitly consider intergroup as well as interpersonal influences. Doing this is critical as it opens the way for understanding the perceptions of the interactants and resulting outcomes for both.

lack of theory and intergroup perspective in health communication

One of the major criticisms of research in health communication is that much of it is atheoretical. While this situation has improved since the early 1990s, it is nevertheless true to say that theory development must continue to be a focal aspect of this discipline (see Kreps, 2001; Thompson, 2003). Beck and colleagues (2004) examined 850 health communication studies, and found that of these 652 did not include a theoretical framework. The lack of theory-driven research is becoming less of an issue as the discipline of health communication matures. For example, Cegala and colleagues have developed *communication competence* as a theoretical framework to understand medical encounters (e.g., Cegala, Gade, Broz & McClure, 2004; Cegala, McNeilis & McGee, 1995; Cegala, McGee & McNelis, 1996; McNelis, 2001). Roter and Hall (1991, 1992) adopted social exchange theory and the *reciprocity principle* to explain the dynamics of the interaction between health providers and patients.

These examples of theoretical approaches to health provider–patient interaction tend to assume an interpersonal relationship between the two interactants. Much of the research cited above lacks a social focus that provides a holistic picture of interactions between health professionals and patients. Thompson (2003) also noted that much of the theory-driven research concentrates on the health provider rather than the patient. One reason for the lack of theoretical focus may be because there is a 'dualism of theory versus practice' (Babrow & Mattson, 2003, p.38). The problem with such dualism is apparent when we consider that much of the value in studying health communication is for its practical application. A major motivation for health communication scholars' desire to improve the quality of communication is to improve health outcomes.

Furthermore, Thompson (2003) pointed to the lack of research that takes account of both health professional and patient, as we noted earlier. It is important to test the commonsense (but under-studied) hypothesis that effective interactions occur when doctors provide information to patients, allow the patients to share the floor, and show empathic concern. In turn, patients have better outcomes if they are not passive but are prepared to ask questions when they do not understand something. Indeed, counts of interruptions by health providers and perceptions of the amount of information a patient has obtained are predictors of patient satisfaction (e.g., O'Hair, 1989; von Friederichs-Fitzwater & Gilgun, 2001). Researchers need to pay more attention than at present to their theoretical frameworks. A practical result of using theory is that researchers can predict when and what type of patients benefit from asking questions and can educate both patients and health professionals appropriately.

We believe that health communication is essentially an intergroup encounter that occurs at the interpersonal level. This assumption has important implications for communication competence training (e.g., Parle, Maguire & Heaven, 1997). The prevalent approach to skills training for health professionals does not take account of the complex intergroup relationships and motivations during any one interaction. It is essential to take account of different levels of miscommunication and problematic talk (Coupland, Wiemann & Giles, 1991), in that there are factors stemming from group memberships and social norms, among other things, that can get in the way of 'good' communication even with the most skilled communicators.

encounters between patients and health professionals: participation and empowerment

Over the past decade or so there has been a significant shift in focus away from the health provider and onto patients, emphasizing the contribution of the patient in interactions. Especially in the areas of disability and chronic illness (e.g., see many chapters in Braithwaite & Thompson, 2000; see also Driedger, Sanders, Gallois, Boyle & Santesso, in press), patients and doctors express the need to develop a team relationship that makes use of the doctor's expertise on disease and the patient's expertise about the experience of illness. Sharf and Street (1997) and Robinson (2003) have similarly stressed the need for research on the perspective of patients. The idea of patient empowerment, including moving away from the term 'patient' to 'client' or 'consumer' are developments over the last ten years that signify this change.

Patient participation during a medical interaction has been a key measure of involvement, orientation, and level of control (or perceived power). Robinson (2003) explained the asymmetry in medical consultations in terms of the structural schema of the doctor–patient interaction. In this sense, the asymmetry is not so much determined by power differences as by individuals' normative expectations of communication in medical interactions. For example, Stivers (2005) found that parents were often actively involved in treatment decision-making for their children; norms for participation changed with the change from patient to carer role. This research does not minimize the status and power of the doctor in the interaction so much as to highlight other variables, such as cultural norms, that define the role of each interactant.

Nevertheless, the rhetoric of patient empowerment has often met with resistance from patients and practitioners alike. Kreps' (2001) discussion of empowerment in health communication raises the problems faced by individuals with minority ethnic backgrounds, lower socioeconomic status, or those from other disadvantaged groups. Members of such groups may face many barriers that preclude active patient participation (see also Barker & Giles, 2003; Cali & Estrada, 1999; Ulrey & Amason, 2001). Doctors may resist sharing power because their training has involved a formulaic approach to the medical consultation that precludes patient participation (Cali & Estrada, 1999). Indeed, as Rimal (2001) comments, the concept of patient empowerment may represent more than anything else a bias on the part of researchers seeking to bring about active patient participation.

There are many patients who do not want to participate. Rimal (2001) classified patients into four types: constrained, active, passive and restrained. Importantly, he acknowledged that patients may have different needs according to their illness status (e.g., chronic versus acute). We have pointed already to this important determinant in health communication. Even among chronically ill or disabled people, however, there are significant individual differences in both identity management and in the desire to participate (cf. Gallois, 2004). The significance of this work is to show how important it is to understand the underlying motivations, goals, and cultural norms in each interaction in order to understand fully the dynamics of medical consultations. Street took this approach further by exploring specific patient variables and how they interact to influence levels of patient interaction with health providers (Street, 2001, 2003b). In doing this, Street developed the linguistic model of patient participation in care (LMOPPC).

chronic or acute illness and participation

One part of LMOPPC that needs further explication is that of patient status (previously highlighted by Fitzpatrick & Vangelisti, 2001). Patients with chronic conditions are likely to have different needs from those with acute illnesses. For example, Driedger and her colleagues (in press) found that women with chronic musculoskeletal conditions (mainly arthritis) needed to maintain close communication with their doctors in order to have appropriate pain management. These women developed a number of strategies, including learning to accommodate to the doctor's vocabulary and pain concepts, trimming the narratives they told doctors, and (less accommodatingly) changing doctors where communication failed. At the same time, doctors, in the view of the women, needed to learn to pay closer attention to the expertise of patients about the experience of their illness. This is a very different kind of participation from that, for example, by a person with tonsilitis who wants temporary pain and symptom relief. In the latter case, there is little need for a relationship between patient and doctor. Clearly, the need to develop a relationship also varies with socio-historical background and health identity; even so, for a patient with inflamed tonsils, a medical prescription is likely to be sufficient. On the other hand, a patient with a chronic condition may not expect symptom relief but may need to obtain support and empathy from the health provider.

The first author has found that patients who differ in medical status also differ in their expectations during medical consultations (Watson, 2005). In 20 interviews with patients who gave self-reports, all patients wanted the physicians to listen to them. Compared to patients who self-rated as chronically ill, effective consultations for acutely-ill patients focused on obtaining information and having their expectations met. In addition, when patients spoke about their experiences of unsatisfactory consultations, chronically-ill patients, when compared to acutely-ill ones, were more concerned about the health provider's manner.

predictors of participation by patients

In the tradition of language and social psychology, Street (2003a) acknowledged the dynamics of the communication process. LMOPPC takes account of patients' beliefs, motivation, and level of rapport with the health provider, as well as their knowledge on the topic and communication repertoire. To some extent the last two features depend on the status of the patient in terms of chronicity. LMOPPC also recognizes that the health provider's responses influence the patient's level of participation. Street (1991) noted that the doctor–patient interaction is commonly characterized by role and power differences. In our current research, which uses a communication accommodation theory framework, we incorporate aspects of LMOPPC but we focus equally on both interactants.

The willingness to communicate model (WTC; see Clément, Noels & MacIntyre, this volume, for a full discussion of the model) in the context of second language acquisition explains communication apprehension from an intercultural perspective. The WTC model provides a theoretical basis for understanding an individual's predisposition to engage in his or her second language across many contexts. Currently Baker and colleagues are applying this model to the health context and using LMOPPC as a framework. Baker (2006) argues that willingness to communicate in the health context has two aspects – a general willingness to communicate in an intergroup encounter, and a specific willingness to communicate about health. The former reflects a predisposing factor in participation by a patient in a health interaction, whereas the latter represents a proximal predictor of patient participation. This work also examines the relationship between a patient's willingness to communicate with a health professional, and variables such as the patient's medical knowledge, rapport with the health provider, and level of anxiety. This novel adaptation of the WTC model is another example of theory driving the investigation of medical interactions, psychological states and communication dynamics.

rapport and relationship building

Street (2001) emphasized rapport building as an important predictor of patient participation and satisfaction. In our current research, we aim to understand in particular those communication behaviours perceived by patients as showing health professionals' affect and empathy. In general, individuals enter an interaction with a psychological accommodative stance that includes both cognitions and affect (see Gallois, Ogay & Giles, 2005). We ask about the extent to which individuals in an encounter wish to maintain their own role and/or suppress the role of the other (cognition), as well as the extent to which they wish to be pleasant (suggesting accommodation) or hostile (suggesting non-accommodation). If we can understand the goals of the individuals as they unfold, we will have moved some way towards understanding their psychological stance. We have been developing the affect component in medical interactions and it is to this area of research that we now turn.

Emotional expression. Many researchers have found that doctors who give positive affect and reassurance aid a patient in his or her disclosure of concerns and symptoms and hence improve patient satisfaction with the consultation (e.g., Duggan & Parrott, 2001; Dutta-Bergman, 2005). Looking at emotional expression from the other side, Bylund and Makoul (2005) examined the components of empathy by patients and the types of responses elicited from doctors. They found that, compared to patients who showed negative empathic expression, patients who gave the doctor opportunities to express positive empathy were more likely to receive acknowledgement and confirmation by the doctor. Doctors, however, did not appear to have the concept of 'shared feeling' in their repertoire for this context. In part, this lack of empathic sharing may stem from medical training, which as Spiro (1992) noted, tends to promote detachment in medical students. A limitation of this work is its lack of a theoretical framework that guides explication of communication behaviour. Taking the perspective of communication accommodation theory allows examination of the dynamics underpinning behaviour in medical consultations.

An important aspect of communication in the medical interaction, at least in many encounters, is the extent to which health professionals provide patients with reassurance and show concern. In spite of calls to do so (Giles, Coupland & Coupland, 1991), emotional expression has not yet been as systematically theorized as the other four CAT strategies have (see Gallois, Ogay & Giles, 2005). The focus on affect, however, is hardly new in health communication research (e.g., Cegala et al., 1995, 1996). What is new is the way in which affect is examined in language and social psychology. First, researchers using CAT have discussed affect in terms of relational communication (Willemyns, Gallois & Callan, 2003) and face maintenance (Gallois, Ogay & Giles, 2005). Thus, *affect* is currently used as an umbrella term, and from this different types of affect (e.g., emotional expression, face maintenance, relational communication) are teased out. The goal is to understand how each of these aspects of affect are negotiated in different types of medical encounters, and to what ends.

To achieve these research aims, we are in the process of recording interactions between health providers and patients. In addition, we ask both interactants to rate their impressions of the interaction and the other person, both prior to and after the consultation. In earlier research we began to theorize emotional expression, but to date have not explicitly linked it with outcomes and with actual behaviour (Watson & Gallois, 1998, 1999, 2002, 2004). We have found, however, that appropriate levels and type of emotional expression by health professionals lead to medical encounters being rated as more satisfying and effective by patients, which is important for understanding the components of effective and satisfying interactions.

Extension of emotional expression. In a study by Watson (2004), 19 allied health professionals (nurses, physiotherapists and occupational therapists) working at a community health centre in a small city were audio-recorded in consultation with their patients. In this study, therefore, interactions were situated outside of the hospital context and within the community. The recordings contained examples of health professionals showing concern and reassuring the patient, in line with earlier research (Watson & Gallois, 2004). However, one aim of this study was to obtain more subtle measures and broaden the concept of emotional expression. Upon a closer analysis of the data, it became apparent that the communication behaviours that typically indicate discourse management (as a strategy in CAT) also serve to reflect emotional expression.

Previous research has indicated clearly that the sociolinguistic strategies in CAT are not mutually exclusive or even orthogonal constructs. In addition, it is crucial to take into account the intentions of interlocutors when categorizing communication behaviour (see Gallois, Ogay & Giles, 2005; Giles et al., this volume). For example, Jones and her colleagues (Jones, Gallois, Callan & Barker, 1995, 1999) noted that an interruption can serve to curb an individual from continuing to talk (using the strategy of interpersonal control). On the other hand, the same interruption can function as a device by one speech partner to encourage the other to say more (through an interruption with a question about a narrative being told, showing the strategy of discourse management). In the same way, disclosing information can serve to encourage the other speaker to share information (discourse management) but it can also be used to reassure the patient (emotional expression).

In the following example, the patient is a 25-year-old drug addict (John – not his real name) who has been in prison for drug-related offences. He has stated that his probation officer wants him to take some educational courses when he has finished rehabilitation to help him understand his past criminal actions. He has expressed doubt about the value of this. The health professional (nurse) shares something of her past and states that she too has had issues about her past. She says:

> Because, John, it mightn't be a bad thing once you finish rehab to actually do that. I visited my past stuff by reading this book and now I'm reading another book and revisiting my past on a different ... and I find it very helpful.

This extract does more than to use self-disclosure to encourage John to talk more. Rather, the nurse appears to use this strategy to provide reassurance and encouragement to her client. She does not necessarily want to encourage John to talk more; rather, she conveys that she too has needed to reflect on and learn from her past.

This is just one example of extending emotional expression as a strategy. The concept of emotional expression is intricately tied to relational communication, but clear definitions are not yet available. Willemyns et al. (2003) discussed the ways in which trust and openness can serve to promote relationships within a supervisor/subordinate context. For a patient, trust of the health provider is also an important aspect of the relationship. Street noted that a patient's level of trust or mistrust 'may be dramatically changed, positively or negatively, depending on the doctor's communicative performance during the interaction' (Street, 2003a, p.74). Importantly though, the emphasis must be on both interactants. Thus, we need to extend our understanding of affect to include health providers. In the past there has been an over-emphasis on the health provider, but we feel that an equal focus on the dynamics of the dyad would bring about a more balanced picture of the medical interaction.

Future research on emotional expression. Thus, there is a need to examine how patients show their need for affect in an interaction and how the health provider responds. Wanzer, Booth-Butterfield and Gruber (2004) investigated the relationship between patient-centred communication (PCC) and satisfaction. Their results indicated that parents were more satisfied with their children's care when they perceived high levels of listening and immediacy from health providers. Interestingly, parents of the sickest children perceived that their children received less PCC than did parents of less sick children. This study should be replicated and extended to an adult population. Even so, one explanation for this worrying finding is that health providers may obtain more rewards for demonstrating empathy and high levels of affect with less sick children because these children reward them by getting well. Of course, it may also be that very sick children are less able to show their need for reassurance, and it is to this that health providers respond. Either way, these results point to a need for further and different training for health professionals in management of affect in interactions with patients.

There is also a need to examine the long-term outcomes for health providers who do engage in high levels of emotional expression. Wanzer and colleagues' (2004) work has relevance for the care of chronic and terminally-ill patients. Relatedly, there is much debate about whether expending emotional labour (see Hochschild, 2003) serves to ameliorate the effects of burnout or increases its incidence. Apker and Ray (2003) discuss findings on this topic and cite the work of Miller, Stiff and Ellis (1988). Miller and colleagues examined emotional labour and differentiated between empathic concern, where an individual has an understanding of another's situation, and emotional contagion, where an individual feels the emotional pain of the other person. The latter is more likely to bring about stress and burnout.

From an intergroup perspective, Willemyns et al. (2003) noted that displaying trust and other positive communication might be expected in one's ingroup and but not for outgroup members. If we understand medical encounters as having intergroup salience, how does demonstrating emotional expression play out? Showing empathy could be stressful for the health provider unless it is seen in intergroup terms. The doctor may feel able to show empathic concern for the patient as an outgroup member, but not so easily if the patient is perceived as an ingroup member. If empathy is shown too often in the latter case, stress and burnout may occur.

interprofessional relations in health contexts

Many of these same variables are important in another intergroup context in health communication, which is the second focus of this chapter.

This area is intergroup interactions between health professionals, and it has received less research attention than has health professional–patient interactions. In the second part of the chapter, we discuss briefly what researchers have accomplished to date. We then discuss the contributions that language and social psychology can make.

As Poole and Real (2003) noted, the scope of this topic is potentially vast. For example, researchers must take account of the interactions that take place between health professionals from the same medical profession who have different expertise (e.g., a cardiovascular specialist discussing patient care with a respiratory physician), between health professionals who are from different backgrounds (nursing, allied health, medical) or health professionals with different status in the organization (seniority and professional experience). In addition, it is increasingly clear that the context within which these interactions occur is an important focus. We are currently examining various interactions in the hospital context, including daily medical and nursing clinical handovers (also known in the USA as handoffs), daily case-conferencing interactions that occur with a group of health professionals that possess a broad range of differing expertise and skills knowledge, working health teams on the wards. We are also following patient care from hospital admission through treatment to discharge. This last study includes both interprofessional and interdepartmental exchanges and addresses the socio-historical background and cultural aspects of the hospital organization. Finally, and equally exciting, we are exploring teleconferencing between health professionals involved in community patient management.

These are large and challenging areas of research and have important implications for a wide range of health outcomes, not only for patients but also for health professionals by increasing the effectiveness and satisfaction of the work environment. We anticipate that different work environments, in terms of health professional combinations, will bring different communication issues. Thus, we envisage that each communication exchange condition will demonstrate both unique and common patterns. This will assist in the development of a sophisticated model of interprofessional health communication.

health care teams

A related dimension of our ongoing research is the investigation of health care teams. Poole and Real (2003) in their review of the literature noted that team function has been a recognized part of health care for the past 100 years. However, they acknowledged that rigorous research into health care teams has been limited. Much of their paper focused on team entitativity and solidarity, as well as team composition in terms of specialization and group structure. This review indicates that previous research has not examined communication as a central construct, but has focused on the components of effective teams and the subsequent issues of error and patient safety (e.g., Carthey, de Leval, Wright, Farewell & Reason, 2003; Kunihide & Reason, 1999; Michan & Rodger, 2000).

Most of the research mentioned above has discussed the problems of communication in generic terms, which, although leaving the reader with an understanding that communication issues are important, give no understanding as to what the problems are. In addition, Poole and Real (2003) pointed out that the research approaches employed have tended not to take account of team characteristics, such as group dynamics and outcomes. These are aspects that need to be studied in a systematic and coherent way in order to understand the processes that help differentiate effective teams and their communication styles. What is required are investigations into team composition in order to understand why what works in one type of team does not work well in another. An effectively functioning team in the operating room may have different needs from a team in the emergency department.

What social psychologists of language can offer to this critical area of health communication is a micro-analysis of team components, aims, levels of solidarity, and team mix. In addition, these researchers can contribute valuable theoretical frameworks guiding the effort to determine the key variables in the dynamics of the team. These features include the culture of the professions from which team members come, the status and power divisions in the group, the purpose of the group, its duration, and the like. Such factors need to be considered alongside the dimensions highlighted by Poole and Real (2003), which include group interdependence, explicit acknowledgement of a group identity, the experiences and knowledge of the group members, and levels of group interaction.

In our own research, we are examining the communication dynamics involved in support by supervisors among nurses. The aim of the research is to design a communication intervention for nursing and multidisciplinary hospital teams that will help the morale and health status of nurses, in a work context where many sources of stress (e.g., shiftwork rosters, pay rates) are out of their control. Pisarski, Lawrence, Gallois, Watson and Bohle (2005) found that communicated supervisor support was a direct predictor of perceived team cohesion and control over the work environment, which in turn predicted level of perceived work–life conflict and psychological and physical wellbeing, for a large sample of hospital-based nurses. Gallois, Watson and Pisarski (2005) developed this theme further through interview and questionnaire studies. They found that support from supervisors and co-workers mediated the influence of organizational, professional, and team identity in predicting team cohesion. Interviews fleshed out the accommodative or non-accommodative communication that made up support, around which the workshop intervention is designed.

communication and patient safety

Currently, in Western society, there is an increased awareness of the need to make health teams accountable and to set in place safe practices. The movement to minimize error and enforce high standards of patient safety is driving much of the research. This follows a similar trend in the aviation industry, which recognizes that error is a natural and human phenomenon, and that safety procedures should be the first consideration of organizations and the teams that work in them (see Reason, 1998).

Lingard and her colleagues have focused on the operating room as a context for examining team functioning and communication problems (Lingard, Espin, Evans & Hawryluck, 2004; Lingard, Espin, Whyte et al., 2004; Lingard, Garwood & Poenaru, 2004; Lingard, Reznick, DeVito & Espin, 2002; Lingard, Reznick, Espin, Regehr & DeVito, 2002). Their work is interesting because, although not coming from a language and social psychology perspective, their research can be reinterpreted through a social-psychological lens. Lingard, Espin, Whyte et al. (2004) analysed team communication in the operating theatre for what they termed 'communication flaws'. Using Burke's (1969) rhetorical factors, they found that out of 421 communication events, 129 were flawed. The most commonly occurring flaw was that of *occasion*, where there were problems with the timing and exchange of communication. Incomplete or inaccurate communication was the next most common communication flaw. The third most common flaw was where objectives were not clearly stated and the fourth communication failure occurred where input from a key team member did not occur owing to his or her absence.

These researchers did not include interpersonal or intergroup communication in their analysis. Intergroup communication adds an important dimension to understanding team communication and dynamics. We see potentially useful comparisons between their levels of communication failure and Coupland et al.'s (1991) integrative model of miscommunication. Some of the research we are currently undertaking uses Lingard et al.'s categorizations in conjunction with Coupland et al.'s model. In this way we can study working contexts investigated by medical experts in the field with our own framework.

Much communication research into team functioning has focused on how individuals engage with one another in the operating theatre environment (e.g., Lingard, Reznick, DeVito et al., 2002; Carthey et al., 2003) or in the emergency department (Eisenberg et al., 2005). Again, in line with our earlier comments, it is noticeable that there is a lack of theory in these studies. On examination these studies lend themselves well to a communication accommodation theory perspective. For example, Lingard, Reznick, DeVito et al. (2002) discussed professional identity and its paramount importance in determining communication behaviour. There is scope for more research on the interplay between professional identities in specific contexts and accommodative stance. As noted at the beginning of this chapter, Parrott (2004) stressed the need to examine communication behaviours and not just perceptions. This point was also echoed by Gardner, Paulsen, Gallois, Callan and Monaghan (2001) and Jones, Watson, Gardner and Gallois (2004). Both these papers address research in organizational communication in general; this research is, of course also highly relevant to communication in health teams.

implications for research in health communication

In this chapter we have argued that merely describing the behaviours occurring in interactions between health professionals and patients, without providing a theoretical framework, is not an effective research approach. In order to understand the communication process, researchers *must* frame their research questions from theory. Taking a more deductive approach to the study of communication does not deny the importance of inductive methodology, particularly when the latter approach uses the rich methodology of conversation analysis or discourse analysis. Rather, the two approaches should work together, with each informing the other and building better theory. In addition, although researchers should continue their recent focus on the patient as an interactant, this focus should not exclude a consideration of the dyad. Communication should be viewed as a two-way process. We also propose that health communication researchers must recognize the benefits of triangulation and, where possible, they should adopt convergent methodologies.

An additional issue that should be addressed in future work is gathering and comparing insider and outsider perceptions with actual behaviour. Our own research (e.g., Watson & Gallois, 1999) has shown that outsiders (potential patients) empathize with the patients and are likely to perceive the interactions in similar ways to insiders (actual patients). There is a need for more systematic research making this kind of comparison, and making similar comparisons for insider and outsider health professionals. This methodology has proved invaluable in many areas of communication, and is very likely to do so here.

In any case, it is essential that researchers remember that health communication is intergroup communication. Like all contexts reflecting societal institutions, like those canvassed in many chapters in this volume, there are different and sometimes competing interests on the part of different health professionals and patients, in spite of the espoused value of 'putting the patient first'. Even so, the intergroup dynamics in these contexts are quite different from those in interethnic, inter-gender, intergenerational, or even inter-ability communication, in part because the group memberships in the health context are so role-bound. Thus, we have consistently found (Watson & Gallois, 1999, 2002, 2004; Watson, in progress) that both patients and health professionals appreciate individuated and accommodative communication that stays within the boundaries of the appropriate roles.

implications for practice

These observations have a clear relevance to the applied aspect of health communication. Health professionals should be made aware that they need to incorporate varying communication strategies to ensure an optimal interaction with a patient. Communication accommodation theory posits that we take with us into new interactions experiences from previous ones. Health professionals should consider the socio-historical context of patients, as well as the immediate situation of the interaction. Thus, health professionals should try to assess a patient's health understanding and identity through carefully phrased comments that encourage the patient to interact with them.

Health professionals need to find ways to allow patients the opportunity to help manage the interaction. Further, they can usefully consider their patients as both patients and as individuals. Our research has found that intergroup identification as patient or health professional is not necessarily negative, provided that it is combined with other accommodative strategies that denote interpersonal salience. Specifically, we have found evidence that health professionals need to focus on the individual as both a patient (his or her presenting problem), and as someone who possesses other personal interests and group identities (e.g., lover of fine wine, member of the local diving club). Health professionals who endeavour to know a little more about the patient's personal interests, encourage the patient to interact, and give reassurance, provides a balance of intergroup and interpersonal salience that facilities an effective and positive consultation.

In interprofessional contexts, the research reviewed in this chapter also has implications for managers in health care organizations as well as for practitioners. There is a recognized need for more communication training for health professionals, as well as more attention to group dynamics and to good relations in multidisciplinary teams. Training programmes, however, are still generally focused on a skills- and skills-deficit approach to effective communication. To be effective, these programmes should be modified to take account of intergroup dynamics and contexts.

conclusion

In this chapter, we have canvassed some new directions for using the approach of language and social psychology to understand how intergroup and interpersonal salience are related in communication, and the influence of communication strategies such as emotional expression in the health provider and patient interaction. We have proposed new avenues of research for interprofessional medical teams, also taking more account of social identity and intergroup dynamics. Overall, in future research, the missing link between micro-level and macro-level aspects of health communication should be made. It is important to study health communication as interpersonal communication, and also as macro-level organizational communication. The intergroup level, however, is equally important, and will add an otherwise missing dimension. The theory and methodology of language and social psychology is very well-suited to this effort.

references

Apker, J. & Ray, E.B. (2003). Stress and social support in health care organisations. In T.L. Thompson, A.M. Dorsey, K.I. Miller & R. Parrott (Eds.), *Handbook of health communication*. Mahwah, NJ: Lawrence Erlbaum.

Babrow, A.S. & Mattson, M. (2003). Theorizing about health communication. In T.L. Thompson, A.M. Dorsey, K.I. Miller & R. Parrott (Eds.), *Handbook of health communication* (pp.35–61).

Baker, S. (2006, June). *Willingness to communicate and participation in health interactions.* Paper presented at the International Conference of Language and Social Psychology, Bonn, Germany.

Barker, V. & Giles, H. (2003). Integrating the communicative predicament and enhancement of aging models: The case of older native americans. *Health Communication, 15(3),* 255–275.

Beck, C.S., Benitez, J.L., Edwards, A., Olson, A., Pai, A. & Torres, M.B. (2004). Enacting 'health communication': The field of health communication as constructed through publication in scholarly journals. *Health Communication, 16(4),* 475–492.

Berry, J.W. (1997). Immigration, acculturation, and adaptation. *Applied Psychology: An international journal, 46,* 5–68.

Braithwaite, D.O. & Thompson, T.L. (Eds.). (2000). *The handbook of communication and physical disability.* Mahwah, NJ: Erlbaum.

Burke, K. (1969). *A rhetoric of motives.* Berkeley, CA: University of California Press.

Bylund, C.L. & Makoul, G. (2005). Examining empathy in medical encounters: An observational study using the empathic communication coding system. *Health Communication, 18(2),* 123–140.

Cali, D.D. & Estrada, C. (1999). The medical interview as rhetorical counterpart of the case presentation. *Health Communication, 11(4),* 355–373.

Carthey, J., de Leval, M.R., Wright, D.J., Farewell, V.T. & Reason, J.T. (2003). Behavioural marks of surgical excellence. *Safety Science, 41,* 409–425.

Cegala, D.J., Gade, C., Broz, S.L. & McClure, L. (2004). Physicians' and patients' perceptions of patients' communication competence in a primary care medical interview. *Health Communication, 16(3),* 289–304.

Cegala, D.J., McGee, D.S. & McNelis, K.S. (1996). Components of patients' and doctors' perceptions of communication competence during a primary care interview. *Health Communication, 8,* 1–27.

Cegala, D.J., McNelis, K.S. & McGee, D.S. (1995). A study of doctors' and patients' perceptions of information processing and communication competence during the medical interview. *Health Communication, 7,* 179–203.

Coupland, N., Wiemann, J.M. & Giles, H. (1991). Talk as 'problem' and communication as 'miscommunication'. An integrative analysis. In N. Coupland, H. Giles & J.M. Wiemann (Eds.), *'Miscommunication' and problematic talk* (pp.1–17). Newbury Park, CA: Sage.

Driedger, S.M., Sanders, C., Gallois, C., Boyle, M. & Santesso, N. (in press). Women and their effective strategies when interacting with health care providers and systems. In D. Driedger & M. Owen (Eds.), *Women and chronic illness anthology.* Toronto: CSPI/Women's Press.

Duggan, A.P. & Parrott, R.L. (2001). Physicians' nonverbal rapport building and patients' talk about the subjective component of illness. *Health Communication Research, 27(2),* 299–311.

Dutta-Bergman, M.J. (2005). The relation between health-orientation, provider–patient communication, and satisfaction: An individual-difference approach. *Health Communication, 18(3),* 291–303.

Eisenberg, E.M., Murphy, A.G., Sutcliffe, K., Wears, R., Schenkel, S., Perry, S., et al. (2005). Communication in emergency medicine: Implications for patient safety. *Communication Monographs, 72(4),* 390–413.

Finnegan, J.R. & Viswanath, K. (1990). Health and communication: Medical and public health: Influences on the research agenda. In E.B. Ray & L. Donohew (Eds.), *Communication and health: Systems and applications*. Hillsdale, NJ: Lawrence Erlbaum Associates, Inc.

Fitzpatrick, M.A. & Vangelisti, A. (2001). Communication relationships and health. In W.P. Robinson & H. Giles (Eds.), *The new handbook of language and social psychology* (pp.541–561). Chichester, UK: Wiley.

Gallois, C. (2004). Intergroup and interpersonal issues in communicating about disability. In S-H. Ng, C-Y. Chiu & C. Candlin (Eds.), *Language matters: Communication, culture, and identity* (pp.355–374). Hong Kong: City University of Hong Kong Press.

Gallois, C., Ogay, T. & Giles, H. (2005). Communication accommodation theory: A look back and a look ahead. In W. Gudykunst (Ed.), *Theorizing about intercultural communication* (pp.121–148). Thousand Oaks, CA: Sage.

Gallois, C., Watson, B.M. & Pisarski, A. (2005, May). *Organizational, professional and team identity and team cohesion in health settings*. Paper presented at the International Communication Association, New York, USA.

Gardner, M.J., Paulsen, N., Gallois, C., Callan, V.J. & Monaghan, P. (2001). Communication in organizations. An intergroup perspective. In W.P. Robinson & H. Giles (Eds.), *The new handbook of language and social psychology* (pp.561–584). London: Wiley.

Giles, H., Coupland, J. & Coupland, N.E. (1991). *Contexts of accommodation: Developments in applied sociolinguistics (Studies in emotion and social interaction)*. Cambridge: Cambridge University Press.

Haslam, S.A. (2001). *Psychology in organizations: The social identity approach*. London: Sage.

Hochschild, A.R. (2003). *The managed heart: Commercialization of human feeling*. Berkeley, CA: University of California Press.

Hummert, M.L., Garstka, T.A., Ryan, E.B. & Bonnesen, J.L. (2004). The role of stereotypes in interpersonal communication. In J.F. Nussbaum & J. Coupland (Eds.), *Handbook of communication and aging research*. Mahwah, NJ: Erlbaum.

Hummert, M.L. & Ryan, E.B. (2001). Patronizing. In W.P. Robinson & H. Giles (Eds.), *The new handbook of language and social psychology* (pp.253–269). New York: J. Wiley.

Jones, E., Gallois, C., Callan, V.J. & Barker, M. (1995). Language and power in an academic context: The effects of status, ethnicity, and sex. *Journal of Language and Social Psychology, 14*, 434–461.

Jones, E., Gallois, C., Callan, V.J. & Barker, M. (1999). Strategies of accommodation: Development of a coding system for conversational interaction. *Journal of Language and Social Psychology, 18*, 125–152.

Jones, E., Watson, B., Gardner, J. & Gallois, C. (2004). Organizational communication: Challenges for the new century. *Journal of Communication, Special Issue: State of the Art in Communication Theory and Research, 54(4)*, 722–750.

Kreps, G.L. (2001). The evolution and advancement of health communication inquiry. *Communication Yearbook, 24*, 231–253.

Kunihide, S. & Reason, J. (1999). Team errors: Definitions and taxonomy. *Reliability Engineering and System Safety, 65*, 1–9.

Larkey, L.K., Alatorre, C., Buller, D.B., Morrill, C., Buller, M.K., Taren, D., et al. (1999). Communication strategies for dietary change in a worksite peer educator intervention. *Health Education Research, 14(6)*, 777–790.

Lingard, L., Espin, S., Evans, C. & Hawryluck, L. (2004). The rules of the game: Interprofessional collaboration on the intensive care unit team. *Critical Care, 8(6)*, 403–408.

Lingard, L., Espin, S., Whyte, S., Regehr, G., Baker, G.R., Reznick, R., et al. (2004). Communication failures in the operating room: An observational classification of recurrent types and effects. *Quality and Safety in Healthcare, 13*, 330–334.

Lingard, L., Garwood, S. & Poenaru, D. (2004). Tensions influencing operating room team function: Does institutional context make a difference? *Medical Education, 38*, 691–699.

Lingard, L., Reznick, R., DeVito, I. & Espin, S. (2002). Forming professional identities on the health care team: Discursive constructions of the 'other' in the operating room. *Medical Education, 36*, 728–734.

Lingard, L., Reznick, R., Espin, S., Regehr, G. & DeVito, I. (2002). Team communications in the operating room: Talk patterns, sites of tension, and implications for novices. *Academic Medicine, 77(3)*, 232–237.

McNelis, K.S. (2001). Analysing communication competence in medical consultations. *Health Communication Special Issue: Coding Provider–Patient Interaction, 13(1)*, 5–18.

Michan, S. & Rodger, S. (2000). Characteristics of effective teams: A literature review. *Australian Health Review, 23*, 201–208.

Miller, K.I., Stiff, J.B. & Ellis, B.H. (1988). Communication and empathy as precursors to burnout among human service workers. *Communication Monographs, 55*, 250–265.

O'Hair, D. (1989). Dimensions of relational communication and control during physician–patient interactions. *Health Communication, 1*, 97–115.

Parle, M., Maguire, P. & Heaven, C. (1997). The development of a training model to improve health professionals' skills, self-efficacy and outcome expectancies when communicating with cancer patients. *Social Science and Medicine, 44(2)*, 231–240.

Parrott, R. (2004). Emphasizing 'communication' in health communication. *Journal of Communication, 54(4)*, 751–787.

Pisarski, A., Lawrence, S., Gallois, C., Watson, B.M. & Bohle, P. (2005, August). *An intervention model of shiftwork tolerance.* Paper presented at the American Academy of Management, Hawai'i, USA.

Poole, M.S. & Real, K. (2003). Groups and teams in healthcare: Communication effectiveness. In T.L. Thompson, A.M. Dorsey, K.I. Miller & R. Parrott (Eds.), *Handbook of health communication* (pp.369–402). Mahwah, NJ: Lawrence Erlbaum Associates Inc.

Reason, J. (1998). Achieving a safe culture: Theory and practice. *Work and Stress, 12*, 293–306.

Rimal, R.N. (2001). Analyzing the physician–patient interaction: An overview of six methods and future research directions. *Health Communication Special Issue: Coding Provider–Patient Interaction, 13(1)*, 89–99.

Robinson, J.D. (2003). An interactional structure of medical activities during acute visits and its implications for patients' participation. *Health Communication, 15(1)*, 27–57.

Roter, D.L. & Hall, J.A. (1991). Health education theory: An application to the process of patient–provider communication. *Health Education Research, 6*, 185–193.

Roter, D.L. & Hall, J.A. (1992). *Doctors talking with patient / patients talking with doctors: Improving communications in medical visits.* Westport, CT: Auburn House.

Ryan, E.B., Bajorek, S., Beaman, A. & Anas, A.P. (2005). 'I just want you to know that "them" is me': Intergroup perspectives on communication and disability. In J. Harwood & H. Giles (Eds.), *Intergroup communication: Multiple perspectives* (pp.117–140). New York: Peter Lang.

Ryan, E.B., Giles, H., Bartolucci, G. & Henwood, K. (1986). Psycholinguistic and social psychological components of communication by and with the elderly. *Language and Communication, 6*, 1–24.

Sharf, B.F. & Street, R.L. (1997). The patient as a central construct: Shifting the emphasis. *Health Communication, 9*, 1–11.

Spiro, H. (1992). What is empathy and can it be taught? *Annals of internal medicine, 116*, 843–846.

Stivers, T. (2005). Parent resistance to physicians' treatment recommendations: One resource for initiating a negotiation of the treatment decision. *Health Communication, 18(1)*, 41–74.

Street, R.L. (1991). Accommodation in medical consultations. In H. Giles, J. Coupland & N. Coupland (Eds.), *Contexts of accommodation: Development in applied sociolinguistics* (pp.131–156). Cambridge, UK: Cambridge University Press.

Street, R.L. (2001). Active patients as powerful communicators. In W.P. Robinson & H. Giles (Eds.), *The new handbook of language and social psychology* (pp.541–561). Chichester, UK: Wiley.

Street, R.L. (2003a). Communication in medical encounters: An ecological perspective. In T.L. Thompson, A.M. Dorsey, K.I. Miller & R. Parrot (Eds.), *Handbook of Health Communication* (pp.63–93).

Street, R.L. (2003b). Interpersonal communication skills in health care contexts. In J.O. Greene & B.R. Burleson (Eds.), *Handbook of Communication and Social Interaction Skills* (pp.909–933). New Jersey: Lawrence Erlbaum Associates.

Tajfel, H. & Turner, J.C. (1979). An integrative theory of intergroup conflict. In W.G. Austin & S. Worchel (Eds.), *The social psychology of intergroup relations* (pp.33–53). Belmont, CA: Wadsworth.

Thompson, T.L. (2003). Introduction. In T.L. Thompson, A.M. Dorsey, K.I. Miller & R. Parrott (Eds.), *Handbook of health communication* (pp.1–8). Mahwah, NJ: Lawrence Erlbaum Associates Inc.

Ulrey, K.L. & Amason, P. (2001). Intercultural communication between patients and health care providers: An exploration of intercultural communication effectiveness, cultural sensitivity, stress and anxiety. *Health Communication, 13(4)*, 449–463.

von Friederichs-Fitzwater, M.M. & Gilgun, J. (2001). Relational control in physician–patient encounters. *Health Communication Special Issue: Coding Provider–Patient Interaction, 13(1)*, 75–87.

Walther, J.B., Pingree, S., Hawkins, R.P. & Buller, D.B. (2005). Attributes of interactive online health information systems. *Journal of Medical Internet Research, 7*.

Wanzer, M.B., Booth-Butterfield, M. & Gruber, K. (2004). Perceptions of health care providers' communication: Relationships between patient-centered communication and satisfaction. *Health Communication, 16(3)*, 363–383.

Watson, B.M. (2004, May). *Effective interactions between health professionals and their clients: Insider and outsider ratings.* Paper presented at the International Communication Association, New Orleans, USA.

Watson, B.M. (2005, May). *Understanding and managing the needs and goals of health professionals and patients during medical consultation.* Paper presented at the International Communication Association, New York, USA.

Watson, B.M. & Gallois, C. (1998). Nurturing communication by health professionals toward patients: A communication accommodation theory approach. *Health Communication, 10*, 343–355.

Watson, B.M. & Gallois, C. (1999). Communication accommodation between patients and health professionals: Themes and strategies in satisfying and unsatisfying encounters. *International Journal of Applied Linguistics, 9*, 167–184.

Watson, B.M. & Gallois, C. (2002). Patients' interactions with health providers: A linguistic category model approach. *Journal of Language and Social Psychology, 21*, 32–52.

Watson, B.M. & Gallois, C. (2004). Emotional expression as a sociolinguistic strategy: Its importance in medical interactions. In S.H. Ng, C.N. Candlin & C.Y. Chiu (Eds.), *Language matters: Communication, culture and identity* (pp.63–84). Hong Kong: City University of Hong Kong Press.

Willemyns, M., Gallois, C. & Callan, V.J. (2003). 'Trust me, I'm your boss...' *International Journal of Human Resource Management, 14(2)*, 1–11.

5

accommodation and institutional talk: communicative dimensions of police–civilian interactions[1]

howard giles, christopher hajek, valerie barker,
mei-chen lin, yan bing zhang, mary lee hummert
and michelle chernikoff anderson

Communication accommodation theory (CAT) has been described as one of the most prominent theories in communication in general (see Littlejohn & Foss, 2005; Tomsha & Hernandez, 2007) as well as in the social psychology of language in particular (Tracy & Haspel, 2004), and has currency in several disciplines (see Meyerhoff, 1998). Indeed, from its initial roots in accent, speech style, and bilingual modifications (see Sachdev & Giles, 2004), CAT has expanded into being an 'interdisciplinary model of relational and identity processes in communicative interaction' (Coupland & Jaworski, 1997, pp.241–242). Research has applied the theory (e.g., Coupland & Giles, 1988; Williams, Gallois & Pittam, 1999) in a wide variety of nations, cultures and languages; to study communication between different social groups (cultures, genders, generations and abilities); in different social and institutional contexts (in organizations, in the health care system, the courtroom, or simply the streets); and through different media (face-to-face interactions, but also radio, telephone, email, etc.). Although the majority of work has been conducted from neo-positivistic and experimental frameworks to enhance control of the variables being investigated, the methodologies and disciplines invoked have, nonetheless, been impressively broad (see Giles, 1984; Giles, Coupland & Coupland, 1991).

In this chapter, we focus on CAT's utility for analysing one under-studied domain of intergroup communication, namely police–civilian encounters

(Giles, 2002). By so doing, we focus on one aspect of institutional talk where a power imbalance is clearly evident. In addition to presenting recent self-report data relevant to this initiative, new intercultural data are also introduced. As an illustrative resource to call upon interpretively throughout this chapter, imagine now a traffic stop where an older male Caucasian police officer engages three young female African American students for allegedly running a stop sign. Think of the variety of social dimensions involved in this situation: gender, culture and ethnicity, social and occupational status, age, and so forth. How are the different personal and social identities negotiated during the interaction? Who changes his or her communicative style to accommodate whom? What are the outcomes of such accommodating behaviours on the relationship between the interactants? In what follows, we make reference to this scenario to show how CAT can be informative to civilian-law enforcement encounters (Giles, Willemyns, Gallois & Anderson, in press). Later in the chapter, we introduce new cross-cultural data on perceptions of accommodation in such encounters. First, however, we overview some important assumptions and concepts of the theory, interlaced with a selection of empirical research studies.

the pillars of CAT

Since its inception in the early 1970s, CAT has undergone several conceptual refinements and theoretical elaborations, as exemplified by moves from speech into the nonlinguistic and discursive arenas (see Gallois, Ogay & Giles, 2005, for a history of its development). Because the extensive amount of CAT research and theorizing can be somewhat overwhelming, predictive models have been developed in an effort to better organize and summarize thinking on these matters (e.g., Street & Giles, 1982; Gallois, Franklyn-Stokes, Giles & Coupland, 1988). However, because of the perpetual refinements of this prepositional format, some expositions of CAT may have become overly dense for some tastes. Hence, in parallel, other reviews have engaged the theory in a more textually flowing fashion, unfettered by propositional frames (e.g., Giles & Noels, 1998; Giles & Wadleigh, 1999; see however, Giles, Willemyns et al., in press). It is in this same reader-friendly spirit (after Giles & Ogay, in press) that we provide a snapshot of the literature here.

CAT provides a wide-ranging framework aimed at predicting and explaining many of the adjustments individuals make to create, maintain or decrease social distance in interaction. It explores the different ways in which we accommodate our communication, our motivations for doing so, and the consequences. For instance, conveyed accommodation often has its desired effect in terms of increasing the likelihood that recipients will feel more positively toward the instigator (Bourhis, Giles & Lambert, 1975). CAT addresses interpersonal communication issues, yet also links communication with the larger context of the *intergroup* stakes of an encounter (see Harwood & Giles, 2005). In other words, sometimes our communications are driven by our personal identities while at others – and sometimes within the very same interaction – our words, nonverbal behaviour, and demeanour are fuelled almost entirely, by our social identities as members of particular groups.

In another example, a speaker (call her Jill) may in a particular context not speak so much *as the individual Jill*, but as someone who represents (as nearly as possible) the prototype of her group, in this case social psychologists, to an audience of (say) lawyers, architects and business people. It is relevant to this chapter that, of all such social encounters, the police officer–civilian one is amongst *the* most visible and salient intergroup-wise across many nations (Molloy & Giles, 2002). An officer's uniform and badge, together with a readily visible array of weaponry, as well as the unique legal authority to use coercive force (Klockars, 1985), can make this a threatening relationship for civilians. Add into the mix the frequent militaristic hairstyle of male officers, in the USA anyway, and another layer of perceived authoritarianism can often be apparent (Giles, Zwang-Weissman & Hajek, 2004). Interestingly as we shall see from data presented in this chapter, the 'intergroupness' of the police–community divide can vary cross-culturally.

Before engaging its theoretical tenets and empirical support, two rather fundamental assumptions of CAT are worth laying out. First, communication is influenced not only by features of the immediate situation and participants' initial orientations to it, but also by the socio-historical context in which the interaction is embedded (see Fox, Giles, Orbe & Bourhis, 2000). For example, an isolated encounter between a particular police officer and citizen could be marred by alleged past hostile relations between *other* members of these two groups in the neighbourhood and/or on the media – as would probably be apparent for many citizens of colour in New York, Los Angeles or Cincinnati (see Lawrence, 2000; Ross, 2000). Current accommodations, or the lack of them, can be borne out of significant *others'* histories of conflict on the one hand, or good will on the other.

Second, communication is not only a matter of exchanging information about facts, ideas and emotions (often called referential communication), as often salient social category memberships are also negotiated during an interaction through the process of accommodation. An example of this could be the decision by a bilingual Latina police officer to use Spanish or English with other Spanish-speaking citizens on her beat. Here she would be negotiating two identities: as an officer of the law and as a Latina. Her choice of language may depend on whether she wishes to emphasize a shared identity (speaking Spanish to show that she and the citizen share a common language and culture) or a discordant identity (speaking English to make salient her position as an authority).

strategies of accommodation and nonaccommodation

CAT posits that individuals use communication in part in order to indicate their attitudes toward each other and, as such, communication is a barometer of the level of social distance between them. This constant movement toward and away from others by changing one's communicative behaviour is called *accommodation*. Among the different accommodative strategies that speakers use to achieve these goals, *convergence* has been the most extensively studied, and can be considered the historical core of CAT (Giles, 1973). Convergence has been defined as a strategy whereby individuals adapt their communicative behaviours in terms of a wide range of linguistic (e.g., speech rates, accents), paralinguistic (e.g., pauses, utterance lengths) and nonverbal features (e.g., smiling, gazing) in such a way as to become more similar to their interlocutor's behaviours (for examples, see Azuma, 1997; Hannah & Murachver, 1999; Levin & Lin, 1988; Niederhoffer & Pennebaker, 2002). Even in the rather socially 'bare' context of communication via email, Thomson, Murachver and Green (2001) have found that women and men converge to the language styles (more female- or male-like) of their net-pals (see also Crook & Booth, 1997; regarding answering machine messages, see Buzzanell, Burrell, Stafford & Berkowitz, 1996).

Accommodation can also vary from slight to full (or even beyond) to the extent to which speakers approximate the communicative patterns of their receivers (Bradac, Mulac & House, 1988; Street, 1982). Moreover, receivers have *expectations* about optimal levels of accommodation. Violation of these expectations can result in a negative evaluation of speakers by their receivers. For instance, Preston (1981) found that full convergence, in the case of foreign language learning, is not always desired by either the speaker or the addressee. He argues that full convergence, or native speaker-like fluency, is often viewed with distrust and seen as controlling by the addressee. These expectations can be based on social *stereotypes* regarding outgroup members (and, in particular, regarding their levels of communicative competence).

It is important to underscore that people are theorized by CAT to accommodate to where they *believe* others are communicatively and not necessarily to how the latter actually speak in any objective or measured senses (see Thakerar, Giles & Cheshire, 1982; Ross & Shortreed, 1990). This is illustrated by Bell's (1984) study of New Zealand broadcasters, who read the same news transcripts on a number of quite different stations, varying their speech according to assumed audience characteristics. It was found that this same content was read in very different ways that accommodated the accent and style of people with the *assumed* socioeconomic status of their listeners.

accommodative motives and communication satisfaction

An important *motive* for convergence is the desire to gain approval from another, particularly in the case where there is a status, power or respect differential (see Fitzpatrick, Mulac & Dindia, 1995). For most organizations, accommodation is also central to their relations with customers and the public in general. Sparks and Callan (1992) applied CAT to the hospitality industry and showed how much a convergent style of communication with consumers is important for customers' satisfaction. This has been observed in a number of settings where, for example, a travel agent accommodated in her pronunciation to the different socioeconomically-based language styles of her Welsh clientele (Coupland, 1984) and in Taiwan, where salespersons converged more to customers than vice-versa (van den Berg, 1986). Not unrelatedly, popular American TV talk show host Larry King was found to change the pitch of his voice as a function of his guests' status; for example, he would converge toward President Clinton (see Al-Khatib, 1995). Conversely, those of King's guests who were held in lower social regard (e.g., Vice-President Dan Quayle) would accommodate more to Larry King than he would to them (Gregory & Webster, 1996).

Bourhis (1984) studied accommodative strategies in Montreal by asking Francophone and Anglophone pedestrians about directions, either in English or in French. He found that 30 per cent of Anglophones maintained English in their responses when they had been addressed in French, even when their linguistic skills would have been sufficient to answer in French. In contrast, only 3 per cent of Francophone pedestrians used French in their answers to the English-speaking interlocutor. The difference in accommodative behaviour displayed by the two groups of pedestrians is explained by the Canadian intergroup context. Traditionally, the Anglophone minority has higher status and power within the Francophone majority setting of Montreal (see also Lawson & Sachdev, 2000).

In another institutional CAT study, this time in Australia, Gardner and Jones (1999) invited superordinates (i.e., supervisors) and subordinates to write down what they would say at 'best' and at 'worst' to their counterparts in a variety of communicative situations offered them (e.g., 'you have an informal chat with your subordinate' or 'you are negotiating a change in your working situation with your superior'). Analysis of the data showed that, for both organizational groups, the best communications were coded, as would be predicted, accommodative. For superordinates, this was indicated by taking the listener's position and knowledge into account and being clear and direct, while for subordinates it was manifest more in listening, asking for input, and being open. The worst communications were clearly *non*accommodative. For superordinates, such talk was overaccommodative, manifest in being overly familiar while, for subordinates, it was more underaccommodative and expressed through being too demanding and aggressive (see also Watson & Gallois, 1999). Hence, participants holding different institutional roles do report varying conversations between themselves in accommodation terms (see also Baker, 1991; Boggs & Giles, 1999).

In a similar vein, research has shown that young people report that conversations considered satisfying with older strangers were imbued with accommodating stances from the latter, while dissatisfying intergenerational encounters tended to be replete with nonaccommodations (Williams & Giles, 1996). In parallel, grandchildren and grandparents in the USA and Taiwan report (although in different ways) that the closeness of their family relationship is contingent on how accommodating their communications were (e.g., they complimented, did not talk down to, each other; see Harwood, 2000; Lin & Harwood, 2003). For grandchildren, this, in turn, has been associated with positive attitudes towards older adults in general (Harwood, Hewstone, Paolini & Voci, 2005). Interestingly, extensive cross-cultural research has shown that elderly people who feel generally accommodated to report better subjective health in terms of lowered depression and heightened self-esteem and life satisfaction (see overview, Giles, McCann, Ota & Noels, 2002).

effectiveness, social identity and nonaccommodation

Accommodating to a common linguistic style and taking into account the listener's interpretive competence or knowledge about a topic (Coupland, Coupland, Giles & Henwood, 1988) also improves the effectiveness of communication. This, in turn, has been associated with increased predictability of the other and hence a lowering of uncertainty, interpersonal anxiety, and an increase in mutual understanding (see Gudykunst, 1995). Bourhis, Roth and MacQueen (1988) found that physicians, nurses and hospital patients considered it more appropriate for health professionals to converge to the patients' everyday language than to maintain their medical jargon. In fact, talking excessively about oneself and one's ailments (Coupland, Coupland & Giles, 1991) and not attending or listening to the other (Giles & Williams, 1994) can be considered *under*accommoda-tive (see Williams & Nussbaum, 2001). Indeed, in the scenario earlier, imagine the police officer does not explain the reason for the traffic stop and emergent citation, nor inquire about the driver's understanding of her transgression and her reasoning for it, and even adopts legalese. Such a nonaccommodating, non-confirming (Sieburg, 1976) stance could instil additional aggravation and irritation in the driver and her passengers, possibly leading to a complaint or even worse.

But accommodation is not only rewarding when it occurs, it may well entail some costs, such as the possible loss of personal or social identity. Again returning to the opening scenario – if the student driver converges towards the officer's communicative style, she may be rewarded by the officer who will perceive her as particularly cooperative and understanding (see Buller, LePoire, Aune & Eloy, 1992), yet the student may also feel deprived of her social identity. Members of her ingroup (e.g., the passengers in the car) who hear her might also perceive her as a 'traitor' and construe and label her derogatorily (Hogg, D'Agata & Abrams, 1989). That said, on reflection passengers may appreciate the prudence of her communicative inclinations for all concerned and especially so if she accounts for her actions to her ingroup as they leave the scene.

Accommodative moves to such outgroups are also variously appreciated by ingroup members, depending on the strength of their attachment to the group. In a study conducted in Hong Kong one year before its handover to the People's Republic of China, respondents with a strong identification to Hong Kong evaluated more favourably their ingroup members who, by using Cantonese, diverged from Mandarin-speaking Chinese people than did respondents who identified themselves with mainland China (Tong, Hong, Lee & Chiu, 1999). Divergence and nonaccommodation can be endorsed as a positive means of maintaining or even accentuating one's social identity (Giles, 1978; Tajfel & Turner, 1986). All in all, it appears that satisfying communication requires a delicate balance between convergence, to demonstrate willingness to communicate, and divergence, to incur a healthy sense of group identity (see Cargile & Giles, 1996). Furthermore, calibrating the amount of perceived non-, under-

and overaccommodation one receives can be an important ingredient in continuing or withdrawing from an interaction.

In what follows, we present some recent and new data which examine accommodative phenomena, albeit self-reported in a context where it is very difficult to access and record ongoing naturalistic data, in civilians' evaluations of their experiences with police officers. Before engaging that, it is important to examine, and be armed with knowledge about, cross-disciplinary studies on attitudes toward law enforcement.

attitudes toward law enforcement

The National Research Council (2004) states that a major dilemma facing police officers is that 'public demands for effective law enforcement may seem to conflict with the responsibility to protect individual civil liberties' (p.57). Correspondingly, many civilians can hold 'contradictory perceptions of the police' (White & Menke, 1982, p.223), with police being construed as almost revered – and yet despised – at one and the same time (Molloy & Giles, 2002). This ambivalence is only one of the many contributors making street police work an emotionally stressful occupation (Howard, Tuffin & Stephens, 2000; see also Toch, 2003) and one where the vast majority of officers themselves concede that they have an image problem (Oberle, 2004). Negative representations of police on fictional drama, reality shows and news programmes are not foreign to TV viewers (e.g., Eschholz, Sims Blackwell, Gertz & Chiricos, 2002; van den Bulck, 1998), with attention often being focused, perhaps overly so, on occasions where police abuses of force have allegedly occurred (e.g., Lawrence, 2000; Ross, 2000). However, incidents such as the Rodney King beating and that of two Mexican immigrants, as well as the videotaped slamming of the head of a Black teenager on a police cruiser in Los Angeles in the 1990s, have hampered police efforts to improve their image. Yet more recent events demonstrating police bravery and dedication in New York City and New Orleans have undoubtedly gone some way to compensate for this (Paulson, 2001).

The public's attitudes are, of course, also shaped by *actual*, rather than parasocial, interactions with officers, many of which occur via traffic stops (Griffiths & Winfree, 1982; Langan, Greenfeld, Smith, Durose & Levin, 2001; see also, Wortley, 1996). Indeed, Hennigan, Maxson, Sloane and Ranney (2002) found in four areas of Los Angeles that, while 35 per cent of respondents believed the mass media were the greatest influence on their opinions of local law enforcement, 65 per cent believed that personal experience was the factor that shaped their views most (see also,

Tyler & Huo, 2002). As the National Research Council (2004) points out, '…the sheer volume of police–citizen contact means that a significant number of individual citizens come away dissatisfied with how they were treated' (p.2), even though, in all likelihood, the vast majority of interactions with the public are non-problematic.

Although no empirically-robust meta-analysis of documented attitudes towards the police exists, many investigations have pointed to the role of socio-demographic factors in predicting such judgements, albeit varying greatly from community to community (e.g., Klyman & Kruckenberg, 1974). Older, female, urban, better educated, higher incomed, married and Caucasian respondents in comparison to their social counterparts consistently manifest more positive views of law enforcement (e.g., Eschholz et al., 2002; Olsen, 2005; Tyler & Huo, 2002; Yates & Pillai, 1996) as do many of those who reside in communities where the level of criminal disorder is purportedly low (Hennigan et al., 2002). Not surprisingly, Cox and White (1988) report that those with negative views of the police have often had disturbing police contacts, felt they were victims of unfair police decisions, and perceived the police as verbally harassing them. Sixty-nine per cent of the participants in their study reported a negative police contact, 35 per cent felt verbally abused, and 15 per cent of their sample 'perceived that the officer had directed profanity at them' (p.120).

The perceptions of various groups about law enforcement, as alluded to above, have received widespread empirical attention. Taylor, Turner, Esbensen and Winfree (2001) found that Caucasians and Asians had the more favourable views of police, followed by Hispanics and Native Americans, and then African Americans. These results, particularly as they relate African Americans' trust in law enforcement (Huo & Tyler, 2000; Tyler, 2001; Tyler & Huo, 2002), have been confirmed by many others (e.g., Parker, Onyekwuluje & Murty, 1995; Prine, Ballard & Robinson, 2001; Smith & Hawkins, 1973; Wortley, 1996). Gratifyingly, contact in some locations between African American juveniles and community-oriented police officers by means of weekly club meetings and collaborative projects has been documented as improving images of the police in general, such as police being seen as less authoritarian (e.g., Derbyshire, 1968; Jones-Brown, 2000; see however, Hopkins & Hewstone, 1992).

accommodative dimensions of attitudes toward police

Previous research has focused as well on other structural factors that affect attitudes towards police (ATP). For example, in an attempt to explore empirically the perceived role of officers' accommodation, Giles, Fortman et al. (2006) studied three fairly large samples of respondents who were asked in a variety of ways and contexts (e.g., after church in Spanish, a community door-to-door survey in English, and at a campus online) about their attitudes towards specified local law enforcement agencies in southern California. The police agencies involved were associated with a small city north of Los Angeles and the local university campus near that location. A range of socio-demographic factors and other questions were posed, such as perceptions of trust in officers, amount of contact with them, and felt anxiety. In addition, depending on the sample, items relating to how accommodating officers appeared to them were included: how well they believed that officers listened to people, took their views into account, and wanted to understand their needs and unique situations.

In general, ratings of and satisfaction with local police agencies were significantly above the neutral mid-point, with males, non-Caucasians, and younger people being less positive in these regards. Furthermore, and invoking separate structural equation models for the three quite different populations, socio-demographic factors (apart from age in one locale) had no direct effects on assessments of local officers and rated satisfaction with them. In other words, socio-demographic variables paled in comparison to perceptions of officers' communication skills. Similarly, even gender, reported income, amount of estimated contact with police, and how safe respondents felt had relatively less bearing on respondents' attitudes when these were built into the evaluative frame. How much respondents perceived officers as accommodating was by far the largest predictor of attitudes toward the police. It was more powerful than rated trust in the police and willingness to call them, both of which also had direct paths to outcomes. Furthermore, not only were trust and accommodation mutually influential, but accommodation also had the same relationship with willingness to call as well as obey the police. Interestingly, when the survey was administered to Spanish-speaking Latinos (mostly Mexican immigrants), it was found that the less people reported police as having been accommodating in their country of origin, the less accommodating they found them in the host community.

Additionally, the amount of contact with officers and how safe respondents felt had little bearing on ATP. Furthermore, communication issues were construed as paramount when generated spontaneously by respondents in their open-ended responses. Whether this potent role for officers' perceived accommodativeness in predicting ATP is not context-specific – and an even more global one – is an empirical question. In order to begin exploring this challenging issue, we examined attitudes toward police in quite contrasting settings.

new vistas for the study of accommodation and ATP

The goal of the current study was to collect reasonably large data sets in three very different locales: one in the USA but this time in Kansas, and the other two in the People's Republic of China (PRC) and Taiwan. In addition to their significant ethnolinguistic differences, these locales were chosen for their histories of police–community conflicts. Therefore, we wondered (besides other questions beyond the remit of the current chapter)[2] if perceived accommodation would have a focal role in ATP predictions in these different locations, and to what extent.

There appears, unfortunately, to be no scholarly research on attitudes towards law enforcement in the Kansan setting. That said, a plethora of articles in the local *Lawrence Journal World* during 2002–03 were highly critical of police practices in the city of Lawrence. Charges levied by the community (as well as a judge) were wide-ranging and hardly contribute to a positive image of law enforcement in the State. Amongst the claims were police harassment, being untrustworthy and irresponsive to complaints, claiming police brutality, conducting unconstitutional searches (during traffic stops), and interrogating without offering those accused their legal rights. Notwithstanding the notion of 'good press' about police actions not surfacing at this time which could provide some sort of media balance, it would seem likely that the communicative climate in this city is probably antithetical – or at least ambivalent – toward local law enforcement.

Turning to Taiwan, it appears that the picture is much bleaker. Police officers (compared with people from other occupations) are not highly regarded in this society. As part of Confucian society, Taiwanese people endorse education (Zhang, Lin, Nonaka & Beom, 2005) and associate higher education with steady and promising careers. The education system separates schools for training police officers from the normal college track and vocational school systems. Most parents discourage their children from entering police schools if there is a possibility of entering any college or university. As a result, and despite recent upgrading of teaching resources for officers, stereotypically they are perceived as intellectually inferior to other college students (Judicial Reformed Foundation, 2002) and their reputation seems to be diminishing almost every year. Moreover, fairly large surveys by Yu (1992) and Lin (2001) found that the public wished that the police would not only protect their property and safety, but would also adopt a more 'customer-oriented approach', responding to the needs of the public in a timely manner and being much more concerned about building positive images of themselves as approachable, trustworthy and friendly.

In Taiwan, the boundaries between police officers, local gangs and politicians can be fairly blurred. Police officers are perceived as abusing their authority, being open to bribes, and being rude to the public. The Judicial Reform Foundation (1999) conducted an online survey about people's understanding of their rights when questioned by the police. Among 623 respondents, only 12 per cent of them believed that they would be treated fairly and reasonably when they were questioned by the police. Not only did participants not trust the police, they would also seek outside sources to intervene to protect their safety. Using a nation-wide telephone interview (n = 4062), and when asked about what should be done to improve safety, the quality of the police recruits was ranked number one, even over preventing drug sales (Ministry of the Interior, 2003). Added to this, feelings of distrust for the police and safety are common ingredients of 24-hour TV news channels.

Finally, we turn to the PRC, where data in English on this topic are infrequently found and where images of the police among the public are often formed from crime fiction (Kinkley, 1993). In the mid-1990s, the police and local judges were under pressure to make the country safer and reduce major crime. Indeed, the force grew by 45 per cent (Gilley, 1996) as did the quality of training, a surge of arrests, and trials lasting a week. Even torture and executions followed. At the start of the new century, a Criminal Justice System Roundtable was formed before the Congressional-Executive Commission on China (Legislative Branch Commissioners, 2002), part of which focused on the elevated fear Chinese people had of the police. This factor is compounded by one authority at the Roundtable reporting that, 'I do not exaggerate, many street level Chinese police probably have less knowledge of modern crime scene management, fingerprinting, blood typing and rudimentary forensic and investigatory skills than the average American viewer of *Law and Order*' (p.7). That said, Cao and Hou (2001) published a comparative study claiming that public confidence in the police was greater in the PRC than the USA.

In sum, and much in contrast to the southern Californian setting discussed above, all three contexts here indicate past consternations with police work and the images that naturally follow about its personnel. And unlike the former setting, efforts are underway in both Kansas and the PRC to raise awareness about alleged police transgressions. Clearly, the Taiwanese situation until very recently has endured a longstanding climate of duress between officers and the communities they serve.

With this backdrop in mind, and in light of research on the roles of perceived trust and communicative accommodation in determining attitudes towards police, we posed just one hypothesis for our purposes in this chapter:

> Perceived trust in and accommodation from officers will be mutually influential of each other, with accommodation being the major predictor of students' ratings of and satisfaction with police in all three cultural contexts.

a cross-cultural investigation

Undergraduate students (n = 682) from universities in Taiwan, the PRC and the USA completed the survey. The study participants in PRC and Taiwan were recruited through flyers and the students in the United States received extra course credit for their participation. The Taiwan sample (n = 216; 112 females) was drawn from undergraduate psychology, communication studies, sociology and law students at a university in Taipei. All participants were of Chinese (Han) ethnic origin, and ranged in age from 18 to 40, with a mean reported age of 21.54 (SD = 3.02). The PRC sample (n = 227; 118 females) was drawn from undergraduate students at a university in Beijing. As with the Taiwan sample, all were of Chinese (Han) ethnic origin, and ranged in age from 17 to 26, with a mean reported age of 19.41 (SD = 1.35). Finally, the United States sample (n = 239; 119 females) was drawn from undergraduate communication students at a Midwestern university. In this sample, the majority of participants were Caucasian (89 per cent), the remainder being of Asian/ Pacific Island (3.8 per cent), African American (2.9 per cent), Latino/a (2.5 per cent), and 'Other American' (1.7 per cent) descent. Their ages ranged from 18 to 32, with a mean reported age of 20.46 (SD = 2.02). At each site, participants completed the questionnaires in small groups under the supervision of a research assistant, resulting in a 100 per cent response rate.

The survey utilized a between-subjects design to examine participants' attitudes toward law enforcement across the three countries. The 38-item instrument was largely comprised of seven-point Likert-type items assessing attitudes toward police in general, as well as a number of demographic items. Assessment items were anchored by 'strongly agree' and 'strongly disagree', or by bi-polar semantic differential items (e.g., 'very unpleasant' to 'very pleasant'). The English version of the questionnaire was translated into Chinese by two of the bilingual authors of this study. Results were compared, and experts in the PRC and Taiwan were consulted in this process. A back translation procedure was adopted to ensure that the translation was sensitive to the cultural contexts, and that the instrument's original meaning was not distorted.

Questionnaire items were adapted from previous surveys of attitudes toward local law enforcement, and included items about perceived contacts with, obligations to obey, trust in, and accommodation from, officers, as well as general feelings of safety (see Table 5.1). Single-item measures – to be comparative with prior studies – were also used to assess satisfaction with the police (i.e., *how satisfied are you with services provided*

Table 5.1 Questionnaire items

Police officer accommodation:
How pleasant overall are the police?
In general, how accommodating are police officers? (i.e., how well do you think they listen to people, take their views into account, and want to understand their needs and unique situations?)
In general, how respectful of students are police officers?
How polite are police officers?
How well do police officers explain things to people (i.e., talk to people in ways that 'sit right' with them, and that they understand)?[*]

Trust:
How much respect do you have for the police?[*]
To what degree do you think police officers are honest?
To what degree do you feel proud of the police?
To what degree do you feel you should support the police?[*]
To what degree do you feel that police decisions are fair?
To what degree do you feel the police protect citizen rights?[*]
I have confidence that the police department can do its job well[*]
I trust the police to make decisions that are good for everyone in the community

Tendency to obey:
People should obey the police even if what the police officers say or do goes against what they think is right
I would always try to follow what a police officer says I should do, even if I thought it was wrong[*]
Disobeying a police officer is seldom justified
Overall, the police are a legitimate legal authority, and people should obey the decisions that police officers make[*]

Safety:
I feel safe at home
I feel safe walking alone in the daytime
I feel safe walking alone at night when it is dark[*]

---

[*] *Item dropped in structural equation models*

by the police?), and evaluations of them (i.e., *overall, how would you rate the police department?*). In addition, participants were asked to report how much police-initiated contact they had experienced, how much they themselves had initiated, and how much contact they had witnessed others experience. Furthermore, two (intergroup) items were used to assess the degree to which participants perceived of themselves and the police as belonging to different social categories (i.e., *if you were to meet a police officer [or when you have interacted with one], how aware would you be that the two of you belonged to different communities?* And, *if you were to meet a police officer [or when you have interacted with one], how aware would you be that you were two people representing the respective groups to which you belong?*). Finally, participants were asked to report their comfort in voicing their concerns to their police department (i.e., *if I have a problem with the police department, I feel I can voice my concern to it*).

findings

Table 5.2 presents the mean differences between the three cultures across all the measures. Multivariate statistics applied to these data showed clear differences between the Kansan, Taiwan and PRC settings,[3] with Taiwan offering, arguably, the least conducive climate for satisfactory police–community relations and Kansas being perceived by far as the safest.[4] Intriguingly, few differences arose between the PRC and USA settings, and when they did it favoured the former on some ways given

Table 5.2 Means and standard deviations for all factors and individual measures by culture

	China	**Taiwan**	**USA**
Factors			
Accommodation	3.94 (1.06)	3.47 (1.04)	3.81 (1.22)
Trust	4.18 (1.13)	3.14 (1.16)	4.36 (1.14)
Tendency to obey	3.49 (1.42)	3.25 (1.24)	4.21 (1.31)
Safety	3.92 (1.48)	3.95 (1.29)	6.28 (0.83)
Individual Measures			
Satisfaction	4.12 (1.40)	3.43 (1.30)	4.58 (1.44)
Rating	4.23 (1.34)	3.48 (1.33)	4.63 (1.36)
Belong to two communities	4.98 (1.61)	5.17 (1.44)	4.37 (1.62)
Represent respective groups	5.09 (1.60)	5.30 (1.43)	4.56 (1.28)
Police-initiated contact	1.41 (0.94)	2.31 (1.46)	3.09 (1.64)
Citizen-initiated contact	2.52 (1.52)	2.21 (1.33)	2.46 (1.34)
Others' contact (witnessed)	3.30 (1.77)	3.45 (1.70)	4.43 (1.61)
Comfort voicing concerns to police	4.91 (1.90)	4.42 (1.75)	4.08 (1.78)

lower police-initiated contacts and more expressed comfort in offering police complaints.

Moving to the main objective of our investigation which was to explore the roles of perceived trust in and accommodation from officers in moulding the public attitudes toward law enforcement, structural equation models were constructed for each country. These models tested for the influence of gender, trust in police officers and perceived officer accommodation on police department ratings and satisfaction with services by police. Additionally, the relationships between these factors and perceived obligation to obey and feelings of safety were assessed (with earlier model construction rendering the various forms of contact with police non-influential).[5]

For each location, a full model was initially tested and non-significant paths were subsequently removed. The PRC and USA models were very similar – a nested models comparison indicated no statistically significant difference ($p = .13$) – and they showed that trust in the police influenced participants' ratings of and satisfaction with the police. Additionally, the results showed strong covariance between perceptions of police accommodation and the two factors, trust in police and the perceived obligation to obey. Also, trust in the police co-varied with perceived obligation to obey. The final model statistics show good fit for both locations[6] and there were no significant relationships for gender or safety in these models. Figure 5.1 is a composite model for the PRC and USA.

The model for the Taiwanese participants shared the paths described by the other two models, but was strikingly different in other ways.[7] The model showed a positive relationship between gender and perceptions of police officers' accommodation and also level of trust in police. This suggests that Taiwanese females perceive police officers as more accommodating and trustworthy than do Taiwanese males. The model also shows covariance between perceived obligation to obey and feelings of safety. Perhaps most telling was the relatively strong influence of police accommodation on ratings of the police department and satisfaction with police services. Thus, while trust in the police is still influential in this model (particularly on ratings of the police department), accommodation is equally as influential among the Taiwanese participants (see Figure 5.2).

It may be recalled that we predicted that perceived trust in and accommodation from officers would be mutually influential of each other, with accommodation being *the major* predictor of ratings of and satisfaction with police in all three cultural contexts. This hypothesis was supported in that accommodation and trust were mutually influential. However, their roles in predicting satisfaction and ratings of police varied

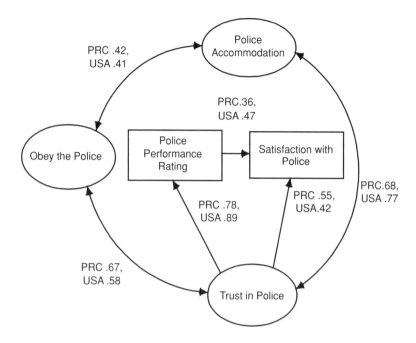

Figure 5.1   Attitudes to police: People's Republic of China and USA

by culture. Interestingly, trust was the *only* predictor of satisfaction and ratings in the USA and the PRC, whereas *both* trust and accommodation were predictors in Taiwan. Indeed, Figure 5.2 (for Taiwan) shares many similarities with models that emerged from investigations in California reported above (Giles, Fortman et al., 2006). Gender – a factor so predictive of ATP in prior research – once again only shapes ratings of and satisfaction of police indirectly through perceived trust and accommodation. As in the USA and PRC model, Taiwanese perceptions of officers' accommodation had more effect in predicting satisfaction with the police in general than trust, although both accommodation and trust figured more equally in this context in forging outcomes. Additionally, perceptions of safety did not have clear pathways to predicting ATP, thereby endorsing Worrel's (1999) views that feelings of safety and police efficacy are quite orthogonal from perceptions of fairness and social support.

There were other markers of commonality in the Taiwanese data and in the models derived from the USA and PRC. Interestingly, gender and safety were inexplicably missing from Figure 5.1 and, as stated above,

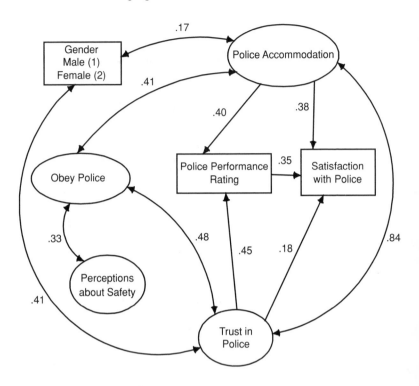

Figure 5.2 Attitudes to Taiwanese police

accommodation gave way to trust which alone predicted the two ATP outcomes. Nonetheless, accommodation and trust were mutually co-determinants and both shaped respondents' expressed obligations to obey the police. Why then did the focal role of communicative accommodation remain in Taiwan, but 'subside' in the other two contexts? Our answer at this juncture relates to the nature of the questions posed respondents in the context of the size of the community targeted. It will be recalled that in the Californian research, views of law enforcement targeted *specifically* the local police agency. In Taiwan, police 'in general' would necessarily be translated as the local police force; their cognitive and affective retrieval mechanisms would locate those proximate officers on the Island. In Kansas and the PRC – both of which are many times larger in size than Taiwan – rating police 'in general' might well have invoked media and generic images beyond that of the local agency. In this sense, particular communicative behaviours might not have assumed primacy as they would have in more localized contexts.

epilogue

Even given the PRC and Kansan data (which derived from very different social contexts, varying as they did in terms of police violence and police reform) and the different questions asked in this study vis-à-vis its predecessors, accommodation did still play an integral role in the construction of ATP. Moreover, a robust link between it and perceived trust was sustained, suggesting that CAT can be useful in understanding domains of criminal justice. As detailed by revised propositions in Giles, Willemyns et al. (in press), this study has implications for a refinement of CAT to the extent that perceived accommodation can yield increased attributions of trust and fashion a climate whereby policies promoting community policing could be more easily fostered. As Oberle (2004) has argued, '…creating a long-term positive image of law enforcement in the minds of the public rests with the support of individual officers and their ability to create a positive image on a daily basis within the communities they serve' (p.27). The results of this study, and other findings elsewhere in the USA and Africa (e.g., Hajek et al., 2006), highlight the perhaps *universal* importance of trust in police and officers' accommodation to meet these ends.

Having presented cross-cultural data which empower accommodative phenomena and processes in the law enforcement domain, we return now to our starting point: the basics as well as inherent complexities of CAT. A number of disciplines have profited from its insights, and in this chapter we have selected an array of experimentally-controlled laboratory and naturalistic studies from around the world designed to explore its dynamics. As readers have seen from recurring treatments of the opening scenario of a traffic stop, there are a plethora of communicative options for, and reactions to, people interacting (who have personal and many social identities). Drawing upon extensive observational data on police roles (Mastrofski, 1983), Roberg, Novak and Cordner (2005) allude to why this context is very relevant to us as social psychologists of language and discourse:

Perhaps the most interesting characteristic of police work revealed by these figures is the importance of *communication* skills. Five of the six most common actions taken by officers consisted entirely of talking and listening. These five were interviewing, interrogating, lecturing or threatening, giving information, and giving reassurance. It is primarily by communicating that police officers determine what is going on… and [reach]…an amicable solution… (p.30, our italics).

We contend that CAT – with its attention to macro-contextual forces, interpersonal and intergroup dynamics, motives, and social consequences – can handle many of these (and other) intricacies. Indeed, a person's accommodative resources and flexibility may make up a hitherto unrecognized statement about his or her communicative competences (see Burleson & Greene, 2003; Spitzberg & Cupach, 1984; Wiemann, 1977), and CAT has the potential to be associated with a very wide range of individuals' uses of communicative actions.

Relatedly, while CAT could be infinitely elaborated to take account of expectancy violations, arousal, cognitive schemas, relational development, and so forth, it was never conceived to be a theory for *all* interpersonal and intergroup eventualities. That said, as we move into new research domains such as police culture, there is the potential for exciting theoretical connections for future development. The law and society literature refers to police behaviours which parallel many forms of accommodation. For example, studying officers seeking compliance with requests for self-control (as opposed to requests for identification or other compliance requests), McCluskey (2003, p.91) found that:

> Citizens who receive respectful treatment from authorities are almost twice as likely to comply, and those receiving disrespectful treatments are nearly twice as likely to rebel. If the citizen's voice is terminated by the police they are more than twice as likely to rebel against the police request for self-control. If the police demonstrate their commitment to making an informed decision by seeking information about the presenting situation, citizens are more than twice as likely to comply with the . . . request for self-control.

Procedural justice theory and CAT are each based solidly in social psychology and acknowledge the prominence of communication in police–civilian interactions and, together, they might swing open the double doors to a better understanding of them.

Finally, let us transform some of the more obviously-relevant aspects of CAT into the police–civilian terrain and with a view to forging an implicit research agenda. As we have seen, police officers have in uncertain, anxious and dangerous situations, such as so-called routine traffic stops and beyond, the obligation and inclination to be accommodatively appealing. They understand that these situations are costly for civilians who may not appreciate that part of the enterprise for them is to be educated appropriately about a violation that may have happened. Officer accommodation – which we have seen from our data above has positive consequences for their ingroup image in general – can reap many immediate rewards in promoting a personal and educative atmosphere where compliance is promoted and frustration and aggravation (or even worse) diminished. Yet such communicative stances can also be motivated – sometimes in parallel – by a nonaccommodative stance in the pursuance of everyone's safety. Empirical questions worthy of following through with actual videotaped data (if possible) for coding and other discursive analyses, then explode in abundance. What specific officer accommodations facilitate what ends? Do civilians (in the moment of social exchange) understand or acknowledge the perspective of the officer and his or her safety challenges? How do civilians construe and respond to actions they perceive as nonaccommodative? Is the ritualistic departure of an officer with, 'Have a nice day!' seen as divergent, or even hostile? What effects, in tandem and in cyclic fashion (as above), do civilians' accommodativeness–nonaccommodativeness have on officers' cognitions, affect, demeanour and ultimately outcome behaviours (e.g., citations, warnings, assistance)? CAT would suggest the value of accommodating. Interestingly, anecdotal experiences by the first author and his police associates suggest, in actuality, the paradoxical preponderance of public *non*accommodations.

Needless to say, theoretically-driven questions about officer–civilian encounters, let alone analogous questions *within* the hierarchical organization of police culture pertaining to office-supervisor/management interactions (see Toch, 2003), could command the foci of numerous studies. Beyond that, we contend that if the policy of community-oriented policing is to fulfil its potential in reducing crime and neighbourhood fear and enhancing subjective feelings of safety (Morash & Ford, 2003), then its mechanics deserve closer attention by social psychologists of language and discourse. Community-oriented policing works from the premise that law enforcement and civilians work in partnership with each other. Interestingly, what constitutes the philosophy and underlying ideology of so-called community-oriented policing varies even across the samples highlighted in this chapter. For instance, the process in the PRC encourages prevention of crime by locating family or clan members who are involved in it and appealing to moral education to remedy the situation. In this way, the police are supplementary to and facilitative of moral education to punish violators more informally (Wong, 2001). Yet whatever model of community-oriented policing is adopted, unhelpful, naïve and inaccurate images where they exist – from *both* sides of this intergroup context – are extremely counterproductive to developing such partnerships. In other words, the microscopy of analysing particularistic discourses and documenting interactional self-reports can serve in the valued direction of helping people live their everyday lives with a minimal need to combat violence, abuse, corruption and (nowadays, technological) exploitation.

notes

1. We are extremely grateful to Cindy Gallois for thorough and insightful feedback on earlier drafts of this chapter and to Val McLean and Carrie Ashley for their invaluable assistance.
2. For instance, and besides gender differences, we were interested in whether Americans would report feeling safer as well as perceive police in general more positively (e.g., satisfaction, trust and accommodation) than would our Asian respondents. In addition, we were interested in what differences (if any) would emerge between the USA, Taiwan and the PRC concerning amounts of contact, group identity salience and voicing concerns to police.
3. Results indicated that both American and PRC participants perceived the police to be more accommodating, and trusted them more, than did Taiwanese informants. With regard to obligation to obey the police and satisfaction with and ratings of them, a staircase USA > PRC > Taiwan pattern emerged. Americans (and not surprisingly men more than women) felt overwhelmingly much safer than respondents from either the PRC or Taiwan. Furthermore, females reported more trust in police than did males overall; however, these differences did not extend to include feelings of satisfaction, tendency to obey police, or accommodation. Findings revealed that Americans, and men more than women, had more contact with police than respondents from either the PRC or Taiwan. Additionally, participants reported low-to-moderate levels of contact with police and claimed to witness more than they personally experienced. Police-initiated contact varied staircase-wise across the locations: USA > Taiwan > PRC. The two Asian samples, as well as males in general, considered themselves and the police as belonging to two different social groups to a greater extent than did those in the USA. Finally, it was the PRC participants who felt the most comfortable voicing their concerns to the police should problems have arisen.

   Given the accommodative foci of the present chapter, the precise details of the multivariate findings will be reported elsewhere (as well as comparatively with other cultural contexts such as South Korea, Japan, Louisiana, Canada and Guam); see the first author for details.
4. As a matter of interest, the relevant means in Table 5.2 for evaluating police are rather lower than in previous work in southern California (Giles, Fortman et al., in press); officers are seen as less trustworthy and accommodating, and ratings of them correspondingly lower.
5. In an initial test of the measurement models, all the indicator variables showed relatively high path coefficients from their latent factors in each location. However, a nested models comparison indicated a lack of measurement invariance across the three models. After several measures were dropped (see Table 5.1), measurement invariance between the PRC and USA was achieved ($p = .23$), but not between these locations and Taiwan. For this reason, true

comparisons can be made between the PRC and the USA only. As stated, it appears that the Taiwan data were somewhat idiosyncratic.

6. PRC: $\chi^2 = 86.34$, $p = .001$, CFI = .99, TLI = .99, RMSEA = .057; US: $\chi^2 = 89.08$, $p = .001$, CFI = .99, TLI = .99, RMSEA = .057.

7. $\chi^2 = 117.24$, $p = .006$, CFI = .99, TLI = .99, RMSEA = .045.

references

Al-Khatib, M. (1995). The impact of interlocutor sex on linguistic accommodation: A case study of Jordan radio phone-in programs. *Multilingua, 14*, 133–150.

Azuma, S. (1997). Speech accommodation and Japanese Emperor Hirohito. *Discourse and Society, 8*, 189–202.

Baker, M.A. (1991). Reciprocal accommodation: A model for reducing gender bias in managerial communication. *Journal of Business Communication, 28*, 113–130.

Bell, A. (1984). Language style as audience design. *Language in Society, 13*, 145–204.

Berg, M.E., van den (1986). *Language planning and language use in Taiwan: A study of language choice behavior in public settings*. Taipei: Crane.

Boggs, C. & Giles, H. (1999). 'The canary in the cage': The nonaccommodation cycle in the gendered workplace. *International Journal of Applied Linguistics, 22*, 223–245.

Bourhis, R.Y. (1984). Cross-cultural communication in Montreal: Two field studies since Bill 101. *International Journal of the Sociology of Language, 46*, 33–47.

Bourhis, R.Y., Giles, H. & Lambert, W.E. (1975). Social consequences of accommodating one's style of speech: A cross-national investigation. *International Journal of the Sociology of Language, 6*, 55–72.

Bourhis, R.Y., Roth, S. & MacQueen, G. (1988). Communication in the hospital setting: A survey of medical and everyday language use amongst patients, nurses and doctors. *Social Science and Medicine, 24*, 1–8.

Bradac, J.J., Mulac, A. & House, A. (1988). Lexical diversity and magnitude of convergent versus divergent style-shifting: Perceptual and evaluative consequences. *Language and Communication, 8*, 213–228.

Buller, D.B., LePoire, B.A., Aune, R.K. & Eloy, S.V. (1992). Social perceptions as mediators of the effect of speech rate similarity on compliance. *Human Communication Research, 19*, 286–311.

Burleson, B. & J. Greene (Eds.) (2003). *Handbook of communicative and social skills*. Mahwah, NJ: LEA.

Buzzanell, P.M., Burrell, N.A., Stafford, S.R. & Berkowitz, S. (1996). When I call you up and you're not there: Application of Communication Accommodation Theory to telephone answering machine messages. *Western Journal of Communication, 60*, 310–336.

Cao, L. & Hou, C. (2001). A comparison of confidence in the police in China and in the United States. *Journal of Criminal Justice, 29*, 87–100.

Cargile, A.C. & Giles, H. (1996). Intercultural communication training: Review, critique, and a new theoretical framework. In W.B. Gudykunst (Ed.), *Communication yearbook 19* (pp.385–423). Thousand Oaks, CA: Sage.

Coupland, J., Coupland, N., Giles, H. & Henwood, K. (1988). Accommodating the elderly: Invoking and extending a theory. *Language in Society, 17*, 1–41.

Coupland, N. (1984). Accommodation at work: Some phonological data and their implications. *International Journal of the Sociology of Language, 46*, 49–70.

Coupland, N., Coupland, J. & Giles, H. (1991). *Language, the elderly and society*. Oxford: Blackwell.

Coupland, N. & Giles, H. (Eds.) (1988). Communication acommodation: Recent advances. *Language and Communication, 8 (3 & 4)*.

Coupland, N. & Jaworski, A. (1997). Relevance, accommodation, and conversation: Modeling the social dimension of communication. *Multilingua, 16*, 235–258.

Cox, T.C. & White, M.F. (1988). Traffic citations and student attitudes toward the police: An examination of selected interaction dynamics. *Journal of Police Science and Administration, 16*, 105–121.

Crook, C.W. & Booth, R. (1997). Building rapport in electronic mail using Accommodation Theory. *Advances Management Journal, 62*, 4–14.

Derbyshire, R. (1968). Children's perception of the police: A comparative study of attitudes and attitude change. *Journal of Criminal Law, 59*, 183–190.

Eschholz, S., Sims Blackwell, B., Gertz, M. & Chiricos, T. (2002). Race and attitudes toward the police, assessing the effects of watching 'reality' police programs. *Journal of Criminal Justice, 30*, 327–341.

Fitzpatrick, M.A., Mulac, A. & Dindia, K. (1995). Gender-preferential language use in spouse and stranger interaction. *Journal of Language and Social Psychology, 14*, 18–39.

Fox, S.A., Giles, H., Orbe, M.P. & Bourhis, R.Y. (2000). Interability communication: Theoretical perspectives. In D. Braithewaite & T. Thompson (Eds.), *Handbook of communication and people with disabilities: Research and application* (pp.193–222). Mahwah, NJ: Erlbaum.

Gallois, C., Franklyn-Stokes, A., Giles, H. & Coupland, N. (1988). Communication accommodation in intercultural encounters. In Y.Y. Kim & W.B. Gudykunst (Eds.), *Theories in intercultural communication* (pp. 157–185). Newbury Park, CA: Sage.

Gallois, C., Ogay, T. & Giles, H. (2005). Communication accommodation theory: A look back and a look ahead. In W. Gudykunst (Ed.), *Theorizing about intercultural communication* (pp.121–148). Thousand Oaks, CA: Sage.

Gardner, M.J. & Jones, E. (1999). Problematic communication in the workplace: Beliefs of superiors and subordinates. *International Journal of Applied Linguistics, 9*, 185–206.

Giles, H. (1973). Accent mobility: A model and some data. *Anthropological Linguistics, 15*, 87–109.

Giles, H. (1978). Linguistic differentiation between ethnic groups. In H. Tajfel (Ed.), *Differentiation between social groups* (pp.361–393). London: Academic Press.

Giles, H. (Ed.) (1984). The dynamics of speech accommodation. *International Journal of the Sociology of Language, 46*.

Giles, H. (Ed.) (2002). *Law enforcement, communication and community*. Amsterdam: John Benjamins.

Giles, H., Coupland, J. & Coupland, N. (1991). Accommodation theory: Communication, context, and consequence. In H. Giles, J. Coupland & N. Coupland (Eds.), *Contexts of accommodation: Developments in applied sociolinguistics* (pp.1–68). New York: Cambridge University Press.

Giles, H., Fortman, J., Dailey, R., Barker, V., Hajek, C., Anderson, M.C. & Rule, N. (2006). Communication accommodation: Law enforcement and the public. In R.M. Dailey & B.A. Le Poire (Eds.), *Interpersonal communication matters: Family, health, and community relations* (pp. 241–270). New York: Peter Lang.

Giles, H., McCann, R.M., Ota, H. & Noels, K.A. (2002). Challenging intergenerational stereotypes across Eastern and Western cultures. In M.S. Kaplan, N.Z. Henkin & A.T. Kusano (Eds.), *Linking lifetimes: A global view of intergenerational exchange* (pp.13–28). Honolulu: University Press of America, Inc.

Giles, H. & Noels, K. (1998). Communication accommodation in intercultural encounters. In J. Martin, T. Nakayama & L. Flores (Eds.), *Readings in cultural contexts* (pp.139–149). Mountain View, CA: Mayfield.

Giles, H. & Ogay, T. (in press). Communication accommodation theory. In B. Whalen & W. Samter (Eds.), *Explaining communication: Contemporary theories and exemplars*. Mahwah, NJ: Erlbaum.

Giles, H. & Wadleigh, P.M. (1999). Accommodating nonverbally. In L.K. Guerrero, J.A. DeVito & M.L. Hecht (Eds.), *The nonverbal communication reader: Classic and contemporary readings* (2nd ed., pp.425–436). Prospect Heights, IL: Waveland Press.

Giles, H., Willemyns, M., Gallois C. & Anderson, M.C. (in press). Accommodating a new frontier: The context of law enforcement. In K. Fielder (Ed.), *Social communication*. New York: Psychology Press.

Giles, H. & Williams, A. (1994). Patronizing the young: Forms and evaluations. *International Journal of Aging and Human Development, 39*, 33–53.

Giles, H., Zwang-Weissman, Y. & Hajek, C. (2004). Patronizing and policing elderly people. *Psychological Reports, 95*, 754–756.

Gilley, B. (1996, July). Rough justice. *Far Eastern Economic Review*, 22–24.

Gregory, S.W. & Webster, S. (1996). A nonverbal signal in voices of interview partners effectively predicts communication accommodation and social status predictions. *Journal of Personality and Social Psychology, 70*, 1231–1240.

Griffiths, C.T. & Winfree, L.T. Jr. (1982). Attitudes toward the police – a comparison of Canadian and American adolescents. *International Journal of Comparative and Applied Criminal Justice, 6*, 128–141.

Gudykunst, W.B. (1995). Anxiety/uncertainty management (AUM) theory: Current status. In R.L. Wiseman (Ed.), *Intercultural communication theory* (pp.8–58). Thousand Oaks, CA: Sage Publications.

Hajek, J., Giles, H., Barker, V., Louw-Potgieter, Pecchioni, L., Makoni, S. & Myers, P. (2006). Communicative dynamics of police–civilian encounters: African and American interethnic data. *Journal of Intercultural Communication Research, 35*, 161–182.

Hannah, A. & Murachver, T. (1999). Gender and conversational style as predictors of conversational behavior. *Journal of Language and Social Psychology, 18*, 153–174.

Harwood, J. (2000). Communicative predictors of solidarity in the grandchild–grandparent relationship. *Journal of Social and Personal Relationships, 17*, 743–766.

Harwood, J. & Giles, H. (Eds.) (2005). *Intergroup communication: Multiple perspectives*. Berlin & New York: Peter Lang.

Harwood, J., Hewstone, M., Paolini, S. & Voci, A. (2005). Grandparent–grandchild contact and attitudes toward older adults: Moderator and mediator effects. *Personality and Social Psychology Bulletin, 31*, 393–406.

Hennigan, K., Maxson, C., Sloane, D. & Ranney, M. (2002). Community views on crime and policing: Survey mode effects on bias in community services. *Justice Quarterly, 19*, 565–587.

Hogg, M.A., D'Agata, P. & Abrams, D. (1989). Ethnolinguistic betrayal and speaker evaluations across Italian Australians. *Genetic, Social, and General Psychology Monographs, 115*, 155–181.

Hopkins, N. & Hewstone, M. (1992). Police–schools liaison and young people's image of the police: An intervention evaluation. *British Journal of Psychology, 83*, 203–221.

Howard, C., Tuffin, K. & Stephens, C. (2000). Unspeakable emotion: A discursive analysis of police talk about reactions to trauma. *Journal of Language and Social Psychology, 19*, 295–314.

Huo, Y.J. & Tyler, T.R. (2000). *How different ethnic groups react to legal authority.* San Francisco: Public Policy Institute of California.

Jones-Brown, D. (2000). Debunking the myth of officer friendly: How African American males experience community policing. *Journal of Contemporary Criminal Justice, 16*, 209–229.

Judicial Reform Foundation (1999, August 15). Jing cha ji guan bu shou ren xing lai, ren min zhi you zi qiu dou fu? [The police are not trustworthy and people can only rely on themselves for their own safety?] [Electronic version]. *Judicial Reformed Foundation Magazine, 37*. Retrieved January 17, 2004, from www.jrf.org.tw/mag/mag_02s2.asp?SN=141

Judicial Reform Foundation (2002, February, 15). Cheng bai guan jian? Jing cha su zhi ti sheng de po que xing [The key to success: Urgent needs to improve quality of the police]. *Judicial Reform Foundation Magazine, 37*. Retrieved January 17, 2004, from www.jrf.org.tw/mag/mag_02s2.asp?SN=795

Kinkley, J.C. (1993). Chinese crime fiction. *Society*, 51–62.

Klockars, C.B. (1985). *The idea of police.* Beverly Hills, CA: Sage.

Klyman, F.I. & Kruckenberg, J. (1974). A methodology for assessing citizen perceptions of police. *Journal of Criminal Justice, 2*, 219–233.

Langan, P.A., Greenfeld, L.A., Smith, S.K., Durose, M.R. & Levin, D.J. (2001). *Contact between police and the public.* Washington, DC: Bureau of Justice Statistics.

Lawrence, R.G. (2000). *The politics of force: Media and the construction of police brutality.* Berkeley, CA: University of California Press.

Lawson, S. & Sachdev, I. (2000). Code-switching in Tunisia: Attitudinal and behavioral dimensions. *Journal of Pragmatics, 32*, 1343–1361.

Legislative Branch Commissioners (2002). *China's criminal justice system roundtable before the congressional-executive commission on China.* Washington, DC: US Government Printing Office.

Levin, H. & Lin, T. (1988). An accommodating witness. *Language and Communication, 8*, 195–198.

Lin, M-C. & Harwood, J. (2003). Accommodation predictors of grandparent–grandchild relational solidarity in Taiwan. *Journal of Social and Personal Relationships, 20*, 537–563.

Lin, Q-T. (2001). *Ti sheng jing zheng fu wu pin zhi ju ti xing wei zhi tan tao: Fu wu daoxing yu jing min he zuo* [In-depth analysis of improving police services:

A customer approach and cooperation between the public and the police]. Unpublished master's thesis, University of Yuan Zhi, Taipei, Taiwan.

Littlejohn, S.W. & Foss, K.A. (2005). *Theories of human communication* (8th ed.). Belmont, CA: Wadsworth.

Mastrofski, S. (1983). The police and noncrime services. In G. Whitaker & C. Phillips (Eds.), *Evaluating the performance of crime and criminal justice agencies* (pp.33–61). Beverly Hills, CA: Sage.

McCluskey, J.D. (2003). *Police requests for compliance: Coercive and procedurally just tactics.* New York: LFB Scholarly Publishing LLC.

Meyerhoff, M. (1998). Accommodating your data: The use and misuse of accommodation theory in sociolinguistics. *Language and Communication, 18,* 205–225.

Molloy, J. & Giles, H. (2002). Communication, language, and law enforcement: An intergroup communication approach. In P. Glenn, C. LeBaron & J. Mandelbaum (Eds.), *Studies in language and social interaction* (pp.327–340). Mahwah, NJ: Erlbaum.

Morash, M. & Ford, J.K. (Eds.) (2003). *The move to community policing: Making change happen.* Thousand Oaks, CA: Sage.

National Research Council (2004). *Fairness and effectiveness in policing: The evidence.* Committee to Review Research on Police Policy and Practices. W. Skogan & K. Frydl (Eds.), Committee on Law and Justice, Division of Behavioral and Social Sciences and Education. Washington, DC: National Academic Press.

Niederhoffer, K.G. & Pennebaker, J.W. (2002). Linguistic style matching in social interaction. *Journal of Language and Social Psychology, 21,* 337–306.

Oberle, A. (2004). Coalition bring positive image to CA law enforcement. *PORAC Law Enforcement News, 36,* 26–27.

Olsen, K. (2005). School of law. *Teaching Tolerance,* Spring, 40–45.

Parker, K., Onyekwuluje, A. & Murty, K. (1995). African Americans' attitudes toward the local police: A multivariate analysis. *Journal of Black Studies, 25,* 396.

Paulson, A. (2001). Reviled no more, N.Y.P.D. is getting 'hugs' from the public. *Christian Science Monitor, 93,* 1.

Preston, D.R. (1981). The ethnography of TESOL. *TESOL Quarterly, 15,* 105–116.

Prine, R.K., Ballard, C. & Robinson, D.M. (2001). Perceptions of community policing in a small town. *American Journal of Criminal Justice, 25(2),* 211–221.

Republic of China Ministry of the Interior. (2003). *Guo min dui mu qian she hui feng qi, lun li dao de yu zhi an zhuang kuang man yi qing xing ji ren wei zheng fu ying gai jia qiang ban li de gai shan gong zuo diao cha jie guo zhai yao fen xi* [Analysis of people's attitudes towards and satisfaction with current morality and safety in Taiwanese society and their suggestions to the government]. Taipei, Taiwan.

Roberg, R., Novak, K. & Cordner, G. (2005). *Police and society* (3rd ed.). Los Angeles: Roxbury.

Ross, J.I. (2000). Making news of police violence: A comparative study of Toronto and New York City. Westport, CT: Praeger.

Ross, S. & Shortreed, I.M. (1990). Japanese foreigner talk: Convergence or divergence? *Journal of Asian Pacific Communication, 1,* 135–145.

Sachdev, I. & Giles, H. (2004). Bilingual speech accommodation. In T.K. Bhatia (Ed.), *Handbook of bilingualism* (pp.353–388). Oxford: Blackwell.

Sieburg, E. (1976). Confirming and disconfirming organizational communication. In J.L. Owen, P.A. Paige & G.I. Zimmerman (Eds.), *Communication in organizations* (pp.129–149). St Paul, MN: West.

Smith, P.E. & Hawkins, R.O. (1973). Victimization, types of citizen–police contacts, and attitudes toward the police. *Law and Society Review, 8,* 135–152.

Sparks, B. & Callan, V.J. (1992). Communication and the service encounter: The value of convergence. *International Journal of Hospitality Management, 11,* 213–224.

Spitzberg, B.H. & Cupach, W.R. (Eds.) (1984). *Interpersonal communication competence.* Newbury Park, CA: Sage.

Street, R.L., Jr. (1982). Evaluation of noncontent speech accommodation. *Language and Communication, 2,* 13–31.

Street, R.L. & Giles, H. (1982). Speech Accommodation Theory: A social cognitive approach to language and speech behavior. In M.E. Roloff & C.R. Berger (Eds.), *Social cognition and communication* (pp.193–226). Beverly Hills, CA: Sage.

Tajfel, H. & Turner, J.C. (1986). The social identity theory of intergroup relations. In W. Austin & S. Worchel (Eds.), *Psychology of intergroup relations* (2nd ed., pp.7–17). Chicago: Nelson Hall.

Taylor, T., Turner, K., Esbensen, F. & Winfree, L. (2001). Coppin' an attitude – Attitudinal differences among juveniles toward police. *Journal of Criminal Justice, 29,* 295–305.

Thakerar, J.N., Giles, H. & Cheshire, J. (1982). Psychological and linguistic parameters of speech accommodation theory. In C. Fraser & K.R. Scherer (Eds.), *Advances in the social psychology of language* (pp.205–255). Cambridge: Cambridge University Press.

Thomson, R., Murachver, T. & Green, J. (2001). Where is the gender in gendered language? *Psychological Science, 12,* 171–175.

Toch, H. (2003). *Stress in policing.* Washington DC: American Psychological Association.

Tomsha, L. & Hernandez, R. (2007). Communication accommodation theory. In R. West & L.H. Turner (Eds), *Introducing communication theory: Analysis and application* (3rd ed.). New York: McGraw-Hill.

Tong, Y-Y., Hong, Y-Y., Lee, S-L. & Chiu, C-Y. (1999). Language use as a carrier of social identity. *International Journal of Intercultural Relations, 23,* 281–296.

Tracy, K. & Haspel, K. (2004). Language and social interaction: Its institutional identity, intellectual landscape, and discipline-shifting agenda. *Journal of Communication, 54,* 788–816.

Tyler, T.R. (2001). Public trust and confidence in legal authorities: What do majority and minority group members want from the law and legal institutions? *Behavioral Sciences and the Law, 19,* 215–235.

Tyler, T.R. & Huo, Y. (2002). *Trust in the law.* New York: Russell Sage.

Van den Bulck, J. (1998). Sideshow Bobby: Images of the police in Flemish film and television. *Public Voices, 4,* 1–8.

Watson, B. & Gallois, C. (1999). Communication accommodation between patients and health professionals: Themes and strategies in satisfying and unsatisfying encounters. *International Journal of Applied Linguistics, 9,* 167–183.

White, M.F. & Menke, B.A. (1982). Assessing the mood of the public toward the police: Some conceptual issues. *Criminal Justice, 10,* 211–230.

Wiemann, J. (1977). A model of communicative competence. *Human Research Communication, 3*, 195–213.

Williams, A., Gallois, C. & Pittam, J. (Eds.) (1999). Communication acommodation in intergroup miscommunication and problematic talk. *International Journal of Applied Linguistics, 9*, 149–245.

Williams, A. & Giles, H. (1996). Intergenerational conversations: Young adults' retrospective accounts. *Human Communication Research, 23*, 220–250.

Williams, A. & Nussbaum, J. F. (2001). *Intergenerational communication across the lifespan*. Mahwah, NJ: Erlbaum.

Wong, K.C. (2001). Community policing in China: Philosophy, law and practice. *International Journal of the Sociology of Law, 29*, 127–147.

Worrel, J.L. (1999). Public perceptions of police efficacy and image: The 'fuzziness' of support for the police. *American Journal of Criminal Justice, 24*, 47–66.

Wortley, S. (1996). Justice for all? Race and perceptions of bias in the Ontario criminal justice system: A Toronto survey. *Canadian Journal of Criminology, 38*, 49–467.

Yates, D.L. & Pillai, V.K. (1996). Attitude toward community policing: A causal analysis. *The Social Science Journal, 33*, 193–209.

Yu, Y-X. (1992). *Jing cha fu wu pin zhi zhi shi zheng yan jiu: Yi Taipei shi zheng fu jing cha ju pai chu suo wei li* [An empirical study on police services: A case analysis using the police department of Taipei government as an example]. Unpublished master's thesis, National Taipei University, Taipei, Taiwan.

Zhang, Y.B., Lin, M-C., Nonaka, A. & Beom, K. (2005). Harmony, hierarchy and conservatism: A cross-cultural comparison of Confucian values in China, Korea, Japan, and Taiwan. *Communication Research Reports, 22*, 107–115.

6
discursive psychology: mind and reality in practice

jonathan potter and alexa hepburn

This chapter will introduce the perspective of discursive psychology. It will introduce its basic theoretical and methodological features, and then flesh them out using a series of recent studies of a child protection helpline. Discursive psychology will be used to make sense of a range of features of what happens on the helpline. In turn, the analysis of the helpline will be used to illuminate the nature of discursive psychology (henceforth DP).

DP is a perspective that starts with the psychological phenomena as things that are constructed, attended to, and understood in interaction. Its focus is on the ways descriptions can implicate psychological matters, on the ways psychological states are displayed in talk, and on the way people are responded to as upset, devious, knowledgeable or whatever. It thus starts with a view of psychology that is fundamentally social, relational and interactional. It is not just psychology as it appears *in* interaction; rather, it understands much of our psychological language, and broader 'mental practices', as organized *for* action and interaction. It is a specifically *discursive* psychology because discourse – talk and texts – is the primary medium for social action.

Most research in modern cognitive and social psychology takes as its central topic mental entities, representations or broad processing systems. Entities such as scripts, schemata, attitudes, attention, theory of mind, perception, memory, and attribution heuristics figure large in such research. DP is not a direct counter to such research (although, as we will show, it raises a range of questions with how such things are theorized and operationalized). Its aim is rather different. Rather than trying to get inside people's heads to get at these entities the focus is on discourse: talk and texts in social practices. It looks for psychology in a completely different place.

Take the central and traditional social-psychological notion of attitudes for example. Rather than considering attitudes as mental entities that drive behaviour (as they are conceptualized in social cognition, such as in Ajzen's, 1991, well-known theory of planned behaviour), in DP they are respecified in terms of a broader concern with the *construction* of evaluations and what evaluations are used to *do*. For instance, in DP research has examined the way food evaluations figure as part of the activity of complimenting the cook, as inducements to an adolescent girl to eat, or as the building blocks of a complaint about child abuse (Wiggins & Hepburn, in press; Wiggins & Potter, 2003). Conversely, DP work has studied how the *absence* of evaluation, and specifically the absence of an individual's attitude, is constructed, such as when making negative comments about minority groups (Potter & Wetherell, 1988; Wetherell & Potter, 1992). So in environments where issues of prejudice and dis- crimination are live it can be important *not* to have a (negative) attitude, but merely to be objectively describing the world (including any putative negative characteristics of minority groups). Indeed, in DP the whole distinction between what is subjective (psychological) and objective (real, in the world) is seen as something that is constructed, attended to and reworked in discourse (Edwards, in press; Potter, 1996).

Put briefly, DP treats discourse as having three key characteristics. First, it is *action-oriented*. Discourse is recognized to be primarily a practical medium and the primary medium for action. Second it is *situated*. It is organized sequentially, such that the primary environment for what is said is, typically, what was said just previously. What is said sets up, but does not determine, what will be said immediately following it. It is situated institutionally in the sense that it is embedded in, and often constitutive of, practices such as news interviews, relationship conflicts or air traffic control instructions. It is situated rhetorically in the sense that constructions may be oriented to counter relevant alternatives. Third, it is both *constructed* and *constructive*. It is *constructed* in the sense that discourse is put together from different elements such as words, categories, commonplaces, interpretative repertoires and other elements. It is *constructive* in the sense that versions of the world, of actions and events, of mental life and furniture are put together and stabilized in talk.

Methodologically, discursive psychology uses careful and systemic analysis of discourse to reveal phenomena of this kind. DP is a package – its topic, discourse, requires an analytic approach that can do justice to the nature of discourse. Discourse works neither in the manner of a mechanical system of weights and pulleys, nor in the manner of a linguistic grammar book with formal rules. The traditional psychological tools of experiment and survey are not tuned for this job. In this chapter we will not say much about methodological issues, although they may become apparent as we describe the development of research. For more elaborate coverage of methodological issues in DP see Potter (2003a,b, 2004) and Wood and Kroger (2000). But first some context and history.

a brief history of discursive psychology

Discursive psychology emerged out of the specific strand of discourse analysis that developed in social psychology in the 1980s. This in turn had its somewhat convoluted roots in the sociology of scientific knowledge, post-structuralism, linguistic philosophy, ethnomethodology and conversation analysis. Let us briefly sketch the outlines of this early work, starting with Potter and Wetherell (1987) which is probably the work that did most to establish the power and nature of a discourse approach to psychological issues.

This book laid out a discourse analytic approach to the psychological topics familiar from traditional social psychology textbooks, such as attitudes, accounts, the self, categories and representations. In each case the focus was on the way these entities figured in interaction. For example, it drew on Harvey Sacks' (1992) work on membership categories to offer a critique of the standard treatment of categories as mental entities that organize (and distort) perception. Thus, this book offers one of the first attempts to apply conversation analysis to a social psychological topic in its critical consideration of the literature on accounts.

One of the central analytic notions of Potter and Wetherell (1987) was that of interpretative repertoires; that is, interrelated sets of terms, used with some stylistic coherence and often organized around particular tropes or metaphors. This notion comes from Gilbert and Mulkay's (1984) study of the different repertoires that scientists use to construct their social world when they are arguing with one another. It was developed in Wetherell and Potter (1992), which studied the way Pakeha New Zealanders constructed versions of social conflict and social organizations to legitimate particular versions of relations between groups. Much of the interest was in ideological questions of how the organization of accounts, and the resources used in those accounts, could be used to help understand the reproduction of broad patterns of inequality and privilege.

This work also drew on Billig's (1986[1987]) rhetorical psychological notions, including the idea of a rhetorical commonplace. Billig suggested that for any culture at any time in history there will be certain phrases or sayings that have a familiar or taken-for-granted quality. Wetherell and Potter (1992) showed how Pakeha New Zealanders draw on a contradictory weave of commonplaces to construct arguments against social change and critique. Billig (1992) also used the notions of rhetorical commonplaces and interpretative repertoires in his study of the way ordinary British people talk about the Royal Family. He showed the way these linguistic resources were fundamental for reproducing certain assumptions about nationality, privilege, equality and change. He suggested that participants are performing 'acts of settlement' in their talk, settling 'ordinary people down into their place within the imagined national community' (Billig, 1992, p.22). For an overview of these major early studies see Hepburn (2003, ch.7).

While these studies are commonly described as discourse *analysis* Edwards and Potter (1992) laid out the basics of a more distinctive discursive *psychology*. Part of the reason for this naming was simply to provide a more clear-cut differentiation from the confusing range of approaches dubbed discourse analysis from across the social sciences (see Jaworski & Coupland, 1999; Wetherell et al., 2001). *Discursive Psychology* was distinctive in applying ideas from discourse analysis specifically to psychological issues. It took as its topic memory and attribution and offered a respecification of both topics in terms of discourse practices. Rather than considering them as mental entities and processes, it treated remembering in terms of situated descriptions and attribution in terms of the way descriptions are organized to manage speaker accountability and to assign blame. A central feature of the work involved taking research in memory and attribution which either used natural interaction or addressed linguistic issues, and showing how its conclusions were distorted by its failure to address the practical nature of language use.

This strand of work was developed more fully in two subsequent works. Potter (1996) offered a systematic rethink of constructionism. This was organized around a consideration of the way descriptions are constructed from different resources (words, membership categories, commonplaces, interpretative repertoires, etc.) and the way these descriptions are organized to perform particular actions. Moreover, it focused on the procedures through which versions of events and actions are produced as literal, credible and independent of the speaker; that is, how they manage the 'dilemma of stake' (Edwards & Potter, 1992) that means all discourse can potentially be treated as motivated or interested in some way.

Edwards (1997) is the other major work. It too considered the role of descriptions. However, its particular focus was on the way descriptions of mental life (categories, emotions, and so on) in all their different forms become parts of particular practices. For example, Edwards noted that when describing actions there are a range of different options. One form of description presents them as tied to the speaker and her or his dispositions. Yet another common form of description presents actions as standard or regular. Both are often highly indirect. Edwards called such descriptions 'script formulations' (1994, 1997). A key feature of such descriptions is that they manage accountability (or 'attribution' in traditional social psychological language). Presenting an action as scripted presents it as not requiring an explanation making reference to the speaker; however, if an action is presented as deviating from script in some way this can be produced as dispositional, and therefore to be explained by reference to the actor. Moreover, Edwards argued that cognitive psychology approaches that look for mental scripts (as frames for information processing) can easily miss the performative nature of the script talk that appears in research materials.

It is notable that as DP developed out of a rather broader discourse analytic approach, there has been much less of an emphasis on the analysis of qualitative interviews. Although such work can still be pertinent and address important issues (Edwards, 2003; Lawes, 1999; Wetherell & Edley, 1999), its limitations have been increasingly apparent (Potter & Hepburn, 2005). At the same time, if records of natural interaction can be analysed so effectively, the reasons for using a research procedure which embodies a range of troubles become less telling.

the disciplinary context of discursive psychology

It is worth briefly distinguishing DP from approaches with which it shares some similarities and differences. In particular, we will consider sociolinguistics, social psychology of language and conversation analysis (henceforth CA). Let us start with sociolinguistics and the social psychology of language. One simple way of separating these approaches is to consider the different ways that they conceptualize language. In much sociolinguistics language appears as a dependent variable. Some feature of language, such as lexical choice or accent, is associated with a variable of interest, such as gender, social groups, status, class or something similar. Social psychology also often treats features of language as dependent variables. For example, work in the 'communication accommodation' tradition has studied the way speakers' accents modify according to the group membership of the addressee, modelling this according to a social psychological process model (see Watson & Gallois, and Giles et al., this volume). Work in both traditions often assumes a telemental view of language, in which it provides a medium for transferring thoughts from one mind to another (Harris, 1988), and such work often assumes that words are associated with mentally encoded categories or concepts.

Discursive psychology does not start out by rejecting such views (although there are pertinent philosophical and sociological critiques – Wittgenstein, 1953; Coulter, 2005). Rather, it brackets issues of cognitive process and reference off, so that it can start somewhere different. Its focus is squarely on language *use* – hence *discursive* psychology rather than psychology *of language* or something similar. In particular, its focus is on discourse practices that are involved in psychological orientations and constructions, or draw on psychological terms. It is important to note, however, that DP provides a sideways respecification and reworking of the whole domain of the psychological, which simultaneously expands it and shrinks it, and questions the very idea that there is a clearly bounded class of psychological terms. For extended overviews of the difference between DP and sociolinguistics see Potter & Edwards (2001a); and for DP and social psychology of language see Edwards & Potter (1993), Potter & Edwards (2001b), and the debate between Schmid & Fiedler (1999) and Edwards & Potter (1999).

DP's relation to CA is a complex one. CA currently offers the most developed and sophisticated approach available to what would traditionally have been called linguistic performance. DP draws heavily on both the analytic tradition of CA and its specific findings. Sacks' (1992) foundational work on CA also offers a sophisticated approach to psychological explanations and language (see Potter & te Molder, 2005, for overview). However, there are two significant areas where there is a difference in emphasis and even potential tension.

First, DP has built a systematic approach to relating the construction of descriptions to the actions that they are involved in. For example, it has studied the way constructions of emotions such as anger in relationship counselling can be part of assigning problems to individuals, nominating them as the party requiring change (Edwards, 1995, 1997). Note that such constructions are mutually inferential – people construct versions of their own thoughts, memories, feelings and so on as part of establishing versions of events or settings and vice versa. This constructionist theme is much less central in CA compared to DP. Moreover, DP draws on the rhetorical tradition of Billig (1996). This highlights the way descriptions are assembled in ways that counter actual or potential alternatives versions. DP is distinct from other constructionist traditions in its focus on the business of constructing versions in talk and texts, and its emphasis on the way constructions are parts of situated practices.

Second, DP is a systematically non-cognitive approach. That is, it brackets off questions about the existence (or not) of cognitive entities and processes, whether they are part of one of the range of *technical* perspectives that make up modern psychology or are part of the *lay* ontologies of mind that are embedded in particular cultures. Its focus is squarely on cognitive entities as they are constructed in and for public, interactional practices. Note that this includes studying the way practices such as therapy or parenting may draw upon basic cognitivist or psychological distinctions, such as between surface and depth, or between public and private. For the most part, CA too has been a non-cognitivist enterprise. However, CA researchers have a more ambivalent approach to cognition, sometimes attempting to connect interactional phenomena to what they understand as cognitive phenomena (for an overview of these issues see papers in te Molder & Potter, 2005, and the debate between Coulter, 1999, and Potter & Edwards, 2003).

So far we have overviewed general features of DP. We now want to go on and illustrate its operation through specific analyses of particular topics.

discursive psychology and child protection

We will base our discussion on a programme of work conducted with the UK NSPCC (National Society for the Prevention of Cruelty to Children). We will focus in particular on studies that can be used to show the contrasting treatment offered to classic psychological concepts: *cognition* (knowledge, attitude), *perception*, and *emotion*. The aim in each case will be to show how a very different understanding is provided by starting with how these things arise in discourse as practical issues to be addressed by participants. Note that we have deliberately selected notions such as emotion and perception that are often treated as prior to, and separate from, what would traditionally be understood as linguistic phenomena. These are 'hard cases' for an approach that focuses on talk and text.

The NSPCC is the major child protection charity in the UK. Central to their work is a 24 hour National Child Protection Helpline that receives several hundred thousand calls each year. This is legally required to pass credible reports of abuse to either social services or the police, whether the caller wishes it or not. The helpline also provides free counselling, information and advice to anyone concerned about a child at risk of ill treatment or abuse, or to children themselves who may be at risk. It is staffed by trained social workers with at least three years field experience of working in child protection; they work under the title Child Protection Officer (henceforth CPO).

Our research is based mainly at the NSPCC's London centre. Calls are highly varied. They come from adults, young people, grandparents, parents and neighbours, from people of different social class and ethnic backgrounds from all over Britain. They can be asking for advice, reporting abuse, or requiring counselling. Issues are varied in severity. Calls average something over 15 minutes although some last for as long as an hour. Where serious abuse is suspected the CPO will follow the call directly with a call to the relevant police force, or, more often, Social Services.

Calls were recorded on minidisk and then digitized for transcription and analysis. All participants to the study consented to their calls being recorded for research and training purposes. CPOs only recorded the call if they were satisfied that informed consent had been given. The calls were transcribed initially by a transcription service. These transcripts were refined using the transcription system developed by Gail Jefferson (Jefferson, 2004) for particular research studies by the second author. Analysis worked with the combination of digitized recording and transcript. The corpus is continually developing but contained more than 250 calls at the time of writing. For more details on methodological, applied or political aspects of the project see Hepburn (2006), and Hepburn and Potter (2003). We will describe further relevant details as we go along.

cognition: knowledge and attitude

Psychologists are often interested in what people know, and what their attitudes are to things. And they have developed a range of more or less sophisticated procedures for testing knowledge and assessing attitudes. For discursive psychologists, in contrast, the starting place is not what people do or do not know and what attitudes they do or do not have, but how knowledge and attitude figure in interaction in particular settings; that is, what kind of things are these for the participants and how are they relevant, or not, to some activities. We will clarify these issues by describing a study of the opening activities in a corpus of the calls (Potter & Hepburn, 2003). Let us emphasize that we have not started with these psychological notions; rather we have started with an attempt to explicate what is going on in the interaction.

For this analysis we worked initially with a corpus of 40 call openings. These were refined from the full collection because they included the core NSPCC practice of reporting abuse. We eliminated calls asking for counselling, offering to donate money, and passing information between different NSPCC sites, and focused only on callers ringing about suspected abuse to a third party.

There is a lot of complexity in the early actions performed in calls; we will focus on an element we have called a C-construction. C-constructions often involve what might loosely be called 'expressions of concern' (hence C-construction). Let us start with an example to help make sense of what they are doing and how they relate to these questions of knowledge and attitude. The following extract comes from the start of a call reporting abuse – the C-constructions are arrowed. The ethics exchange has been removed to save space. The transcription conventions are provided in the Appendix of this volume.

extract 1: LB neighbour concern

```
01              ((phone rings))
02    CPO:      Hello NSPCC Helpline can I help you:?
03    Caller:   Good after[ noon >I      won]der if y'
04    CPO:                 [((clears throat))]
05              could< .hhh
06    CPO:      [ Ye:s  certainly:,  ]
07    Caller:   [I'm concerned about-]                    ←1
08              (0.2)
09    CPO:      Yeh,
10              (0.2)
11              .h
12    Caller:   about a child that lives next
13              door to me.
14    CPO:      Tk.h ri::ght, could- before you go on
15              ((ethics exchange))
16    CPO:      ↑o↓kay: fine yeh go on:, sorry to stop you,
17    Caller:   Yeah I'm- I'm concerned about °h° (0.2)    ←2
18              my next door neighbours an they got a
19              little girl about six. an she's
20              always cry:in',
21              (0.2)
22              .Hh
23    CPO:      R[i:ght,]
24    Caller:   [I  can] hear them through the wa:ll now
25              an mum's shoutin at 'er like anything.
26              (0.7)
27              Tk 'I don't want to see you get away from
28              me:,' an (0.3) °.hh° an I mean it's
29              really loud.=huh
30              (0.3)
31    CPO:      Ri::ght.
```

```
32  Caller:  I mean I didn' 'ave a too brilliant
33           upbringin so I w'd know what it's li:ke
34           so. Hh
35           (0.4)
36  CPO:     Ye- ri:ght yeah:=an this: is: something
37           that you've >been worried about for a<
38           whi:le [have you?]
39  Caller:         [It has  ] yes I've got a friend
40           who works in child protection and she's
41           told me to ri- if I'm worried, ring in.
```

We will start with a number of observations about this extract.

First note that at line 14 the CPS says 'before you go on', thereby treating the caller as having more to say and being about to go on to say it. This directly follows the first C-construction and so treats it as incomplete. The CPO's 'sorry to stop you' (line 16) treats the caller as having been stopped from something. Second, note the CPO's 'right' on 14 and again on line 23. Of particular interest for us is what these turns are *not* doing. They are not assessments of the prior turn, nor are they moves to new business. They are simply acknowledgement tokens (Schegloff, 1982). Taken together, these things show that the CPO is treating the C-construction as the *start* of something rather than something that is complete.

The third point to note is that after the intrusion of the ethics exchange the caller resumes with a further C-construction. This suggests that the C-construction is structurally important for the early activities of the call. After the intrusion the activities are restarted with the C-construction. The fourth point to note is that the caller continues after the CPO's acknowledgement token (line 23) with a range of descriptions that suggest violence and abuse, and attend to his knowledge of events and motive for calling.

Let us try and specify more precisely what the C-constructions are doing, and therefore why they are important for the unfolding of the call.

1. C-constructions are prefacing moves. As we have noted, C-constructions are hearably incomplete. They are treated by both caller and CPO as elements of talk that project a possibly extended set of turns. The CPO's acknowledgement tokens treat these turns as, at least potentially, appropriate to the institutionally relevant issues.

2. C-constructions project collaborative unpacking of the abuse description. C-constructions project collaborative unpacking by not starting with a definitive claim about the status of the abuse. Instead, they operate by invoking a concern (or similar 'psychological' item), which can be worked up as more (or less) definitive in the course of conversation with the CPO. The caller starts with a stance that is open with respect to what actions the NSPCC will respond with.

3. C-constructions display the caller's (appropriate) stance. C-constructions display the caller's 'attitude' toward the object of the call, typically some kind of abuse. The topic is treated as serious, potentially damaging or upsetting. Conversely, and relevantly here, this object is not treated as something that the caller feels good about, is entertained by, or gets pleasure or sexual excitement from. The C-construction is the caller's first opportunity to establish appropriate motivations for making the call.

4. C-constructions manage knowledge asymmetry. Constructions orient to, and manage, a basic asymmetry. The caller is treated by both parties as knowing about the particular events and actions that they are calling about. The CPO is treated by both parties as knowing about the procedures of child protection work, the policies of the NSPCC, and what reports should be acted on. This is similar to the situation in medical consultations where patients are treated as knowing about their particular symptoms and doctors are treated as knowing about medicine (Gill, 1998). The C-construction is a terrific way of managing the potential difficulties that the asymmetry throws up. In projecting the unpacking of concerns the caller allows the child protection status of the report to be decided by the CPO. In doing acknowledgement tokens (e.g. line 31) and follow-up questions (e.g. lines 36–38) the CPO collaborates in this unpacking.

In terms of attitude and knowledge we can see how both of these things appear as participants' issues and constructions. Attitude is displayed with a C-construction, and it is embedded as a practical part of the interaction. It is locally relevant rather than something that the speaker necessarily carries around as a fully formed mental object. Its production is fitted to the task at hand, of reporting abuse. Likewise with knowledge, differences are a practical issue to be managed in the interaction, and the C-construction is one effective way of doing this. Again, we should not confuse the local construction of, and management of, knowledge with the idea that these participants have particular cognitive states or entities in any simple way. Attitude and knowledge are important, but right here, right now, for the specifics of the interaction.

Note also that the C-construction itself has an interesting mind/reality tension built in. It simultaneously invokes mental or psychological states, and also the states of affairs in the world that generate those states. In effect, it wires in the basic mutual inference feature that is part of DP's topic. Although the word 'concern' is an item that does this job very effectively, in our analysis we found a range of other psychological objects that could be used instead. For example, the word 'worried' could be used to do this job, as could an idiom such as 'I'm going out of my bleedin head' or 'gut feeling' (see Potter, 2005).

We can see in this example the way psychological matters are bound up with the practical and institutional business of the helpline. We need to understand attitude and knowledge as matters of participant concern that are produced and attended to for their local relevance. Likewise C-constructions such as 'I'm a bit concerned' and 'it's a gut feeling' have a subtle institutional job of managing the caller's appropriate stance and the speakers' knowledge asymmetries, as well as projecting collaborative unfolding of the report.

perception: noise and hearing

A central feature of cognitive psychology is that the person is seen to be receiving information through the perceptual system, and this information is then processed. Perception is seen as something fundamental, often bound up with physiology and mechanical processes. Although there has been a tradition of social perception for many years, this has typically been conceptualized in terms of 'higher level' cognitive processes acting on perceptual 'input' when other people or social groups are the 'stimulus material' (Zebrowitz, 1990).

Since the early 1990s there has been a rather different tradition of work that has considered 'perception' as a feature of situated practices. For example, Goodwin and Goodwin have studied situations where airline workers, say, or oceanographers 'see' particular planes or features of the ocean floor (Goodwin, 1995; Goodwin & Goodwin, 1996). Goodwin suggests that 'seeing' involves a range of criteria, and is oriented to particular local practices. Picking up from this alternative tradition, Stokoe and Hepburn (2005) worked with a corpus of the NSPCC materials that included references to noise. Rather like Goodwin's studies of seeing, the aim was to study hearing. In this case, however, the topic was not professional hearers (audiometrists, say, or musicians) but the constructions of sounds in the reporting of abuse.

Let us illustrate this with an example. The extract below starts immediately after the caller has been taken through the ethics exchange.

extract 2: AD neighbour worried

```
01  CPO:     So how can I help yo(h)u °hheh°=
02  Caller:  =Well I'm- (0.6) hhh (0.6) I've
03           just moved into a new hou:se.=
```

```
04                oo a[bout (.) th]ree months ago.
05    CPO:            [ M ↓m ::,  ]
06                (0.4)
07    Caller:    .Hh and they're: (0.3) terraced
08                houses.
09                (0.2)
10    Caller:    With quite thin wall:s. Hh
11                (0.3)
12    CPO:        R:ight.
13    Caller:    And you can hear a lot through the
14                wa:lls: an: what I ↑seem to be
15                hearing quite* a lot of is children
16                screaming and crying.
17    CPO:        R[i : : g h t. ]
18    Caller:      [the neighbour]s.
19                (0.2)
20    CPO:        Ri [ : : g h t.  ]
21    Caller:        [An I'm gettin] a bit c(h)onc(h)erned.
22                  (0.4)
23    CPO:        R[i: g h t.]
24    Caller:    [I dowanna] make a big dea:l out of
25                it but I've just- (0.2) >ye know I'm
26                sittin 'ere in the livin r'm< (.) .hh
27                an I've just hear:d* 'please don't do:
28                that. please don't do: that. dad. dad.'
29                (0.3)
30    Caller:    °.Hh°
31    CPO:        R:i:gh[t.]
```

Let us offer a number of observations about this extract and how the various noise constructions are operating.

By describing her house as 'terraced' and having 'thin walls' (lines 7 and 10) the caller starts to manage both the epistemic status of her reports and her identity as a listener. She then spells out the implications with 'you can hear a lot through the walls' (lines 13–14). Note here the way this is constructed: 'you can hear', not 'I can hear', 'I am able to hear', 'if I am really quiet I can pick up…'. The construction presents the hearing in scripted terms (see above, and Edwards, 1997). This presents it as an anybody hearing. Put another way, it heads off the idea that she spends time carefully trying to listen to what is going on; she is not a busybody.

The first specific noise construction is done cautiously:

what I ↑seem to be hearing quite* a lot of is children screaming and crying.

The 'seem to be hearing' displays the caller as not rushing to conclusions and allows any confirmation of NSPCC relevance to be arrived at collaboratively. The construction 'screaming and crying' is also interesting, as in other data sets examined the construction 'crying and screaming' was much more common (see Stokoe & Hepburn, 2005). It is possible that more common 'crying and screaming' would make available the inference that what is heard is a problem child. However, 'screaming' followed by 'crying' makes available the inference that they have been first frightened or hurt and then responding to this event with tears.

The second noise construction also attends to the passivity of the hearing. The caller is not trying hard to hear what is going on next door, as a 'nosey neighbour' might. Rather she is 'sitting here in my living room' (lines 25–26). She constructs herself as doing what an ordinary person would do. Note the importance that this is treated as having for the narrative, because the caller breaks off what would probably have been 'just heard' (line 25) and inserts the living room description. In the actual noise description the caller reports direct speech: 'please don't do: that. please don't do: that. dad. dad.' (lines 27–28). This does a number of things. First, reporting speech like this as if verbatim (we have no record, of course), manages the objectivity of the caller. They are not going beyond what they have heard. The rather flat 'as if read out' delivery further contributes to this sense of being objective. Second, the words present a puzzle. What would make a child say those particular words? One solution to the puzzle is that the father is doing something abusive to the child. By offering the puzzle rather than the conclusion the caller further bolsters her status as a reliable witness, and allows the upshot to be a collaborative production with the CPO.

In their study Stokoe and Hepburn (2005) bring out an important further level of detail in the noise reporting by comparative analysis with a set of calls to a neighbour mediation service. There too, there are a large number of calls reporting noise from neighbours and children. However, calls to the mediation service typically construct what they can hear as noise, as well as being inappropriate (e.g., over loud or very late at night). Such reports are systematically different from the NSPCC abuse reports. In the NSPCC calls the callers are not complaining – they are concerned (note the C-construction in line 21) about the child, not bothered for their own comfort. Their motives are produced, in the detail of the noise reporting, as altruistic rather than selfish.

What we see in this study is the way aspects of perception – sound, things that are heard – are constructed in specific ways as parts of the discrete conversational practices. There are subtle but systematic differences when calling a child protection helpline and calling a neighbour mediation line. These reflect the hearing of 'indications of child abuse' or 'unwarranted disturbance'. In this setting hearing is public and interactional. This shows how 'perception', whatever its biological underpinning, is inextricably bound up with practices of interaction.

emotion: crying and empathy

Emotion is a theoretically interesting topic for discursive research as it too is something of a 'hard case'. That is, it is often treated as something close to biology, something lying underneath language and maybe even culture. Often in social psychology emotion is treated as a causal variable that exerts a distorting effect on cognition (Park & Banaji, 2000). However, Edwards (1997) has suggested that the very category 'emotion' needs to be treated cautiously. The boundaries and contrasts of what makes up 'emotion' are different across cultures and settings. Indeed the category 'emotion' itself is a feature of a particular modern and Western idea of the person. As Edwards (1999, p.273) suggests:

> Emotions are not only *contrasted* with cognitions (whether rational or not), both in 'folk' and in professional psychology, but there are also cognitive theories *of* emotions, and indeed cognitive models that virtually do away with, or explain away, emotion categories altogether. But there are also emotion-based explanations of cognition, of what people think, what they think about, and why they think one thing rather than another (because of envy, jealousy, prejudice, obsession, etc.).

Edwards has used ideas from conversation analysis, cultural anthropology and constructionism, as the basis for a respecification that focuses research on: (a) the use of 'emotion' categories; (b) orientations to objects and actions as 'emotional'; and (c) displays of 'emotion'. Some of these features appear in a further development of our child protection project where callers' crying and CPO's responses to crying are the topic of analysis (Hepburn, 2004).

One of the features of psychological work on crying is that it has overwhelmingly worked with participants' reports of crying (in question-naires or rating scales). There is no work that uses direct observation, or attempts to provide situated descriptions of crying. This meant that one of the early research tasks was to develop an extension to the Jeffersonian transcription scheme (Jefferson, 2004) that would represent different features of crying such as sobs, whispers, wet sniffs and wobbly voice (Hepburn, 2004). Again, a list of the transcription symbols used can be found in the Appendix of this volume. This fine-grained description of crying provides a way of seeing how the different activities in crying and crying recipiency are organized together. We can illustrate this with the following extract. Various characteristic elements of crying on the helpline are highlighted, such as caller apologies (A), and CPO actions such as 'right-thing' descriptions (RT), 'take-your-times' (TYT) and what we have termed 'empathic receipts' (ER).

extract 3: JK distraught dad

```
01   Caller:    >.Hhih .hhihhh<
02   CPO:       D'you want- d'y'wann'ave [a break for a ] moment.=  ←TYT
03   Caller:                             [ Hhuhh >.hihh<]
04              =>hhuhh hhuhh<
05              (0.6)
06   Caller:    .shih
07              (0.3)
08   Caller:    °°k(hh)ay°°
09              (1.8)
10   Caller:    .shih >hhuh hhuh[h]<
11   CPO:                       [S]'very har:d when              ←ER
12              they're not there with you isn't it.=            ←ER
13              and [you're-] (.) you're tal:kin about it.       ←ER
14   Caller:        [>.hhih<]
15              (0.8)
16   Caller:    >.Hhuh .HHuh<
17              (2.1)
18   Caller:    .shih
19              (0.2)
20   Caller:    °.shih° (.) °°(Need) hhelp(h)°°
21              (2.5)
22   Caller:    .HHhihh°hh°
23              (0.5)
24   Caller:    HHhuhh >.hih .hih<
25              (0.7)
26   CPO:       .Htk.hh Well you're doing what you can now to    ←RT
27              actually offer them protection and help though   ←RT
28              are:n't you.                                     ←RT
29   Caller:    .Skuh (.) Huhhhh
30              (0.5)
31   Caller:    °°I:'m not the(hehheh)re. Hh°°
32              (3.2)
33   Caller:    .Shih
34              (0.4)
35   Caller:    ~↑I'm ↑sorry.~                                   ←A
36   CPO:       An they als- well E-E-Eddie obviously al- thought ←RT
37              you were the person to contact to get he:lp.     ←RT
38   Caller:    Yeh. hh
```

```
39   CPO:     F'which (.) ye know he turned to you: .hh          ←RT
40            (0.7)
41   Caller:  .Hh[h°hhh°     ]
42   CPO:        [T'help 'im.]=didn't he.                        ←RT
43   Caller:  °°Yhhehhh°°
44   CPO:     So 'e saw you as a person who could help in this   ←RT
45            situa[tion ] for him:.                             ←RT
46   Caller:       [.Shih]
47            (0.9)
48   Caller:  .Hdihhhh hhhuhh
49            (0.2)
50   Caller:  H↑oh: s(h)orry.                                    ←A
51            (0.4)
52   CPO:     .Htk s'↑oka:y. kay.
53            (1.3)
54   Caller:  .SKUH
55            (0.3)
56   CPO:     It's distressing but it's also quite a shock       ←ER
57            isn't it I guess [(for you)]                       ←ER
58   Caller:                   [.HHHHhih ]hh HHHhuhhhh
59            (1.7)
60   Caller:  ((swallows)) °Hhhoh dhear.°
```

Once we have a description that allows this level of detail to be revealed we can start to observe a range of interesting features about the way the extract develops. First, note the way the take-your-time in line 2 is occasioned by the caller's sobbing that starts in line 1 and continues through to line 4. We can see how delicate the mutual attention in this interaction is as, despite the sobbing, the caller responds to the take-your-time with a whispered 'khhay' (line 8).

Second, note further on in the sequence the caller's wobbly voiced apology (line 35). We might think that the caller is apologizing for the transgressive nature of sobbing with a stranger or something similar. However, a careful examination of where apologies appear in crying sequences suggests that they are more likely to be apologies for disruption of ongoing actions or failing to provide normatively expected contributions. That is, they are explicated better by understanding conversational organization. For example, in this case the CPO's assessment in 26–28 is followed by an extremely quiet and very disrupted second assessment on 31 (the normatively expected turn). The following delay from the CPO would allow the turn to be recycled, and the apology could be specifically apologizing for the absence of this recycling.

Third, note the right-thing descriptions on 26–28 and through 36–45. These are constructed from information already provided by the caller, redescribed to present him having done the right thing. Such descriptions seem designed to reassure the caller and move him out of crying. These descriptions are often accompanied by tag questions (e.g. 28 and 42), which may be designed to move the caller out of crying by encouraging agreement with the right-thing description.

Finally let us consider the interesting topic of empathy. Recently some researchers have started to develop an interactional account of empathy (Pudlinski, 2005; Ruusuvuori, 2005). We have marked segments of this extract where the CPO does 'empathic receipts'. The category empathy comes from psychology rather than interaction analysis; however, there are a cluster of features that tend to go together in empathic receipts. Typically there is a formulation of the experience from the recipient's point of view or of the recipient's 'mental state'. Thus on line 11 there is the formulation it's 'very hard' and on line 56 the formulation 'it's distressing but it's also quite a shock'. Interactional contributions such as this are potentially tricky as the speaker is offering a version of something that the recipient is normally expected to know best. Features such as the tag questions (12 and 57) and displays of epistemic caution (e.g. 'I guess' on 57) may be a way of managing this.

More generally, although emotion is often thought of as something that is beyond the purchase of DP, studies of this kind show the way that issues and actions which we understand as emotional can be tractable to interaction analysis. This is not surprising once we remind ourselves of the practical and communicative role that emotions play in social life (Planalp, 1999). DP offers the possibility of understanding the various phenomena loosely glossed as emotion in terms of what they are doing and where they appear in people's lives.

discourse, psychology and interaction

Work in contemporary DP is made up of a number of closely related themes. These NSPCC studies illustrate a number of them:

- They are studies of the procedures through which the psychological implications of talk are managed.
- They consider the practical use of the mental thesaurus (terms such as 'concern', 'hearing', 'screaming'), although it simultaneously makes problematic a simple distinction between a mental thesaurus and other terms.
- They are studies that respecify core theoretical notions from orthodox cognitive and social cognitive psychology (knowledge, attitudes, perception, emotions).

- They focus on the 'embodiment' of psychological states in displays, for example in the sobs and sniffs of crying.
- They address the relationship of psychological and institutional issues, exploring the way the business of the helpline (reporting abuse, orienting to expertise, and so on) is actively accomplished, in part by the use of psychological terms and practices.

There is another theme of DP research that is focused specifically on psychological research methods in practices. It studies both the interactional accomplishment of the method and the constitution of particular findings. There has not been space to overview this work here (but see Antaki, 2005; Puchta & Potter, 2002; and, from a more specifically CA perspective, Schegloff, 1999).

In addition to these research themes there is a developing interest in the potential for DP doing practical or applied work. For a discussion of the problems and possibilities here see Hepburn (2006) as well as a range of the contributions to Hepburn and Wiggins (in press).

In general then, discursive psychology offers a way of theorizing and analysing psychology as a feature of people's practices. It starts with records of what people actually do. In the examples discussed here we have focused on interaction on a helpline, but DP work has been done in a wide range of different settings, and the research is limited only by the imagination of the researcher and the possibility of gaining appropriate access. It offers a picture of psychology that is embedded in practices rather than abstracted from those practices.

references

Ajzen, I. (1991). The theory of planned behaviour. *Organizational Behavior and Human Decision Processes, 50*, 179–211.

Antaki, C. (2006). Producing a 'cognition'. *Discourse Studies, 8*, 9–15.

Billig, M. (1992). *Talking of the royal family.* London: Routledge.

Billig, M. (1996[1987]). *Arguing and thinking: A rhetorical approach to social psychology* (2nd edn). Cambridge: Cambridge University Press.

Coulter, J. (1999). Discourse and mind. *Human Studies, 22*, 163–181.

Coulter, J. (2005). Language without mind. In H. te Molder & J. Potter (Eds.), *Conversation and cognition* (pp.79–92). Cambridge: Cambridge University Press.

Edwards, D. (1994). Script formulations: a study of event descriptions in conversation. *Journal of Language and Social Psychology, 13*(3), 211–247.

Edwards, D. (1995). Two to tango: Script formulations, dispositions, and rhetorical symmetry in relationship troubles talk. *Research on Language and Social Interaction, 28*(4), 319–350.

Edwards, D. (1997). *Discourse and cognition*. London and Beverly Hills, CA: Sage.

Edwards, D. (1999). Emotion discourse. *Culture & Psychology, 5*(3), 271–291.

Edwards, D. (2003). Analysing racial discourse: The discursive psychology of mind–world relationships. In H. van den Berg, M. Wetherell & H. Houtkoop-Steenstra (Eds.), *Analysing race talk: Multidisciplinary approaches to the interview* (pp.31–48). Cambridge: Cambridge University Press.

Edwards, D. (in press). Managing subjectivity in talk. In A. Hepburn and S. Wiggins (Eds.), *Discursive research in practice: New approaches to psychology and interaction*. Cambridge: Cambridge University Press.

Edwards, D. & Potter, J. (1993). *Discursive psychology*. London: Sage.

Edwards, D. & Potter, J. (1999). Language and causal attribution: A rejoinder to Schmid and Fiedler, *Theory & Psychology, 9*, 849–863.

Gilbert, G.N. & Mulkay, M. (1984). *Opening Pandora's box: A sociological analysis of scientists' discourse*. Cambridge: Cambridge University Press.

Gill, V. (1998). Doing attributions in medical interaction: Patients' explanations for illness and doctors' responses. *Social Psychological Quarterly, 61*, 342–360.

Goodwin, C. (1995) Seeing in depth. *Social Studies of Science, 25*, 237–274.

Goodwin, C. & Goodwin, M.H. (1996). Seeing as situated activity: Formulating planes. In Y. Engeström & D. Middleton (Eds.), *Cognition and communication at work* (pp. 61–95). Cambridge: Cambridge University Press.

Harris, R. (1988). *Language, Saussure and Wittgenstein: How to play games with words*. London: Routledge.

Hepburn, A. (2003). *An introduction to critical social psychology*. London: Sage.

Hepburn, A. (2004). Crying: Notes on description, transcription and interaction. *Research on Language and Social Interaction, 37*, 251–290.

Hepburn, A. (2006). Getting closer at a distance: Theory and the contingencies of practice, *Theory & Psychology*.

Hepburn, A. & Potter, J. (2003). Discourse analytic practice. In C. Seale, D. Silverman, J. Gubrium & G. Gobo (Eds), *Qualitative research practice* (pp.180–196). London; Sage.

Hepburn, A. & Wiggins, S. (Eds.) (in press). *Discursive psychology in practice*. Cambridge: Cambridge University Press.

Jaworski, A. & Coupland, N. (Eds.) (1999). *The Discourse Reader*. London: Routledge.

Jefferson, G. (2004). Glossary of transcript symbols with an introduction. In G.H. Lerner (Ed.), *Conversation analysis: Studies from the first generation* (pp.13–31). Amsterdam: John Benjamins.

Lawes, R. (1999). Marriage: An analysis of discourse. *British Journal of Social Psychology, 38*, 1–20.

Park, J. & Banaji, M.R. (2000). Mood and heuristics: The influence of happy and sad states on sensitivity and bias in stereotyping. *Journal of Personality and Social Psychology, 78*, 1005–1023.

Planalp, S. (1999). *Communicating emotion: Social, moral and cultural processes*. Cambridge: Cambridge University Press.

Potter, J. (1996). *Representing reality: Discourse, rhetoric, and social construction*. London and Thousand Oaks, CA: Sage.

Potter, J. (2003a). Discourse analysis and discursive psychology. In P.M. Camic, J.E. Rhodes and L. Yardley (Eds.), *Qualitative research in psychology: Expanding perspectives in methodology and design* (pp.73–94). Washington: American Psychological Association.

Potter, J. (2003b). 'Discourse analysis'. In M. Hardy & A. Bryman (Eds.), *Handbook of Data Analysis* (pp.607–624). London: Sage.

Potter, J. (2004). Discourse analysis as a way of analysing naturally occurring talk. In D. Silverman (Ed.), *Qualitative analysis: Issues of theory and method*, 2nd edition (pp.200–221). London: Sage.

Potter, J. (2005). A discursive psychology of institutions. *Social Psychology Review, 7*, 25–35.

Potter, J. & Edwards, D. (2001a). Sociolinguistics, cognitivism and discursive psychology. In N. Coupland, S. Sarangi & C. Candlin (Eds.), *Sociolinguistics and Social Theory* (pp.88–103). London: Longman.

Potter, J. & Edwards, D. (2001b). Discursive social psychology. In W.P. Robinson and H. Giles (Eds.), *The new handbook of language and social psychology* (pp.103–118). London: John Wiley & Sons Ltd.

Potter, J. & Edwards, D. (2003). Rethinking cognition: On Coulter, discourse and mind. *Human Studies, 26(1)*, 165–181.

Potter, J. & Hepburn, A. (2003). I'm a bit concerned – Early actions and psychological constructions in a child protection helpline. *Research on Language and Social Interaction, 36*, 197–240.

Potter, J. & Hepburn, A. (2005). Qualitative interviews in psychology: Problems and possibilities. *Qualitative Research in Psychology, 2*, 38–55.

Potter, J. & te Molder, H. (2005). Talking cognition: Mapping and making the terrain. In J. Potter and H. Te Molder (Eds.), *Conversation and cognition* (pp. 1–56). Cambridge, UK: Cambridge University Press.

Potter, J. & Wetherell, M. (1987). *Discourse and social psychology: Beyond attitudes and behaviour*. London: Sage.

Potter, J. & Wetherell, M. (1988). Accomplishing attitudes: Fact and evaluation in racist discourse. *Text, 8(1–2)*, 51–68.

Puchta, C. & Potter, J. (2002). Manufacturing individual opinions: Market research focus groups and the discursive psychology of attitudes. *British Journal of Social Psychology, 41*, 345–363.

Pudlinski, C. (2005). Doing empathy and sympathy: Caring responses to troubles tellings on a peer support line. *Discourse Studies, 7*, 267–288.

Ruusuvuori, J. (2005). Empathy and sympathy in action: Attending to patients' troubles in Finnish homeopathic and GP consultations. Social *Psychology Quarterly.*

Sacks, H. (1992). *Lectures on conversation.* Vols. I & II, edited by G. Jefferson. Oxford: Basil Blackwell.

Schegloff, E.A. (1982). Discourse as an interactional achievement: Some uses of 'uh huh' and other things that come between sentences. In D. Tannen (Ed.), *Georgetown University Round Table on Language and Linguistics, 1981: Text and Talk*. Washington, DC: Georgetown University Press.

Schegloff, E.A. (1999). Discourse, pragmatics, conversation, analysis. *Discourse Studies, 1*, 405–436.

Schmid, J. & Fiedler, K. (1999). A parsimonious theory can account for complex phenomena: A discursive analysis of Edwards and Potter's critique of nondiscursive language research. *Theory & Psychology, 9(6)*, 807–822.

Stokoe, E.H. & Hepburn, A. (2005). 'You can hear a lot through the walls': Noise formulations in neighbour complaints. *Discourse & Society, 16*, 647–674.

te Molder, H. & Potter, J. (Eds) (2005). *Conversation and cognition.* Cambridge: Cambridge University Press.

Wetherell, M. & Edley, N. (1999). 'Negotiating hegemonic masculinity: Imaginary positions and psycho-discursive practices'. *Feminism and Psychology, 9(3)*, 335–356.

Wetherell, M. & Potter, J. (1992). *Mapping the language of racism: Discourse and the legitimation of exploitation.* Hemel Hempstead: Harvester/Wheatsheaf and New York: Columbia University Press.

Wetherell, M., Taylor, S. & Yates, S. (Eds.) (2001). *Discourse theory and practice: A reader.* London: Sage.

Wiggins, S. & Hepburn, A. (in press). Food abuse: Mealtimes, helplines and troubled eating. In A. Hepburn & S. Wiggins (Eds.), *Discursive research in practice.* Cambridge: Cambridge University Press.

Wiggins, S. & Potter, J. (2003). Attitudes and evaluative practices: Category vs. item and subjective vs. objective constructions in everyday food assessments. *British Journal of Social Psychology, 42*, 513–531.

Wittgenstein, L. (1953). *Philosophical investigations.* Oxford: Blackwell.

Wood, L.A. & Kroger, R.O. (2000). *Doing discourse analysis: Methods for studying action in talk and text.* Thousand Oaks, CA: Sage.

Zebrowitz, L.A. (1990). *Social perception.* Buckingham: Open University Press.

part three
gender and sexuality

7
gender and communication in context

tamar murachver and anna janssen

Gender is a pervasive aspect of social life. The gender category one belongs to may shape the clothes worn, the activities selected, the books and news articles read, or the roles played. It might also shape the language spoken, signed or written. These choices, habits and preferences are influenced, in part, by gender stereotypes and expectations. One consequence of the pervasiveness of gender performances is that in many contexts it seems to reflect fixed and stable gender differences in behaviour. In this chapter, we explore the topic of gender differences in language use. We consider how gendered behaviours, in particular those found in language and communication, are shaped by social expectations, stereotypes, and the need for social identity. We also briefly explore whether gendered communication styles might be shaped by biological bases. Our destination, so to speak, is the claim that gender differences in language use are contextual. Understanding how gender is done through language in different contexts tells us more about the social use of language than simply arguing whether gender differences do or do not exist.

We find it useful to draw a parallel between gender differences in dress and those in language use. From our observations, we have noticed that women and men, girls and boys, often dress differently. Nonetheless, we also note that variations within a gender are substantial, and in some situations there are no discernible gender differences in dress. Does this invalidate the initial observation of gender difference in dress? Drawing back on the parallel between dress and language, we argue that gender differences in language use are observable and well-documented. At the same time, there are large variations within a gender, and there are many contexts in which gender differences in language use are non-existent.

Moreover, the specific language features that vary between women and men are not the same across contexts. This is true of dress as well; sometimes gender differences are noted in fabric or colour, and sometimes the difference is more apparent in accessories or cut of the garment. We adopt a perspective whereby we try to understand patterns within the variations within and across contexts. We believe that there is nothing subversive or reactionary in accepting that there are gender differences in how language is used, just as there is nothing subversive in accepting the existence of gender differences in dress.

Both forms of dress and language use are social behaviours that can be used to mark gender. How does a speaker know whether they are addressing a woman or a man? Clothing, language use, titles and names, voice quality, and mannerisms all provide cues. The specific cues vary across cultures. For example, skirts mark the female gender in many cultures, but in traditional Scottish settings, a skirt is not a predictable marker of women. Similarly, in some societies indirect language is considered more common among women, but this norm is not universal. In a Malagasy community in Madagascar, it is the men who are indirect, whereas the women are direct (Keenan, 1974). Of course, language does far more than mark gender. Language use reveals individuals' social standing – desired or otherwise. It tells stories about where they are from, how long they have been schooled, what groups they think they belong to, and how they feel towards their audience.

gender and language stereotypes

Stereotypes are based on perceivers' experiences and knowledge. Stereotypes are more than a description of an average of one's observations, however. They function to maximally differentiate one category from another. Using the clothing parallel, although the average grown woman does not spend the majority of her life dressed in shades of pink, or adorned with lace, sequins or beads, these features maximally distinguish aspects of women's dress from that of men's. Similarly, most women do not say such stereotype-based statements as, 'Oh dear! I meant to take that lovely aubergine blouse to the cleaners, didn't I?' Because stereotypes establish maximal distance between groups, they are easily recognizable. Thus, one or two features are adequate to elicit the appropriate social category.

From observations of gender-related differences in styles of communication, people form stereotypes about how and why men and women communicate. Stereotypes reinforce the notion that gender is marked in communication. Such stereotypes about communication also fit well with those people have regarding the priorities that women and men hold in daily life. For example, whereas women are seen as more relationship- and people-focused, men are stereotyped as more independent, ego-driven and agentic (e.g., Carli, 2001; Eckert & McConnell-Ginet, 1992; Lakoff, 1990; Zimmerman, Holm & Haddock, 2001). By their very nature, stereotypes about gender and its role in communication are easily formed, helpful to use (Macrae, Milne & Bodenhausen, 1994) and commonly accepted. As a result, these stereotypes are difficult to avoid as a framework for making sense of the social world.

Research on gender stereotypes about language use show that by primary school, children attribute certain statements as ones spoken by either women or men. Edelsky (1976) found that by six years, children classified statements such as, 'That's an adorable story' as more likely to be said by women and 'Damn it, I lost my keys' as more likely to be said by men. By 11, children judged that men would more likely say, 'I'll be damned, there's a friend of mine' and 'You're damn right', whereas women would more likely state, 'Won't you please close the door' and 'My goodness, there's a friend of mine.' Adolescents and adults do not hesitate when asked to surmise the gender of a speaker or author. When judging the origin of verbal statements (Edelsky, 1976), email messages (Thomson & Murachver, 2001) or authored text (Janssen & Murachver, 2005), participants readily make attributions about the originator's gender, and their guesses are often correct.

Stereotypes about gendered communication often focus on topic or content, rather than form. For her honour's thesis, Melanie Hills (2000) asked university students to send each other email messages with the goal of convincing the reader that they were the 'other' gender. She found that students were less systematic in altering the form of their messages towards expected gender-based behaviour. Instead, they greatly exaggerated the gendered content. Compared to the frequency with which male university students normally discussed 'male' topics such as rugby and beer drinking (determined by an independent set of raters), female university students pretending to be males greatly increased their talk on such topics. Similarly, male university students pretending to be females mentioned 'female' topics such as exercise and appearance far more often than female students in normal email conversations. This exaggeration is akin to what happens when women and men are asked to role-play the other gender. Voice pitch becomes much deeper or higher than normal, body positions become humorously 'too feminine' or 'too masculine', and very few role-plays approach the behaviour of the ordinary woman or man.

To view communication through the lenses of social stereotypes about gender is to oversimplify the nature of human social interaction and the role of gender therein. Stereotypes are not necessarily an accurate predictor of the communication behaviour exhibited by females and males. Gender stereotypes, by necessity, are simplifications and exaggerations. They are the creation of binary categories where the reality is an overlapping continuum. Although gender differences might exist in our interactions, they are not necessarily large or opposing. In certain situations they do not exist at all. So, gender differences in communication behaviours are highly variable. An indicator of gender in one interaction may be inconspicuous in another interaction.

gender differences in language use

Although gender differences in language use vary across situations, there is a wealth of evidences that differences, on occasion, do exist. Some of the features more commonly produced by girls and women appear to be a reflection of the time and focus placed on dyadic relationships. Women more frequently produce references to emotion (Mulac & Bradac, 1995; Mulac & Lundell, 1994; Thomson & Murachver, 2001), and are more likely to apologize, compliment, and make self-derogatory statements (Holmes, 1988, 1995). Men, who seem to be more focused on their standing within a much larger group, are less likely to talk about emotions or offer statements of submission such as apologies and self-derogatory statements. Instead, males are more likely to use self-promoting language, including brags, insults or teasing (Thomson & Murachver, 2001; Thorne, 1993), and they more frequently give opinions (Aries, 1982; Thomson & Murachver, 2001). Men and boys are more likely to use directives (e.g., 'you do that'; Leaper, 1991), whereas girls and women are likely to use more inclusive and suggestive forms (e.g., 'let's do that'; Leaper, 1991) or indirect requests (Mulac & Bradac, 1995). Other linguistic differences include men's more frequent references to quantity and place (Janssen & Murachver, 2004a; Mulac & Lundell, 1986) and women's more frequent use of intensifiers, particularly high frequency ones such as 'really' and 'very' (Janssen & Murachver, 2004a; Mulac & Bradac, 1995).

biological beginnings

It is not our intention to explain the origins of gender differences in language. It seems likely that multiple factors underpin the separation of female and male behaviour. Three explanatory contenders include biology, social expectations, and social identity. Although we do not regard biology as a strong determinant of gender differences, we believe that it is premature to suggest that biology has no impact on the expression of gender. Even among non-human primates, there are gender differences in interest shown towards the young and in rough-and-tumble play (Maccoby, 1998). There are also subtle gender differences in receptivity to social stimuli. For example, Lutchmaya and Baron-Cohen (2002) found sex differences in 12-month-old infants' preferences to view social and non-social stimuli. In their study, male infants preferred to look at videos of mechanical motion, whereas girl infants preferred videos of people talking. A similar preference has been shown with neonates (Connellan, Baron-Cohen, Wheelwright, Ba'tki & Ahluwalia, 2001). These biologically based differences do not explain adult behaviour, but they may be foundational. Biological differences are fairly small, but they foster stereotypes and change the behaviours directed toward the child, which then amplify prevailing differences. For example, adults are more persistent in attempting to engage female babies in interaction (Goldberg & Lewis, 1969). This might be a result of, in part, the greater initial interest in social stimuli shown by these babies. As a consequence, the initially small gender difference is enhanced by the increased encouragement given to girl babies. The end result is that gender difference becomes more substantial through the interaction between biologically based tendencies and environment.

expectations and social identity

Human behaviour is influenced by that of others. Once individuals are identified as members of social categories, there is pressure to behave according to what is expected of category members. Behaviour that is congruent with expectations is often reinforced by others. Women who speak more tentatively have greater influence on men's opinions than those who speak more assertively (Carli, 1990). Children who act more like others of their own gender are more accepted and have more positive social behaviour directed towards them (Maccoby, 1998). Behaviour that deviates too far from societal expectations is not reinforced and may be punished. Janssen (2004) demonstrated this in a recent study by asking participants to read scripts of mixed-gender dyadic conversations in which speakers' gender labels, language styles, and goals in conversation were manipulated. Participants rated speakers' perceived levels of competency, likeability, friendliness, and respectfulness towards their conversational partners. Ratings were consistently lowest for female-labelled speakers who displayed male-typed approaches to conversation (e.g., competitive, argumentative, problem-solving). Participants showed clear disapproval for female speakers who show gender-inconsistent behaviour. Research also shows that boys and men, in particular, react strongly towards other males whom they regard as feminine (Hajek, Abrams & Murachver, 2005).

Societal expectations work together with social identity to shape the behaviour of individuals who identify with a particular social group. Individuals identify themselves as a particular gender, and then adhere to expected behaviours to show themselves and others that they are a good exemplar of that gender. A quote attributed to Gloria Steinam, which has been circulated by women in humorous electronic mailings is, 'I have never heard a man ask for advice on how to combine a career and family.' Why do women find this quote humorous? A man does not have to be a good caregiver in order to be an example of a 'good man'. But women recognize that no matter how much they believe that women can and do have meaningful careers, if they have a family, they feel the need to adhere to expectations and be a 'good woman' too. It is not just that others want them to be good examples of women and men – they want to belong to these groups, and they quite willingly do what is necessary to show their belongingness.

the variable relationship between language and gender

With changes in context come changes in social expectations regarding the expression of gender. Once again, our clothing analogy is useful. When women and men go out for a run, a cycle, or sail around the harbour, they dress very much alike. In other contexts, such as a wedding, a pub visit, or dinner at a restaurant, the differences between women and men's dress is noticeable. Similarly, gender differences in language use are not found in every context. Moreover, the subset of features that might differ between genders can vary across different contexts. As we will explain shortly, contexts can make specific demands about roles to play, including the salience or importance of gender. When the demands of other roles are greater than that of gender, gender differences are less noticeable. When gender is salient, or no other gender-neutral roles compete, then gender differences will become more prominent.

Our goal is to understand and explain actual communication behaviour. This requires us to look beyond those behaviours that support our assumptions and expectations. Experience often calls one's expectations and assumptions into question. Using examples of this as well as pertinent theory and framework, it is possible to begin to explain those behaviours that are contrary to expectations and assumptions about gender.

gender is not stable

Contrary to what prevailing stereotypes might suggest, gender is not a stable trait within each individual. Gender may be better described as an array of behaviours that individuals may or may not express. As discussed earlier, people are unlikely to engage in behaviours that are gender marked to the same extent in every instance. We believe it is possible to identify the features of social transactions that shape the expression of gender behaviours. Some evidence of this comes from a study by Fitzpatrick and colleagues in which the same speakers conversed in both same- and mixed-gender dyadic conversations (Fitzpatrick, Mulac & Dindia, 1995). Only when talking with someone of the same gender did participants use gender-typed features of language use. In other words, the gender of the communicator's partner was a factor that determined speakers' gendered language use.

A further example comes from talk arising during children's play activities. Typically, boys show a preference for play that is action-focused, whereas girls prefer play that is cooperative and people-focused. The language that arises in these play settings is often compatible with our gender stereotypes about communication (Leaper, 1991; McCloskey & Coleman, 1992; Thorne, 1993). But how can we be sure that the language is a result of the speakers' gender as opposed to the activity they choose to engage in? This was a question that Leaper and Gleason (1996) sought to answer. Rather than observe naturally occurring conversations in which children selected their activities, Leaper and Gleason designed a study to independently control play activity while assessing language use. Their research showed that when the choice of activity was removed, the language children and their parents used when playing was a better reflection of the activity than their gender. Child–parent pairs who were given a socially-focused activity (playing grocer) used language that was more female-typical. On the other hand, pairs involved in action-focused play (building a car) used language more typical of males. The participants' styles of expression were determined by their activities, not their gender.

It is possible to move beyond the binds of gender stereotypes and make sense of such findings by borrowing from a social constructionist perspective of gender (Leaper, 2000). Like the findings above, a social constructionist perspective challenges the assumption that gender is a static, inherent trait. Instead, it frames gender as a dynamic, socially-created entity that exists in our interactions (Crawford, 1995). Rather than being a particular gender, individuals 'do' gender (Beall, 1993; West

& Zimmerman, 1987). Using this framework we will demonstrate that it is the social context hosting interactions that determines expressions of gender behaviours.

gender differences are subtle and overlapping

Even when a gender difference does exist, it is not necessarily large. At times there are more similarities than differences in females' and males' approaches to language use. For example, Bogoch (1997) assessed how female and male lawyers talk to their clients. Minor differences were noted. For instance, female lawyers displayed a greater tendency to highlight their professional status and consider clients' emotional concerns than did male lawyers. On the other hand, lawyer gender was not marked by their approaches to cooperating, establishing control, or building rapport with the client. In other words, these findings did not support gender-role stereotypes. When playing the role of lawyer, these individuals' gender was marked more subtly than our stereotypes would suggest.

The previous example brings us to another interesting point. Even when women and men are in gendered roles, they do not necessarily behave in opposing fashions. It may be that although men and women tend to speak in gender stereotypically consistent ways, one gender does so to a slightly greater or lesser extent than the other. A good example of this is the use of expletives. This is often seen to be a marker of communicator gender. According to stereotypes, males are more likely than females to use expletives (Bayard & Krishnayya, 2001). Also typically, expletives are more common in casual conversation than in purpose-oriented discussions (e.g., making specific arrangements or decisions). A recent study into expletive use by young adults found that gender was marked by the amount of difference in expletive use between the two types of talk (Bayard & Krishnayya, 2001). Whereas all communicators increased their use of expletives when in casual, as opposed to purpose-oriented talk, males did so to a greater extent than females. In other words, along with any differences, there is much overlap in the styles of communication used by each gender. Gender differences are often a matter of degree rather than direction.

our styles of expression may be no indictor of our gender

There is no reason to assume that styles of communication will provide any suggestion of gender. For example, Janssen and Murachver (2004b) asked people to write passages on three different topics. A range of language variables were coded for in participants' written passages, including intensifiers, hedges, personal information, references to emotion, opinions, and references to quantity or place. All of the coded variables had been found to vary as a function of gender in previous research. In this context gender had no bearing on the language used by the passage authors. Language use varied only as a function of passage topic.

Similar findings arose in a study by Thomson, Murachver and Green (2001, Study 1) in which participants each wrote to a female-labelled and a male-labelled netpal. These netpals were confederates in the study. Although participants' language use varied as a function of the netpals' gender labels and communication style, no effect of participant gender was found. Such findings demonstrate that our gender need not play any significant role in the way we express ourselves.

the conflict between stereotypes and experience

Gender stereotypes fail to take into account the types of behaviour women and men show across a range of situations. Fundamental to gender stereotypes is the notion that women and men are members of separate social groups. Stereotypes are socially shared generalizations about a group. Stereotypes can function to disguise variability between individuals within a particular social group. For example, in addition to being female, a woman has a list of other traits and attributes that determine the types of roles she may play in a given situation, depending on her age, job, ethnicity, marital status, political views, pastimes and religious persuasion, for example.

Moreover, to fully appreciate how gender functions in communication, it is important to remember that gender does not operate in a vacuum. Because it is a major part of the social world, gender can bear noticeably upon the situations in which individuals communicate. Nonetheless, the very nature of the social world means that it is host to numerous additional factors that can also come into play when people communicate. Stereotypes overlook the numerous possible variations between the situations in which these individuals interact. These factors need to be considered to fully understand the patterns of communication observed in daily life.

the role of context in the expression of gender

Individuals do not necessarily behave in gendered ways to the same extent on every occasion. The extent to which gender is evident in behaviour varies enormously depending on a host of factors. These factors can include peoples' physical location, who they are with, what they are discussing, and why they are discussing it. The presence or absence of such factors, and therefore the likelihood of engaging in gender stereotyped behaviours, is related to the context in which the behaviour is taking place. In the following section we will look at the impact that context can have on the extent to which people do gender when communicating and some possible explanations for this. We begin with a brief discussion of the methodology that has helped us to better understand the contextual expression of gender.

methodological choices

Our approach to studying gender in context is to systematically study context while independently varying context and gender. Leaper and Gleason (1996) controlled children's activity choices so that they could determine whether activity or gender was related to children's and parents' language. Our research adopts a similar strategy. If we believe that a number of factors are influencing a behaviour, we attempt to create situations where these influences can be teased apart. In our study of electronic communication, we asked whether writers of email messages wrote differently to people who appeared female or male in their language style, and whether this influence was separate from their knowledge of the other writer's gender. We trained one writer to systematically vary the type of language used (i.e., more typical of a male or female), and we also independently varied whether their email correspondent thought they were a woman or a man. We see this empirically-based strategy as a complement to more naturalistic observations, and believe that multiple strategies can be used to converge on a shared understanding of the contextual nature of gender and language use.

co-communicator language style

With a change in context often comes a change in the people engaged in the communication. There is much evidence showing that the communication partner or audience can have a key role in determining how the communicator uses language. For example, communication partner gender can influence speaker behaviour. Revisiting Fitzpatrick and colleagues' (1995) work, participants were found to vary their language style depending on the gender of their conversation partner. One question is whether participants altered their language style because they were talking to a female or a male, or because they were talking to someone who was using a gender-preferential language style. Often these two factors vary together, and it is difficult to separate the influence of each. One study that sought to disentangle the relative contribution of each factor involved email communication (Thomson et al., 2001, Study 2). It showed that partner language style, which can often be predicted by gender, is a better determinant of communicator language use than partner gender. Thomson and colleagues assigned netpals (confederates) to participants. These netpals interacted electronically over a two-week period. Netpal gender label and language style (female-preferential or male-preferential) were independently manipulated. Half of the participants were told that their netpal was a woman and half were told that their netpal was a man. Within each of these groups, the confederate used more female-preferential language features for half of the participants and more male-preferential language features with the remaining half. These features were relatively easy to control in the context of electronic communication. Analysis of participants' language use showed that although there was a small effect of participant gender, netpal language style was the strongest predictor of participants' language style. Female-preferential language features such as intensifiers, hedges, references to emotion, and personal information were more common in participants' messages when emailing netpals who used a female-preferential language style. In contrast, netpals who used a male-preferential style received messages from participants that featured more opinions. Netpal gender label had no effect on participants' language use.

Such effects are also found in face-to-face conversation. Hannah and Murachver (1999) asked participants to talk with female and male confederates who used either a female-preferential (facilitative) style of conversation, or a male-preferential (non-facilitative) style of conversation. As in the email study, confederate gender and gender-preferential language use were independently controlled. Thus, the influence of each could be assessed. Hannah and Murachver found that confederate speech style was a stronger predictor of participant speech style than either participant or confederate gender.

communication accommodation theory

What drives people to alter their communication styles to reflect those of their communication partners? According to communication accommodation theory (CAT; Shepard, Giles & LePoire, 2001), communicators adapt their language to be more like (convergence) or less like (divergence or maintenance) that of their communication partner. Convergence is motivated by peoples' desire to create rapport, gain approval, and display a liking for those they are communicating with. It reduces the differences between speakers and their audience and marks a willingness to gain social approval. Divergence, on the other hand, increases the differences between communicators and their discussion partner(s). This is thought to reflect the communicators' desire to emphasize their social identity as distinct from that of the people they are communicating with. Maintenance, whereby communicators do not alter their style of expression in relation to that of their partner, can be interpreted as the communicator disregarding or consciously reacting to the partner's style.

Children are likely to show communication accommodation in a similar way to adults. For example, when playing in a mixed-gender dyad, girls and boys tend to attenuate their use of gender-preferential styles of communication relative to that when playing in a same-gender dyad (Leaper, 1991). In a similar study design, Mulac and colleagues (1988) found that adults used more gender-preferential language when interacting with another individual of their gender as opposed to someone of the other gender. Both studies show that in typical, everyday interactions, people are driven to reduce the social distance between themselves and others. Their styles of communication are a useful tool for achieving this.

Research also shows that children not only accommodate to their co-communicators in their use of particular language devices, but also on a higher-order level of self-expression. When deciding upon a writing topic, girls-only writing groups selected more pro-social topics, whereas boys-only groups chose more overtly aggressive topics. Children writing in mixed-gender dyads chose a more pro-social topic than did boys writing in boys-only groups (Strough & Diriwachter, 2000). It seems the children were influenced by the situation they were in, which in turn influenced their topic selection.

Does divergence occur when the atmosphere is less congenial, as CAT would suggest? Research into language use during a debating context indicates that this is so. Hogg (1985) asked participants to report on their perceptions of speakers who were debating. This is a style of interaction that is more closely associated with males than females, in that it is competitive, direct and confrontational. In line with this, it affords a male-preferential style of communication, as the study showed. In mixed-gender groups, more male-preferential language was perceived overall. Judges noted females' convergence towards a more male-preferential language style. In other words they adapted their language to fit the context (i.e., either the mode of communication, the male co-communicators' language style, or both). On the other hand, males were seen to diverge. Judges viewed an increase in their use of male-preferential language along with a reduction in their use of female-preferential language. This is not surprising, for two reasons: There was a competitive, as opposed to amiable, context; and gender was more salient in the mixed- as opposed to same-gender debating groups. Using a CAT framework for interpretation, males were driven to emphasize their social identity as distinct from their female co-communicators in this mixed-gender, competitive setting.

Divergence behaviour can also be observed in everyday settings. People may use it when communicating with those of a different social group (e.g., race, age, religion, or political persuasion), in order to express and increase their social distance from the other person. Such behaviour is well-documented as creating intergroup boundaries in the workplace (see Boggs & Giles, 1999). For example, Willemyns, Gallois and Callan (2003) interviewed people who work in a range of settings. They found that managers often showed a counter-accommodative style of communication when interacting with their employees. Such supervisors appeared driven to highlight their social group as separate from that of the employees.

For divergence or maintenance to occur there need not be social tension or dislike. The emphasis of a person's own social identity as distinct from that of their co-communicator can be helpful to the relationship where interpersonal differences are valued. For example, Kolaric and Galambos (1995) found that adolescents conversing in mixed-gender dyads differed markedly in their use of certain 'display' behaviours, such as chin strokes (male-preferential), hair flips, head tilts and coy looks (female-preferential). The authors argue that such displays were used in an effort to develop a heterosexual relationship with the co-communicator. Arguably, the communicators thought these behaviours to be attractive to the other gender. Because there was no obvious social tension in the majority of these interactions, it comes as no surprise that alongside their diverging displays, communicators also converged in certain ways. The authors found that the only difference among other verbal and nonverbal behaviours of adolescents in mixed-gender dyadic conversations was frequency of smiling. Contrary to literature supporting gender stereotypes, female and male speakers did not differ significantly in their use of questions, interruptions, speaking time and verbal uncertainty, for instance.

Moreover, maintenance behaviour can be performed unconsciously as a result of a lack, or undeveloped repertoire, of communication skills appropriate for a particular context (Boggs & Giles, 1999). For example, a male working in a stereotypically male-orientated setting (e.g., building site) who has never had a female co-worker before may fail to accommodate to the communication style of a new female counterpart. Rather than a marker of dislike, this may reflect his inexperience interacting with someone in such apparently paradoxical work- and gender-related social categories.

non-social contextual factors influencing our styles of expression

There is more to a communication scenario than the range of people involved. One important factor in many communication contexts is discussion topic. In such events, it is not a question of who is communicating so much as the issue that they are communicating about, that most strongly predicts the language they use. Conversation topic was the best predictor of speaking time in adolescents' mixed-gender dyadic conversations (Kolaric and Galambos, 1995). Although speaking time is often portrayed by stereotypes as greater among females (e.g., Tannen, 1994), the authors found that females only spoke more than males where the discussion topic was female-oriented. Male-oriented topics elicited more talk from male speakers.

Another study in point is that by Janssen and Murachver (2004b). As previously outlined, language use varied between topics, but not between female and male authors. Authors were not doing gender. Rather, they employed language that displayed the gender of the topic. Whereas the female-oriented topic elicited female-preferential language, the male-oriented topic elicited male-preferential language from the authors, irrespective of their gender. In other words, as the dominant contextual factor, topic determined writers' language use.

There are times when people communicate without the company or response of another communicator. Such contexts include writing and lecturing to a silent audience. What, of these contexts, might predict an individual's style of communication? What does the communicator have to guide or shape their style of expression? We argue that in such instances, communicators use stereotypes and social schemas or scripts to guide their behaviour. In this, they accommodate to the social expectations of appropriate behaviour for that context.

A person giving a lecture, for instance, is likely to perform according to social norms and expectations for this context. In this, they are likely to stand and speak more formally than they would when holding a friendly, informal discussion about their weekend activities, for instance. Further, they are likely to be dressed more formally than they were while gardening at the weekend. There will be language devices and behaviours that they use rarely while lecturing, such as questions, laughter, personal information, and references to emotion. Some they are unlikely to use at all, such as minimal responses and interruptions. On the other hand, there are likely to be a higher frequency of devices such as facts and indirect attention-getting devices (e.g., 'The point is...', 'Strictly speaking...', 'In fact...', 'Now, what...') relative to casual conversation. Language use may also be determined by a combination of the setting and the individual speaking. For example, the use of fillers and hedges is likely to depend on the speaker's levels of preparation and anxiety within the setting.

This adaptation of communication style to fit the context is highly comparable to convergence in a more interactive social setting. Communicators converge with their co-communicators in order to develop rapport and gain approval. In a similar way, communicators in a non-responsive setting (e.g., a lecture theatre, writing on a particular topic) shape their expressions to fit with the implied expectations of that context.

The ability to follow a 'script' or schema whereby communication is aligned with the context has been found to begin at a young age. Revisiting Leaper and Gleason's (1996) research, it is clear that the predictive power of children's play activities on their language use eclipsed that of gender. Parent–child pairs were using gendered language, but that language matched the gender-orientation of the activity, not that of the communicators. Arguably, the children were accommodating to the parents' language as well. This would suggest that the children were guided by the scripts their parents perform. Whatever the main influence here, these findings suggest that children accommodate to contextual factors in a similar way to adults.

the implications of contextual factors on gender

When generalizing about gender, disregarding the major role that contextual factors can play, it is easy to think of language devices, behaviours, and styles of expression that mark gender. This thinking is guided by stereotypes. When context is considered, however, those features of communication that stereotypically had been clear markers of gender often become more subtle. In some cases they are invisible. One example is references to emotion, which are often considered a female-preferential language device. Anderson and Leaper (1998) asked participants to hold unstructured and self-disclosure conversations. More emotion talk was used in the self-disclosure conversations, and no effect of gender was found. Emotion talk acts as a gender marker in many situations not because of gender differences in ability to use emotion talk, but because of different inclinations among women and men to express themselves in this way (Anderson & Leaper, 1998). Arguably, these differences are a result of social expectations. Consistent with our argument, they can be removed altogether in certain contexts.

What does our investigation into the role of context say about individual styles of communication? Gender is more fluid and flexible than is often supposed within popular culture or from stereotypes. People do gender often, but not always. They are highly capable of stepping outside the boundaries of gender stereotypes when they interact. As we have shown, just because behaviour differs as a function of gender in one setting does not mean it will in another setting. Thanks to constant variations in context, and willingness to meet the demands of these contexts, people only do gender in so far as gender is demanded of them. It just happens that in the highly gendered world in which individuals live, gender performance is often expected.

future directions

We have taken a simple idea – that women and men differ in their use of language – and shown that this is an inadequate description of the world. The study of how these supposed differences fluctuate across different contexts adds a valuable contribution to our understanding. We have found it useful to employ CAT to explain many of these variations, but CAT alone does not fully explain or predict the range of behaviours we see. We are also somewhat uneasy about the powerfulness of CAT to explain many phenomena when much of CAT remains untested. This reveals something about us (the authors) and something about CAT. We are trained as empiricists, and we believe that theories must do more than explain the data after the fact; theories should be able to make clear predictions that are testable. CAT is able to explain why convergence, maintenance or divergence has taken place. If communicators converge, they must be motivated to seek affiliation. If communicators diverge, they must be motivated to show that they are members of different groups. But does such motivation *cause* accommodation?

Our lab has gathered some support for the notion that communicators' motivation to affiliate shapes their language accommodation. As part of his PhD research, James Green (2004) asked university students to interact with netpals of the other gender via email. These netpals, who in reality were the experimenter, systematically used female- or male-preferential language. Before their first interaction, Green sent each participant a digital photo of their netpal. These photos had been rated beforehand as being either less attractive or highly attractive. Based on CAT, Green predicted that participants would converge more to emails written by highly attractive netpals than to those written by less attractive netpals. His results supported this prediction. Further support for CAT has been shown in our lab with a similar email study design. In two experiments (Hows, 2004; Thomson et al., 2001), participants converged more to netpals who used language consistent with their supposed gender than to netpals who used language inconsistent with their gender. In this situation, convergence can be interpreted as a signal of acceptance, and overall, gender consistent behaviour is regarded as more acceptable than gender inconsistent behaviour (Janssen, 2004).

There are a number of factors that might influence a speaker to converge, maintain or diverge, and few of these have been rigorously tested. The degree to which people like their communication partner, how much they feel they belong to the social group of their communication partner, and the salience of the social groups relevant to the communicators might all influence accommodation behaviour. Reid, Keerie and Palomares (2003) tested the importance of group salience on communication behaviour and found that when gender was salient, participants were more likely to maintain their more stereotyped language than when gender was not salient.

Giles and his colleagues (Coupland, Coupland, Giles & Henwood, 1991; Giles & Powesland, 1975) have already noted that it is too simplistic to state that convergence is a positive social behaviour and maintenance or divergence is a negative behaviour. When speakers converge toward an expected stereotype, the message conveyed can be far from positive. Speakers who converge their speech too much (overaccommodation) to the expected roles of the very old, for example, convey a strong negative message about the presumed competence of their audience. When others converge towards social roles we do not value or wish to be part of, their behaviour is insulting.

Giles and Powesland (1975) depict another example of non-convergence that is generally perceived as positive and that was mentioned earlier in this chapter. In initial encounters between women and men that have a romantic potential, women and men are likely to maintain some gender-consistent language behaviours as a way of conveying femininity and masculinity, respectively. One issue our research group has struggled with but not resolved is how to predict which language features are to be maintained as markers of a salient social category, and which features will converge as a means of signalling strong approval. Possibly the choice depends on how strongly correlated certain features are with one or another social group. For example, men might converge towards women's disclosure of personal information and mentions of emotion because these remain acceptable behaviours for men in the context of conversing with a woman, as long as they are not overdone. The increased use of certain terms that might be associated with homosexuality as well as the female role, however, would more likely be avoided (Hajek et al., 2005).

Our analysis of context has made us realize that we do not yet have an adequate set of constraints that allows us to predict which contextual factors will have an impact in a given situation. Individuals fill many different roles, and each role exerts some influence on behaviour. We are able to look at the behaviour after the fact and attribute it to specific roles. These explanations should also be tested in a forward manner by manipulating speakers' willingness to adhere to one of many roles and predicting their subsequent language use.

An adequate model of gendered language behaviour will need to consider both features of the individual as well as features of the situation. Features of the individual that would likely impinge on gendered language use include degree of identification with and sense of belongingness to gender group, attitudes towards own and other gender group, the extent to which a person seeks to moderate their self-presentation, and their social awareness of the expectations arising from the situational context. Traditional attitudes towards gender roles, for example, are associated with greater maintenance and less convergence in mixed-sex interactions (Fitzpatrick et al., 1995) and in interactions with those using language considered typical of the other gender (Robertson & Murachver, 2003). The situation might afford certain behaviours, either through social roles and expectations, or by limits placed on the types of behaviour possible. Gender role expectations should be more likely to impinge on behaviour at a social gathering than in a workplace meeting. Situational factors also can explain the variable use of particular language features. For example, there are far fewer opportunities to interrupt and provide minimal responses ('mmmm', 'uh huh') in a lecture than in office hours.

conclusion

We maintain that gender is a choice made by individuals as they interact with others; it also can function as a set of behavioural expectations placed upon individuals by others and themselves. On the one hand, it can be empowering to know that gender-preferential language use varies across situations. Individuals do gender more – or less – or even not at all. On the other hand, people have strong expectations that push themselves and others towards or away from certain gender-preferential behaviours. We hope that the continued exploration of the flexibility shown within the rich repertoire of communication behaviours will help to break down gendered barriers both in behaviour and expectations.

references

Anderson, K.J. & Leaper, C. (1998). Meta-analyses of gender effects on conversational interruption: Who, what, when, where, and how. *Sex Roles, 39*, 225–252.

Aries, E. (1982). Verbal and nonverbal behavior in single-sex and mixed-sex groups: Are traditional sex roles changing? *Psychological Reports, 51*, 127–134.

Bayard, D. & Krishnayya, S. (2001). Gender, expletive use, and context: Male and female expletive use in structured and unstructured conversation among New Zealand university students. *Women and Language, 24*, 1–15.

Beall, A.E. (1993). A social constructionist view of gender. In A.E. Beall & R.J. Sternberg (Eds.), *The psychology of gender* (pp.127–147). New York: Guilford Press.

Boggs, C. & Giles, H. (1999). 'The canary in the coalmine': The nonaccommodation cycle in the gendered workplace. *International Journal of Applied Linguistics, 9*, 223–245.

Bogoch, B. (1997). Gendered lawyering: Difference and dominance in lawyer–client interaction. *Law and Society Review, 31*, 677–712.

Carli, L.L. (1990). Gender, language, and influence. *Journal of Personality and Social Psychology, 59*, 941–951.

Carli, L.L. (2001). Gender and social influence. *Journal of Social Issues, 57*, 725–739.

Connellan, J., Baron-Cohen, S., Wheelwright, S., Ba'tki, A. & Ahluwalia, J. (2001). Sex differences in human neonatal social perception. *Infant Behavior and Development, 23*, 113–118.

Coupland, N., Coupland, J., Giles, H. & Henwood, K. (1991). Intergenerational talk: Goal consonance and intergroup dissonance. In K. Tracy (Ed.), *Understanding face-to-face interaction: Issues linking goals and discourse*. Hillsdale, NJ: Lawrence Erlbaum Associates.

Crawford, M. (1995). *Talking difference: On gender and language*. London: Sage.

Eckert, P. & McConnell-Ginet, S. (1992). Think practically and look locally: Language and gender as community-based practice. *Annual Review of Anthropology, 21*, 461–490.

Edelsky, C. (1976). The acquisition of communicative competence: Recognition of linguistic correlates of sex roles. *Merrill-Palmer Quarterly, 22*, 47–59.

Fitzpatrick, M.A., Mulac, A. & Dindia, K. (1995). Gender-preferential language use in spouse and stranger interaction. *Journal of Language and Social Psychology, 14*, 18–39.

Giles, H., Fortman, J., Dailey, R., Barker, V., Hajek, C. & Anderson, M.C. (2007). Communication accommodation: Law enforcement and the public. In A. Weatherall, B. Watson & C. Gallois (Eds.), *Language and social psychology*. Basingstoke, England: Palgrave Macmillan.

Giles, H. & Powesland, P.F. (1975). *Speech style and social evaluation*. European Monographs in Social Psychology, No. 7. London: Academic Press.

Goldberg, S. & Lewis, M. (1969). Play behavior in the year-old infant: Early sex differences. *Child Development, 40*, 21–32.

Green, J. (2004). *Communication accommodation theory: Understanding language use in social interaction*. PhD thesis, University of Otago, Dunedin, New Zealand.

Hajek, C., Abrams, J.R. & Murachver, T. (2005). Female, straight, male, gay, and worlds betwixt and between: An intergroup approach to sexual and gender identities. In J. Harwood & H. Giles (Eds.), *Intergroup communication: Multiple perspectives* (pp.43–64). New York: Peter Lang.

Hannah, A. & Murachver, T. (1999). Gender and conversational style as predictors or conversational behavior. *Language and Social Psychology, 18*, 153–174.

Hills, M. (2000). *You are what you type: Language and gender deception on the internet*. Unpublished honours thesis, University of Otago, Dunedin, New Zealand.

Hogg, M.A. (1985). Masculine and feminine speech in dyads and groups: A study of speech style and gender salience. *Journal of Language and Social Psychology, 4*, 99–112.

Holmes, J. (1988). Paying compliments: A sex-preferential politeness strategy. *Journal of Pragmatics, 23*, 445–465.

Holmes, J. (1995). *Women, men, and politeness*. Essex: Longman Group Limited.

Hows, L. (2004). Nicola or Nicholas – does it make a difference? Reactions to gender-inconsistent language use in electronic communication. Unpublished Honours research project, University of Otago, Dunedin, New Zealand.

Janssen, A. (2004). *Communication in context: How writers, speakers, readers, and listeners do gender*. PhD thesis, University of Otago, Dunedin, New Zealand.

Janssen, A. & Murachver, T. (2004a). The role of gender in New Zealand literature: Comparisons across periods and styles of writing. *Journal of Language and Social Psychology, 23*, 180–203.

Janssen, A. & Murachver, T. (2004b). The relationship between gender and topic in gender-preferential language use. *Written Communication, 21*, 344–367.

Janssen, A. & Murachver, T. (2005). Readers' perceptions of author gender and literary genre. *Journal of Language and Social Psychology, 24*, 207–219.

Keenan, E. (1974). Norm-makers, norm-breakers: Uses of speech by men and women in a Malagasy community. In R. Bauman & J. Sherzer (Eds.), *Explorations in the ethnography of speaking* (pp.125–143). Cambridge: Cambridge University Press.

Kolaric, G.C. & Galambos, N.L. (1995). Face-to-face interaction in unacquainted female–male adolescent dyads: How do girls and boys behave? *Journal of Early Adolescence, 15*, 363–382.

Lakoff, R.T. (1990). *Talking power: The politics of language*. New York: Basic Books.

Leaper, C. (1991). Influence and involvement in children's discourse: Age, gender, and partner effects. *Child Development, 62*, 797–811.

Leaper, C. (2000). The social construction and socialization of gender during development. In P.H. Miller & E.K. Scholnick (Eds.), *Towards a feminist developmental psychology* (pp.1–22). New York, NY: Routledge Press.

Leaper, C. & Gleason, J.B. (1996). The relationship of play activity and gender to parent and child sex-typed communication. *International Journal of Behavioral Development, 19*, 689–703.

Lutchmaya, S. & Baron-Cohen, S. (2002). Human sex differences in social and non-social looking preferences, at 12 months of age. *Infant Behavior & Development, 25*, 319–325.

McCloskey, L.A. & Coleman, L.M. (1992). Difference without dominance: Children's talk in mixed- and same-sex dyads. *Sex Roles, 27*, 241–257.

Maccoby, E.E. (1998). *The two sexes: Growing up apart, coming together.* Cambridge, MA: The Belknap Press.

Macrae, C.N., Milne, A.B. & Bodenhausen, G.V. (1994). Stereotypes as energy-saving devices: A peek inside the cognitive toolbox. *Journal of Personality and Social Psychology, 66*, 37–47.

Mulac, A. & Bradac, J.J. (1995). Women's style in problem solving interaction: Powerless, or simply feminine? In P.J. Kalbfleisch & M.J. Cody (Eds.), *Gender, power, and communication in human relationships* (pp. 83–105). Hillsdale, NJ: Lawrence Erlbaum.

Mulac, A. & Lundell, T.L. (1986). Linguistic contributors to the gender-linked language effect. *Journal of Language and Social Psychology, 5*, 81–101.

Mulac, A., Wiemann, J.M., Widenmann, S.J. & Gibson, T.W. (1988). Male/female language differences and effects in same-sex and mixed-sex dyads: The gender-linked language effect. *Communication Monographs, 55*, 315–335.

Reid, S.A., Keerie, N. & Palomares, N.A. (2003). Language, gender salience, and social influence. *Journal of Language and Social Psychology, 22*, 210–233.

Robertson, S. & Murachver, T. (2003). Children's speech accommodation to gendered language styles. *Journal of Language and Social Psychology, 22*, 321–333.

Shepard, C.A., Giles, H. & LePoire, B.A. (2001). Communication accommodation theory. In W.P. Robinson & H. Giles (Eds.), *The new handbook of language and social psychology.* John Wiley & Sons.

Strough, J. & Diriwachter, R. (2000). Dyad gender differences in preadolescents' creative stories. *Sex Roles, 43*, 43–60.

Tannen, D. (1994). *Talking from 9 to 5.* London: Virago Press.

Thomson, R. & Murachver, T. (2001). Predicting gender from electronic discourse. *British Journal of Social Psychology, 40*, 193–208.

Thomson, R., Murachver, T. & Green, J. (2001). Where is the gender in gendered language? *Psychological Science, 12*, 171–175.

Thorne, B. (1993). *Gender play: Girls and boys in school.* New Brunswick, NJ: Rutgers University Press.

West, C. & Zimmerman, D.H. (1987). Doing gender. *Gender & Society, 1*, 125–151.

Willemyns, W., Gallois, C. & Callan, V.J. (2003). Trust me, I'm your boss: Trust and power in supervisor–supervisee communication. *International Journal of Human Resource Management, 14*, 117–127.

Zimmerman, T.S., Holm, K.E. & Haddock, S.A. (2001). A decade of advice for women and men in the best-selling self-help literature. *Family Relations, 50*, 122–133.

8

conversation analysis, gender and sexuality

sue wilkinson and celia kitzinger

This chapter explores the use of conversation analysis in studying gender and sexuality from a feminist perspective. We are both long-time feminist researchers and activists (see, for example, Kitzinger, 1987, 2004; Kitzinger & Wilkinson, 2004; Wilkinson 1986, 2007; Wilkinson & Kitzinger, 1993). Feminism means developing an understanding of oppression on the basis of gender and sexuality and acting to end it. Oppression operates at many levels – from rape, physical violence and intimidation (Amnesty International, 2001), through discriminatory legislation and institutional practices (Wilkinson & Kitzinger, 2006), to beauty practices (Jeffreys, 2005), offensive joking, banter and innuendo (Hall & Bucholtz, 1995). In our current research, we focus on mundane, routine, everyday forms of oppression: the 'micro-inequalities' of social life (Haslett & Lipman, 1997). We are committed to understanding how sexist and heterosexist presumptions are threaded through the ordinary practices of talk and interaction that, cumulatively, constitute an oppressive social order. Conversation analysis offers a powerful and rigorous method for exposing the mundane oppressions of everyday life.

Conversation analysis (CA) is a theoretically and methodologically distinctive approach to the study of social life. It was developed in the late 1960s and early 1970s by Harvey Sacks, in collaboration with Emanuel Schegloff and Gail Jefferson, from intellectual roots in the sociological tradition of ethnomethodology. Ethnomethodology (from the Greek *ethno* = people or members of a society; and *methodos* = way or method) is concerned with social members' ways of making sense of the everyday social world (Weeks, 1995). For ethnomethodologists, social phenomena such as power and oppression are primarily *accomplishments* (Garfinkel, 1967), processes continually created, sustained (and sometimes resisted) through the practices of social members in interaction. Ethnomethodology offers a model of people as agents, and of a social order grounded in contingent, ongoing interpretive work – an interest in how people *do* social order, rather than in how they are animated by it. For Sacks, talk-in-interaction was simply one site of human interaction that could be studied for what it revealed about the production of social order. Talk as such is not given any *principled* primacy in CA: the key interest of CA is in talk not as *language*, but in talk as *action*: that is, in what people *do* with talk. CA 'describes methods persons use in doing social life' (Sacks, in Psathas, 1995, p.53). For more on the early history and development of CA, see Lerner (2004), Psathas (1979), or Turner (1974).

The methodology of CA was shaped by the availability to Sacks of tape-recorded calls to a suicide prevention centre, which provided its earliest data set:

> It was not from any large interest in language or from some theoretical formulation of what should be studied that I started with tape-recorded conversation, but simply because I could get my hands on it, and I could study it again and again, and also consequentially, because others could look at what I had studied and make of it what they could, if, for example, they wanted to be able to disagree with me. (Sacks, in Heritage, 1984, p.235)

In contrast to the self-report or experimentally-generated data typical of (much of) social psychology, or the invented data typical of (much of) linguistics, CA works with *actual instances* of talk-in-interaction. The analytic procedure depends upon the repeated inspection of recorded naturalistic data[1] (either ordinary everyday conversation, or institutional talk in settings such as courts, classrooms or doctors' surgeries). It focuses upon the organized, recurrent, *structural features* of talk-in-interaction, which stand independently of the characteristics of particular speakers. Knowledge of these structural features, and an understanding of the actions they typically perform, is a key part of social members' competence as communicators: it influences both our own conduct in talk-in-interaction and our interpretation of the conduct of others. CA is defined by a cumulative body of empirical research that describes the basic characteristics of talk-in-interaction. It develops technical specifications of the recurrent patterns, structures and practices that constitute key interactional phenomena. These interactional phenomena, several of which we draw upon below, include sequence organization and preference structure (e.g., Schegloff, 2005); turn-taking and turn-design (e.g., Sacks, Schegloff & Jefferson, 1974); repair and error correction (e.g., Schegloff, Jefferson & Sacks, 1977); storytelling (e.g., Sacks, 1972); word selection, person reference and membership categorization (e.g., Sacks & Schegloff, 1979); and the overall structural organization of interaction (e.g., Jefferson, 1980). This reliance on, and contribution to, a set of cumulative empirically-derived, technical specifications of interactional phenomena is what differentiates CA from discourse analysis and discursive psychology: an argument developed further in Kitzinger (2006).

In any CA project, analysis begins with transcription of the recorded data, preserving fine-grained details such as in-breaths, sound stretches and (timed) pauses. This is necessary because CA research has shown that such apparently tiny and insignificant details of the talk are oriented to by the participants in the conversation; that is, they systematically affect what they do next, and how they do it. If, as analysts, we want to understand how people do things in and through talk, then we need to attend to their talk at the same level of detail as they do. The data extracts below include symbols representing various characteristics of the timing and delivery of the talk, using a transcription notation originally developed by Jefferson. There is a key to the transcription symbols used in this chapter in the Appendix at the end of the volume; for a fuller list, see Jefferson (2004).

Some recent critics of CA – feminists and others (e.g. Billig, 1999; Lakoff, 2003; Wetherell, 1998) – have proposed that, because of its attention to the fine detail of talk, CA is not well-suited to the feminist agenda of understanding power and oppression. These critiques incorporate various 'misunderstandings or misreadings' of CA (Schegloff, 1999, p.559; see also Stokoe, 2005), and we have laid out in more detail elsewhere (Kitzinger, 2000) our arguments for the use of CA in feminist research (including the kinds of research for which it is *not* suited). In this chapter we do not want to pursue a theoretical argument, but rather to show how some of the technical tools that define CA as a discipline – specifically, sequence organization, person reference and repair – can be deployed within a feminist framework.

There is a body of classic feminist work on gender which draws on CA, including West and Zimmerman's explorations of interruptions in cross-sex conversations (e.g., West, 1979; Zimmerman & West, 1975) and Goodwin's analyses of girls' talk (e.g., Goodwin, 1990). In addition, in the last five years or so, there has been a dramatic increase in CA and CA-influenced research on gender and sexuality by feminists and other critical researchers: see, for example, Stokoe (2000), Speer (2005), Tainio (2003), Rendle-Short (2005), Weatherall (2002), and several contributions to the collections edited by McIlvenny (2002) and Stokoe and Weatherall (2002). Our focus in this chapter is on a number of our own projects: talk about sexual refusal, lesbians and breast cancer, and coming out as lesbian or gay. We will show instances of data analysis drawn from these three studies, in each case highlighting the contribution of a different technical CA tool in exposing the operation of gender and sexuality in everyday talk. In the following three sections we focus on sequence organization and preference structure, person reference and category memberships, and repair and error correction.

talk about sexual refusal: sequence organization and preference structure

One of our earliest feminist CA projects was on young women's talk about sexual refusal (Kitzinger & Frith, 1999). There is a substantial literature indicating that young women report difficulty in refusing unwanted (hetero)sex. This literature proposes that many instances of date rape are the result of women not communicating clearly to men the fact that they do not want sex (e.g., Campbell & Barnlund, 1977; Howard, 1985; Warzak & Page, 1990). This, in turn, has led to the development of so-called 'refusal skills training'; a variety of date rape prevention, assertiveness training and social skills programmes and manuals which teach women to be assertive in refusing sex and to 'just say no' clearly, directly and unapologetically (e.g., Kidder, Boell & Moyer, 1983). These typically advise young women that refusals are best accomplished through plain, unvarnished – and preferably repeated – 'no's. For example:

> It is crucial that you give a simple 'no' rather than a long-winded statement filled with excuses, justifications, and rationalizations about why you are saying 'no'. It is enough that you do not want to do this, simply because you do not want to do it. (Phelps & Austin, 1987, pp.123–4)

However, CA analyses of how refusals are actually *done* shows us something very different. Based on empirical analysis of naturally-occurring conversations in which people receive invitations and respond to them (with acceptance or refusal), conversation analysts have found that acceptances and refusals follow very different patterns. In a nutshell, acceptances do indeed often involve 'just saying yes', but refusals very rarely involve 'just saying no'.

Two key CA interactional phenomena underwrite research on (sexual) refusal: sequence organization (Schegloff, 2007) and preference structure (Sacks, 1987). Sequence organization is based on the empirical finding that actions typically occur in sequences. The most basic type of sequence involves two (adjacent) turns at talk by different speakers, the first constituting an *initiating* action, and the second an action *responsive* to it (Schegloff, 2007). Most initiating actions can be followed by a range of *sequentially-relevant* (i.e., appropriately 'fitted') next actions. For example, an invitation can be followed by an acceptance or a refusal, a request by a granting or a denying, a proposal by an acquiescence or a rejection, and so on. But these alternative responsive actions are not equivalent (Sacks, 1987). In CA terminology, an acceptance of an invitation, a granting of a request or an acquiescence to a proposal are *preferred* next actions, while a refusal of an invitation, a rejection of a request or a rejection of a proposal are *dispreferred*. 'Preference' is a structural concept, rather than a psychological one: thus, the fact that an invitation 'prefers' an acceptance is independent of the personal preference of the recipient of that invitation. Most of us will have had the experience of accepting an invitation that we would personally have preferred to have refused.

Preferred and dispreferred responses run off very differently (Pomerantz, 1984; Sacks, 1987). Preferred responses are characteristically offered without delay, and are clear and direct. Here are two examples of a recipient *accepting* an invitation:

Acceptance 1
```
[SBL:10:12, in Atkinson and Drew, 1979, p.58]
A:  Why don't you come up and see me some[time
B:                                        [I would like to
```

Acceptance 2
```
[Davidson, 1984, p.116]
A:  We:ll, will you help me [ou:t.
B:                          [I certainly wi:ll.
```

Dispreferred responses, by contrast, are often delayed, hedged, and accompanied by explanations, excuses or justifications. Here are two examples of a recipient *refusing* an invitation:

Refusal 1
```
[Potter and Wetherell, 1987, p.86]
Mark:  We were wondering if you wanted to come over Saturday,
       f'r dinner.
       (0.4)
```

Jane: Well (.) .hh it'd be great but we promised Carol
        already.

Refusal 2
[SBL:10:14, in Heritage, 1984, p.266]
A: Uh if you'd care to come and visit a little while this
    morning I'll give you a cup of <u>co</u>ffee.
B: hehh Well that's awfully sweet of you, I don't think I
    can make it this morning .hh uhm I'm running an ad in the
    paper and-and uh I have to stay near the phone.

In the first refusal we see a silence (of four tenths of a second) before the refusal; the refusal is softened by a palliative (the compliment 'it'd be great'); and it is explained with reference to a prior commitment ('we promised Carol already'), proposing an inability, rather than an unwillingness, to accept the invitation (Drew, 1984). In the second, we see a filled silence (hehh) before the refusal; again it is softened by a compliment ('that's awfully sweet of you'); and explained by reference to a prior commitment ('I have to stay near the phone').

CA work on preferred and dispreferred responses shows us that if young women find it difficult to give immediate, clear, direct 'no's in sexual situations, that might be because that is not how refusals are normatively done. Refusal skills training manuals seem to be offering advice that does not capture social reality. Further, young women themselves are able to articulate this. Although we don't have the ideal data in which young women are actually *doing* sexual refusals (see Tainio, 2003, for an example of this), we do have data in which they *talk about doing* such refusals – and their discussions embody a lay version of CA discoveries (of course, they don't use terminology such as 'dispreferred' or 'palliative'). When asked why they don't 'just say no', young women explain that that would feel 'rude' or 'foolish'. They describe the 'best' explanations or excuses as those which assert their inability, rather than their unwillingness, to engage in sex (illness, menstruation, a parent's imminent arrival home). They say it is a good idea to qualify or mitigate refusals ('I'm not ready yet'), and to soften the blow with what CA calls palliatives ('well it's very flattering of you to ask'). They know very well how refusals are normatively done, and are able to use this knowledge to criticize and resist the advice to 'just say no'.

On the basis of this analysis, and from a feminist perspective, we suggest that the insistence of date rape educators on the importance of 'just saying no' is counter-productive in that it requires women to engage in conversationally abnormal actions. CA shows us that refusals are not typically done in such a direct and unvarnished way. The advice to 'just say no' also allows rapists to persist in their claim that if a woman hasn't actually said no, then she hasn't actually refused to have sex with him. CA shows us that it is not necessary to say the word 'no' in order to be heard as doing a refusal (Davidson, 1984; Levinson, 1983).[2] Using CA specifications of sequence organization and preference structure, examination of how refusals are normatively done shows us the mundane, everyday operation of the practices of oppression and resistance.

lesbians and breast cancer: person reference and category memberships

A second area in which CA offers us tools for looking at power relations is person reference and category memberships. There is a substantial body of CA work on how persons are referred to in talk-in-interaction, particularly as members of various social categories (e.g., Sacks, 1972; Sacks & Schegloff, 1979; Schegloff, 1996).

Social scientists and linguists have sometimes written about 'men's talk' (Coates, 2003), 'women's talk' (Coates, 1996), or 'gay men's talk' (Leap, 1996), as though the fact that the speakers whose talk is being analysed *are* men, or women, or gay is sufficient warrant for treating them as *speaking* as men, or women or gays. But any given individual can be characterized by a wide range of category terms taken from many different category sets: sexual identity (which we focus on here), gender, ethnicity, age, nationality, religion, occupation, place of residence, health status, dietary preference, and so on. One consequence of this is that we cannot explain the choice of any given category term to refer to a person simply 'by saying that they *are*, after all, such a one' (Schegloff, 1997, p.165). It is not enough to justify referring to someone as a 'lesbian' just because she *is* a lesbian, when she is also, for example, a Northerner, British, forty-something, vegetarian (and many others). There are always alternative forms of reference that are equally *accurate*. However, they are not, of course, all equally *relevant* on any given occasion. The key question, then, is what is the relevance on any particular occasion of using a particular way of referring to someone – why that now?

For conversation analysts the answer to this question is generally in terms of which of their categorical identities participants can be seen to be oriented to on any particular occasion. This can shift over the course of an interaction, depending on what they are using these categorical identities to do. For example, drawing on a corpus of out-of-hours calls to a doctor's office, we have shown how in phoning to get medical help for a family member, callers routinely selected person reference terms drawn from the category set 'family', such as 'husband' or 'wife', thereby producing themselves as the spouse of the person so referred to (Kitzinger, 2005b). Presumably, of course, the people so referred to *are* the 'husband' or 'wife' of the caller, but this is not enough to mandate so categorizing them, since they are also 'a diabetic', or 'a seventy-year-old', and so on. Data analysis showed that the selection of family terms in this data corpus was deployed to obviate the need for an account as to why it was they who were calling on behalf of the patient, since a woman calling on behalf of her husband or a man calling on behalf of his wife is engaged in a culturally-understood-as-normal-activity: nothing special is happening in terms of the relationships displayed. By contrast, callers in the same data corpus who contacted the doctor on behalf of (for example) an 'old friend' or a 'next door neighbour's baby' provided accounts for why it was they who were making the call. In these instances, then, category terms drawn from the device 'family' are deployed to facilitate the process of getting medical assistance for the person so referred to. This constitutes a mundane instance of heterosexual privilege, since this option is not generally available to people in same-sex relationships.[3]

Conversely, a person who is, in fact, a husband can be referred to with reference to other categorical memberships for local interactional purposes. For example, in an analysis of talk between women with breast cancer, we have shown how a woman accounts for her husband's problems in coming to terms with her post-mastectomy body by positioning him within the category 'men'. He is exonerated from individual culpability for his difficulties because it is a cultural commonplace that – as most of the participants in the discussion agree – 'all men like boobs' (Wilkinson & Kitzinger, 2003).[4]

Most research on person reference and categorization focuses on talk about third persons, since third persons are often referred to using non-recognitional reference forms which take the form of categories ('the old guy', 'the white woman', 'the teenager', etc.), whereas first person references are normally accomplished with a simple 'I' (Schegloff, 1996). We focus here on how speakers produce *themselves* as category members, in part through the deployment of a collective first person reference form ('we') and in part through the use of categorical self-declarations ('I am a [category member]'). In particular, we show how a speaker whose contribution to a research enterprise has been invited on the basis of her 'lesbian' identity, speaks instead as a 'Lancashire lass' (Lancashire is a county in the north of England, and 'lass' is a northern term for a woman/girl). The data extract below comes from a focus group discussion about breast cancer between a group of self-identified lesbians recruited *as lesbians* (by a known-to-be lesbian moderator) and asked to identify 'risk factors' for breast cancer, particularly any that might affect lesbians differently from heterosexual women (as part of a larger study on lesbians and breast cancer: e.g., Fish & Wilkinson, 2003; Wilkinson, 2002).

The category membership foregrounded by the focus group moderator, both in recruiting the participants and in asking her questions, is the sexual identity category 'lesbian'. 'Lesbian' is produced *as* a sexual identity category (that is, as one of the category set of which 'heterosexual' and 'bisexual' are also members), by virtue of the contrast repeatedly invoked by the focus group moderator (and, as we shall see, by focus group participants), between 'lesbians' and 'heterosexual women'. We might note, in passing, that 'lesbian' is not *necessarily*, in practice, a category of sexual identity. Most category terms belong to a range of *different* category sets – as Sacks (1995a, p.247) has famously argued, 'baby' is one of the category set 'family' (of which, mother, father, uncle, and so on, are also members) and also one of the category set 'stage of life' (of which toddler, teenager, adult, and so on, are also members) – and, on any given occasion of use, may be deployed as a term from *either* category set. Likewise, the category set relevantly invoked by 'lesbian' can be 'gender', rather than 'sexual identity' (in a context where the contrast is between 'lesbian' and 'gay man'), or 'grounds on which discrimination is banned' (where the contrast is between 'lesbian' and 'black person', 'Jewish person', 'person with a disability', etc.).

In the following extract (and in this focus group more generally), however, 'lesbian' is produced *as* a sexual identity by virtue of the question the moderator poses after each risk factor identified by the participants: 'Do you think that affects lesbians any differently?' (implying a contrast category of 'heterosexual women'), and by and large the participants speak *as lesbians*. One participant says, for example: 'I think we're just as likely to be either slim or (.) overweight as (.) as heterosexual women' – where (as is clear from the contrast category 'heterosexual women') 'we' clearly means 'lesbians' – and 'sexual identity' is thereby produced as the relevant category set. In the discussion of smoking and drinking which immediately precedes the data extract below, another participant comments 'I think as a group we <u>do</u> drink. To excess.' The 'group' to which she refers, and in which she includes herself (through using the pro-term 'we') is treated by the moderator as meaning 'lesbians' (and as invoking the sexual identity category set) when she poses her follow-up question, 'You think we drink more than heterosexual women?' Note that the moderator is also speaking *as a lesbian* (marking her own inclusion in the category 'lesbian' through her repeat of the pro-term 'we'). One way of producing a first person speaker as a member of a category, then, is to use a collective pronoun, thereby invoking a collectivity – identifiable here, for the reasons outlined above, as 'lesbians'.

Here, then, is a moment from the focus group discussion in which one of its lesbian participants speaks – in contradistinction to the others – not as a lesbian, but as something *other* than a lesbian: as a Lancashire lass. As the extract below opens, Karen is disagreeing with a prior assertion (not shown here) that meeting and drinking in bars is a key part of lesbian culture:

Lancashire lass[5]

```
[JF: LBC1: 10-12]
01 Kar:  [>Well I mean<] I've never sort of- [ (0.2)   ]
02 ():                                       [((Sniff))]
03 Kar:  I've never been a frequenter of ba:rs anyway
04       I've- I've never felt the nee:d.
05       (0.5)
06 Kar:  To- (.) to be a frequenter of bars <an' I
07       certainly don't drink a lot.
08 Lou:  No:.=I don't.
09       (.)
10 Pen:  <My experience is that (.) most of my friends
11       don't drink a lot either.=
12 Mod:  =Ri:ght.
13 Pen:  Uh:m (.) so:[: ]
14 Mod:            [Mo]st of your lesbian f[riends.]
15 Pen:                                    [ Yeah. ]
16 Mod:  °Mm hm.°=
17 Pen:  =Yeah.
18       (0.2)
19 ():   ((Sniff))
20       (0.5)
21 Pen:  I'm just ( .)
22 ():   °O:h n(h):[o.°]
23 ():          [hu ]h >hah hah< ha[ h]
24 ():                            [°N]o.° °°No.°°
25 Deb:  >But I mean you- like the statistic-< (.) that
26       kind of statistic could apply: like i-in the
27       No:rth-South divide you know=you have that
28       kind of thing. .hh[hhhh uh]:::m: [ (.)] you know
29 ():                     [Yea:h. ]
30 ():                                    [Mmm.]
31 Deb: >which especially-< (.) I'm a Lanc- $I'm
32       a Lancashire lass$ .hhh >say a lot of (.)
33       <y'know< people in Lancashire drink a lot
34       more >I mean there are-< an' you do
35       get these kind of statistics don't you.
```

```
36  Mod:   Ah.
37  Deb:   <That uh:m (.) >you know< that people in
38         the North smo:ke mo:re.
39         (0.2)
40  Deb:   You know. Therefor:e this happens. .h So: I-I- I
41         don't think it's necessarily: a: >such a< (.)
42         >you know< a gay and straight thing.
43         (0.2)
```

In this extract, Karen and Louise speak *as lesbians*, and are treated as so
speaking by the moderator and by the other group members. Having been
recruited to the focus group as lesbians, they treat their lesbian identities
as already-known-in-common by other group members, invoking them as
presuppositions in their talk. So, Karen's claim that she has 'never been a
frequenter of bars' (line 3) is produced as a disagreement with the claim
that lesbians meet and drink in bars. She makes it *as a lesbian*, claiming
her own experience as offering evidence to counter the generalization.
The relevance of her assertion that she doesn't go to bars presupposes her
own inclusion in the category 'lesbian'. Likewise, her emphatic negative
assertion that she doesn't 'drink a lot' (line 7) is made *as* the lesbian she is
already known to be, in order to counter the prior assertion that lesbians
'as a group' are prone to drinking 'to excess'. In this turn (lines 1–7), then,
Karen is (separately) challenging both of the category attributes (earlier)
made to lesbians as category (going to bars and drinking a lot): since she
is a lesbian, and they don't apply to her, they can't possibly be true. In
so doing, she is speaking as a lesbian.

Louise's support for Karen's challenge to the heavy drinking attribution
(her 'no', line 8, agrees with Karen's negatively-polarized assertion, 'I
certainly don't', lines 6–7) and her stress on the 'I' (of the assertion 'I
don't', line 8) indicates that it is *as another lesbian* – that is, in addition to
Karen – she also cannot be characterized by the behaviour attributed to
the category 'lesbians' (drinking a lot). Louise's assertion, then, supports
Karen's position, in claiming her own exclusion from the category-
attribution of excessive drinking, and again the relevance of her claim
presupposes her own inclusion in the category 'lesbian'.

When Penny builds on this, claiming exclusion from the category
attribution (of heavy drinking) for others beyond the room ('most of
my friends don't drink a lot either', lines 10–11), the moderator seeks
clarification of the sexual identity of Penny's friends (line 14): only if they
are lesbian is their not drinking a lot relevant to the ongoing discussion.
In checking her understanding of the sexual identity of Penny's moderate-
drinking friends, the moderator displays that she has treated Karen and

Louise as having spoken 'as lesbians' when they staked a claim to their own alcoholic moderation.

By contrast, Debbie (who is also a lesbian) speaks instead as a 'Lancashire lass', using a category term drawn from a set related to geographical region, not sexual identity. Her turn (at lines 25–42[6]), like those of Karen, Louise and Penny, is built as a disagreement with prior assertions about lesbian drinking (and smoking). At lines 25–28, she begins to advance the argument that differences in alcohol and tobacco use ('that kind of statistic') could equally well be based on categorical identities related to the device geographical region ('the North-South divide'[7]), using the self-identification 'Lancashire lass' (lines 31–32) to claim experiential authority on the drinking and smoking habits of 'people in Lancashire' (line 33) and 'people in the North' (lines 37–38). Although all of the participants are known to be lesbian, in the context of a discussion held 'down South', Debbie is likely to know (or at least reasonably presume) herself to be the only 'Lancashire lass' present. What she does here, by foregrounding a categorical identity of geographical region, rather than sexual identity, is to invoke a new 'partitioning' (Sacks, 1995b, pp.104–113) of the group: between Southerners (many/most of those present) and Northerners (possibly only herself). In this partitioning, of course, only Northerners have the experiential authority to speak *as Northerners* (in contrast to the previous partitioning, based on sexual identity, in which all of the group members were partitioned as lesbian, with concomitant rights to speak *as lesbians*).

The particular person reference form Debbie selects – 'Lancashire lass' – is hearably idiomatic, as well as alliterative, which may account for the cut-off on her first try at self-identification as a member of this category ('I'm a Lanc-', line 31), and her redoing of the self-identification with a smile voice (as indicated by the $ symbols, lines 31–32). This hearable amusement may also display an awareness that reconstituting her categorical identity in geographical terms, in a context where she has been specifically invited to speak as a lesbian, could be seen as rather mischievous. More generally, it may also display an orientation to the somewhat transgressive nature of the action in which she is engaged – just as Heritage (personal communication) has noted the use of a smile voice when reporting medical misdemeanours (such as diet-breaking or resumption of smoking) to the doctor.

The particular categorical self-identification Debbie selects, challenges the foregrounding of membership in one category (lesbian) by invoking an *alternative* category of which she is also a member (Lancashire lass). She questions the category attributes (heavy drinking and smoking) made to lesbians by pointing out that these attributes could also apply to people from Lancashire/the North. If these risk factors are not specific to lesbians, then there is no reason to assume lesbians are at particular risk of developing breast cancer. Through her invocation of an alternative category of self-identification, then, Debbie challenges the idea that cancer risk is related to sexual identity. As she says (at lines 40–42): 'I don't think it's necessarily a gay and straight thing.'

Our analysis of this focus group interaction has shown two ways in which lesbians speak *as lesbians*: by using the pro-term 'we' in sequential contexts and with turn designs that make lesbians the relevant collectivity; and by using the pro-term 'I' in invoking their own experience to dispute some attribute allegedly attached to the category lesbian, such that their own lesbianism is presupposed. In the context of this lesbian-only focus group, lesbian identities are presupposed and indexed rather than explicitly articulated (as heterosexual identities are in presumed heterosexual-only contexts: see Kitzinger, 2005a). The challenge Debbie faces in this focus group, then, is to be heard as speaking as something *other* than a lesbian, even though she *is* a lesbian and is not denying it. Her explicit claiming of a categorical identity ('I'm a Lancashire lass') stakes a claim to speak outside the 'lesbian' identity she has been assigned, on the basis of another not incompatible, but, in this context, competing, categorical identity. She is claiming that it is not enough to justify treating her as a 'lesbian' just because she *is* a lesbian, when she is also a Lancashire lass – and thereby illustrating precisely Schegloff's (1997) point.

For social scientists and linguists interested in how categories of people (men, women, gays, Northerners) speak, or in how they 'perform' their identities, conversation analysis provides a method that actively engages with, and offers empirical resources to analyse, multiple, fractured and constantly shifting identities, as they are mobilized in interaction. Using the tools of CA to examine the deployment of particular person reference forms and the category memberships they invoke can enable us to see how these are implicated in the operation of power and oppression.

coming out as lesbian or gay: repair and error correction

A third major technical area of CA to provide us with a set of resources for examining how power and oppression may be accomplished (and resisted) in everyday talk-in-interaction is the domain of repair and error correction. We will illustrate this with reference to a project on coming out to others as lesbian or gay.

The significance of coming out for lesbians/gay men and for their families is reflected both in the extensive self-help literature (e.g., Borhek, 1983; Signorile, 1996) and in psychological research (e.g., Fields, 2001; Markowe, 2002). It is often assumed that coming out is inevitably done as big news announcement ('Mum, Dad, I've got something to tell you – I'm gay'), and self-report studies (as well as published 'coming out stories') tend to bear this out. Coming out (particularly to significant others) may indeed sometimes be done this way, but there is no empirical evidence of this because previous work on coming out is based entirely on self-report data, rather than examining *actual instances* of coming out itself. By contrast, we have examined some *actual* comings out that just happen to have been captured 'live' on audiotape – in small group seminar sessions with undergraduate students (Kitzinger, 2000), and in phone conversations from lesbian households (Land & Kitzinger, 2005). These are rather less dramatic instances than coming out to Mum and Dad, but our analysis of how these 'mundane' comings out are done provides a rather different picture from the big news announcement, as we will see.

'Repair' is the technical CA term for what takes place when the interactional business-in-hand is temporarily suspended in order to deal with some kind of 'trouble' in the talk. The term 'repair' is used to cover a range of practices used by conversational participants to address ostensible problems in speaking, hearing or understanding – problems that apparently need to be dealt with before the participants can resume the ongoing interactional business. Conversation analysts differentiate between repairs initiated (and usually performed) by speakers on their *own* talk (self-intiated repair), and repairs initiated on the speaker's talk by someone *other* than the speaker (other-initiated repair), which is a far less frequent practice, particularly if it also involves performing the repair (see Schegloff, Jefferson & Sacks, 1977; Schegloff, 2000). This latter kind of repair involves *correction*, as in the following example:

Exposed correction
```
[GTS:II:2:54, from Jefferson, 1987, p.87]
01  Ken:  And they told me how I could stick a th-uh::
02        Thunderbird motor? (0.5) in my Jeep? And I
03        bought a fifty five [Thunderbird motor.
04  Rog:                      [Not motor, engine. You
05        speak of [electric motor and a gasoline engine
06  Ken:           [Okay
07  Ken:  Engine. [Okay-
08  Rog:          [Internal combus:tion.
09  Ken:  Alright, So [lookit, I moved this thing in the Jeep
```

Here, at line 4, Roger initiates repair on Ken's prior turn, naming the trouble source ('not motor') and also providing the repair solution, the correction ('engine'). The whole of Roger's turn at lines 4–5 is devoted to correcting Ken's error, and that he does this *instead* of producing a next action that is sequentially-relevant to this stage of a telling (such as a receipt, or a continuer, or an assessment of Ken's purchase). And Ken's turns at lines 6 and 7 are devoted to an acceptance of the correction, rather than to a continuation of his telling, which is suspended until line 9 (although here he uses the term 'thing' rather than the correction provided by Roger).

This kind of overt or 'exposed' error correction is rare in ordinary conversation. What's more common is what Jefferson (1987) calls 'embedded' correction of errors. By contrast with exposed correction, which, as we have seen, suspends the ongoing business of the talk in order to deal with some trouble, an embedded correction allows the interactional business-at-hand to continue without disruption. Instead, the correction takes place entirely within the context of the ongoing interactional business: it is *embedded* within it. In the following example (another exchange between the same two young offenders in a group therapy session), Roger offers a candidate correction ('cops', line 4) as an alternative to the term Ken has used in his prior turn ('police', line 1). However, Roger's correction is embedded within a relevant next action and so does not disrupt the interactional business in any way:

Embedded correction
```
[GTS:II:60:ST, from Jefferson, 1987, p.93]
01  Ken:  Well- if you're gonna race, the police have
02        said this to us.
03  Rog:  That makes it even better. The challenge of
04        running from the cops!
05  Ken:  The cops say if you wanna race, uh go out at
06        four or five in the morning on the freeway
              ((continues))
```

Here, Roger's candidate correction ('cops') is embedded within his assessment (lines 3–4) of the information Ken has just conveyed (lines 1–2). Because the production of such an assessment is a sequentially-relevant next action to this stage of a telling, the correction does not disrupt the interactional business-at-hand: it continues smoothly. Nor does Ken interrupt his telling in order to accept Roger's proffered alternative (as in the exposed correction example): he does this simply by incorporating the alternative term ('cops') into the continuation of his telling (line 5).

We turn now to an application of this technology to the process of coming out. The two data extracts below come from the Land corpus: a series of telephone calls made to and from five lesbian households in England.[8] The first is taken from a series of calls in which a lesbian couple, Janice and Sylvia, is trying to arrange car insurance. As we know from other calls in the corpus, Janice and Sylvia habitually refer to each other as 'my wife' (a practice not uncommon among established lesbian couples, although 'my partner' is more usual); however, in this particular call, Janice first uses the gender-neutral term 'spouse' (line 2) – perhaps fitted to the insurance context. She subsequently finds herself performing an exposed correction (lines 12–13) on the word 'husband' (line 11):

```
Car insurance
[Land: SC03]
01  Jan:  .hhh I'm wanting insurance fo:r uhm: (.),
02        two named drivers self and spous:e.=
03  Clt:  =>Yeah< 'v cou:rse.
04        (13.0)
05  Clt:  (Right) I've got you down as a doctor. Do
06        you have the use of any other vehicle
07        within the househo:ld.
08  Jan:  Yes I do.
09        (0.8)
10  Clt:  An: (.) you said you'd like to insure your
11        husband to drive the car.
12  Jan:  mcht Uh:::m It's not my husband it's my
13        wi:fe and yes I would l[ike t- ]
14  Clt:                         [Oh I do] beg your
15        pardon.
16  Jan:  I would like to insure her.
17  Clt:  Yep >thank you<
18        (11.5)
19  Clt:  ('Kay) Could I take your wife's name
20        please.
```

At lines 10–11, the call-taker offers an understanding check of Janice's insurance requirements. However, this understanding check, through the call-taker's use of the gendered term 'husband', incorporates the presumption that Janice's 'spouse' (line 2) is male. In her immediately following turn (lines 12–13) Janice suspends the business-in-hand (confirming her insurance needs) in order to initiate repair upon this presumption and offer the alternative, appropriate term ('wife') instead, as an exposed correction. In doing so, of course, she also comes out to the call-taker as lesbian. The call-taker explicitly apologizes (lines 14–15) for his presumption and displays his acceptance of the alternative term 'wife' by using it himself in his next question (line 19).

As we noted in an earlier analysis of mundane, everyday, comings out (Kitzinger, 2000), the action of coming out is generally embedded into a longer turn such that recipients do not have to deal with it there and then. Janice's coming out above is relatively atypical, both for its overtness, and for being done as an exposed correction (in fact, across our data sets, it is the only 'in your face' coming out of this type). It is far more common for comings out to be done as embedded corrections. In our second example, taken from another call in the Land corpus, Nicola is trying to register her partner, Sandra, as a new patient at a dentists' surgery.[9] Like Janice (who used the term 'spouse'), Nicola initially uses a gender-neutral term ('partner', line 13), and finds herself performing an embedded correction upon the masculine pronoun 'he' (line 23):

Dentist
[Land: OC04]
```
01          ((ring-ring ring-ring))
02   Rec:   Good afternoon Johnson Olivier and
03          Tilsley?
04   Nic:   Hello. >uhm< I was wondering if it would
05          be possible to find out if I could r-uhm
06          register as a new patie:nt.
07   Rec:   Yes. certainly.= Miss Boon's thee (.) only
08          patient taking NHS: .hh any- only dentist
09          taking N-H-S patient[s.
10   Nic:                        [Mm hm¿
11   Rec:   mcht U:hm: I'll just take some
12          detail[s from you. ]
13   Nic:         [Well it's for my part]ner actually.
14   Rec:   Ri:ght.
15          (0.5)
16   Rec:   'Scuse me a moment.
17   Nic:   Okay than[k you
18   Rec:            [Mr Leggett¿ ((off phone))
19          (.)
20   Rec:   Would you like to go: up. hh ((off phone))
21          (0.8)
22   Rec:   An' what was the na:me¿
23          (0.8)
24   Nic:   >Sorry my name.<
25   Rec:   What was his name.
26   Nic:   Oh uhm it's S:andra Ferry
27          (0.5)
```

```
28        (( [another phone [ringing))]
29  Rec:     [ Ferry¿ ]
30  Nic:                      [ Yes::. ]
31        (3.5)
32  Rec:  Ye- Just hold the line a second.
33  Nic:  >Okay< Thank you.
34        (10.5)
35  Rec:  Sorry about that.= We've got (.) dentists
36        swapped surgeries 'n' .hh one's come
37        downstairs and one's gone upstairs an' the
38        patients don't know whether they're
39        co(h)ming [or go(h)ing.
40  Nic:            [Huhuh huh huh
41        [No](h) prob(h)lem don't [worry about it
42  Rec:  [So]                     [Ferry did you
43        say¿
44  Nic:  .hh Yes. F double R Y.
45        (.)
46  Rec:  A:n' the Christian n:ame¿
47  Nic:  It's: Sandra. hh
48        (0.5)
49  Rec:  F- Is it for him or for you:.
50  Nic:  It's for her.
51        (.)
52  Rec:  Oh for her- O:h °sor(h)ry° .hh[h     ]
53  Nic:                               [.hh $I]t's
54        oka:y$
55  Rec:  Uh huh huh huh huh Sandra.
56  Nic:  Yes:.
57  Rec:  .hh Right. An::d date of birth¿
```

The receptionist's use of the masculine pronoun 'he' (line 25), in asking for the name of the new dental patient, incorporates the presumption that Nicola's 'partner' (line 13) is male. However, in her immediately following turn (line 26), Nicola does not suspend the interactional business-in-hand in order to perform an exposed correction (which might have looked something like: 'not his name, her name'); rather she produces the sequentially-relevant next action: providing the name that has been asked for. Nicola's provision of a culturally-known-to-be female first name may be seen as (at least) a partial embedded correction, and thereby a partial coming out – in that it makes available to the receptionist that her partner is female. However, it is the surname that the receptionist first repeats for confirmation (both at line 29, and again after an apology sequence following an interruption to the call while the receptionist deals with a patient, at line 42), only then returning to the problematic first name (at line 46). The receptionist's treatment of Nicola's repetition of 'Sandra' suggests an attempt to solve the puzzle of why she has been given a female name rather than the male one she showed herself to expect. She checks out the possibility that she has misunderstood which of the two members of the presumed-heterosexual couple is being registered (line 49). In response, Nicola produces an embedded correction: she continues with the interactional business-in-hand (answering the question about which of them is the new patient), but incorporates an alternative pronoun ('her', line 50, instead of 'him', line 49). The receptionist subsequently accepts the correction, and apologizes for her presumption (line 52). Through her embedded correction, Nicola has come out as a member of a lesbian couple.

This is typical of the comings out in our collection. In these (relatively safe) environments there is no fuss or fanfare: nobody makes a big news announcement, and nobody expresses disgust, condemnation – or congratulations. Rather, speakers convey the information about their sexuality in an embedded way. This enables them to avoid having to initiate repair, because other-initiated repair is dispreferred, as we have noted. It also enables them to keep lesbianism (largely) off the surface of the conversation, and so avoid the necessity of their or their interlocutors having to deal with it directly (the dental receptionist is rather unusual in choosing to do so, through offering an apology for her presumption).

What does this practice tell us about the conditions of lesbian and gay oppression? First, in coming out in this way, speakers are attentive to the (common) accusation of 'flaunting' their sexuality. Their embedded corrections are precisely designed *not* to flaunt, not to make an issue of it, but to slip it into the conversation in a way that gets it into the public arena, but does not foreground it. A second reason why coming out might be done like this is to mark some kind of resistance to the necessity of coming out (such that not to do so is to be presumed heterosexual). This 'not news' kind of coming out, then, can be seen both as collusion with the heterosexual imperative *not* to be public about lesbian or gay sexuality, and as resistance to the whole notion that coming out should be necessary at all. Third, there is a protective element in play here, both for speakers and for recipients. In coming out in this embedded way, speakers protect recipients from necessarily having to produce a response. The location of the information as an embedded correction, which does not suspend the ongoing interaction in any way, provides for recipients to hear the information and yet not necessarily have to engage with it there and then (or at all). And if there is no response, the speaker, in turn, protects herself from having to deal with such a response. In sum, the organization of repair and error correction provides a resource for speakers to come out 'discreetly'[10] in ordinary, everyday contexts.

conclusion

In this chapter, we have demonstrated how some of the tools of CA – the technical domains of sequence organization and preference structure, person reference and category memberships, and repair and error correction – can be used in studying gender and sexuality from a feminist perspective. We have shown how talk about sexual refusal, and about lesbians and breast cancer, as well as everyday phone calls to insurance salesmen and dental receptionists, embodies the sexist and heterosexist presumptions that are imbricated into social life. Using the methodology of CA on such data sets, we have demonstrated how oppression – and, sometimes, resistance – can be seen at work in the ordinary, mundane practices of talk and interaction.

As feminists, we have found that CA offers a powerful and rigorous method for exposing the micro-inequalities of everyday social life. In the particular projects presented here, it has enabled us to see that sexual refusals are not normatively done by 'just saying no' (as young women well know); that presuppositions of particular categorical identities powerfully affect what can be said and how it is understood; and that coming out (at least in relatively mundane, safe environments) is often discreetly embedded into the structure of conversation. These kinds of understandings of how an oppressive social order is produced, and reproduced, in ordinary, everyday life can inform feminist political action to end oppression.

notes

1. Conversation analysts sometimes also study interaction in non-naturalistic settings such as interviews and focus groups. In this case, the interactions taking place there and then, in the interview or focus group itself, constitute the data, rather than (as is the case in most interview or focus group research) participants' *reports* of interactions that have taken place in other contexts (see Wilkinson 2004, 2006, for a more extended discussion and examples of this).
2. For empirical evidence that young men do, indeed, know this, see O'Byrne, Rapley and Hansen (2006).
3. Family reference terms (such as husband, wife, in-laws) are not available in any unproblematic way to lesbian or gay couples in countries where same-sex marriage is not permitted under law. At the time of writing (October, 2005) only The Netherlands, Belgium, Spain, Canada and the US state of

Massachusetts accorded the right to marry to same-sex partners (see Wilkinson & Kitzinger, 2003). In the third section below, we show two examples of the interactional difficulties that may arise in referring to a same-sex partner; see also Land and Kitzinger (2005).

4. This offers another example of mundane heterosexual privilege, as our more extended analysis shows. The commonplace does not, of course, apply to gay men; and the lesbian moderator of the discussion disassociates herself from the assumption that (as a woman) she would know what men like.

5. With thanks to Julie Fish for permission to use this data extract, of which a preliminary analysis was presented (by the first author) at the international conference on 'Talking Gender and Sexuality', held at Aalborg University, Denmark, in November 1999.

6. This is a very long turn, and it is worth noting that Debbie uses several of the turn-holding devices identified by conversation analysts (e.g., Schegloff, 1982): a pivot (lines 26–27), compressed transition spaces (lines 27 and 32), and increments (lines 37–38 and 40).

7. This idiom refers to the common understanding that, in England, there is a divide between the relatively prosperous south of the country and the economically poorer north.

8. With thanks to Vicky Land for permission to use these data extracts.

9. For a more detailed analysis of this data extract, and for a deferred coming out (which depends upon an embedded correction performed by the call-taker rather than by the lesbian caller), see Land and Kitzinger (2005).

10. We have shown elsewhere (Land & Kitzinger, 2005) how coming out may be *delayed* by the exigencies of sequence organization; or indeed may not happen at all, despite having been relevantly occasioned by an interlocutor's question about marital status (Wilkinson & Kitzinger, 2003).

references

Amnesty International (2001). *Crimes of hate, conspiracy of silence*. London: Amnesty International.

Atkinson, J.M. and Drew, J. (Eds.) (1979). *Order in court: The organisation of verbal interaction in judicial settings*. London: Social Sciences Research Council.

Billig, M. (1999). Whose terms? Whose ordinariness? Rhetoric and ideology in conversation analysis. *Discourse & Society, 10(4)*, 543–558.

Borhek, M.V. (1983). *Coming out to parents: A two-way survival guide for lesbians and gay men and their parents*. Cleveland, OH: The Pilgrim Press.

Campbell, B.K. & Barnlund, D.C. (1977). Communication patterns and problems of pregnancy. *American Journal of Orthopsychiatry, 47*, 134–9.

Coates, J. (1996). *Women talk: Conversation between women friends*. Oxford: Blackwell.

Coates, J. (2003). *Men talk: Stories in the making of masculinities*. Oxford: Blackwell.

Davidson, J. (1984). Subsequent versions of invitations, offers, requests and proposals dealing with potential or actual rejection. In J.M. Atkinson & J. Heritage (Eds.), *Structures of social action: Studies in conversation analysis* (pp.102–128). Cambridge: Cambridge University Press.

Drew, P. (1984). Speakers' reportings in invitation sequences. In J.M. Atkinson & J. Heritage (Eds.), *Structures of social action: Studies in conversation analysis* (pp.152–164). Cambridge: Cambridge University Press.

Fields, J. (2001). Normal queers: Straight parents respond to their children's coming out. *Symbolic Interaction, 24(2)*, 165–187.

Fish, J. & Wilkinson, S. (2003). Understanding lesbians' healthcare behaviour: The case of breast self-examination. *Social Science & Medicine, 56(2)*, 235–245.

Garfinkel, H. (1967). *Studies in ethnomethodology.* Englewood Cliffs, NJ: Prentice-Hall.

Goodwin, M.H. (1990). *He-said-she-said: Talk as social organization among black children.* Bloomington, IA: Indiana University Press.

Hall, K. & Bucholtz, M. (Eds.) (1995). *Gender articulated.* London: Routledge.

Haslett, B.B. & Lipman, S. (1997). Micro-inequalities: Up close and personal. In N.V. Benokraitis (Ed.), *Subtle sexism: Current practice and prospects for change* (pp.34–51). Thousand Oaks, CA: Sage.

Heritage, J. (1984). *Garfinkel and ethnomethodology.* Cambridge: Polity Press.

Howard, M. (1985). How the family physician can help young teenagers postpone sexual involvement. *Medical Aspects of Human Sexuality, 19*, 76–87.

Jefferson, G. (1980). On 'trouble-premonitory' response to inquiry. *Sociological Inquiry, 50(3–4)*, 153–185.

Jefferson, G. (1987). On exposed and embedded correction in conversation. In G. Button & J.R.E. Lee (Eds.), *Talk and social organization* (pp.86–100). Clevedon: Multilingual Matters.

Jefferson, G. (2004). Glossary of transcript symbols with an introduction. In G.H. Lerner (Ed.), *Conversation analysis: Studies from the first generation* (pp.13–31). Amsterdam: John Benjamins.

Jeffreys, S. (2005). *Beauty and Misogyny.* London: Routledge.

Kidder, L.H., Boell, J.L. & Moyer, M.M. (1983). Rights consciousness and victimization prevention: Personal defence and assertiveness training. *Journal of Social Issues, 39*, 155–170.

Kitzinger, C. (1987). *The social construction of lesbianism.* London: Sage.

Kitzinger, C. (2000). Doing feminist conversation analysis. *Feminism & Psychology, 10*, 163–193.

Kitzinger, C. (2004). Afterword: Reflections on three decades of lesbian and gay psychology. *Feminism & Psychology, 14(4)*, 527–534.

Kitzinger, C. (2005a). Speaking as a heterosexual: (How) is sexuality relevant for talk-in-interaction. *Research on Language and Social Interaction, 38*, 221–266.

Kitzinger, C. (2005b). Heteronormativity in action: Reproducing the heterosexual nuclear family in after-hours medical calls. *Social Problems, 52(4)*, 477–498.

Kitzinger, C. (2006). After post-cognitivism. *Discourse Studies, 8(1)*, 67–83.

Kitzinger, C. & Frith, H. (1999). Just say no? The use of conversation analysis in developing a feminist perspective on sexual refusal. *Discourse & Society, 10(3)*, 293–316.

Kitzinger, C. & Wilkinson, S. (2004). Social advocacy for equal marriage: The politics of 'rights' and the psychology of 'mental health'. *Analyses of Social Issues and Public Policy, 4(1)*, 173–194.

Lakoff, R. (2003). Language, gender and politics: Putting 'women' and 'power' in the same sentence. In J. Holmes and M. Meyerhoff (Eds.), *The handbook of language and gender* (pp.161–178). Oxford: Blackwell.

Land, V. & Kitzinger, C. (2005). Speaking as a lesbian: Correcting the heterosexist presumption. *Research on Language and Social Interaction, 38,* 371–416.

Leap, W. (1996). *Word's out: Gay men's English.* Minneapolis, MN: University of Minnesota Press.

Lerner, G.H. (Ed.) (2004). *Conversation analysis: Studies from the first generation.* Amsterdam: John Benjamins.

Levinson, S.C. (1983). *Pragmatics.* Cambridge: Cambridge University Press.

McIlvenny, P. (Ed.) (2002). *Talking gender and sexuality.* Amsterdam: John Benjamins.

Markowe, L.A. (2002). Coming out as lesbian. In A. Coyle and C. Kitzinger (Eds.), *Lesbian and gay psychology* (pp.68–80). Oxford: Blackwell.

O'Byrne, R., Rapley, M. & Hansen, S. (2006). 'You couldn't say "no", could you?': Young men's understandings of sexual refusal. *Feminism & Psychology, 16,* 133–154.

Phelps, S. & Austin, N. (1987). *The Assertive Woman.* 2nd edn. San Luis, CA: Impact Publishers.

Pomerantz, A. (1984). Agreeing and disagreeing with assessments: Some features of preferred/dispreferred turn shapes. In J.M. Atkinson & J. Heritage (Eds.), *Structures of social action: Studies in conversation analysis* (pp.57–101). Cambridge: Cambridge University Press.

Potter, J. & Wetherell, M. (1987). *Discourse and social psychology.* London: Sage.

Psathas, G. (Ed.) (1979). *Everyday language: Studies in ethnomethodology.* New York: Irvington.

Psathas, G. (Ed.) (1995). *Conversation analysis: The study of talk-in-interaction.* London: Sage.

Rendle-Short, J. (2005) 'I've got a paper-shuffler for a husband': Indexing sexuality on talk-back radio. *Discourse & Society, 16(4),* 561–578.

Sacks, H. (1972.) On the analyzability of stories by children. In J.J. Gumperz & D. Hymes (Eds.), *Directions in sociolinguistics: The ethnography of communication* (pp.329–345). New York: Holt, Rinehart and Winston.

Sacks, H. (1987). On the preferences for agreement and contiguity in sequences in conversation. In G. Button & J.R.E. Lee (Eds.), *Talk and social organisation* (pp.54–69). Cleveland: Multilingual Matters.

Sacks, H. (1995a). Lecture 1 (R): 'The baby cried. The mommy picked it up'. *Lectures on Conversation, Vol. 1* (pp.243–251). Oxford: Blackwell.

Sacks, H. (1995b). Lecture 3: 'Patients with observers' as 'performers with audience'. *Lectures on Conversation, Vol. 2* (pp.104–113). Oxford: Blackwell.

Sacks, H. & Schegloff, E.A. (1979). Two preferences in the organization of reference to persons in conversation and their interaction. In G. Psathas (Ed.), *Everyday language: Studies in ethnomethodology* (pp.15–21). New York: Irvington.

Sacks, H., Schegloff, E.A. & Jefferson, G. (1974). A simplest systematics for the organization of turn-taking for conversation. *Language, 50(4),* 696–735.

Schegloff, E.A. (1982). Discourse as an interactional achievement: Some uses of 'uh huh' and other things that come between sentences. In D. Tannen (Ed.), *Analyzing discourse: Text and talk* (Georgetown University Roundtable on Languages and Linguistics 1981) Washington, DC: Georgetown University Press.

Schegloff, E.A. (1996). Some practices for referring to persons in talk-in-interaction: A partial sketch of a systematics. In B. Fox (Ed.), *Studies in anaphora* (pp.437–485). Amsterdam: John Benjamins.

Schegloff, E.A. (1997). Whose text? Whose context? *Discourse & Society, 8*, 165–187.

Schegloff, E.A. (1999). 'Schegloff's texts' as 'Billig's data': A critical reply. *Discourse & Society, 10(4)*, 558–572.

Schegloff, E.A. (2000). When 'others' initiate repair. *Applied Linguistics, 21(2)*, 205–243.

Schegloff, E.A. (2007). *Sequence organization: A primer in conversation analysis.* Cambridge: Cambridge University Press.

Schegloff, E.A., Jefferson, G. & Sacks, H. (1977). The preference for self-correction in the organization of repair in conversation. *Language, 53*, 361–382.

Signorile, M. (1996). *Outing yourself: How to come out as lesbian or gay to your family, friends and coworkers.* New York: Fireside.

Speer, S.A. (2005). *Gender talk: Feminism, discourse and conversation analysis.* London: Routledge.

Stokoe, E. (2000). Toward a conversation analytic approach to gender and discourse. *Feminism & Psychology, 10(4)*, 552–563.

Stokoe, E. (2005). Analysing gender and language. *Journal of Sociolinguistics, 9(1)*, 118–133.

Stokoe, E. & Weatherall, A. (Eds.) (2002). Gender, language, conversation analysis and feminism. Special issue, *Discourse & Society, 13(6)*.

Tainio, L. (2003). 'When shall we go for a ride?' A case of the sexual harassment of a young girl. *Discourse & Society, 14(2)*, 173–190.

Turner, R. (Ed.) (1974). *Ethnomethodology: Selected readings.* London: Penguin.

Warzak, W.J. & Page, T.J. (1990). Teaching refusal skills to sexually active adolescents. *Journal of Behavioral Therapy and Experimental Psychiatry, 21*, 133–9.

Weatherall, A. (2002). *Gender, language and discourse.* London: Routledge.

Weeks, P.A.D. (1995). The microsociology of everyday life. In S.M. Hale (Ed.), *Controversies in sociology* (pp.449–472). Toronto, ON: Copp Clark Ltd.

West, C. (1979). Against our will: Male interruptions of females in cross-sex conversations. In J. Orasanu, M.K. Slater & L.L. Adler (Eds.), *Language, sex and gender.* Annals of the New York Academy of Sciences, 327: 81–97. New York: New York Academy of Sciences.

Wetherell, M. (1998). Positioning and interpretative repertoires: Conversation analysis and post-structuralism in dialogue. *Discourse & Society, 9(3)*, 387–412.

Wilkinson, S. (Ed.) (1986). *Feminist social psychology: Developing theory and practice.* Milton Keynes: Open University Press.

Wilkinson, S. (2002). Lesbian health. In A. Coyle & C. Kitzinger (Eds.), *Lesbian and Gay Psychology* (pp.117–134). Oxford: Blackwell.

Wilkinson, S. (2004). Focus group research. In D. Silverman (Ed.), *Qualitative research: Theory, method and practice* (pp.177–199). 2nd edn. London: Sage.

Wilkinson, S. (2006) Analysing interaction in focus groups. In P. Drew, G. Raymond & D. Weinberg (Eds.), *Talk and interaction in social research methods* (pp.50–62). London: Sage.

Wilkinson, S. (2007). Breast cancer: Lived experience and feminist action. In O. Hankivsky, M. Morrow & C. Varcoe (Eds.), *Women's health in Canada: Critical health theory, policy and practice.* Toronto, ON: University of Toronto Press.

Wilkinson, S. & Kitzinger, C. (Eds.) (1993). *Heterosexuality: A* Feminism & Psychology *reader.* London: Sage.

Wilkinson, S. & Kitzinger, C. (2003). Constructing identities: A feminist conversation analytic approach to positioning in action. In R. Harré & F. Moghaddam (Eds.), *The self and others: Positioning individuals and groups in personal, political, and cultural contexts* (pp.157–180). Westport, CT: Praeger.

Wilkinson, S. & Kitzinger, C. (2006). In support of equal marriage: Why civil partnership is not enough. *BPS Psychology of Women Section Review, 8,* 54–57.

Zimmerman, D.H. & West, C. (1975). Sex roles, interruptions and silences in conversation. In B. Thorne & N. Henley (Eds.), *Language and sex: Difference and dominance.* Rowley, MA: Newbury House.

part four
discourse, rhetoric and politics

9

contemporary racist discourse: taboos against racism and racist accusations

martha augoustinos and danielle every

During the last twenty years there has been a burgeoning literature on the language of contemporary racism in Western liberal democracies such as Australia, New Zealand, Britain, Europe and the United States. Much of this literature has been informed by discursive psychology, which not only analyses everyday talk and conversation, but also formal institutional talk that can be found in parliamentary debates, political speeches and newspaper articles. One of the most pervasive features of contemporary racist discourse is the denial of prejudice. Increasing social taboos against openly expressing racist sentiments have led to the development of discursive strategies that present negative views of outgroups as reasonable and justified, while at the same time protecting the speaker from charges of racism and prejudice. This research has demonstrated the flexible, contradictory and ambivalent nature of contemporary racist discourse, which is organized by common and recurring tropes used by majority group members to justify and rationalize existing social inequities between groups. These justifications are premised largely on the flexible and rhetorical use of liberal and egalitarian commonplaces that draw on principles of freedom, fairness, and individual rights.

In this chapter we outline the theoretical and analytic approach of discursive psychology and its implications for the study of prejudice and racism. We review discursive research conducted in Australia, New Zealand, the UK, Europe and the United States to illustrate how majority group members manage issues such as indigenous rights claims, immigration and racism in their talk. This review highlights some of the discursive resources and strategies that majority group members deploy to justify and rationalize negative outgroup evaluations, while at the same time positioning themselves as non-prejudiced. Finally, we consider a largely ignored phenomenon that appears to be closely associated with the denial of prejudice: while there are increasing social taboos against the expression of racism, there are also increasing social taboos against making racist accusations. Such charges and accusations are invariably met not only with strong denials, but also with moral outrage. We demonstrate how speakers, in particular anti-racist critics, attend to this taboo by avoiding making such explicit accusations, and instead frame their criticisms in indirect and subtle ways.

discursive psychology

Discursive psychology, broadly defined, describes a number of social psychological approaches that are predominantly concerned with analysing the socially constitutive nature of language (see also Potter & Hepburn, this volume). Most contemporary psychology, in particular social psychology, adheres to the notion of internal mental representation. As such, social psychology has been concerned predominantly with examining the cognitive contents of the mind, making use of notions such as attitudes, stereotypes and representations, and has focused on how such cognitions are generated by cognitive mechanisms and processes. From this perspective, cognition is conceptualized as prior to language. Language is viewed primarily as a communicative medium through which cognition finds expression. Most social psychologists also subscribe to a realist epistemology: that there is a knowable domain of facts about human experience and consciousness that can be discovered through the application of reason and rationality (science) or through hermeneutic interpretative methods.

The emergence of the social-constructionist movement in psychology (Gergen, 1985) challenged this realist epistemology and the dominant paradigm of cognitivism. This challenge can be attributed to the increasing interest in the role and function of language as a socially constitutive force in consciousness and experience. This 'turn to language', which was part of a larger intellectual tradition in the humanities and social sciences during the 1980s, emphasized the role played by language in creating and reproducing meaning in everyday social interaction and practice. Conceptualized as a social practice, language has no fixed meaning outside the context in which it is used. Further, this approach argues that the language we use to describe our world shapes our perceptions: objects, activities, events and categories derive their epistemological status from the definitions we create for them.

One influential application of these ideas was that of Potter and Wetherell's early work on discourse analysis and its application to social-psychological topics. In their seminal book, *Discourse and Social Psychology*, Potter and Wetherell (1987) combined the theoretical and empirical foundations of speech act theory, ethnomethodology and semiology to arrive at a distinctive approach to the analysis of discourse. Based on Austin's speech act theory (1962), a central emphasis running through this approach is that people use language 'to do things'. Words are not simply abstract tools used to state or describe things; they are also used to make things happen. People use language to justify, explain, blame, excuse, persuade and present themselves in the best possible light. Thus, language is functional. As in ethnomethodology, the focus is on the ordinary, everyday use of talk that has practical consequences for participants: how people use language to understand and make sense of everyday life. Language is viewed as reflexive and contextual, as constructing the very nature of objects and events as they are talked about.

Because language in social interaction is the site where meanings are created and changed, and because it is the primary way of performing actions, discursive psychology argues that language itself should be the object of study rather than used as a conduit to 'other things'. Discursive psychology considers language in its situated use, within the process of an ongoing interaction. It examines how accounts are constructed: how people do things such as present their accounts as factual (Potter, 1996). Discursive psychology also identifies patterns of language that constitute aspects of society and the people in it. This second aspect draws attention to the social nature and historical origins of the world 'out there'. It involves the study of power and resistance based on the assumption that the language available to people enables and constrains their actions (Wetherell & Potter, 1992).

The approach to discourse adopted by us in our own research is informed by the early work of Potter and Wetherell (1987), in addition to more recent theoretical developments and extensions in this tradition (Billig, 1991, 1998; Edwards, 1997; Edwards & Potter, 1992; Potter, 1996; Wetherell, 1998). Broadly, this approach analyses how talk and texts are socially organized to achieve local actions, such as identity management, as well as ideological effects that rationalize and legitimate oppression. It examines both the broad patterns and themes within talk (interpretative repertoires or discourses), as well as the techniques and linguistic tools through which accounts are imbued with the status of fact and truth. It also examines how accounts are organized argumentatively, i.e. how they are designed to compete with alternative versions of social reality.

discursive psychology and racism

Traditional social psychologists have generally sought to understand racism as an aspect of cognition. This may be contrasted with discursive psychologists, who seek to understand racism as a social practice: as an aspect of discourse and communication that is primarily linguistic rather than cognitive.[1] Discursive research on the language of racism has examined the ways in which discursive resources and rhetorical arguments are put together to construct notions of race, disadvantage, identity, and how majority group members use these resources in everyday talk to justify and legitimate current social practices. Discursive psychology locates these language practices or 'ways of talking' at a societal level, as products of a racist society rather than as individual, psychological and/or cognitive products (Wetherell & Potter, 1992). The analytic site therefore is not the 'prejudiced' or 'racist' individual, but the rhetorical and discursive resources that are available within an inequitable society.

The implications of this work for the study of racism may be explored with reference to discursive psychology's challenges to a central explanation of racism in traditional social psychology: categorization and stereotyping. The stereotype construct has played a pivotal role in social-psychological approaches to racism and prejudice in the last sixty years (for a history of this see Condor, 1988; Hopkins, Reicher & Levine, 1997). The increasing dominance of social cognition as a theoretical framework during the past ten years within social psychology has led to a proliferation in the stereotyping literature. In this framework, stereotyping is regarded as the outcome of a pervasive cognitive tendency to categorize people into their respective group memberships – a process that is understood as either serving to simplify an overly complex world (e.g., Fiske & Taylor, 1991) or to render it more intelligible (Macrae & Bodenhausen, 2000). Stereotypes are conceptualized as a stable set of descriptions and attributes of a particular social group that are highly consensual, pervasive and resistant to change. These approaches also document negative consequences of categorization and stereotyping that include objectification, distortion, bias and prejudice.

Discursive psychology argues that some of the subtlety and complexity of intergroup relations may be obscured by this social cognitive approach. In particular, it ignores the social nature of categorization and its links with power. Discourse analysts treat categorization as something people do, in talk, in order to accomplish social actions: to deny racism; to present the self positively and the other negatively; and to classify a group as worthy or not worthy of particular entitlements. Categorization also serves a broader social, political and cultural function: to maintain (or challenge) existing social inequalities. Indeed, social cognitive research on categorization may itself be examined as part of the discourse of racism. Both Condor (1988) and Hopkins et al. (1997) argue that accounts of race categorization and stereotyping as general, potentially benign, evaluatively-neutral cognitive processes ignore the specific meanings and implications of the use of 'racial' categorizations and their place in the exclusion and oppression of other groups. These researchers argue that such an account of stereotyping as a natural human process may itself be used to legitimate racism by denying the moral accountability of racist practices, rendering invisible the links between racism, power and politics, and entrenching racism as inevitably defining intergroup relations.

There have been a number of discursive studies of social categorization and racism that demonstrate the flexibility of social categorization and its links with maintaining power relationships. Wetherell and Potter (1992) investigated the way white middle-class New Zealanders (Pakeha) used the particular categories of 'race', 'culture' and 'nation' in their talk of Maori–Pakeha relations, and how these rhetorical constructions were used to legitimate the existing social order of inequality and Maori disadvantage. While many of the respondents spoke favourably of Maori cultural identity, ultimately this identity was viewed as secondary to homogeneous and unifying 'national' identity. The category of 'nation' was used in Pakeha talk to limit and constrain the aspirations of Maori identity, which in its 'radical' form was seen to undermine and threaten national unity. Attempts to identify as 'Maori' and to tie category entitlements of land rights, cultural recognition and affirmative action programmes to this identity were denied by redefining Maoris as 'New Zealanders' and thereby constructing a Maori identity as divisive and threatening. What this contextual selectivity demonstrates is the important rhetorical and ideological work that is being accomplished by the use of particular categorizations in different contexts. In some contexts a 'Maori' cultural identity is valorized, but in others, it is seen as problematic and to be replaced by a superordinate national identity as a 'New Zealander'.

The flexible content and strategic functions of social categories are also clearly demonstrated in research in the UK and Europe examining the construction of immigrants. A common rhetorical device observed in arguments in the UK asylum seeker debates is the division of immigrants into 'good' immigrants and 'bad' immigrants (Lynn & Lea, 2003). 'Good' immigrants were represented as already in the country, invited and as arriving 'legally', whilst 'bad' immigrants were those who arrived without authorization. However, in Austrian discussions of the relationship of immigrants to the category of 'native Austrians', they were categorized as 'immigrants', an homogeneous group who represented a burden and threat to the Austrian people (Sedlak, 2000).

The construction of categories also normatively binds entitlements to those categories and is an essential rhetorical move in politics. Le Couteur et al. (2001) examined the 'Address to the Nation' of the Australian Prime Minister John Howard. They demonstrate in Howard's speech how the categories of Indigenous Australians and farmers were constructed in order to bind certain entitlements to these categories. The category of farmers was represented as the symbolic expression of Australian-ness, as positive, productive and socially beneficial. They were described as important to the future of our country in terms of their generation of wealth, which was tagged as the source of assistance for the less fortunate (implicitly, in this speech, the indigenous communities). Their claims on the land and on the government were positioned as indisputable and compelling. By contrast, 'Aboriginals' were constructed as passive, inactive and unproductive. Indigenous Australians were described as people we must continue our effort to improve. Their relationship with the land was represented as a 'special affinity' that did not contribute to wealth production. Their claims to a place in the negotiation over land could thus be dismissed as less compelling and indisputable than the entitlements of the farmers. By prefacing his policy of the severe restriction of indigenous land rights with the above categories, Howard paved the way for these changes to be seen as normal, obvious and right, whilst preserving a positive presentation of his government, and effectively removing the claims of Indigenous Australians from serious consideration in the debate. Research such as this demonstrates the links between social categorization and political and social power, and clearly posits stereotyping as a social rather than solely as an internal, cognitive process.

Examining social categorization from a discursive perspective demonstrates that categorization, rather than being a natural phenomenon reflecting cognitive processes and uncontested external objects, is a complex and subtle social accomplishment. The categories of the 'other' briefly examined here reveal that these categories are flexible and variable in their deployment in arguments to maintain existing social inequities.

discursive research on racism

Discursive studies on the language of racism have been conducted for a range of sites, including the media, parliament and everyday talk, and in many countries, including the Netherlands (van Dijk, 1984, 1987, 1991, 1993, 1997; Verkuyten 1998, 2001), Belgium (Blommaert & Verschueren, 1998), Europe (Wodak & Van Dijk, 2000), Spain (Rojo, 2000), South Africa (Seidel, 1998), the UK (Billig, 1988; Jones, 2000; Reeves, 1983; Lynn & Lea, 2003), the USA (Mehan, 1997; Santa Ana, 1999; Thiesmeyer, 1995), New Zealand (Abel, 1996; McCreanor, 1993a, 1993b, 1993c; Nairn & McCreanor, 1990, 1991; Wetherell & Potter, 1992), and Australia (Augoustinos, Tuffin & Every, 2005; Augoustinos, Tuffin & Rapley, 1999; Augoustinos, Tuffin & Sale, 1999; Le Couteur, Rapley & Augoustinos, 2001; Rapley, 1998, 2001; O'Doherty, 2001).

This research reveals a commonality in the discursive resources (i.e. interpretative repertoires, rhetorical devices) of the contemporary language of racism across topics, arenas (public, private, political, media) and countries. One of the crucial properties of contemporary racism is its denial, typically illustrated by the ubiquitous disclaimer 'I'm not racist, but...' (van Dijk, 1992). Those who argue against the interests of minorities typically deny that they are prejudiced. Reeves (1983) in his study of British political discourse, uses the term 'discursive deracialization' to describe the strategy by which politicians avoid using racial categories. For example, calls for immigration restrictions, although ostensibly relating to non-whites, are phrased in such a way that race is not mentioned.

American researchers have referred to this as the 'new racism', which denies being racist, in contrast to 'old-fashioned racism', which was unambiguous in terms of its racist agenda. This new racism appropriates liberal individualist principles such as the work ethic and self-reliance to argue for 'racist' and discriminatory practices. Negative feelings and attitudes are justified by 'matter of fact' observations that minority groups transgress central values such as hard work, thrift and self-reliance (Katz & Hass, 1988; Kinder & Sears, 1981; McConahay, 1986; Pettigrew & Meertens, 1995). However, the distinction between old and new racism in this way is less than clear cut, as there is evidence that even 'old fashioned' racists choose their terms and arguments strategically (Billig, 1988).

Billig (1988) argues that contemporary political leaders, the media and citizens are faced with a social taboo against expressing *unjustified* negative views against outgroups. General norms and values prohibit blatant forms of prejudice (Billig, 1988; van Dijk, 1992). Billig (1988) suggests that the concept of 'prejudice', a product of Enlightenment liberalism, is associated with irrationality. Thus speakers attempt to maintain a subject position of being 'rational' by constructing their views as 'reasonable' and framing their talk in such a way as to undermine or prevent possible charges of prejudice. Those who wish to express negative views against outgroups take care to construct these views as justified, warranted and rational (Rapley, 2001). This serves a number of functions. On a local level, people, institutions and countries deny, mitigate, justify or excuse negative acts and views towards minorities in order to position themselves as decent, moral, reasonable citizens. Condor, Abell, Figgou, Gibson and Stevenson (in press), note that denials of racism protect the reputation of ingroups as well as the individual. These denials also function on a political, social and cultural level to marginalize claims of prejudice, thereby controlling resistance and disruption and maintaining existing social advantages and power.

The discursive resources used for denying, rationalizing and excusing negative views of outgroups can be loosely grouped into three types of strategies: (a) framing negative views as ostensibly based on conditions external to one's self, rather than on internal, psychological motivations; (b) re-defining racism as 'extreme, violent behaviour', as 'doing equity', as 'honesty' and as 'over-sensitivity'; and (c) deploying liberal and egalitarian principles of fairness and 'treating everyone the same', regardless of social group membership.

external rationales for negative views

Research has found that speakers use a 'reasonable prejudice' repertoire, constructing negative views as based on incontrovertible, external reasons, rather than as stemming from an internal, psychological cause (Billig et al., 1988). Two popular externalized justifications for negative views of outgroups are to argue that the negative view is a response to the negative characteristics of the outgroup (blaming the victim); and to re-present racist views as economic concerns.

Blaming the victim. Attributing inequality to the characteristics of the outgroup is a strategy van Dijk (1991) calls 'blaming the victim'. In this classic neo-liberal trope, problems are described not in terms of social or historical causes, but as caused by individuals' characteristics and destructive choices (Le Couteur, Rapley & Augoustinos, 2001).

Augoustinos, Tuffin and Rapley (1999) found evidence of victim blaming in their study of everyday discourse on Aboriginal and white relations in Australia. Participants constructed the issue of Aboriginal poverty as a consequence of their '(wilful) disengagement from productive activity' (p.355) and Aboriginal alcoholism the result of an individual choice to drink. Similarly, the Aboriginals' 'failure to achieve' was attributed to the 'dead weight' of other problematic Aborigines, who prevented progress. By shifting the responsibility for poverty and alcoholism onto the individual, white speakers were able to reject claims that these issues were the result of systemic racism and discrimination.

Victims of racism are not only blamed for problems such as inequality, unemployment and alcoholism, but are also constructed as the cause of the majority group's racism. Reeves (1983), van der Valk (2000), Jones (2000) and Verkuyten (1998) found that politicians and focus group participants argued that immigration and the presence of immigrants caused racism and was responsible for the rise of extremism. The participants in Verkuyten's (1998) study argued their negative views of 'foreigners' grew out of their experiences living in a multiethnic community: they were not racist until they lived with immigrants and observed their unhygienic and immoral lifestyles.

Economic arguments. Negative views of an outgroup can also be externalized by framing them as a concern with economic practicalities. Blommaert and Verschueren (1998) found that immigration was consistently constructed in the Belgian media as a threat to prosperity, to the future of 'our' children, the viability and integrity of the social security system and majority group employment. An ostensible concern for cost-efficiency was often used to legitimate the refusal to grant asylum to refugees. Refugees were depicted as a drain on the economy, requiring a large financial outlay for little return (often juxtaposed with the financial benefits of 'other immigrants': Blommaert & Verschueren, 1998).

Economic arguments can also be used to re-frame negative views of an outgroup as a concern with economic practicalities. Augoustinos, Tuffin and Rapley (1999) found that participants rationalized racism as 'justifiable anger' over 'unfair' government handouts to Indigenous Australians. Participants argued that negative feelings towards Aborigines were not based on 'the colour of a person's skin' but on the 'social advantages they are seen to have'. One participant framed the pervasive dislike of Aboriginal people as 'taxpayers [...] worried about where their money is going', rather than racism.

redefining racism

Contrary to the assumptions of much research on racism, the category of racism, and attributions of race and racism, are not static, nor are they value-free, empirical scientific statements about observable objects in the natural world. Rather, the category of racism is constructed flexibly and variably in ways that manage the moral accountability and identity of the speaker as non-racist. By re-drawing the boundaries of what may legitimately be defined as 'racist', the category of racism may be used to position individuals as non-racist by placing their own behaviour and views outside of the boundaries of 'racism'. This is demonstrated by the variety of constructions of racism observed across sites of formal and informal talk about 'race'. These constructions include racism as violence, racism as equity, racism as honesty and racism as over-sensitivity.

Racism as violence. The 'reasonable prejudice' repertoire, outlined above, is coincidental with a repertoire of 'unreasonable prejudice', in which the reasonably prejudiced argue that the 'real' racists are those who engage in violence (Billig et al., 1988). The use of extremism as the measure of racism is often used to allow the 'reasonably prejudiced' to distance themselves from racism: the identification of 'real' racism opens the way for the expression of negative views as 'not' racism (van Dijk, 1991).

This was found by Verkuyten (1998) in his study using focus groups in the Netherlands. Participants constructed 'real racism' as the Nazi extermination of the Jews and the violent protests of extreme right-wing political groups. By defining racism as extreme actions, they were able to distinguish themselves as not racist.

Racism as equity. Billig et al. (1988) suggest that linked to the concept of prejudice is the notion of equality, as to be non-prejudiced is to treat all people equally. Thus it is imperative, in order to avoid charges of racism, that the reasonably prejudiced uphold the values of equality whilst formulating unequal views. This is demonstrated in arguments opposing affirmative action that are expressed as a concern that no group should receive special treatment or more than their fair share (Augoustinos, Tuffin & Every, 2005).

In his study of the maiden speech of Pauline Hanson, an Australian right-wing political candidate, Rapley (2001) found that the speech drew upon locally nuanced, culturally pervasive discourses of egalitarianism, mateship and the notion of a 'fair go' to construct a version of self as representing 'equity'. Hanson redefines her negative views of Indigenous land rights and affirmative action as a defence of the right of white Australians to be treated equally, rather than as a prejudicial view of persons on the basis of their race.

As Billig et al. (1988) argue, the argument that it is 'we' who are unfairly treated and thus the 'real' victims of prejudice, re-casts oppressor and oppressed. This was found by Verkuyten (1998); participants in his study redefined themselves as the object of discrimination from anti-racists. In this argument, the injustice of discrimination is not questioned, but who is being discriminated against is challenged. This allows participants to define themselves as part of the moral community, as upholders of equality, whilst espousing negative views of others (Verkuyten, 1998).

Racism as honesty. Rapley (2001) also found that a key strategy in Hanson's speech was to redefine racially negative views as the expression of frank, down-to-earth, common sense. This was also noted by van Dijk (1991) who found the British media argued that articles on 'blacks' and crime, for example, were reporting the 'truth' and therefore were not racist.

Racism as 'over-sensitivity'. In this argument, racism is redefined as the victims of racism being over-sensitive. This was found by Nairn and McCreanor (1990) in their study of submissions to the Human Rights Commission on race relations in New Zealand. They examined the use of notions of 'sensitivity' in Pakeha (white New Zealanders) constructions of a fight between Pakeha and Maori students after the Pakeha students performed a mock Haka (Maori dance). The behaviour of the Pakeha was attributed to 'insensitivity', rather than racism, whilst the Maori response to the mock Haka was attributed to 'over-sensitivity'. This functioned to allocate blame for racial tension to the undue sensitivity of the Maori, whilst minimizing the responsibility of the Pakeha.

The attribution of racism to the over-sensitivity of the oppressed was also found by van Dijk (1997), Augoustinos, Tuffin and Rapley (1999) and Augoustinos, Tuffin and Sale (1999). Augoustinos et al. (1999, p.95) give the following example from a majority group member:

> Also too they often look for *reasons* that are not there. Ahh they feel that because they're Aborigines if something doesn't happen it's because they're Aboriginals (Ah ha). Umm often, ok I admit that sometimes it may be the case in jobs and whatnot but ahh I think often it's not warranted?

In this account, experiences of racism by Aboriginal people are contested with the suggestion that Aboriginal people are claiming racism where it does not exist. Such strategies locate the source of racism in the individual psyches of Aboriginal people, and infer that racism is more imagined than real. The magnitude of racism is minimized with the suggestion that, while some claims are justified, 'often' these are unwarranted.

liberal arguments for 'illiberal' ends

Wetherell and Potter's systematic analysis of racist discourse in New Zealand (1992) found that the intellectual resources of Western political democracies structure the discourse of race politics. Discursive resources such as human rights, egalitarianism and equality have been utilized in anti-racist discourse, and are perhaps common-sensically associated with liberalism and democracy. However, Wetherell and Potter (1992) found that these same intellectual resources are also successfully deployed to support arguments whose effects or aims could be claimed to be 'illiberal' and undemocratic. They found that these intellectual traditions were mobilized as 'rhetorically self-sufficient arguments'; that is, they were used by participants without further explanation, allowing the ethical principles of liberal philosophy to do their rhetorical work. When these ethics raised potentially opposing or problematic issues, participants then drew on the discursive resource of 'practicality', most frequently in the form of the principle/practical dichotomy in which a principle is cited, but is excluded as impractical in the current situation.

Wetherell and Potter (1992) identified ten rhetorically self-sufficient arguments utilized by white speakers to justify the inequality between Pakeha and Maori citizens:

1. Resources should be used productively and in a cost-effective manner
2. Nobody should be compelled
3. Everybody should be treated equally
4. You cannot turn the clock backwards
5. Present generations cannot be blamed for the mistakes of past generations
6. Injustices should be righted
7. Everybody can succeed if they try hard enough
8. Minority opinion should not carry more weight than majority opinion
9. We have to live in the twentieth (twenty-first) century
10. You have to be practical.

All of the strategies for denying racism outlined in the previous sections can be seen to draw on these intellectual resources. For example: redefining racism as 'equity' draws on the argument that 'everybody should be treated equally'; the categorization of Indigenous Australians as unproductive relies on the argument that 'resources must be used productively'; and the construction of inequality as the fault of minorities draws on several arguments such as 'present generations cannot be blamed for the mistakes of past generations' and 'everybody can succeed if they try hard enough'.

Although these rhetorically self-sufficient arguments were used extensively in the Pakeha discourse examined by Potter and Wetherell, the researchers emphasized that they were deployed in flexible and often contradictory ways. They stressed that these maxims should not be viewed as cognitive templates or schemas that structured and organized Pakeha discourse, but rather as 'tools' or 'resources' which were combined in variable ways by the respondents to do certain things, most notable of which was to avoid a 'racist' identity and to justify existing Maori–Pakeha relations.

accusations of racism

So far we have examined talk and text that, whilst avowing non-racism, reasonableness and liberal values, functions to maintain and justify social inequality and existing power relationships between white majorities and non-white minorities. However, this language of prejudice and racism is intertwined with, responds to and shapes a counter anti-racist discourse. As yet, there has been little research examining talk by majority-group members that accuses other majority-group members of racism.

The pervasive, negative positioning of anti-racists and majority-group accusations of racism plays a significant role in shaping a counter anti-racist discourse. Van Dijk (1992, p.90) writes:

the person who accuses the other as racist is in turn accused of inverted racism against whites, as oversensitive and exaggerating, as intolerant and generally as 'seeing racism where there is none'…Accusations of racism then soon tend to be seen as more serious social infractions than racist attitudes or actions themselves, e.g. because they disrupt ingroup solidarity and smooth ingroup encounters: they are felt to ruin the 'good atmosphere' of interactions and situations. Moreover, such accusations are seen to impose taboos, prevent free speech and a 'true' or 'honest' assessment of the ethnic situation. In other words, denials of racism often turn into counter-accusations of intolerant and intolerable anti-racism.

Indeed, van Dijk (1992, p.93) goes on to argue that: 'the very notion of "racism" may become virtually taboo in accusatory contexts because of its strong negative connotations'.

Examples of this negative characterization of anti-racists and accusations of racism have been documented in studies conducted in the United States, Britain, Europe and Australia. In the USA, supporters of an anti-discrimination bill were categorized as the 'human rights industry' and as 'demagogic', constructing them as incompatible with American values of democracy and freedom of speech (van Dijk, 1997). In the UK, refugee sympathizers were derisively tagged as 'white liberals': wealthy elites who espoused humanitarianism but, duplicitously, did not disadvantage themselves by providing for asylum seekers but forced this burden on to others (Lynn & Lea, 2003). The theme of anti-racists as out of touch with the mainstream was also found in the Netherlands. Participants in Verkuyten's (1998) focus groups positioned anti-racists as ignorant of the reality of living in a multiethnic community and therefore without legitimate right to speak of the 'facts'. These participants also presented anti-racists as discriminatory towards the majority white population.

In Australia the construction of accusations of racism as a violation of free speech was popularized during debates over indigenous and white Australian race relations (McIntyre & Clark, 2003). For example, notable political journalist Paul Sheehan (1998) alleged that 'racist' was a loaded term employed by the 'Thought Police' (post-modern academics, Labor politicians and members of the 'elite multiculturalism industry') to silence their opponents. As in Belgium and the UK, 'the elites' has become a powerful derogatory categorization applied to those who oppose conservative and reactionary policies on immigration, refugees and indigenous peoples. As such, anti-racists are constructed as an out of touch, privileged minority. As part of the maintenance of social inequity, the construction of anti-racists as pernicious, oppressive, discriminatory or just plain crazy (the 'loony left') is a potent way of silencing prejudice claims.

The work of Jones (2000) in the UK suggests that majority group members who are critical of immigration policies attend to these accusations against anti-racists by framing their criticisms as reasonable and rational, and avoiding overt allegations of racism. She found that in the UK political debates on new asylum laws, beyond very general statements, opposition speakers rarely openly addressed race and racism. She examines a speech from Labour MP Chris Davies, in which he argues against a clause barring asylum seekers from employment because it 'will mean worse employment prospects for the Asian community...and black people'. He goes on to state 'I believe that the Government are playing the race card...and they are appealing to the white, Conservative-minded vote'. He later claims that the government will fail because most people in Britain are 'fair minded'. Jones argues that Davies avoids direct statements regarding racism by claiming that Asians and blacks will experience 'worse employment prospects' rather than prejudice and discrimination. She also suggests that 'Conservative-minded' is a euphemism for the white racist vote, and 'fair-minded' a euphemism for 'not racist'. The function of these euphemisms is to construct the policy negatively whilst maintaining a 'reasonable' self-presentation.

Jones's research, together with that on the negative construction of anti-racists, suggests that those criticizing racist policies and outcomes must attend to pervasive concerns that accusations of racism are unreasonable and discriminatory by presenting their position as reasonable and rational. The remainder of this chapter turns to consider recent evidence examining the increasing pervasiveness of taboos against making racist accusations taken from the Australian parliamentary debates on asylum seekers. Specifically, it examines the subject position performed by a politician criticizing asylum seeker policy in Australia, how racism is defined in this criticism and the local and ideological functions of this construction.

making and managing accusations of racism in the australian parliament

The data for this analysis comes from a corpus of the 2001 Australian Senate Hansard speeches on the *MV Tampa*, amendments to the *Migration Act*, and the *Border Protection Bill 2001*. In 2001, 438 asylum seekers were shipwrecked off the Australian coast, rescued by the Norwegian container ship the *MV Tampa*, and subsequently refused entry into Australia by the Australian government. Australian troops boarded the vessel and removed the survivors to hastily established processing camps on Pacific islands, where many remain incarcerated today. After this incident several bills were passed through the Australian parliament: retrospectively legalizing the hostile takeover of the *Tampa*, excising islands from Australia's migration zone to prevent persons landing there from invoking asylum obligations, allowing strip searching of asylum seekers in detention from the age of ten, reducing avenues of appeal for migration decisions, and restricting the definition of refugee. The Australian Labor Party (ALP), then (and now) in opposition, supported the legislation proposed by the conservative government, as did the far-right Senator of the One Nation Party, with the result that some ALP ministers, independents, Greens and Australian Democrat senators were the only voices of dissent.

Parliamentary discourse such as these Senate debates has been called 'elite discourse', and it is studied to examine the role of politicians in the reproduction of racism and anti-racism (Wodak & van Dijk, 2000). The choice of parliamentary debates allows a continuation of, and comparison with, previous work reviewed here, particularly that of Jones (2000) and van Dijk (1992). Wodak and van Dijk (2000) also suggest that parliamentary debates are useful sites of analysis, because it is in this forum that policies are legitimized and legislation is adopted that directly affects the lives of minority groups such as asylum seekers.

The analysis that follows draws attention to the ways in which participants/speakers attend to the accountability of their talk and thus construct their talk to take account of possible challenges. Rather than attempting to define what 'really' constitutes 'racism', in this analysis we sample the production of racism as an everyday phenomenon as it is produced by social members in talk-in-interaction. In this way, it attends to the indexicality and contingency of the meaning of this construct in a changing political climate. It is thus well placed to offer insight into the changing face of the race debate in Australia and internationally.

The extract below is taken from Senator Andrew Bartlett's (immigration spokesperson for the Australian Democrats) speech on the *Tampa* crisis. It features justifications and warrants for his opposition to the government's border protection bills that position him as reasonable and rational. It also features two redefinitions or euphemisms of racism which have been commonly deployed in accusations of racism in the Australian parliament: racism as the One Nation Party and/or Pauline Hanson; and racism as 'playing the race card'.

1   I do not think we want to have an election played on the race card. We have
2   had debate about people putting One Nation last on their how-to-vote cards.
3   There is not much point putting them last on how-to-vote cards if we are
4   going to adopt their policies at the same time.
    (Senator Andrew Bartlett, Senate Hansard, 28/8/01, p.26794)

This account does much work to position the speaker (and his claims) as reasonable, rational and representative (rather than the accusation of a wealthy minority elite). In the first line, Bartlett establishes a race-based election as not only something he is against but others also oppose, through his use of 'we'. He also presents the decision to put One Nation last on how-to-vote cards as the outcome of a 'debate'. This positions the decision as the result of a participatory democratic process and thus the result of deliberate and rational group decision-making. Both position the speaker's claims as reasonable and legitimate, as well as consensual.

As well as attending to accountability in these ways, the speaker also constructs two versions of racism, which have both local identity management functions and ideological effects. Firstly, Bartlett uses the phrase 'played on the race card'. This construction was also found in parliamentary speeches in the UK (Jones, 2000). It does not accuse the politicians of being racist themselves, but of generating racism for political gain. It constructs racism as readily aroused and manipulable by politicians. This is interesting in light of the 'blaming the victim' strategy outlined previously, which argues that immigrants themselves are responsible for generating racism. In this construction, responsibility is shifted on to politicians, which has important implications for addressing racism, an issue discussed further below.

This repertoire of 'racism as playing the race card' recognizes that racism may be a political tool wielded through electioneering such as speeches, advertising and pamphlets. This is somewhat different from social psychology's conceptualization of racism as located within the person. This construction still has a strong negative connotation, possibly as strong as accusing a person of being racist. To generate racism, for one's own gain, constructs the accused as manipulative, immoral and unrepresentative of the national good (a very important position for a politician). By accusing the government of playing the race card Bartlett avoids more explicit or problematic terminology, whilst still hearably calling the government to moral account for their actions. This repertoire of 'playing the race card' encompasses the generation of racism for political gain as a morally accountable act.

As a second construction of racism, Pauline Hanson's One Nation Party is used to stand in for racism (line 2). Pauline Hanson won a seat in the 1996 Australian general election as an Independent, after being dropped from the conservative Liberal/National Party for 'racist' comments. Her election, achieved with a large swing in the vote in her favour, was accompanied by a media furore. The 'race debate', as it was coined by the Australian media, came to be identified with her. She was named in many media reports as the 'spark' that ignited the debate (Rapley, 1998). She was widely vilified in the general press as anti-Aboriginal, anti-Asian and anti-free trade. Her party campaigned for asylum seekers arriving by boat to be turned away. That One Nation has also been equated with racism here (note that this is the only party named in the account, it is closely associated with the term 'race card', and the speaker highlights that the party has been placed last on how-to-vote cards, effectively denying them another seat in parliament), without explanation or elaboration, suggests that this equation of racism with One Nation has entered the Australian consciousness as 'common sense'.

As noted in the previous section, definitions of racism as extreme behaviour such as the Nazi holocaust are commonly deployed in order to distance a speaker's negative views about others as not racist. The identification of racism with the One Nation Party is interesting in this context, because it locates racism in contemporary Australian society, rather than in the distant past or in other countries. This definition of racism also encompasses the new racism. As noted by Rapley (2001), Hanson claimed her anti-Aboriginal stance was actually a defence of the Australian principle of egalitarianism and also that her use of terms which may be heard as racist was actually 'honesty'. The equation of racism with this kind of new racism, albeit still one of the most direct examples of overt racist talk in recent Australian political history, redefines racism as talk and policies that discriminate against indigenous peoples, refugees and migrants, despite their ostensibly liberal justifications.

These two definitions of racism feature as part of a critique of the majority-group as racist and have functions at both a local and ideological level. Locally, they accomplish an accusation of racism that is indirect, complex and subtle. By accusing the government of playing the race card and adopting the policies of One Nation, speakers avoid more explicit terminology (such as racist or bigot), whilst still hearably calling the government to moral account for their actions. These definitions of racism, together with the use of rhetorical tools such as the consensus warrant noted above, act as a prolepsis against charges commonly levelled at accusations of racism. Ideologically, they engage in a struggle for meaning over what may be criticized as racist. These definitions attempt to encompass actions such as the generation of racism for political gain and new racist talk as morally accountable racist acts. In this way actions, such as the exclusion of asylum seekers under discussion in these debates, may be challenged as morally unacceptable, with the view to mobilizing the populace to accept asylum seekers.

They also play a role in establishing solutions to racism. In both instances, these definitions lend themselves to the idea of combating racism through political change: by voting against the government and the One Nation Party. However, in some respects the identification of racism with politicians, particularly the personalization of racism to one person/party, may prove problematic. In its equation of racism with a minor political party and its leader, the repertoire of racism as Hanson is similar to definitions of racism as extremism reviewed in the section on new racism. It was noted there that the equation of racism with extremism is used to define a subject position for the speaker as 'not racist'. In the current context, racism as Hanson may potentially sideline a focus on the institutionalized racism of social structures participated in by all Australians.

conclusion

The issue of the exclusion of minority groups remains an entrenched and difficult one. As demonstrated by the discursive research on the language of contemporary racism, race talk has effectively adapted to a social and moral taboo against overt expressions of prejudice. Through adopting rhetorical strategies that deny racism, such as presenting one's negative views as reasonable and rational, defining racism in such a way that one's own actions may be categorized as non-racist and the deployment of tropes of equality and fairness, the discursive construction of an unequal society is re-produced and re-constructed daily. However, as our analysis of a speech from the Australian Senate debates on asylum seekers demonstrates, anti-racist counter discourses are also adapting to this new racist discourse. Speakers manage the socially delicate act of making an accusation of racism through presenting themselves as reasonable and rational, whilst also defining racism in such a way that new racism is still called to moral account. Defining racism as 'playing the race card' calls politicians to account for inciting racism in others, whilst allowing the speaker to avoid making explicit accusations of racism that may prove to be problematic. There are also some problems posed, however, by the re-definition of racism as Pauline Hanson/One Nation that may work to obscure widespread and institutionalized racism by locating racism within an extreme but minor political party.

The study of counter arguments has not yet been a major focus of discursive research. However, the initial exploration here suggests that it is an area ripe for further study that may contribute to the elucidation of contemporary race talk. Most importantly, it is hoped that such analysis will contribute to strengthening efforts to combat racism.

note

1. Of course, it seems that both these perspectives ignore a fundamental aspect of racism: the material means through which oppression is expressed and experienced. Discursive psychologists address this argument in two ways. Firstly, they point out that to claim something is 'constructed' does not mean it is non-existent or not 'real'. Secondly, they point out that discourse is the primary way in which physical realities such as apartheid are established

and maintained. Such a system must be made sense of, legitimated, justified and supported by the populace. However, there are a number of researchers who argue that discursive psychology has not sufficiently tackled issues of subjectivity and the body (e.g. Parker, 1988) and this remains a contentious issue in the field.

references

Abel, S. (1996). 'Wild Maori' and 'Tame Maori' in television news. *New Zealand Journal of Media Studies, 3(2)*, 33–38.

Augoustinos, M., Tuffin, K. & Every, D. (2005). New racism, meritocracy and individualism: Constraining affirmative action in education. *Discourse & Society, 16(3)*, 315–339.

Augoustinos, M., Tuffin, K. & Rapley, M. (1999). Genocide or a failure to gel? Racism, history and nationalism in Australian talk. *Discourse and Society, 10(3)*, 351–378.

Augoustinos, M., Tuffin, K. & Sale, L. (1999). Race Talk. *Australian Journal of Psychology, 51*, 90–97.

Austin, J.L. (1962). *How to do things with words*. Oxford: Clarendon Press.

Billig, M. (1988). The notion of 'prejudice': Some rhetorical and ideological aspects. *Text, 8*, 91–110.

Billig, M. (1991). *Ideology and opinions: Studies in rhetorical psychology*. London: Sage.

Billig, M., Condor, S., Edwards, D., Gane, M., Middleton, D. & Radley, A. (1988). *Ideological dilemmas: A social psychology of everyday thinking*. London: Sage.

Blommaert, J. & Verschueren, J. (1998). *Debating diversity: Analysing the discourse of tolerance*. London: Routledge.

Condor, S. (1988). Race Stereotypes and Racist Discourse. *Text, 8*, 69–89.

Condor, S., Abell, J., Figgou, L., Gibson, S. & Stevenson, C. (in press). 'They're not racist...': Prejudice denial, mitigation and suppression in dialogue. *British Journal of Social Psychology*.

Edwards, D. (1997). *Discourse and cognition*. London: Sage.

Edwards, D. & Potter, J. (1992). *Discursive psychology*. London: Sage.

Fiske, S.T. & Taylor, S.E. (1991). *Social Cognition*. (2nd edn). New York: McGraw-Hill.

Gergen, K.J. (1985). The social constructionist movement in modern psychology. *American Psychologist, 40*, 266–275.

Hopkins, N., Reicher, S. & Levine M. (1997). On the parallels between social cognition and the 'new racism'. *British Journal of Social Psychology, 36*, 305–329.

Jones, L. (2000). Immigration and parliamentary discourse in Great Britain: An analysis of the debates related to the 1996 Asylum and Immigration Act. In R. Wodak & T.A. van Dijk (Eds.), *Racism at the top* (pp.283–310). Austria: Drava Verlag.

Katz, I. & Hass, R.G. (1988). Racial ambivalence and American value conflict: Correlational and priming studies of dual cognitive structures. *Journal of Personality and Social Psychology, 55*, 893–905.

Kinder, D.R. & Sears, D.O. (1981). Prejudice and politics: Symbolic racism versus racial threats to the good life. *Journal of Personality and Social Psychology, 40*, 414–431.

Le Couteur, A., Rapley, M. & Augoustinos, M. (2001). 'This very difficult debate about Wik': Stake, voice and the management of category memberships in race politics. *British Journal of Social Psychology, 40*, 35–57.

Lynn, N. & Lea, S. (2003). 'A phantom menace and the new Apartheid': The social construction of asylum-seekers in the United Kingdom. *Discourse and Society, 14(4)*, 425–452.

Macrae, C.N. & Bodenhausen, G.V. (2000). Social cognition: Thinking categorically about others. *Annual Review of Psychology, 51*, 93–120.

McConahay, J.B. (1986). Modern racism, ambivalence, and the modern racism scale. In J.F. Dovidio & S.L. Gaertner (Eds.), *Prejudice, discrimination and racism*, (pp.91–125). Orlando, FL: Academic Press.

McCreanor, T. (1993a). Mimiwhangata: Media reliance on Pakeha commonsense in interpretations of Maori actions. *Sites, 26*, 79–90.

McCreanor, T. (1993b). Pakeha ideology of Maori performance: A discourse analytic approach to the construction of educational failure in Aoteoroa/New Zealand. *Folia Lingistica, 27*, 293–314.

McCreanor, T. (1993c). Settling grievances to deny sovereignty. *Sites, 27*, 45–73.

McIntyre, S. & Clark, A. (2003). *The history wars*. Melbourne: Melbourne University Press.

Mehan, H. (1997). The discourse of the illegal immigration debate: A case study in the politics of representation. *Discourse and Society, 8(2)*, 249–270.

Nairn, R.G. & McCreanor, T.N. (1990). Insensitivity and hypersensitivity: An imbalance in Pakeha accounts of racial conflict. *Journal of Language and Social Psychology, 9(4)*, 293–309.

Nairn, R.G. & McCreanor, T.N. (1991). Race talk and common sense: Patterns in Pakeha discourse on Maori/Pakeha relations in New Zealand. *Journal of Language and Social Psychology, 10(4)*, 245–261.

O'Doherty, K. (2001). *'Asylum seekers', 'boat people' and 'illegal immigrants': Social categorisation and fact construction in the media.* Unpublished Honours Thesis, University of Adelaide, Adelaide.

Parker, I. (Ed.) (1988). *Social constructionism, discourse and realism*. London: Sage.

Pettigrew, T.F. & Meertens, R.W. (1995). Subtle and blatant prejudice in Western Europe. *European Journal of Social Psychology, 25*, 57–75.

Potter, J. (1996). *Representing reality: Discourse, rhetoric and social construction*. Sage: London.

Potter, J. & Wetherell, M. (1987). *Discourse and social psychology: Beyond attitudes and behaviour*. London: Sage.

Rapley, M. (1998). 'Just an ordinary Australian': Self-categorisation and the discursive construction of facticity in 'new racist' political rhetoric. *British Journal of Social Psychology, 37*, 325–344.

Rapley, M. (2001). How to do X without doing Y: Accomplishing discrimination without 'being racist' 'doing equity'. In M. Augoustinos & K. Reynolds (Eds.), *Understanding prejudice, racism and social conflict*. London: Sage.

Reeves, F. (1983). *British racial discourse. A study of British political discourse about race and race-related matters*. Cambridge: Cambridge University Press.

Rojo, L.M. (2000). Spain, outer wall of the European fortress: Analysis of the Parliamentary Debates on the immigration policy in Spain. In R. Wodak & T. A. van Dijk (Eds.), *Racism at the top: Parliamentary discourse on ethnic issues in six European parliaments* (pp.169–220). Austria: Drava Verlag.

Santa Ana, O. (1999). 'Like an animal I was treated': Anti-immigrant metaphor in US public discourse. *Discourse and Society, 10(2)*, 191–224.

Sedlak, M. (2000). You really do make an unrespectable foreigner policy: Discourse on ethnic issues in Austrian Parliament. In R. Wodak & T.A. van Dijk (Eds.), *Racism at the top: Parliamentary discourses on ethnic issues in six European states* (pp.107–168). Austria: Drava Verlag.

Seidel, G. (1988). Verbal strategies of the collaborators: A discursive analysis of the July 1986 European Parliamentary debate on South African sanctions. *Text, 8*, 111–125.

Sheehan, P. (1998). *Among the barbarians: The dividing of Australia.* Sydney: Random House.

Thiesmeyer, L. (1995). The discourse of official violence: Anti-Japanese North American discourse and the American internment camps. *Discourse & Society, 6(3)*, 319–352.

van der Valk, I. (2000). Parliamentary discourse on immigration and nationality in France. In R. Wodak & T.A. van Dijk (Eds.), *Racism at the top* (pp.221–260). Austria: Drava Verlag.

van Dijk, T.A. (1984). *Prejudice in discourse.* Amsterdam: Benjamins.

van Dijk, T.A. (1987). *Communicating racism: Ethnic prejudice in thought and talk.* Newbury Park, CA: Sage.

van Dijk, T.A. (1991). *Racism and the press.* London: Routledge.

van Dijk, T.A. (1992). Discourse and the denial of racism. *Discourse & Society, 3(1)*, 87–118.

van Dijk, T.A. (1993). Elite discourses and racism. London: Sage.

van Dijk, T.A. (1997). Political discourse and racism: Describing others in Western parliaments. In S.H. Riggins (Ed.), *The language and politics of exclusion: Others in discourse* (pp.31–64). London: Sage.

Verkuyten, M. (1998). Personhood and accounting for racism in conversation. *Journal for the Theory of Social Behaviour, 28(2)*, 147–168.

Verkuyten, M. (2001). 'Abnormalisation' of ethnic minorities in conversation. *British Journal of Social Psychology, 40*, 257–258.

Wetherell, M. (1998). Positioning and interpretative repertoires: Conversation analysis and post-structuralism in dialogue. *Discourse & Society, 9(3)*, 387–412.

Wetherell, M. & Potter, J. (1992). *Mapping the language of racism: Discourse and the legitimation of exploitation.* London: Harvester Wheatsheaf.

Wodak, R. & van Dijk, T.A. (Eds.) (2000). *Racism at the top: Parliamentary discourses on ethnic issues in six European states.* Drava Verlag: Austria.

10
political language and persuasive communication
peter bull

There is now a widespread international interest in the analysis of political language and rhetoric (e.g., Beer & De Landtsheer, 2004; Billig, 2003; Bull, 2003; De Landtsheer & Feldman, 2000; Feldman & De Landtsheer, 1998). Research topics have included political metaphors (e.g., Beer & De Landtsheer, 2004; Wilson, 1990; Lakoff & Johnson, 1980), rhetoric (e.g., Billig, 2003; Atkinson, 1984a), issues of stake and interest (e.g., Dickerson, 1997), equivocation (e.g., Bavelas et al., 1990), and the use of pronouns (e.g., Wilson, 1990; Bull & Fetzer, 2006). The aim of this chapter is to review three particular aspects of political language: equivocation, rhetorical devices used by politicians to invite applause, and the use of metaphor. Their significance is also considered in the context of traditional research on persuasive communication.

equivocation

Politicians are often castigated for their evasiveness in political interviews, as the sort of people who can never give a straight answer to a straight question. But are the questions in political interviews always so straight? To what extent is the evasiveness of politicians a response to the kinds of questions they receive? An alternative perspective can be derived from a theory of equivocation, proposed by Bavelas, Black, Chovil and Mullett (1990).

the theory of equivocation
According to Bavelas et al. (1990, p.28), equivocation is '...nonstraight-forward communication; it appears ambiguous, contradictory, tangential,

obscure or even evasive'. More recently, it has been defined as the 'intentional use of imprecise language' (Hamilton & Mineo, 1998). Bavelas et al. stress that although it is individuals who equivocate, such responses must always be understood in the context in which they occur. According to their situational theory of communicative conflict, people typically equivocate when posed a question to which all of the possible replies have potentially negative consequences, but where nevertheless a reply is still expected.

Bavelas et al. (1990) further argue that equivocation needs to be understood as a multidimensional concept. They specify four main dimensions: sender, content, receiver and context. They state (Bavelas et al., p.34): 'All messages that would (intuitively or otherwise) be called equivocal are ambiguous in at least one of these four elements.' The sender dimension refers to the extent to which the response is the speaker's own opinion; a statement is considered more equivocal if the speaker fails to acknowledge it as his own opinion, or attributes it to another person. Content refers to comprehensibility, an unclear statement being considered more equivocal. The receiver dimension refers to the extent to which the message is addressed to the other person in the situation, the less so the more equivocal the message. Context refers to the extent to which the response is a direct answer to the question – the less the relevance, the more equivocal the message.

Bavelas et al. (1990) have conducted a series of experiments in which a number of conflictual situations are described. Their results clearly showed that responses to conflictual questions were judged as significantly more equivocal on these four dimensions than responses to non-conflictual questions. It should be noted that their theory is not just intended to explain political equivocation, but how equivocation occurs in a wide variety of social contexts. For example, a person receives a highly unsuitable gift from a well-liked friend, who then asks directly 'Did you like the gift?' In responding, the person has two negative choices: saying, falsely, that they like the gift or saying, hurtfully that they do not. According to equivocation theory, the person will if possible avoid both of these negative alternatives, especially when a hurtful truth serves no purpose. What they do instead is equivocate; for example, someone might say 'I appreciate your thoughtfulness' with no mention of what they thought of the actual gift.

In this chapter, the focus is specifically on political equivocation. Particular attention is given to the two main features of equivocation theory: firstly, the conceptualization of equivocation as multidimensional; secondly, the situational theory of communicative conflict.

equivocation as a multidimensional construct

Studies of televised political interviews clearly show that politicians equivocate on what Bavelas et al. (1990) call the context dimension. In an analysis of 33 interviews with four British party political leaders (Margaret Thatcher, Neil Kinnock, John Major, Paddy Ashdown), politicians' responses were coded as *replies* (direct answers) only if they gave the information requested in the question (Bull, 1994). The term *non-reply* was coined to refer to those responses in which the politician failed to provide any of the information requested in the question. *Reply rate* (the proportion of questions which receive a direct answer) was then used as a measure of equivocation: the lower the reply rate, the more equivocal the politician. Results showed a mean reply rate of just 46 per cent. In effect, the politicians replied to only slightly more than two out of five questions. In an independent study of a completely different set of interviews (but again with Margaret Thatcher and Neil Kinnock), the politicians were found to give direct answers to only 39 per cent of questions (Harris, 1991).

In comparison, it is interesting to consider reply rates in televised interviews with people who are not politicians. The late Diana, Princess of Wales, in her celebrated interview with Martin Bashir, replied to 78 per cent of questions (Bull, 1997). Louise Woodward, the British au-pair who was convicted for the manslaughter of eight-month-old Matthew Eappen, in an interview with Martin Bashir replied to 70 per cent of questions (Bull, 2000a). Monica Lewinsky replied to 89 per cent of questions posed by Jon Snow in an interview concerning her affair with President Clinton (Bull, 2000a). The mean reply rate of 79 per cent across all three interviews is significantly higher than the mean reply rate of 46 per cent for the 33 political interviews reported above (Bull, 2000a).

Bavelas et al.'s (1990) sender dimension was the focus of a study by Bull and Fetzer (2006). Their analysis was based on 20 interviews from the British general elections of 1997 and 2001, together with one subsequent interview (February 6, 2003) between Jeremy Paxman and Labour prime minister Tony Blair (from the time of the Iraq war). Over all 21 interviews, 17 examples were identified in which the politician avoided replying to the question through the strategic use of personal pronouns. In most cases, the interviewers were asking questions about the politicians' personal role or political beliefs ('you' in the singular), but the politicians typically responded in terms of the collective 'we', thereby not replying to the question. For example, Jonathan Dimbleby asked Tony Blair in the 2001 general election, 'Mr Blair, before the last election *you* said: *I* love the pound. Um, can *you* be trusted to go on loving the pound?' Tony Blair replied, 'Well, if the economic conditions are right, I believe *we* should join the single currency.' In this example, the 'you' was clearly personal (second person singular), because the interviewer referred to something Tony Blair said in the previous general election. Because Tony Blair responded in terms of 'we', his response was regarded as equivocal on the sender dimension.

All four equivocation dimensions provided the framework for a study by Feldman (2004) of televised interviews with Japanese politicians. The politicians' responses were rated by observers on 6-point Likert-type scales ranging from (1) 'straightforward, easy to understand' to (6) 'totally vague'. The mean ratings were: context 3.51, content 2.79, sender 3.39, and receiver 1.68. A content analysis was also conducted, in which the politicians' responses were categorized into replies and non-replies: to be regarded as a *full answer*, responses had to be unequivocal on all four dimensions. This showed a reply rate of only 9.9 per cent, markedly lower than that for British politicians reported above (Bull, 1994; Harris, 1991). But as Feldman points out, the British data were based on only the context dimension; the responses of the Japanese politicians were analysed on all four dimensions. Even so, when responses of Japanese politicians were coded on the context dimension alone, barely 15.8 per cent of responses were direct answers to the question (Feldman, 2004).

Feldman (2004) also analysed reply rates for televised interviews with Japanese who were not politicians (broadcast during the same period as the political interviews). Six interviews with five public figures (experts on social, economic and educational issues) were studied. These public figures gave full answers (in the sense defined by Feldman) to 88.5 per cent of the questions (N = 78 questions). These figures suggest that the low reply rates for Japanese politicians are not simply a reflection of the oft-noted tendency towards equivocation in Japanese culture. Notably, in both British and Japanese televised interviews, politicians seem to equivocate far more than non-politicians; in that respect, the politicians seem to resemble each other more than members of their own indigenous cultures (Feldman, 2004; Bull, 1994, 1997, 2000a).

the situational theory of communicative conflict

Communicative conflicts were analysed by Bull (2003) and Bull, Elliott, Palmer and Walker (1996) in the context of British televised political interviews. In this social situation, they proposed that face and face management are of prime importance. Specifically, they hypothesized that interviewer questions create what are termed *threats to face*. That is to say, questions are formulated in such a way that politicians constantly run the risk of making *face-damaging* responses (responses which make themselves and/or their political allies look bad). Communicative conflicts may occur when *all* the principal ways of responding to a question are potentially face-damaging.

For example, when Tony Blair stood for re-election as Labour prime minister in the 2005 British general election, he was asked by the BBC interviewer Jeremy Paxman 'Do you accept any responsibility at all for the death of Dr David Kelly?' Dr David Kelly was a microbiologist and chief scientific officer for the Ministry of Defence. He apparently committed suicide after his identification as the source of revelations to the BBC, that intelligence officers were unhappy with the government's dossier on Iraq's weapons of mass destruction (the so-called 'dodgy dossier'). Because it was the Ministry of Defence who identified Dr Kelly, the government was widely assumed to bear some responsibility for his death. Thus, if Blair had replied no to Paxman's question, his response would have lacked credibility, and he might also have been perceived as unsympathetic and uncaring. But if Blair had replied yes, it would have reflected extremely badly on his own and his government's perceived competence. If Blair had equivocated, this would also be face-damaging, because it would make him look evasive: both politicians in general and Tony Blair in particular have an unenviable reputation for such slipperiness. Thus, Paxman's question created a classic communicative conflict, in which either confirmation or denial by Blair would have been extremely face-damaging; equivocation was arguably the least face-threatening option. In fact, Paxman posed the question four times, and each time Blair equivocated; after Blair's fourth equivocal response ('...it's maybe not a question you need to give a yes or no answer to'), Paxman moved on to a new topic.

Not only can equivocation be explained in terms of the concept of face, it also can be used to explain when and why politicians *do* reply to questions. So, for example, in an interview during the 1992 British general election, Labour leader Neil Kinnock was posed the following question by David Frost: 'Now can you give me a picture of the future if Neil Kinnock is prime minister after twelve months can you give me a specific vision of how our lives will be different?' Not replying or equivocating in response to such a question would be extremely face-damaging, it would have made Neil Kinnock look totally incompetent. The face-threatening structure of the question is such that it can be predicted with confidence that the politician would reply.

Eighteen televised interviews from the 1992 British general election were analysed by Bull et al. (1996) in terms of the face-threatening structure of questions. If *all* the possible principal responses to a question were regarded as potentially face-damaging, the question was judged as creating a communicative conflict. It should be noted that even an equivocal response was regarded as face-damaging, especially given that politicians are widely criticized for being evasive. Nevertheless, equivocation was still predicted as the most likely response, because arguably it is typically less face-damaging than other possible responses. Conversely, in non-conflictual questions, where a response that was not face-damaging was considered possible, this was also the predicted response. Overall, 41 per cent of questions were judged as conflictual, and the modal response was to equivocate (64 per cent of questions). In the remaining 59 per cent of questions (non-conflictual), the politicians typically produced a response that was not face-damaging (87 per cent of questions); furthermore, they also tended to *reply* to such questions (60 per cent of responses).

A second study was conducted, based on six interviews from the 2001 British general election (Bull, 2003). These differed from the traditional 'one-on-one' interview, in that ordinary voters were given the opportunity alongside professional political interviewers to put questions directly to the leaders of the three main political parties. What made this situation so potentially interesting is that voters may differ from political interviewers in the kinds of questions which they ask. In particular, given the more complex structure of conflictual questions, voters might be expected to ask them less frequently. Whereas interviewers might seek through such questions to highlight inconsistencies in policy, voters may be more concerned simply to establish where a party stands on a particular issue. Consequently, if voters pose fewer communicative conflicts, then politicians might be expected to give them significantly more replies.

Results showed that politicians replied to 73 per cent of questions from members of the public, and to 47 per cent of questions from political interviewers ($p<.025$). This latter figure is almost identical to the 46 per cent reply rate for the set of 33 political interviews reported above (Bull, 1994). Conversely, the reply rate of 73 per cent to questions from voters is directly comparable to that of 79 per cent for interviews with people who are not politicians, also reported above (Bull, 1997, 2000a). In addition, it was found that political interviewers used a significantly higher proportion of conflictual questions than ordinary voters (58 per cent cf. 19 per cent, $p<.025$). Finally, a significant Phi correlation of 0.76 ($p<.05$) between questions and responses showed that equivocation by the politicians was associated with conflictual questions from the political interviewers. The comparable correlation for responses to questions from voters just missed significance (Phi = 0.70, $p>.05$).

conclusions

Overall, the two main propositions of equivocation theory have received impressive support from the research reviewed above. Equivocation in televised political interviews can usefully be understood as a multidimensional construct (Feldman, 2004; Bull, 1994, 2003; Bull & Fetzer, 2006); it also does occur principally in response to questions which create a communicative conflict (Bull et al., 1996; Bull, 2003). Thus, politicians typically equivocated to conflictual questions and replied to non-conflictual questions (Bull et al., 1996). Furthermore, professional political interviewers asked significantly more conflictual questions than members of the general public, and received significantly fewer replies (Bull, 2003). But an important modification of equivocation theory has also been proposed: in the context of political interviews, the prime source of communicative conflicts are threats to face. Indeed, questions may be understood as having a face-threatening structure, from which it is possible to predict whether or not a politician is likely to give a reply. Not only does this approach provide a means of analysing questions in political interviews, it also demonstrates that the occurrence of both replies and non-replies can be understood within the same theoretical framework.

applause and political rhetoric

applause invitations in political speeches

How politicians invite applause to their speeches was analysed in detail by Atkinson (e.g., 1983, 1984a, 1984b). According to Atkinson, applause occurs in response to a relatively narrow range of actions on the part of the speaker, e.g., supporting the speaker's own party or attacking the opposition. The timing of applause is also characterized by a high degree of precision. Typically it occurs either just before or immediately after a possible completion point by the speaker, while speakers usually wait until the applause has finished before continuing to speak. Thus, just as conversationalists take it in turn to speak, so speaker and audience also take turns, although audience 'turns' are essentially limited to gross displays of approval or disapproval (such as cheering or heckling).

Atkinson's critical insight (e.g., 1984a) was to identify key rhetorical devices whereby politicians invite applause from their audiences. These are formulaic features embedded in the structure of talk that indicate when to applaud through the projection of appropriate completion points. One such device is the three-part list. In conversation, the completion of a list can signal the completion of an utterance – a point at which another person can or should start talking. Such lists also typically consist of three items, so that once the listener recognizes that a list is under way, it is possible to anticipate the completion point and hence the end of the speaker's utterance (Jefferson, 1990). In political speeches, Atkinson proposed that the three-part list may serve a comparable function, but in this case signalling to the audience appropriate places to applaud. For example, in a speech to the British Labour Party conference (October 1, 1996), Tony Blair was applauded when he famously said: 'Ask me my three main priorities for Government, and I tell you: education, education and education.'

Another comparable rhetorical device is the contrast. Blair was applauded in a more recent speech when he said (Brighton, September 28, 2004), 'But the point is: Britain doesn't need a ruling class today, the rulers are the people' (thereby contrasting 'ruling class' with the 'people'). To be effective, the second part of the contrast should closely resemble the first in the details of its construction and duration, so that the audience can the more easily anticipate the point of completion. Atkinson (1984a, pp.86–123) argued that the skilled use of both three-part lists and contrasts is characteristic of 'charismatic' speakers, and that such devices are often to be found in those passages of political speeches selected for presentation in the news media (Atkinson, 1984a, pp.124–163).

Heritage and Greatbatch (1986) extended Atkinson's (1984a) work by analysing all the 476 speeches televised from the British Conservative, Labour and Liberal Party conferences in 1981 – a truly heroic study! They identified another five rhetorical devices for obtaining applause, and found that more than two thirds of the collective applause was associated with all seven rhetorical devices. Most effective were contrasts and lists, the two devices originally identified by Atkinson as significant in evoking applause; these accounted for almost half the incidences of collective applause.

re-evaluating atkinson's analysis of rhetoric

Atkinson's (1984a) analysis has proved remarkably enduring, and provides some compelling insights into the stage management of political speeches. However, his research suffers from one important limitation: as an analysis of how applause occurs in political speeches, it is incomplete. In fact, it is possible to identify several significant features of political applause not accounted for in Atkinson's original research (Bull, in press); these are listed below:

1. In the 476 speeches analysed by Heritage and Greatbatch (1986), 68 per cent of the collective applause was associated with the seven rhetorical devices. Thus, almost a third of collective applause occurred in the *absence* of rhetorical devices.
    How and why does this occur?
2. Rhetorical devices do not always receive applause. For example, Heritage and Greatbatch (1986) analysed what they called *external attacks* (statements critical of outgroups, e.g., other political parties). Seventy-one per cent of external attacks accompanied by rhetorical devices received applause.
    But why were the other 29 per cent of external attacks not applauded?
3. Heritage and Greatbatch did not analyse all applause incidences, they specifically excluded isolated applause in which only one or two people clap.
    How often does isolated applause occur?
4. According to Atkinson (1984a, p.33), applause is typically closely synchronized with speech. In the vast majority of cases, it starts either just before or immediately after the speaker reaches a completion point.
    But how often and why does asynchronous applause occur?

The focus of Atkinson's (1984a) analysis was on synchronous applause invited by the speaker through rhetorical devices. But applause which is asynchronous, isolated or which occurs in the absence of rhetorical devices may be of considerable significance for a comprehensive account of how and why applause occurs in political speeches. The author has carried out a series of studies intended to address these questions (Bull, 2003); key findings from this research are summarized below with regard to six central issues in Atkinson's analysis of political rhetoric.

studies evaluating atkinson's analysis of rhetoric

Synchrony. According to Atkinson (1984a, p.33), '...displays of approval are seldom delayed for more than a split second after a completion point, and frequently start just before one is reached...'; that is, applause is characteristically synchronized with speech. But neither Atkinson nor Heritage and Greatbatch (1986) analysed *all* the incidents of applause which occur in political speeches. This task was carried out by Bull and Wells (2002) on the basis of 15 speeches delivered by the leaders of the three main British political parties at party conferences between 1996 and 2000. They found only 66 per cent of applause incidents were fully synchronized with speech. Thus, it would seem Atkinson overestimated the degree of speech/applause synchrony.

Rhetorical devices. From three leader speeches at the 1996 British party political conferences, Bull (2000b) analysed 15 statements which received collective applause in the absence of clear applause invitations. In these incidences, the applause was invariably asynchronous with speech; it was either clearly interruptive, or started well before the speaker had reached a completion point. Furthermore, whereas Atkinson (1984a) found that applause occurred typically in response to praise of the politician's own party and/or attacks on the opposition, in these examples applause occurred in response to statements of political policy. Arguably, the content of such policy statements is of greater significance than mere ingroup praise or outgroup derogation. Accordingly, Bull (2000b) argued that applause may occur in the absence of rhetorical devices in response to speech content alone, and that Atkinson overestimated the importance of rhetorical devices in inviting applause.

Speech content. Atkinson (1984a) never denied the role of speech content in evoking applause; but he argued that audiences are much *more* likely to applaud if content is expressed through appropriate rhetorical devices. An alternative view was proposed by Bull (2000b). In some messages, the content may be so significant that they will be applauded whether or not they are expressed through rhetorical devices. According to this view, Atkinson underestimated the role of speech content.

Spontaneous applause. According to Atkinson (1984a, pp.45–46), 'Professional politicians would no doubt prefer us to think of displays of approval as wholly spontaneous responses to the depth and wisdom of their words. Unfortunately, however, the available evidence provides few grounds for so doing.' Thus, he was highly dismissive of the notion that applause at political rallies can ever be spontaneous. However, if audiences on occasions applaud the content of speech in the absence of rhetorical devices, this would suggest that applause can also be spontaneous (Bull, 2000b). From the author's perspective, Atkinson underestimated the possibility of spontaneous applause.

Uninvited and invited applause. A fundamental distinction was proposed between invited and uninvited applause (Bull, 2000b). Uninvited applause may occur either directly in response to the content of speech (Bull, 2000b), or through a misreading of rhetorical devices (Bull & Wells, 2002). In the latter case, the audience may mistakenly respond to a rhetorical device when the associated delivery (body language and/or tone of voice) suggests it was not intended as an applause invitation, but rather that the speaker wished to continue. So, for example, if a speaker employs a three-part list but at the same time is visibly taking in another breath, still using hand gestures, or even starting another sentence, this would seem not to be an applause invitation, rather the speaker intended to continue with the speech. Uninvited applause was never discussed by Atkinson (1984a); this concept represents a significant modification of his analysis.

Delivery. A further significant modification concerns the role of delivery. Whereas Atkinson (1984a) argued that appropriate delivery increases the chance of a rhetorical device receiving applause, Bull and Wells (2002) proposed that delivery indicates *whether or not* a rhetorical device is intended as an applause invitation. In their analysis of 15 conference speeches, almost all the incidents of synchronous applause (98 per cent) occurred in response only to rhetorical devices accompanied by delivery appropriate for inviting applause. That is to say, appropriate delivery would seem to be as important as the use of rhetorical devices for speech/ applause synchrony. Thus, it would appear that Atkinson underestimated the importance of delivery.

conclusions

Atkinson's (1984a) insights into the techniques of applause invitation have made an enormous contribution to our understanding of political rhetoric. This author's intent has not been to devalue the significance of Atkinson's analysis, rather to re-evaluate it in the light of more recent research. The main argument proposed is that as an account of how applause occurs in political speeches, Atkinson's analysis is incomplete (Bull, 2006). Whereas Atkinson overestimated the importance of rhetorical devices and speech/applause synchrony, he underestimated the potential role of speech content, spontaneous applause and delivery. The varying roles of these different factors can be more adequately reflected in terms of a fundamental distinction between invited and uninvited applause.

political metaphor

introduction

Metaphor plays an important role in political rhetoric. According to Lakoff and Johnson (1980), political metaphors represent ways of thinking about political issues. If a politician can persuade us to think in terms of their metaphors, they can lead us to adopt their political viewpoint. So, for example, a bicycle metaphor has sometimes been used in connection with the expansion of the European Union (Emerson, 1988). To keep a bicycle moving, you have to keep pedalling. From this perspective, EU enlargement and integration should continue; if you accept the bicycle metaphor, you are persuaded of the argument. But if you think of the EU in terms of a different metaphor, say as a transatlantic liner like the *Titanic*, a very different picture emerges!

The word metaphor itself is taken from two Greek words, meaning to carry something from one place to another (Haddon, 2003). Essentially, metaphor involves trying to comprehend and understand something in terms of something else (Lakoff & Johnson, 1980). So for example, 'Make poverty history' is a metaphor based on the concept of time; if we imagine that poverty one day may belong to the past, we may strive for a future in which poverty no longer exists.

But metaphor is not just a matter of language, of mere words; according to Lakoff and Johnson (1980), human thought processes are intrinsically metaphorical. In politics and economics, metaphors are of particular importance. Inspired by Lakoff and Johnson's (1980) seminal work, an extensive research literature has developed on the use of political metaphors (e.g., Beer & De Landtsheer, 2004). The role of metaphor in modern British politics is discussed below, based on a recent article by the author (Bull, 2005).

metaphor in modern british politics

In the context of British politics, there have been two powerful political metaphors in recent decades. During the 1980s, the idea of an 'enterprise culture' emerged as a central motif in the political thought of Margaret Thatcher's Conservative government (Keat, 1991a). The term was used in at least two ways. Firstly, a wide range of institutions and activities were to be remodelled along the lines of commercial enterprise. Secondly, the acquisition of enterprising qualities (such as initiative, boldness and self-reliance) was to be encouraged. Central to the philosophy of the enterprise culture were institutional reforms intended to introduce market principles into areas such as health and education, which had traditionally been protected from market forces by public funding or subsidy. These intrusions were vociferously attacked by critics, who maintained that the introduction of market forces distorted or undermined values and standards (Keat, 1991b) – that is to say, in the context of health or education, the enterprise metaphor was inappropriate.

In response to the Conservative electoral successes of the 1980s, the Labour Party under Neil Kinnock embarked on a series of fundamental changes, which became widely known as 'modernization'. These changes led eventually to New Labour's historic landslide election victory in 1997 under Tony Blair. The term modernization did not just refer to the process of change, it also provided a powerful form of rhetoric in its own right – a metaphor of both fashion (Lakoff & Johnson, 1980) and technology (Beer & De Landtsheer, 2004). Through this metaphor, radical change which might have been seen as a betrayal of traditional values could be justified as keeping up with the times and adapting to the demands of modern technology and techniques. Thus, analyses of televised interviews broadcast during the 1997 general election campaign showed how Blair used this metaphor to great effect (Bull, 2000a). Not only was he able to acknowledge explicitly the policy changes which had taken place, but also to present them as principled – an adaptation of the traditional values of the Labour Party to the contemporary political situation. In this way, he could equivocate skilfully in response to awkward questions and also present a positive face for his party, as both principled and moving with the times.

metaphors in the 2005 general election

By 2005, the rhetoric of the enterprise culture and modernization was stale and passé, perhaps dead metaphor already. As time goes on, metaphors can become hackneyed and lose their effect. Thus, novelty is an important aspect of political metaphor. The linking together of two hitherto unconnected ideas can provide new political insights, stimulating and mobilizing popular support. But no such new powerful metaphors emerged in the 2005 election, it will not stand out as a watershed alongside the elections of 1979 and 1997.

Thus, in contrast with the dynamism of the metaphor of the enterprise culture of the Thatcher years, the Conservative campaign of 2005 was marked only by timidity and negativity. 'Are you thinking what we're thinking?' was scarcely a clarion call. As a slogan, it made the Conservatives sound as if they were too frightened to put what they thought into words. Similarly, their immigration policy with its slogan 'It's not racist to impose limits on immigration' was widely perceived by many as just the opposite, as insidiously or even manifestly racist. If the Conservatives had one big idea, it was 'accountability' – the proposal that politicians should be subject to the discipline of the workplace. But this metaphor was neither new nor exciting; the Conservatives remained becalmed in the opinion polls throughout the campaign.

The Labour manifesto was entitled 'Britain forward not back', about as bland and pedestrian a slogan as can be imagined. According to Tony Blair's preface, 'Our case rests on one idea more than any other – that it is the duty of government to provide opportunity and security for all in a changing world.' Would any modern democratic political party disagree with such sentiments? After the preface, there was an encomium to New Labour's record, and then nine separate chapters, spelling out policy in exhaustive detail; to read the document in full is 112 pages. Throughout the campaign, Labour complained that their policies were not given sufficient attention because of media preoccupations with the war in Iraq. But Labour's positive vision, if it had one, lacked an overarching metaphor with which to enthuse the voters.

The Liberal Democrats in their manifesto put themselves forward as 'The REAL alternative'. But this gave no indication of what they stood for, simply that they were not the other two parties. The manifesto further stated that their leading themes were 'Freedom, Fairness, Trust. These are the qualities of the British people at their best, and they are the guiding principles of the Liberal Democrats.' Again, it would be surprising to find any modern democratic political party that would not subscribe to these values. In the 2005 election, Liberal Democrats increased their representation from 52 to 62 seats. But in the context of disillusion with Labour and disaffection with the Conservatives, they might have expected to do much better. According to Tony Blair (Brighton speech, September 28, 2004) 'The great advantage of the Lib Dems is precisely that no-one knows what they stand for.' If the Liberal Democrats are to make the historic breakthrough for which they have so long aspired, this may also be their greatest disadvantage.

the dangers of metaphor

Political and economic ideologies are often framed in metaphorical terms. But metaphors can conceal as much as they illuminate: in enabling us to focus on one aspect of a concept, we may overlook other important features inconsistent with the metaphor (Lakoff & Johnson, 1980). In politics and economics this matters more, because misleading metaphors can so seriously affect our lives. Thus, in *Metaphor and War*, Lakoff (1991) baldly stated that 'Metaphors can kill'. In that article, he showed in detail how the political and economic situation in Iraq was conceptualized in metaphors which systematically concealed the consequences of US government action. Thus, business metaphors which presented war in terms of 'costs' and 'benefits' obscured the pain, dismemberment, starvation, death and injury of loved ones incurred by conflict: these are not metaphorical, but only too real. However, Lakoff does not condemn the use of metaphors outright; he has always acknowledged that metaphorical thought is unavoidable and ubiquitous (Lakoff &

Johnson, 2003). It is the misuse of inappropriate metaphors in a political context which can be so dangerous.

conclusions

In the novel *The Curious Incident of the Dog in the Night-Time*, the literal-minded Christopher Boone states that '....I think it [a metaphor] should be called a lie because a pig is not like a day and people do not have skeletons in their cupboards' (Haddon, 2003). Metaphors can be misleading, even deceitful, but they are also intrinsic to human cognition. In politics, metaphors can be a powerful means of mobilizing popular support. Despite this, the analysis of metaphor has played no part in the traditional social-psychological study of persuasive communication. In the final section below, research on persuasive communication is reviewed, and discussed in the context of the analysis of political language.

persuasive communication

introduction

Traditionally, research on persuasion has been focused on the significant components of persuasive messages (Stiff & Mongeau, 2003). These have been summarized as 'who says what to whom with what effect' (Hovland, Janis & Kelley, 1953). 'Who' refers to characteristics of the source of the message. 'What' refers to the message itself, so for example, comparisons between so-called 'rational message appeals' and 'emotional message appeals'. 'To whom' refers to characteristics of the receivers of the message. 'With what effect' has been studied in terms of a number of models of persuasion.

Message source. Credibility is an important feature of a message source. Two principal dimensions of credibility are expertise and trustworthiness, which both have significant effects on persuasion (Hovland et al., 1953). Although these dimensions are often related, this is not necessarily the case. For example, the source of a message may be perceived as expert but untrustworthy, or as trustworthy but lacking in expertise. Two other factors which can also affect persuasion are the physical attractiveness of the source and his or her similarity to the message receivers. Thus, when the message is relatively unimportant to the receivers, they are more likely to be affected by the attractiveness of the source. Again, when characteristics of the source that are relevant to the message are similar to characteristics of the audience, this may also enhance persuasiveness (Stiff & Mongeau, 2003).

Message characteristics. Message characteristics have been studied particularly in terms of the contrast between the use of reason and emotion as means of persuasion. Rational messages have been analysed in terms of how receivers process evidence, and when it is likely to be most effective; comparisons have also been made between one-sided and two-sided messages. Emotional messages have been analysed in terms particularly of the use of fear as a means of persuasion (so-called *fear appeals*), although more recent research has also been focused on messages which seek to arouse guilt as a means of persuasion (Stiff & Mongeau, 2003).

Message receivers. The role of receivers in response to persuasive messages has been studied in relation to four particular characteristics: gender, message discrepancy, involvement and function matching (Stiff & Mongeau, 2003). Traditionally, it was believed that women are more persuasible than men. But when Eagly and Carli (1981) carried out a meta-analysis of studies on gender and persuasion, they found that although women were more susceptible to influence, the effect size was very small.

Message discrepancy research is concerned with how the difference between a receiver's opinion and the position advocated in the message affects its persuasiveness. Message discrepancy can enhance attitude change, unless the discrepancy is so large as to appear ridiculous, or if it seriously contradicts the values of the message recipients (Stiff & Mongeau, 2003).

Involvement can also affect persuasion in a variety of ways. So, for example, values which are strongly held will be much more resistant to attitude change. Again, when people are concerned about the impressions they make on others, they may be reluctant to endorse positions which are incompatible with those of the source of the message (Stiff & Mongeau, 2003).

Finally, several studies have found that successful persuasion contains messages that match the functions underlying receivers' attitudes. So, for example, an individual whose attitudes serve the functions of obtaining rewards may be persuaded by a message that promises rewards, but not by one that stresses underlying values (Stiff & Mongeau, 2003).

Models of persuasion. A number of models have been proposed to account for persuasion. According to the elaboration likelihood model of persuasion (Petty & Cacioppo, 1986), there are two distinct alternate routes to persuasion, referred to as *central* and *peripheral* processing. Central processing is characterized by a careful scrutiny of message content, whereas when people are unable or unwilling to carefully scrutinize message content, they rely on peripheral cues, such as aspects of the source of the message, or message length. Although the elaboration likelihood model has been enormously influential, a key criticism is that central and peripheral processing are not necessarily alternate modes of message processing; people may be able to use both modes in parallel. Critics have also questioned whether the model can in principle be falsified.

According to the heuristic model, persuasion also involves two distinct cognitive processes (Chaiken, 1987). *Systematic processing* involves the careful scrutiny of message content and is similar to the concept of central processing. *Heuristic processing* involves very little cognitive effort by message receivers: *heuristics* are simple decision rules that allow people to evaluate messages without too much cognitive effort. So, for example, the heuristic that 'experts are usually correct' allows people to make a quick evaluation of the message based on a quick assessment of the source's expertise. Unlike the careful scrutiny of message content, this process requires little cognitive effort beyond the application of a heuristic to a particular situation. But in contrast to the elaboration likelihood model, it is explicitly acknowledged that systematic and heuristic processing can occur at the same time in parallel.

Although these models are very much open to debate, they have been the leading theories of persuasion for nearly two decades (Stiff & Mongeau, 2003). However, both models have been criticized on the grounds that it is unnecessary to postulate two distinct cognitive processes. Thus, according to the unimodel proposed by Kruglanski (e.g., Kruglanski & Thompson, 1999), persuasion is a process in which beliefs are formed on the basis of appropriate evidence; message arguments and peripheral/heuristic cues may all be seen as forms of evidence, which are evaluated in terms of the same cognitive processes. For example, appraising the source of a message is not necessarily simpler than appraising its contents. Indeed, under certain circumstances, it may require a great deal of cognitive effort – as witnessed by the enormous attention paid to the issue of Tony Blair's credibility following British involvement in the Iraq war in 2003. From the perspective of Kruglanski's unimodel, the source and the content of a message are not processed in different ways, they simply reflect different forms of evidence.

persuasive communication and political language

The study of persuasive communication represents a very different research tradition from that of the study of political language. But in a democratic society, a prime aim of politicians is to win electoral support through persuasion. Thus, the interrelationship between persuasive communication and political language is of considerable significance. In this final section, the implications of political language research for the analysis of persuasive communication are considered.

Certainly, the analysis of political language has important implications for what in the traditional study of persuasive communication is termed a 'message characteristic'. But political language research has never been considered in this context. Whereas persuasive communication research has been focused in particular on the contrast between rational and emotional appeals (Stiff & Mongeau, 2003), there has been no consideration of the role of features such as equivocation, political rhetoric and applause, or political metaphors.

Yet the microanalysis of political language does present significant possibilities for enhancing our understanding of political persuasion. The most obvious link is with the study of political metaphors. If politicians can beguile us to think in terms of their metaphors, we may be persuaded of their arguments without even being aware of how we are being persuaded. This is an interesting hypothesis, certainly worthy of further empirical research.

Research on applause and political rhetoric has arguably been less concerned with persuasion than with social influence. Since rhetorical devices in political speeches are intended to invite applause, manifestly they are a form of social influence. But does the use of such devices make the message more persuasive? Whether political messages become more persuasive if skilfully formatted in appropriate rhetorical devices is an interesting question, but not one which has been considered in traditional persuasive communication research.

Equivocation might seem less obviously related to persuasion. In terms of Bavelas et al.'s (1990) theory, equivocation is regarded very much as a means of avoiding the negative consequences of questions which pose communicative conflicts. But equivocation is not always negative. As discussed above, Tony Blair in televised interviews during the 1997 British general election made skilful use of the metaphor of modernization, not only to equivocate in response to awkward questions about Labour's policy about-turn over the preceding decade, but also to present a positive face for New Labour as both principled and moving with the times (Bull, 2000a). As such, this equivocal rhetoric of modernization was a key element in Blair's campaign to persuade the British electorate that New Labour was now fit to govern the country. Thus, equivocal messages may be used not only to avoid communicative conflicts but also as a significant means of persuasion.

Overall, political language research does have significant implications for what in traditional persuasive communication research are termed 'message characteristics'. Furthermore, our understanding of the other major dimensions ('message source', 'message receivers' and 'cognitive models of persuasion') should also benefit greatly from this kind of approach. Thus, techniques whereby politicians seek to establish themselves as a credible source should certainly repay detailed linguistic analysis. So too would the analysis of how politicians tailor their messages to different receivers, given that in a democratic society, they must seek to attract the widest possible support from the electorate. Again, political language analysis should be highly relevant to evaluating different models of persuasion, particularly with regard to whether it is necessary to postulate two distinct kinds of cognitive processing.

conclusions

In this chapter, recent research on three aspects of political language has been reviewed, and their implications for the analysis of persuasive communication discussed. The study of political language is now a burgeoning field of academic study, but as yet has failed to impact on the traditional study of persuasion. Currently, these two research traditions exist as if in a parallel universe, there has been no interplay between them. But in a democratic society, a prime aim of politicians is to win popular support for their policies through skilled communication; thus, political language is integral to political persuasion. In this author's view, analysis of all the major dimensions of traditional persuasive communication research – message source, message characteristics, message receivers and cognitive models of persuasion – would benefit greatly from the application of techniques used in the study of political language. Thereby, our understanding of both political language and political persuasion would be greatly enhanced.

references

Atkinson, J.M. (1983). Two devices for generating audience approval: A comparative study of public discourse and text. In K. Ehlich & H. van Riemsdijk (Eds.), *Connectedness in sentence, text and discourse* (pp.199–236). Tilburg, Netherlands: Tilburg papers in Linguistics.
Atkinson, J.M. (1984a). *Our masters' voices*. London and New York: Methuen.
Atkinson, J.M. (1984b). Public speaking and audience responses: Some techniques for inviting applause. In J.M. Atkinson & J.C. Heritage (Eds.), *Structures of social*

action: Studies in conversation analysis (pp.370–409). Cambridge & New York: Cambridge University Press.

Bavelas, J.B., Black, A., Chovil, N. & Mullett, J. (1990). Equivocal communication. Newbury Park: Sage.

Beer, F.A. & De Landtsheer, C. (2004). Metaphors, politics, and world politics. In F.A. Beer & C. De Landtsheer (Eds.), Metaphorical world politics (pp.50–52). Michigan: Michigan State University Press.

Billig, M. (2003). Political rhetoric. In D.O. Sears, L. Huddy & R. Jervis (Eds.), Oxford handbook of political psychology (pp.222–250). New York: Oxford University Press.

Bull, P.E. (1994). On identifying questions, replies and non-replies in political interviews. Journal of Language and Social Psychology, 13, 115–131.

Bull, P.E. (1997). Queen of hearts or queen of the arts of implication? Implicit criticisms and their implications for equivocation theory in the interview between Martin Bashir and Diana, Princess of Wales. Social Psychological Review, 1, 27–36.

Bull, P.E. (2000a). Equivocation and the rhetoric of modernisation: An analysis of televised interviews with Tony Blair in the 1997 British general election. Journal of Language and Social Psychology, 19, 222–247.

Bull, P.E. (2000b). Do audiences only applaud 'claptrap' in political speeches? An analysis of invited and uninvited applause. Social Psychological Review, 2, 32–41.

Bull, P.E. (2003). The microanalysis of political communication: Claptrap and ambiguity. London: Routledge

Bull, P. (2005). Communicating claptrap. The 2005 general election. Behind the Spin (11 October), 30–31.

Bull, P.E. (2006). Invited and uninvited applause in political speeches. British Journal of Social Psychology, 45, 563–578.

Bull, P.E., Elliott, J., Palmer, D. & Walker, L. (1996). Why politicians are three-faced: The face model of political interviews. British Journal of Social Psychology, 35, 267–284.

Bull, P.E. & Fetzer, A. (2006). Who are we and who are you? The strategic use of forms of address in political interviews. Text and Talk, 26, 1–35.

Bull, P.E. & Wells P. (2002). By invitation only? An analysis of invited and uninvited applause. Journal of Language and Social Psychology, 21, 230–244.

Chaiken, S. (1987). The heuristic model of persuasion. In M.P. Zanna, J.M. Olson & C.P. Herman (Eds.), Social influence: The Ontario symposium (Vol. 5, pp.3–39). Hillsdale, NJ: Erlbaum.

De Landtsheer, C. & Feldman, O. (Eds.) (2000). Beyond public speech and symbols: Exploration in the rhetoric of politicians and the media. Wesport, CT: Praeger.

Dickerson, P. (1997). 'It's not just me who's saying this...' The deployment of cited others in televised political discourse. British Journal of Social Psychology, 36, 33–48.

Eagly, A.H. & Carli, L.L. (1981). Sex of researchers and sex-typed communications as determinants of sex differences in influenceability: A meta-analysis of social influence studies. Psychological Bulletin, 90, 1–20.

Emerson, M. (1988). 1992 and after: The bicycle theory rides again. Political Quarterly, 59(3), 289–299.

Feldman, O. (2004). *Talking politics in Japan today*. Brighton: Sussex Academic Press.

Feldman, O. & De Landtsheer, C. (Eds.) (1998). *Politically speaking: A worldwide examination of language used in the public sphere*. Wesport, CT: Greenwood Publishing Group.

Haddon, M. (2003). *The curious incident of the dog in the night-time*. London: Jonathan Cape.

Hamilton, M.A. & Mineo, P.J. (1998). A framework for understanding equivocation. *Journal of Language and Social Psychology, 17*, 3–35.

Harris, S. (1991). Evasive action: How politicians respond to questions in political interviews. In P. Scannell (Ed.), *Broadcast talk* (pp.76–99). London: Sage.

Heritage, J. & Greatbatch D. (1986). Generating applause: A study of rhetoric and response at party political conferences. *American Journal of Sociology, 92*, 110–157.

Hovland, C.I., Janis, I.L. & Kelley, H.H. (1953). *Communication and persuasion*. New Haven, CT: Yale University Press.

Jefferson, G. (1990). List-construction as a task and resource. In G. Psathas (Ed.), *Interaction competence* (pp.63–92). Lanham, MD: University Press of America.

Keat, R. (1991a). Introduction: Starship Britain or universal enterprise? In R. Keat & N. Abercrombie (Eds.), *Enterprise culture* (pp.1–17). London & New York: Routledge.

Keat, R. (1991b). Consumer sovereignty and the integrity of practices. In R. Keat & N. Abercrombie (Eds.), *Enterprise culture* (pp.216–230). London & New York: Routledge.

Kruglanski, A.W. & Thompson, E.P. (1999). Persuasion by a single route: A view from the unimodel. *Psychological Inquiry, 10*, 83–109.

Lakoff, G. (1991). Metaphor and war: The metaphor system used to justify war in the Gulf. Retrieved August 19 2005, from http://lists.village.virginia.edu/sixties/HTML_docs/Texts/Scholarly/Lakoff_Gulf_Metaphor_1.html

Lakoff, G. & Johnson, M. (1980). *Metaphors we live by*. Chicago: Chicago University Press.

Petty, R.E. & Cacioppo, J.T. (1986). *Communication and persuasion: Central and peripheral routes to attitude change*. New York: Springer-Verlag.

Stiff, J.B. & Mongeau, P.A. (2003). *Persuasive communication* (2nd edn). New York: The Guilford Press.

Wilson, J. (1990). *Politically speaking: The pragmatic analysis of political language*. Oxford: Basil Blackwell.

11

false beliefs and unsound arguments promoted by authorities

w. peter robinson

rhetoric and reality in post-1979 britain: socio-political perspectives

By the time the British electorate had returned a third successive Conservative government in 1992, any academic interested in the psychology and sociology of the operation of false beliefs and invalid and weak arguments in the public domain of socio-politics had more than enough naturally occurring data on which to base extensive analyses. There were numerous recorded examples of government rhetoric bearing more than problematic relationships to the realities they were referring to. Many of the claims and arguments to support these were suspect or worse.

The two preceding administrations had shattered or shaken most of the core institutional social orders of the country. From 1979 governments trumpeted the virtues of competition as a necessary spur to the achievement of efficiency and improved performance in all occupational walks of life. The first Thatcher government acted on this belief with decisions to privatize nationalized industries, a number of public services, and several centrally directed public organizations. Market forces were claimed to be the key driving force for economic progress. In addition, self-help and self-reliance were exalted as core values for individuals to replace what was represented as the undeserved comfort of being cosseted by a nanny Welfare State. The writings of Adam Smith, Samuel Smiles and Milton Friedman were cited as general references to justify the conclusions drawn, but without detailed citations. Could the conclusions drawn by the Thatcher government in fact be derived from the writings? For example, when Adam Smith was arguing for the advantages of competition among businesses, his frame of reference was of many small enterprises competing to provide goods or services to customers who had equal access to all of them. How such an idea could be elaborated to suggest that the transport, gas, water or electricity industries should be privatized was not, and could not be plausibly, explicated. In fact Smith had warned about the disadvantages for society of massive companies. Samuel Smiles was particularly interested in the biographies of extraordinary historical persons who had shown great imagination and persistence in the pursuit of extraordinary goals, such as the manufacture of fine Chinese porcelain in Europe. His cases had no relevance to the problems of whole communities of coal-miners suddenly sacked and advised to 'get on their bikes' to find jobs.

The arguments were mostly formal, sloganized appeals to authority entirely lacking in any substantial, supportive empirical evidence. Simultaneously the government devised indices to measure gains in efficiency, mostly in terms of income less expenditure. In sectors where 'efficiency' gains could not be assessed in simple terms of reduced public expenditure, the government just slashed its financial support and imposed targets to be achieved. For example, universities had their government support cut year on year, were given set quotas of British undergraduates for each degree course, and were penalized for exceeding or undershooting these. Fees remained fixed by the government and not by Friedman's market forces. This obliged universities to reduce staffing and to increase their recruitment of students from overseas.

Throughout the public sector, annual staff reviews were made compulsory, with both 'customers' and 'managers' filling in evaluation forms of colleagues. Since it was very difficult, if not impossible, legally to sack incompetent and inefficient individuals, and re-training them was not a feasible option, these measures did not lead to either increased competence or the weeding out of ineffectual staff.

The consequences of the privatization of nationalized industries were far more serious for both employees and society. Procedures differed, but a common pattern permitted the existing senior managements and others in opportune positions to write themselves into very large shareholdings very cheaply. The Chief Executive Officers (CEOs) of the larger industries then quickly awarded themselves enormous pay increases and greatly improved contracts, with a strong ripple effect spreading to senior management in the public sector, e.g. top civil servants, and to members of parliament, with neither targets nor reviews for the latter. 'Self-help' became 'Help yourself'. The management of the newly privatized industries laid off large numbers of the less well-paid workers, leaving them to solve their own employment problems. With bus and coach services, a large number of small competitors did appear briefly, but these were quickly squeezed out, leaving just a few companies with virtual regional monopolies, and some very rich people running them. This absurd outcome was defended in terms of efficiency gains, and benefits to society as a whole, but fares had spiralled, and rural services had plummeted. Worse, many of the statistics produced about the efficacy of the changes were more than massaged to hide the true consequences. For example, formulae for calculating unemployment rates were revised over 25 times by the Conservative administrations, always in the direction of lowering estimates. One crude device used was to re-allocate many chronically unemployed into other administrative categories such as Sickness Benefit, where many Welsh coal-miners remain, 30 years on.

In addition, a significant number of senior politicians secured well-paid directorships for themselves in privatized companies. Reports of a succession of financial and other scandals were at first denied by the identified members of the government, but were then shown to be well-founded. More than twenty ministers resigned over these exposures and other more personal self-indulgences. Such activities were sadly at variance with the values proclaimed by Mrs Thatcher and her successor. The word 'sleaze' came into circulation as a shorthand to refer to such events. Regrettably, it has to be noted that the conduct of the subsequent New Labour governments and their spokespeople has resulted in the adoption of the word 'spin' as a euphemism to apply to much of their discourse, and sleaze has continued as well. These examples illustrate just a few of the seriously flawed beliefs and arguments used by government to bring about devastating changes to the lives of literally millions of British people. Treating all public organizations as businesses designed to maximize profits by selling their products to their customers was a misleading analogy taken much too far. Other abuses of reasoning lay in using faulty premises to derive faulty conclusions, generating and sustaining a rhetoric of success based on invalid and dysfunctional measures, making unexplained claims about wealth at the top 'trickling down', and changing statistical indices to hide unpalatable numbers, e.g. crime rates. Honest evaluations and corrective strategies to counteract undesirable consequences were not undertaken. In parallel personal conduct was too often at variance with what was being proclaimed to the public at large.

Evidence to support this critique is to be found in a host of official documents of the times as well as in reliable media reports. For present purposes, it is to be hoped that these few examples mentioned are sufficient to index the strong flow of false beliefs and invalid arguments in the rhetoric of the governments as well as of other authorities, and that the public were expected to accept these beliefs and the inadequate arguments used to support them.

Hence, with education in secondary schools in disarray as a result of clearly dysfunctional enforced changes, around 1990 I abandoned research into ways of improving the chronically debilitating situation of 'below average' children, and began to investigate what the public were thinking, feeling and doing about government 'sleaze' and its accompanying discourse, and about the trustworthiness of other authorities who had been publicly called to account for misrepresenting reality. Were people believing what they were being told? If not, what did they feel about the delusions and deceptions being propagated? What were they doing about such matters, if anything?

public faith in institutional authorities

Data from Gallup Polls Social Trends in the UK and the University of Michigan in the USA had shown dramatic results in public attitudes to those in positions of authority. From 1973 to 1993 the US data indicated substantial losses of public confidence in almost all the social institutions considered in the surveys: Congress down 43 per cent, the Executive 31 per cent, financial institutions 32 per cent, the press 36 per cent, and TV 22 per cent. By 1993, just 9 per cent of Americans felt able to say that hardly any government personnel were *not crooked* (see Lipsett and Schneider, 1983 and Dionne, 1991 for commentaries). In the UK an ICM quota survey (1994) reported distrust/trust percentage levels for various institutions: government 60/11, Parliament 47/13, the civil service 33/21, the judiciary 42/23, the police 28/44. Gallup Polls (1993, Social Trends Report) provided a similar picture in their monitoring of perceived honesty and ethical standards of various professions (1993 percentages of 'very high' ratings are given, with declines since 1982 in square parentheses): government ministers 9[13], MPs 7[8], civil servants 15[5], lawyers 37[11], the police 38[18]. Only 9 per cent of journalists were seen as having high ethical standards. Across a number of opportunity samples, I found frequencies of lying often of over 80 per cent for the *Sun* newspaper, advertisers and governments, and over

50 per cent for politicians of each of four named political parties and CEOs (Robinson, 1996).

Following a variant of Lincoln's warning to politicians, it would appear that in these matters most of the people were not being fooled most of the time, and it was not just politicians who were disbelieved. Given that people would have been in error to have adopted many of the particular beliefs being propagated by authorities, generally UK and US citizens were not fooled by the propaganda machinery of their authorities. There are comparable results from other quasi-democracies, and, even without surveys, it had been evident for years that most citizens of the ex-communist bloc countries had not been fooled by the propaganda of their governments either.

What did people think and feel about the (unsuccessful) lies communicated to them? A standard British national sample was asked about their reactions to a number of widely reported specific incidents involving attempts to deceive people. They expressed very strong disapproval of all cases, and especially in those where the likely consequences were life-threatening and the victims were powerless, e.g. needy and poor (Robinson, 1996). In later interviews of adults, more than resignations were expected of the perpetrators, with long prison sentences and the stripping of deception-related wealth being recommended for some of the most serious other-harming, self-benefiting offences. There was strong disapproval of the leniency with which culprits were being treated, especially if they were still rich and powerful, as most were. There was disgust and resentment that 'they' were allowed to 'get away with it', whatever it was.

Among a further sample of similar people with similar views questioned later, none had done anything about any of the topics raised or any other contestable matters. These latter participants were also asked some 'why' questions, so as to begin to find out what arguments they would advance to support their beliefs and (in)action. Responses to such enquiries were minimal in the extreme, and what was said was very insubstantial.

The tentative general conclusion drawn was that the misdemeanours of those in authority and their attempts to cover these up served mainly as useful topics for everyday conversation, and could occasionally give rise to expressions of contrastive self-righteousness along Us versus Them lines. Strong opinions were asserted baldly, but not argued. The data were certainly consistent with the claims of those discourse analysts who stress that the speech itself can be the significant stratum of reality. Although the original thrust of the interviews was directed towards finding out about reactions to false statements of authorities and reasons for these, the results gave rise to questions about the foundations of people's beliefs and the quality of the arguments of which these beliefs were conclusions. (For immediate purposes arguments will be treated as the reasons people can give for holding their beliefs, although elsewhere I try to explicate a more complicated story [Robinson, 2006]. To abbreviate the political, legal, moral and social aspects relevant to the issues considered here, the term 'socio-cultural' will be used to embrace all four.)

production of arguments to support empirical claims

In some further as yet unpublished studies, criminal culprits were asked to give reasons for some of their actions, e.g. burgling and making false insurance claims. In others, content analyses were made of arguments used in several TV discussion programmes and newspaper articles. Suffice it to say that it was evident from these analyses that politicians and other persons in authority have no monopoly of false beliefs and inadequate arguments, but these people were not inciting the public to believe them. Rather than quote from these unpublished studies however, it is more appropriate to summarize the essentially similar main findings of Kuhn's published study (1991). She engaged persons differing in age, education, gender, and specialist training in extended semi-structured interviews in which the opening questions invited respondents to comment on the causes of three social phenomena:

What causes prisoners to return to crime after they're released?
What causes children to fail in school?
What causes unemployment?

Although each of these questions is initially explanation-seeking, Kuhn's procedure developed the interview dialogue into an interrogatory which focused on arguments. Respondents were asked first to provide *evidence in support* of their preferred explanations and then to offer *alternative* explanations. Then they were asked what counter-arguments could be advanced against their position, and how these *counter-arguments* could be *rebutted*.

How successful were interviewees in offering 'genuine evidence' for their explanation/s, alternative explanations, counter-arguments and rebuttals? Less than half the main sample could advance any genuine evidence to support their preferred explanations. For alternative explanations, the percentages were somewhat higher, but for counter-arguments they were somewhat lower. In the procedure, those participants who did not offer either an alternative explanation or a counter-argument were provided with an acceptable alternative explanation and then asked to rebut it. Hence everyone had an opportunity to provide a rebuttal; 47 per cent succeeded. Educational level was the strongest intergroup discriminator, yielding on average a 20 per cent advantage. The five PhD students all succeeded on all four counts.

This quantitative summary does not do justice to Kuhn's more detailed analysis, and a number of further points can be made:

1. A substantial minority of participants offered only a single cause to explain each putative fact.
2. Participants were reported as holding their beliefs with 'considerable conviction'.
3. Those who offered 'genuine evidence' for their preferred explanations were prone to mix this with pseudo-evidence, the most common form being plausible descriptive narrative scripts, devoid of expressed causal linkages.
4. Those who did not generate alternatives were more likely to view their version of reality as the only reality; the way things happen to be could not be different. Concurrently, they were happy to tell the interviewer that, 'everyone has his own views' and mix this with 'everyone has a right to their own views' or 'everyone's opinion is equally right'. Although they quoted positive examples for their views, they did not see counter-examples as evidence against them.
5. Rebuttals followed the same diversity as counter-arguments: simple re-assertions of the thesis, acceptance of relativism for which evidence was irrelevant, etc.
6. Those offering a single-cause explanation were also more likely to offer pseudo-evidence, and least likely to offer alternatives, counter-arguments or rebuttals.
7. There were persons for whom their explanations were virtually a frame of reference of self-supporting beliefs for which further empirical evidence or other arguments were irrelevant; counter-arguments were assimilated to what were neither coherent nor consistent schemata.
8. There were also persons who did not think the claimed facts needed specific explanations; their attitudes implied a tolerance of fatalistic anarchic diversity in human affairs.

Kuhn's issues for studying arguing skills were confined to empirical matters of socio-cultural importance in the domain of the human sciences, and the features of arguments exposed were in relation to explanations rather than descriptions and to general co-variations rather than particular occurrences.

Ignoring possible methodological criticisms, just two observations will be made. The topics of the three initial questions asked are commonly voiced concerns in election campaigns in prosperous quasi-democracies ('democracy' is a much abused term now euphemistically used to refer to individualistic capitalist oligarchies which allow electors to choose their governing elite at intervals). Further, if Kuhn's results are indicative of the general understanding and competence of voting populations, then such States are far from being well-educated and well-informed democracies. From a theoretical and scientific perspective, it can be asked how it can be that so many people who have been 'schooled' for so long can emerge without seeing the relevance of systematically collected and properly processed empirical evidence for answers to such questions. Since education in elementary moral philosophy, 'scientific thinking', 'critical thinking' and 'general problem-solving' is very rare in school systems, plausible answers to that question may not be too difficult to discover.

Kuhn was exploring the nature of general and differential competence of argumentation in the domain of the human sciences, and did not pursue explanations for the inadequacies. In cognitive psychology there is tradition of concern with rationality in conclusion-drawing and decision-making in laboratory-based experiments, using both everyday conversational issues for investigations of general reasoning and constructed puzzles about probabilities, often in the areas of health and criminal convictions for example (see Baron, 2000; Kahneman & Tversky, 2000; Gigerenzer, 2002; Nisbett, 1993; Oaksford & Chater, 1998). Some explanations offered have focused on forms of presentation which reduce errors. Others have generated 'explanations' for the errors and biases manifested, but then confined these to summarizing labelling at proximal levels of analysis (e.g. anchoring). Yet others have examined the role of different undergraduate specialisms in facilitating transfer of competencies. These last have focused on the characteristics of the disciplines being studied. Generally, the studies have not included post-study interviews in which the reasoning of respondents has been probed, à la Kuhn.

In a virtually separate tradition, personality and social psychologists have looked at sources of biases and other distortions in causal attributions and in beliefs held about persons and social categories of people. There have been numerous studies within the frameworks of attribution theory (see Hewstone, 1981; Hewstone & Fincham, 1996) and social identity theory (Tajfel & Turner, 1979), later modified to social categorization theory (Turner et al., 1987). Many of these investigations have been methodologically immaculate, but they have relied heavily or solely on box-ticking paper and pencil exercises completed by university students required to give answers to multiple-choice questions about features of clearly under-determined vignettes. With that reservation, the weight of evidence for causal explanations shows that Western students asked about events are more likely to cite persons than situations as causes of positive and negative outcomes. Among particular persons cited, respondents are more likely to attribute positive causes and outcomes to themselves and to their own social groups and negative outcomes to others and their social groups. The many studies within the social identity ambit reveal similar biases and errors. Beyond causal events, people are disposed to perceive themselves and their own social groups positively and other individuals and other groups negatively. Both their beliefs and their arguments display such biases. Unfortunately again, such studies have neglected to ask participants for the grounds of their judgements and beliefs, and probing systematic post-experimental interviews have not been conducted.

Psychologists in both fields tend to confine motivational explanations to the level of human needs for positive evaluation, e.g. self-esteem, where such esteem is based on social comparisons with others, and over-estimations of the self (Taylor, 1989). This restriction is extraordinary, given the wide array of motives and reasons people refer to in everyday talk and that motivation theorists list (e.g. Engler, 2003).

Psychologists are not the only academics concerned with these issues. Other disciplines focused on human activities yield the same types of selectivity, biases and errors: communication, media, political and socio-cultural studies, sociology, and history. Using their own particular methods, they have severally charted who selects which propositions within which framework to communicate which messages by which means to whom – and why. At the risk of over-generalizing, my speculative hypothesis would be that the motivational explanations used in these areas most often call upon the relevance of the sociological trio of motives: increasing and/or preserving power, wealth and/or status. Certainly this trinity looks to be more immediately relevant to the behaviour of people in societies in which so much emphasis is placed on success measured against such criteria. Gaining and preserving power, wealth and status look to be more plausible explanations than self-esteem issues for the false beliefs and inadequate arguments used by authorities to justify actions and their attempts to cover up possible misdemeanours, although some of the biases and errors investigated by psychologists relate to both.

It is not surprising that the ruling and power elites of societies have endeavoured to ensure that the interests of themselves and their associated groups are enhanced and protected in their societies – and have been from before time immemorial. Throughout history the struggles for resources including wars have been motivated by other and more fundamental motives than self-esteem enhancement.

Members of British governments and their associated elites of the last two decades have indeed differentially increased their power and wealth, but their rhetoric has not fooled most of the people much of the time. That granted, there is scant evidence that the general public is equipped to evaluate the validity of claims made by authorities or the strengths of arguments advanced to support them. Neither the high incidence nor the importance to our species of these phenomena of false beliefs and unsound arguments should be under-estimated. They are embedded in the verbal justifications of the whole social structure. Here, it is apposite to mention just three of the myths that continue to have a reactionary rather than conservative influence on the organization and distribution of resources and opportunities in our societies. Given the current frame of reference, the three are explicated primarily in terms of language use in referential communication generally and argumentative discourse in particular. Plato (1955, original work 4th century BC) was so concerned with the value of truth, that in his ideal republic there was to be no poetry, plays or stories that misrepresented reality. There would be just one magnificent myth (unfortunately generally mistranslated as 'noble lie'), and this would provide a set of false beliefs sufficient to serve as a justification for the division of the society into three main castes: men of gold, men of silver, and men of iron and bronze. For all its longevity, variants of comparable myths continue to be major determinants of the structure and functioning of *all* the States represented in the United Nations. For many of these, the castes have become classes, but there is still massive historical intergenerational reproduction of power, wealth and status in all (Bourdieu, 1977; Bourdieu & Passeron, 1977), and there are accompanying myths to justify the status quos extant.

myth 1: the rhetoric of the authorities controlling educational establishments reflects a plausible construction of what happens in those organizations

It does not. Schools, colleges and universities are required to publish 'mission statements' for their clients, customers, etc. Typically, these statements refer to the promotion of the full potential or optimal development of the whole person, with more specific claims about intellectual and practical competence, along with personal and social development. They may mention enhancing capacity to function adaptively in adult society. Such aims imply the use of criterion-referencing or at least progress-referencing as the bases of recording student achievements, and yet the system is pervaded with age-related norm-referencing testing through which more and more children are selected out of the routes to higher education. The higher the institution the fewer the places available, and of course the well-paid jobs and sinecures subsequently open are even more strictly rationed. The rhetoric is of selection by merit and competence, but again from time immemorial the best single predictor of final academic achievement has been social status and most recently in the form of social class at birth, with the sponsoring into the ultimate elites being strongly related to the social networks of parents, relatives, and friends of the family (see Sampson, 1965). This selective differentiation is a major function of the national educational system, and it works by preventing the optimal development of the many to the advantage of a predictable very few. The social reproductive story of Bourdieu and others is the most plausible account of the filtering process.

What is taught through the curriculum of schools? If 'democracy' is a form of government of the people, by the people, for the people, why is it that core information about the structures and functioning of society is omitted from the national curriculum? To be well-informed, citizens need to be familiar with the facts about their society and its cultures, and with its relevant applied ethical basis. They need to know about their laws, and how these came to be what they are. The mastery of this propositional knowledge requires a corresponding mastery of the language, but this is not sufficient. It needs to be combined with the procedural knowledge of how to question, analyse, integrate and evaluate, so that people can become constructive general problem-solvers who can check the claims of other people and the adequacy of their arguments, resulting in the end at sensible well-founded decisions. However, neither representational nor procedural knowledge are transmitted from generation to generation freely or randomly. Those with power can and do control who gains access to how much of what kind of knowledge. Historically, rulers and their associates have striven to retain control of knowledge relevant to the preservation of and increase in their power, wealth and status (see Robinson, 2006). How they have justified this is taken up under Myth 2. There is nothing novel in these ideas. They achieved a measure of flowering in the 1960s, with consequences to be mentioned later.

myth 2: statements for which it is pragmatically appropriate to assign a truth-value are generally true rather than false

When statements are made and their truth-value is of primary importance, the default expectation is that they are true rather than false. More than one line of argument can be used to support this case. Perhaps most powerful is the one that observes that since language was only invented and developed as a system to perform communicative functions, it would be absurd if any other assumption were the default. It would be pragmatically impossible if we had to first decide whether every statement uttered was true or false before we reacted to it. The ontological evidence is that developing children have to learn to lie rather than learn to tell the truth and to be wary rather than trusting.

Parenthetically it should be noted that much of what each of us learns is not true, simply because knowledge is advanced within each of our lifetimes. Much of what we are offered is told in good faith, but just happens to be wrong because the species as a whole or our particular sources are ignorant or ill-informed. This applies massively on the historical scale, as mistaken beliefs of the species are replaced by less obviously mistaken ones: the earth is not flat, diseases have medical rather than supernatural explanations, the tests for witchcraft were not valid, ad infinitum. There is an enormous but innumerable class of such mistaken beliefs, which are explained by an ignorance which has not been engineered by other human beings. Furthermore, the amount of knowledge now extant is so enormous that each individual can cope with only a miniscule amount of it, and societies have long relied on a division of expertise as an efficient means of people within groups benefiting from each other. However, over and above these considerations there is engineered ignorance.

In co-operative situations telling the truth may be the common intention, but in competitive and conflict situations other considerations come into play. Co-operation and competition co-exist in our societies, and in any struggle for power, wealth and status the emphasis is on winning. Successfully persuading others that you deserve more than they do is a formidable weapon in that competition. It is not surprising then that there is a large sub-class of false beliefs, which have been discovered, devised and propagated by the elites of power, wealth and status. As noted above, controlling greater knowledge of relevant kinds has always been a component in the struggle for dominance within and between human groups; measures to ensure this will include both maximizing knowledge for self and the ingroup, and minimizing it for others and outgroups. In addition to controlling who had access to how much and which kinds of knowledge and promoting particular false beliefs, rulers and their acolytes have constructed and re-constructed whole belief systems to justify their special rights and privileges. *The truth-value of these claims may be what is of primary importance, but what is being promoted is in fact false.* Historically, rulers often achieved this by asserting personal divine rights and authority to argue for massively differentiated distributions of rights and resources. Such behaviour has not been confined to societies in which religious bases have been asserted to justify discriminations. Among the secular, ideologically inspired States that have replaced those claiming a religious justification for the differentials, the plot of Orwell's *Animal Farm* has come to be prophetic; many successful revolutionaries have quickly adopted the privileged life-styles they overthrew, simultaneously condemning their citizens to lives with the nasty, brutish and short qualities of Hobbes (1914, original work published 1651). In brief, citizens of many States have been encouraged to accept or required to conform to false beliefs associated with unsound arguments on a truly enormous scale; they have been deceived to a massive extent. And Orwell's *1984*? Perhaps that too is approaching in a number of quasi-democracies where any such trend would be vigorously but incorrectly denied.

myth 3: The past is another country – history has nothing to teach us

Myths 1 and 2 have focused on knowledge and truths to which access is denied to most people by those with power to manage this, and on falsehoods which they have propagated to justify their own positions. At the present time, the still wealthy and powerful descendants of those who might be described in President Teddy Roosevelt's words as 'malefactors of great wealth' are permitted to continue to enjoy the fruits of the deeds of their distant ancestors without any requirement to justify their inheritances; for almost a thousand years in England for some families. Histories are written that pay little attention to the awfulness of the lives lived by the great majority of human beings. When tourists see the grandiose and massive palaces and pyramids of past ages, in China, India, Central Asia, Vietnam or the Americas, they may marvel. Do they pause to ask how many labourers spent their lives and died, so that some king or emperor could glory in *his* achievements? Thousands died building Versailles, Mafra and the great cathedrals of Europe. Millions of ordinary people died and were enslaved in the conquests of the Egyptians,

Persians, Romans and Mongols. More recently similar fates befell the populations in the colonial conquests by European powers in Africa, the Americas, Asia and Australasia. Imperial histories are a succession of stories of powerful individuals and groups having millions of the less powerful robbed, enslaved and slaughtered to enhance their own power, wealth and status. This is not what emerges in the sanitized and indirectly if not directly censored school history texts, but it is true. Even more recently, how many died as a result of the rhetorical competence and actions of Hitler, Mao Zedong, Stalin and Tojo? Over 100 million is frequently quoted. What false beliefs and inadequate arguments were used to justify these atrocities? What has changed?

The myth propounded to publics nowadays is that such extravagant and inhuman behaviour is now confined to the authoritarian rulers of countries in the Third World. Certainly there are many regimes in which the powerful very few continue to display indifference to the subsistence poverty in which they keep the very many in their own countries. The UN and its IMF and World Bank continue to hand out money to such rulers, but require the populations to repay the loans (Stiglitz, 2003). And the regimes of the quasi-democracies? Those which report statistics record that in the last 25 years their rich and absurdly rich have become very much richer, whilst their poor have not (Hutton, 1996; Wilkinson, 1994). Increases in mean GNPs are meaningless figures to quote when distributions of wealth and income range from 5,000,000 pounds or so a year to the 5,000 or so received by the elderly as a basic state pension. A number of quasi-democracies have significant underclasses of people in poverty, particularly among the elderly, the long-term unemployed, certain ethnic minorities, ex-prison inmates, the psychiatrically disturbed, young single mothers and homeless youths. In several, unemployment is high and crime rates have risen, as have prison populations, drug takers and pill dependent depressives. Additionally, most rich societies have now imported a significant legal and illegal migrant work-force to do jobs that their own nationals cannot or will not do at the rates of pay and conditions of work offered. Certainly the British government has done nothing to stop the widespread exploitation of such workers by the 'gangmasters' who organize such trafficking. These then are the consequences of the impositions of the beliefs and arguments for the allegedly free market economy ideals of governments post-1980. While Britain's leaders have certainly done some nest-feathering, they are not in the same league as the Bushes, Cheney, Rumsfeld, Baker and their colleagues in the USA. Poverty continues to be created both nationally and internationally, and the victims continue to be blamed for their condition, just as they always have been.

More dramatic still have been the beliefs and arguments propounded to justify recent military interventions (Coll, 2004), and of these, the invasion of Iraq occasioned a wide variety of reasons being offered by the US President and the British Prime Minister. There are parliamentary records as well as video recordings of what the British Prime Minister actually said about the threat of Iraq to Britain and other countries: the presence of Weapons of Mass Destruction, the 45 minute readiness to deploy WMD, the links to Al Qaida, etc. There are records of the arguments used to justify the invasion that can be examined for their inadequacy. There was Blair's statement that the intelligence was 'detailed, authoritative, and extensive', whereas the intelligence services had noted the sporadic and limited nature of that intelligence. An out-of-date American higher degree thesis was quoted as evidence, initially without an identification of the source. Niger was reported to have supplied raw materials for WMD. That the public has been denied sight of some of the reasoning and some of the intelligence 'to protect sources' simply added to the disbelief and distrust. The injunction of 'Trust me. I am your Prime Minister' became an utterance for getting a quick satirical laugh on TV. The Americans report now that their intelligence was wholly inadequate in quantity and quality. It is admitted that there were no WMD. (Ferguson, 2005 mentions some less inadequate and dishonest arguments that might have been used to justify the invasion, but that is a separate issue.) How a British Prime Minister who was so deluded could justify staying in office defies my imagination. Nevertheless, both Bush and Blair were subsequently re-elected, and to that extent the script departs from that of *1984*, but both have continued to trade on fears of future terrorist attacks, without recognising that their own continuing conduct is almost certainly encouraging these. Blair has dared to claim that bombs in London are unconnected with the British invasion of Iraq, but has failed to explain why Britain was selected. Rights and freedoms have been reduced, and surveillance of the public increased, both indicative of *1984*-type attitudes.

the public predicament

Evidence has been provided to argue that the public is aware of the falsification of claims made by authorities about economic, social and political-military matters. People think it wrong that authorities 'get away' with telling lies, feathering their own nests, and continuing to be prosperous and occupying powerful positions. The reactions of public resentment and retreat into apathy are not sociologically surprising, given their perceived impotence. In the UK the Labour government may have been re-elected, but only 25 per cent of the electorate voted for them. Perhaps it is surprising that there has been no coming together to form new political parties with transparent honesty and establish a better and less unequal society as central manifesto values, but Runciman (2006) discusses less creditable explanations.

If the data of Kuhn (1991) can be generalized to the UK, any general disillusionment and apathy of the electorate is conjoined with a widespread ignorance about the role of evidence in the furtherance of establishing sound conclusions to claims being made. Mastery of the dialectical mode of enquiry and argument publicized over 2,000 years ago in Plato's Socratic dialogues is not included in school education as yet; neither are the multitude of ways of faulty reasoning, again extant from the times of Plato and Aristotle. It appears that many people are not even aware that there are ways of resolving disagreements about empirical facts or matters of justice and morality.

If the bulk of the population has not been educated into the knowledge, understanding and skills necessary for independent problem-solving and disagreement resolution about socio-cultural issues, there is no reason for them to be more than passive victims of the status quo. Furthermore, if they have not acquired sufficient substantive information in the various relevant domains of knowledge and they are unaware of the special criteria of relevance to the assessment of claims and arguments in them, they are ill-equipped even to ask critical questions.

For the socio-cultural issues in focus here, the main potential sources of information for adults are personal experience, the mass media, and educational courses they might choose to take. Alas the media are now primarily concerned to achieve high audience and circulation figures. In the case of commercial media their overriding purposes are to generate profits and enhance the power of the owners and managers. Public service media are under political (and hence funding) pressure to maximize audience coverage. Most of what is presented on TV and radio and in newspapers and magazines is in fact concerned to gain audiences and hence entertain, even when the apparent function is to inform through intelligent discussion. Personal problem discussion programmes are carefully pre-programmed to generate expressions of opinions but seldom move towards sensible resolutions. Political or current affairs debating matches are arenas in which winning certainly takes precedence over truth-seeking. The same is true of news broadcasts. News on TV has long been demonstrated to emphasize the visual and the sensational. Bad news is preferred to good news, wars and disasters being particularly newsworthy, especially if individual suffering victims can be brought before the cameras. Crimes of violence likewise (Galtung & Ruge, 1973; Glasgow Media Group, 1976, 1982; McChesney, 1999). In such broadcasts, the arguments, if any, frequently focus on the cases of the individuals on camera, with alternative perspectives being ignored. When keeping audiences switched on is the immediate priority, 'truth' is a secondary or even lesser consideration. Even the so-called quality newspapers and magazines are remarkably devoid of well-structured, evidence-based and principled arguments.

An extreme variant on this theme is the dispensing of the use of propositions altogether. Much political discourse is just peppered with buzz words: 'freedom', 'liberty', 'choice', can be uttered as good appeals. 'Education', 'health', 'crime', 'terrorism', 'immigration' are offered as priorities in elections, but without further explication. No mention may be made of either the ends of or means to achieve these, except in the vaguest terms. In short, no arguments are offered to support what, how or why. The simultaneous claims by authorities of their commitment to evidence-based research for the construction and implementation of policies are inconsistent with the slogans.

round-up

This text has ignored interpersonal communication. It has ignored several domains of knowledge: formal calculi, aesthetics, metaphysics. It has not discussed issues of evaluating claims about morality and justice, although value positions on social injustice and the unethical have been transparent. The emphasis has been on the evaluation of empirical matters, both in respect of some specific events in their contexts and general explanations of human behaviour. A socio-cultural perspective has dominated the orientation and selection, mainly because issues of the trustworthiness and competence of those occupying positions of power and authority have been central to much public debate and media coverage in those quasi-democracies where most of the data have been collected. The socio-cultural arena also has the further two advantages that everyone has potential access to much of the data, and the enactment of relevant policies affects their lives. Given the facts, what are the research implications?

implications for research

At the risk of being branded a traitor to the common academic plea for more funds for more research, my initial suggestions relate to research that does *not* need to be done. Governments are past-masters at setting up diversionary devices to avoid enacting policies or having their inefficiencies or worse exposed. Setting up committees of inquiry is one device. Giving money to critics to conduct research is even better, because their energies are then applied to the research rather than to continuing criticism; that is what happened in Britain in the 1960s to a variety of potential educational reforms. Beware of governments offering gifts!

It is also true that the knowledge base about what needs to be achieved if the peoples of the quasi-democracies are to be competent to act as responsible citizens is already sufficient for many of the necessary educational measures to be enacted, evaluated and improved. Intervention programmes relevant to the inadequacies and weaknesses discussed earlier could be introduced and properly assessed. (The reformation of the conduct of authorities is a more difficult challenge.)

Updated and extended lists of Aristotle's forms of unsound and weak reasoning exist (Fischer, 1971; Thouless, 1930 through 1974; Walton, 1989). The scientific methods of relevance to the substantive evaluation of empirical claims were not available to Aristotle, and it was only from the nineteenth century that scientifically respectable surveys and observational field studies of human behaviour began to be conducted. During the twentieth century, statisticians developed analytic techniques for assessing the strength of co-variations and the probabilities of differences occurring. Post-1960 technologists developed computers of awesome calculative power to provide best estimates of relationships in data sets, to test the efficacy of interventions, and to examine the likely applicability of theoretical models as explanatory frameworks for results found. Descriptions and explanations of human experience and behaviour have been the last sub-domain to receive scientific treatment, but advances in the psychology and sociology of knowledge mastery and in problem defining and solving are now far enough advanced to evaluate whether or not means adopted to increase these are progressing towards provisional ends being aimed at.

To begin with some of the more tractable research issues, courses aimed at increasing competence with general problem-solving, decision-making and statistical appreciation are common in further and higher education, and they afford natural opportunities for systematic evaluation. It should be relatively easy to examine necessary and sufficient conditions for these skills to be transferable from their contexts of learning to all other issues where they are relevant. Universities include courses labelled 'transferable skills' but do not check for transfer. Courses on critical thinking in general problem-solving are standard options in North American and some British universities. Does experience of such courses have effects on performance in other courses and generalize to everyday living? If not, why not? If so, which courses, under what circumstances, for whom, and why? These courses typically involve argumentation itself as the central formal theme, and the texts used often take socio-cultural issues as the substantive content of arguments. However, they do not always proceed to discuss what kinds of reasons and evidence would lead to sensible resolutions and decisions. If such critical thinking is presented simply as a means for challenging assertions, it runs the risk of being nihilistic, just as much British twentieth-century analytic philosophy became agnostic about almost everything (see Magee, 1997 for a critique and Toulmin, 2001 for a constructive commentary). If students following such courses treat them as means of gaining isolated course credits, they are not performing their manifest functions. England and Wales have just introduced an AS level qualification in critical thinking, and this does extend coverage to looking at how arguments can be strengthened (van den Brink-Budgen, 2005), but does not separate criteria by domains of knowledge (Robinson, 2006), and no evaluation studies of transfer have yet been published.

There is some well-designed constructive research on inter-subject transfer on conditional and statistical reasoning (Nisbett et al., 1995), but not nearly enough, and just as that research did, other similar research will need to include post-tests with ecological validity; transfer to other tests is not sufficient. With so many potentially relevant courses already extant, naturally-based field studies could be conducted and their results publicized by authorities with minimal expense. Alas, even if such research is successful what will be crucial for societies will be the implementation of its findings. As noted at various points in this chapter, those with the power and wealth have always endeavoured to secure the positions of themselves and their networks, and until publics demand and achieve changes in education and in other social orders, gross differentiation will remain.

More generally, 'thinking scientifically and probabilistically' still appears to be relatively rare in standard curricula, and certainly so in public discourse, and yet it has become an essential perspective for many policy decisions affecting human lives. How can students who have not learned sciences come to think scientifically about human activities?

When can children begin to cope with the kinds of issues Gigerenzer (2002) writes about? How are members of the public going to learn that drugs and operations cannot yield certain outcomes? Could judges trying cases where such issues arise learn not to permit nonsense being admitted as evidence? There has been a massive cultural lag in the incorporation of such developments into the highest arenas of decision-making. Gross mistakes are made by 'experts'. Crazy models of death rates from disease spreading are broadcast to the public. Can journalists learn to question unlikely models? How one can persuade professionals to undergo courses relevant to the exercise of their expertise and have the courses evaluated is clearly a difficult matter, but that is what is needed if sensible decision-making is to be promoted. Governments insist on life-long learning and re-training for persons in other jobs, but undergo no pre-service or in-service training themselves. Research into why this remains so and how the situation might be changed could have a massive cascade effect.

Sadly however, a debased legal model of prosecution versus defence still dominates political debates in the highest legislative assembly, reaching a nadir in the point-scoring verbal boxing matches of the Prime Minister and the leader of the main opposition party. Self-serving arguments from one authority co-exist with negative ad hominem arguments against the other. Claims about facts are treated as though they can be decided by decrying the status of the antagonist and asserting personal integrity and competence. There is no or little negotiation to agree the facts and seek best answers to policies and practices in relation to these. Similar gladiatorial contests occur daily between TV and radio interviewers and their victims, who are likely to be treated as being incompetent, deceitful and evasive. Are these exchanges just a left-over from traditional ways of proceeding? Does the government believe that its parliamentary procedures are an effective means of ensuring that the country is well-served by its legislature? These matters do not need more research to underpin sensible changes, but they do need research into why outmoded ways of debating and resolving matters of fact are still endemic. The influence of the rhetoric of Gorgias and the amorality of Thrasymychus remain strong.

Myth 3 is not solely concerned with the distant past. In the 1960s in the USA there was a mass political movement to enfranchise and raise the life-chances of the poor white, black and hispanic communities especially, and this was followed by arguments about gender discrimination against girls and women. These arguments met with considerable success in respect of gender discrimination. Considerable funding was made available to boost educational opportunities for the children of the most disadvantaged groups of people, and to fund programmes that treated children as active learners who would benefit from 'guided discovery' methods of learning as well as from more traditional teaching knowledge and skills. An over-simplification of the outcomes would note that great educational successes were achieved (see Schweinhart, et al., 1993), but that these were dwarfed by an enormous waste of money on ill-considered projects, and by political alarm about the likely social consequences of those successful programmes that were raising questions about the nature of society, including the extent of and the rationale for the differentiation of power, wealth and status of different social groups. Those devising and teaching such courses were quickly labelled as communist sympathizers or worse by both politicians and the media, and with the Vietnam war and other anti-communist military interventions in progress, the potential educational advances faded fast.

Civil Rights campaigners for Blacks in the USA suffered killings and violence on a large scale. At Kent State University, the National Guard opened fire on students, killing a number of them. Critical thinking about the status quo of society was not answered with well-founded arguments, but with force. As an early end-game, the power elites who control the police and armed forces do use them – allegedly in the interests of preserving peace – and of course the status quo. In the past the top formal and informal institutions of the State have welcomed 'critical thinking', but only about matters that are irrelevant to the valued vested interests of those with power (e.g. cloning, abortion, adolescent misbehaviour) or advantageous to them (advances in science and technology). This has been true of States and their powerful institutions throughout history. The mistake made by the populations of the quasi-democracies is to believe that their own States now are different from what they used to be, and from other States. Perhaps the time is ripe once to introduce into secondary and tertiary education studies of how our societies work, human geography, and honest history, combined with training in competence to evaluate the political, social and moral issues these can be used to raise. We are still a long way from the Ancient Greek dreams in which civilized and cultivated societies would be realized through actions founded on true beliefs and sound arguments.

references

Baron, J. (2000). *Thinking and deciding* (3rd edn). Cambridge, UK: Cambridge University Press.
Bourdieu, P. (1977). *Distinctions*. London: Routledge.

(Original work 4th century BC.)

Publishing Cooperative Society.

Hewstone, M. (1981). *Causal attribution*. Oxford, UK: Blackwell.

Bourdieu, P. & Passeron, J.C. (1977). *Reproduction in education and culture*. London: Sage.

Dionne, E.J. (1991). *Why Americans hate politics*. New York: Simon & Schuster.

Engler, B. (2003). *Personality theories: An introduction* (6th edn). Boston, MA: Houghton-Mifflin.

Ferguson, N. (2005). *Colossus*. London: Penguin.

Fischer, D.H. (1971). *Historians' fallacies*. London: Routledge.

Gallup Polls (1993). *Social trends*. London: Gallup.

Galtung, J. & Ruge, M. (1973). Structuring and selecting news. In S. Cohen & J. Young (Eds.), *The manufacture of news* (pp.52–62). London: Constable.

Gigerenzer, G. (2002). *Reckoning with risk*. London: Allen Lane.

Glasgow Media Group (1976). *Bad news*. London: Routledge.

Glasgow Media Group (1982). *Really bad news*. London: Writers and Readers Publishing Cooperative Society.

Hewstone, M. (1981). *Causal attribution*. Oxford, UK: Blackwell.

Hewstone, M. & Fincham, F. (1996). *Attribution theory and research*. In M. Hewstone, W. Stroebe & G.M. Stephenson (Eds.), *Introduction to social psychology* (2nd edn), pp.167–204). Oxford, UK: Blackwell.

Hobbes, T. (1914). *Leviathan*. London: Dent. (Original work published 1651.)

Hutton, W. (1996). *The state we're in*. London: Vintage.

Kahneman, D. & Tversky, A. (Eds.) (2000). *Choices, values and frames*. Cambridge, UK: Cambridge University Press.

Kuhn, D. (1991). *The skills of argument*. Cambridge, UK: Cambridge University Press.

Lipsett, S.M. & Schneider, W. (1983). *The confidence gap: Business, labor and government in the public mind*. New York: Free Press.

Magee, B. (1997). *Confessions of a philosopher*. London: Weidenfeld and Nicolson.

McChesney, R.W. (1999). *Rich media, poor democracy*. Urbana, IL: University of Illinois Press.

Nisbett, R.E. (Ed.) (1993). *Rules for reasoning*. Hillsdale, NJ: Erlbaum.

Oaksford, M. & Chater, N. (1998). *Rationality in an uncertain world: Essays on the cognitive science of human reasoning*. East Sussex: Psychology Press Ltd.

Plato (trans. H.D.P. Lee, 1955). *The republic*. Harmondsworth, UK: Penguin Classics. (Original work 4th century BC.)

Robinson, W.P. (1996). *Deceit, delusion and detection*. Thousand Oaks, CA: Sage.

Robinson, W.P. (2006). *Arguing to better conclusions*. Mahwah, NJ: Lawrence Erlbaum.

Runciman, W.G. (2006). What happens to the Labour party? *London Review of books, 28(12)*, 17–20.

Sampson, A. (1965). *New anatomy of Britain today*. London: Hodder and Stoughton.

Schweinhart, L.J., Barnes, H.V., Weikart, D.P., Barnett, W.S. & Epstein, A.S. (1993). *Significant benefits: The High-Scope Perry preschool study through age 27*. Ypsilanti, MI: High/Scope Press.

Stiglitz, J.E. (2003). *Globalization and its discontents*. London: Penguin.

Tajfel, H. & Turner, J.W. (1979). An integrative theory of intergroup conflict. In W.G. Austin and S. Worchel (Eds.), *The social psychology of intergroup relations* (pp.33–46). Monterey, CA: Brooks/Cole.

Taylor, S. (1989). *Positive illusions*. New York: Basic Books.
Thouless, R. (1974). *Straight and crooked thinking* (Rev. edn). London: Pan. (Original work published 1930.)
Toulmin, S. (2001). *Return to reason*. Cambridge, MA: Harvard University Press.
Turner, J.C., Hogg, M.A., Oakes, P.J., Reicher, S.D. & Wetherell, M. (1987). *Rediscovering the social group*. Oxford, UK: Blackwell.
van den Brink-Budgen, R. (2005. *Critical thinking for students* (2nd edn). Oxford, UK: How to Books.
Walton, D.N. (1989). *Informal logic*. Cambridge, UK: Cambridge University Press.
Wilkinson, R. (1994) *Unfair shares*. Ilford, UK: Barnardos.

appendix
transcription notation

The transcription notation used in chapters 6 and 8 of this volume is most fully described in: G. Jefferson (2004), Glossary of transcript symbols with an introduction. In G.H. Lerner (Ed.), *Conversation analysis: Studies from the first generation* (pp.13–31). Amsterdam: John Benjemins.

general transcription notation

[ ]	Square brackets mark the start and end of overlapping speech.
↑↓	Vertical arrows precede marked pitch movement, over and above normal rhythms of speech. They are for marked, hearably significant shifts. The aim is to capture interactionally significant features, hearable as such to an ordinary listener.
→	Side arrows are not transcription features, but draw analytic attention to particular lines of text.
Underlining	Signals vocal emphasis; the extent of underlining within individual words locates emphasis, but also indicates how heavy it is.
CAPITALS	Mark speech that is obviously louder than surrounding.
°↑I know it,°	'Degree' signs enclose obviously quieter speech (i.e., hearably produced-as quieter, not just someone distant).
that's r*ight.	Asterisks precede a 'squeaky' vocal delivery.
(0.4)	Numbers in round brackets measure pauses in seconds (in this case, 4 tenths of a second).
(.)	A micropause, hearable but too short to easily measure.
((text))	Additional comments from the transcriber, e.g. context or intonation.

she wa::nted	Colons show degrees of elongation of the prior sound; the more colons, the more elongation.
hhh	Aspiration (out-breaths); proportionally as for colons.
.hhh	Inspiration (in-breaths); proportionally as for colons.
Yeh,	'Continuation' marker, speaker has not finished; marked by fall-rise or weak rising intonation, as when enunciating lists.
y'know?	Question marks signal stronger, 'questioning' intonation, irrespective of grammar.
Yeh.	Periods (full stops) mark falling, stopping intonation ('final contour'), irrespective of grammar.
bu-u-	Hyphens mark a cut-off of the preceding sound.
>he said<	'Greater than' and 'lesser than' signs enclose speeded-up talk.
solid.=	'Equals' signs mark the immediate 'latching' of successive talk, whether of
=We had	one or more speakers, with no interval.
heh heh	Voiced laughter. Can have other symbols added, such as underlinings, pitch movement, extra aspiration, etc.
sto(h)p i(h)t	Laughter within speech is signalled by h's in round brackets.
( )	Transcriber doubt about the talk.
<word	'A left push' or hurried start.
¿	Weaker intonation rise than a question mark.
$	Smile voice.

features of crying

See chapter 6 in this volume, and A. Hepburn (2004), Crying: Notes on description, transcription and interaction. *Research on Language and Social Interaction, 37*, 251–290.

°°help°°	Whispering – enclosed by double degree signs.
.shih	Wet sniff.
.skuh	Snorty sniff.
~grandson~	Wobbly voice – enclosed by tildes.
↑↑Sorry	High pitch – represented by one or more upward arrows.
k(hh)ay	Aspiration in speech – an 'h' represents aspiration:
hhhelp	in parenthesis indicates a sharper more plosive sound outside parenthesis indicates a softer more breathy sound.

Huhh .hhih	Sobbing – combinations of 'hhs', some with full stops before them to indicate
Hhuyuhh	inhaled rather than exhaled, many have voiced vowels, some have voiced
>hhuh<	consonants. If sharply inhaled or exhaled – enclosed in the 'greater than/less than' symbols (> <).

index